웰컴 영어

개정증보판

WELCOME TO ENGLISH GRAMMAR & READING

정재창·윤천기 지음

Helping Learners with the Essential Grammar & Advanced Reading

한국문화사

웰컴영어

WELCOME TO ENGLISH GRAMMAR & READING

1판 1쇄 발행 2004년 2월 27일
2판 1쇄 발행 2010년 9월 1일

저 자 · 정재창, 윤천기
펴낸이 · 김진수
펴낸곳 · **한국문화사**
주 소 · 서울특별시 성동구 성수1가 2동 656-1683 두앤캔 B/D 502호 133-823
전 화 · (02)464-7708 / 3409-4488
팩 스 · (02)499-0846
등록번호 · 제2-1276호
등록일 · 1991년 11월 9일
Homepage · www.hankookmunhwasa.co.kr
E-mail · hkm77@korea.com

책값은 뒤표지에 있습니다.

ISBN 978-89-5726-810-0 93740

Welcome to English Grammar & Reading

정재창 · 윤천기 지음

한국문화사

머리말

영어를 여러 해 공부해도 외국인과 의사소통을 제대로 못한다는 의견이 집중적으로 제기된 적이 있습니다. 그에 따라 영어 교육의 방향이 읽기와 쓰기에서 듣기와 말하기 중심으로 전환된 지 십 여 년이 지났습니다. 그 덕분에 듣기와 말하기 능력이 그 전에 비하여 훨씬 향상된 것이 사실입니다. 이는 참 다행스러운 일이 아닐 수 없습니다. 그러나 문제는 지나치게 듣기와 말하기를 강조한 나머지 읽기와 쓰기를 상대적으로 소홀하게 취급한 것도 부인할 수 없는 사실이라 하겠습니다. 실제로 최근 적지 않은 대학 신입생들이 일정 수준 이상의 읽기와 쓰기에 여간 큰 어려움을 겪는다고 토로하는 것도 그 때문이라 생각합니다.

우리가 외국어로서의 영어를 제대로 학습하기 위해서는 어느 시점에서든지 반드시 문법을 공부해야 합니다. 문법과 문형을 이해함으로써 읽기와 쓰기 능력을 향상시킬 수 있을 뿐만 아니라 말하기와 듣기 능력도 아울러 향상시킬 수가 있습니다. 진정한 의미에서, 외국어를 잘 한다고 하는 것은 이 네 가지를 동시에 잘 한다는 것을 의미하기 때문입니다. 정확한 문법 실력 없이 대충 읽도록 훈련받은 학습자는 영어실력이 어느 수준에 도달한 후 더 이상의 향상을 기대할 수 없는 상황에 부딪치기 쉽습니다. 우리가 문법을 확실하게 공부해야 하는 까닭이 여기에 있습니다.

따라서 이 책은 문법과 독해에 초점을 맞췄습니다. 제1부에서는 대학수학능력시험에서 토익, 토플 수준에 이르는 핵심 문법을 체계적으로 정리하였습니다. 아울러 학습한 문법 내용을 곧 바로, 다양한 지문에 적용함으로써 쉽고 재미있게 읽기 훈련을 할 수 있도록 구성하였습니다. 독해와 문법을 따로 따로 공부하는 것은 비생산적입니다. 그 둘은 결국 하나이기 때문입니다. 제2부에서는 제1부에서 공부한 내용을 더욱 더 심도 있게 두루 공부할 수 있도록 정치, 경제, 사회, 문화 그리고 문학 분야의 명문장을 엄선하여 싣고, 이에 대한 해설도 곁들였습니다.

이 책은, 따라서, 이렇게 공부하면 좋을 것입니다. 문법과 독해에 훈련이 덜 된 학습자는 먼저 제1부의 동사와 관련된 부정사, 분사, 동명사, 수동태, 관계사, 그리고 비교 단원을 공부하는 것이 바람직합니다. 이런 단원들은 그 이외의 단원에 비해 훨씬 더 독해와 밀접한 관련을 맺고 있기 때문입니다. 또 이미 탄탄한 문법 지식을 가진 학습자라면, 각 장의 'Basic Reading' 부분과 'Advanced Reading' 부분을 먼저 공부해도 괜찮을 것입니다. 그리고 이런 부분을 다 학습한 독자라면, 제2부의 각 단원을 공부하면서 영어권의 문화와 사회에 대한 이해의 폭을 넓히는 것이 효과적인 학습 방법이 될 것입니다. 물론 전체를 차례로 다 학습해도 좋고, 필요한 부분만 골라 학습해도 좋을 것입니다.

아울러 외국어로서의 영어를 잘 구사하려면, 우리말을 잘 구사할 수 있어야 한다는 점을 강조하여 말씀드리고자 합니다. 훌륭한 우리말 구사 능력 없이, 훌륭한 영어 구사 능력을 기대하기 어렵기 때문입니다. 우리가 외국어로서의 영어를 배우고 익히는 일은 쉽지 않지만, 집중적인 반복훈련에 대한 즐거움, 굳건한 학습의지와 목표, 그리고 꾸준한 실천력을 가지고, 산을 오르듯이, 한 걸음 한 걸음 끊임없이 전진한다면, 반드시 좋은 성과가 있을 것입니다.

끝으로 이 책이 나오기까지 노고를 아끼지 않으신 한국문화사 두유미 선생님과 최은경 선생님께 감사를 드립니다. 또 이 책을 흔쾌히 출판해 주신 김진수 사장님과 김정희 실장님께도 깊은 감사를 드립니다. 작은 책을 내고 여간 긴장되는 것이 사실이지만, 아무쪼록 이 조그만 책이 독자 여러분들의 영어 공부에 보탬이 된다면 더 없이 큰 기쁨이 될 것입니다.

지리산 옆 연구실에서

정재창 · 윤천기

Part 1

Grammar

Part 2

Advanced Reading for making a full man

Section 1. Reading & Language

Section 2. Culture & Society

Section 3. Nature & Science

Section 4. History & World

Section 5. Insight & Interpretations

Section 6. Life and Literature

Grammar

Part I

Grammar

제1장. 문장

- A 품사
- B 문장의 성분(成分)
- C 문장의 기본 5형식
- D 어군(語群)
- E 문장의 종류

제1장 문장 Sentence

A 품사

❶ 품사의 유래

품사를 part of speech라고 하는 것을 보면 낱말을 집합의 개념으로 분류한 것을 알 수 있다. 그리스시대 플라톤(Plato, 429~347 B.C.)은 품사를 명사와 동사 두 개로 분류했으나 아리스토텔레스(Aristotle, 382~322 B.C.)가 거기에서 '접속사'를 구별해냄으로써 '3품사론'이 생겨났다.

영어로 쓰여진 최초의 영문법서인 윌리암 블로카(William Bullokar)의 『간략 영문법(Brief Grammar)』(1586)에서 그는 라틴문법의 8품사를 영어의 품사분류에 그대로 적용하여 명사, 대명사, 동사, 분사, 부사, 접속사, 전치사, 감탄사의 8품사로 나누었다. 그 당시 초기 영문법학자들은 라틴어문법의 영향을 받아 형용사를 형용명사(noun-adjective)라 하여 명사의 하위범주로 분류하였다. 그 때문에, 분사가 품사였던 반면 형용사는 품사의 범주로 인정되지 못했다.

조셉 프리슬리(Joseph Priestly)는 『기본 영문법(The Rudiments of English Grammar)』(1761)에서 분사를 하나의 품사로 간주하는 대신에 영어의 형용사는 성, 수, 격의 어미변화를 하지 않는다는 점을 들어 명사의 범주에서 분리하여 형용사를 하나의 독립된 품사로 인정하였다. 오늘날 우리가 사용하고 있는 명사, 형용사, 대명사, 동사, 부사, 접속사, 전치사, 감탄사의 8품사는 그런 과정을 통해 확립되었다.

❷ 품사의 종류

1. 명사(Noun)
사람이나 사물의 이름을 표시하는 말.
명사(구)는 문장 안에서 주어, 보어, 목적어 등으로 쓰인다.
ex. book, John, the whale

2. 형용사(Adjective)
(대)명사를 한정하거나 서술하는 말.
ex. good man, He is nice.

3. 대명사(Pronoun)
명사 대신에 사용할 수 있는 말.
ex. he, she, they, him, her

4. 동사(Verb)
사람이나 사물의 동작, 상태를 표시하는 말.
동사만 유일하게 문장의 구조에 대한 정보를 가지고 있다.
ex. John walks.

5. 부사(Adverb)
동사, 형용사, 다른 부사, 절(문장)을 수식하는 말.
ex. He speaks English easily and correctly. a very fast swimmer

6. 접속사(Conjunction)
절(문장)을 하나의 단위로 묶는 말.
ex. I believe that he is honest.

7. 전치사(Preposition)
(대)명사 앞에 놓여서 구를 형성하는 말.
ex. of no use, in the sky, for sale

8. 감탄사(Exclamation)
감정을 나타내는 말.
문장과 독립하여 있다.
ex. oh, alas

B 문장의 성분(成分)

❶ 주어(主語)와 술어(術語, predicate)

(1) 주부 : 주어의 중심으로 된 말

The blond girl is my sister.
(The blond girl: 주부 / is my sister.: 술부)

(2) 술부 : 술어의 중심으로 된 말

My brother learned a great many new words.
(My brother: 주부 / learned a great many new words.: 술부)

※ 품사명칭인 동사를 구별하여, 문장을 구성하는 요소로서의 동사를 술어라 한다.

❷ 보어(補語, complement)

다른 말의 보충을 필요로 하는 동사와 같이 써서, 그 의미를 보충하는 말

• 보어의 기능

(1) 명사보어: 주어와 동일한 '=' 관계를 형성한다.

John is a student. (John = a student)

(2) 형용사 보어: 주어의 상태나 속성을 나타낸다.

John is happy. (John ≒ happy)

※ 주어나 목적어는 의미면에서 동사와 일차적인 관계가 있는 반면, 보어는 의미면에서 동사보다는 주어나 목적어와 일차적인 관계가 있는 문장의 요소이다.

❸ 목적어(目的語, object)

목적어는 동사가 타동사인 경우에만 쓰인다.
목적어는 주어와 마찬가지로 명사, 명사구, 명사절로 실현된다.

(1) 타동사(他動詞) : 반드시 목적어와 같이 문장에 나타난다.

1. I met yesterday. (×)
2. I met her yesterday. (○)

(2) 자동사(自動詞) : 목적어가 필요 없다.

다만, 자동사+전치사는 타동사구가 되어 목적어를 취할 수 있다.

1. He kept silent.
2. He looked for his brother. (look(자동사) + for = 타동사구)

❹ 수식어(修飾語, modifier)

수식어(Modifier)란 주어, 술어동사, 목적어, 보어 등을 설명하거나, 한정하는 말을 말한다. 즉, 형용사 및 부사 상당어구를 지칭한다. *modify: 단어 · 구를 수식(한정)하다

(M) S + (M) V + (M) O + (M) C

The people **of the city** appointed **the most brave young** man mayor **of the city**.

주어 동사 목적어 보어

C 문장의 기본 5형식

1형식	The plane landed safely.	(S + V + (adv))
2형식	The meal was absolutely delicious.	(S + V + C + (adv))
3형식	She cleaned the house thoroughly.	(S + V + O + (adv))
4형식	Father gave me a watch.	(S + V + I.O. + D.O.)
5형식	I believe him an honest man.	(S + V + O + C)

D 어군(語群, word-group)

❶ 구(句, phrase)

두 개 이상의 단어가 결합하여 의미를 형성하며 절(문장)보다는 단위가 작다.

(1) 명사구: 명사(구)는 문장 안에서 주어, 보어, 목적어 등으로 쓰이는 표현이다.

1. **To see** is **to believe**.
2. My dream is **to build a beautiful house on a hill**.

(2) 형용사구: 명사(구)를 수식하거나, 보어로 쓰인다.

1. It is **of no use**.
2. I am **to build a beautiful house on a hill.**
3. He has no house **to live in.**

(3) 부사구: 절, 구, 동사, 형용사, 부사, 분사를 수식한다.

1. You should work hard **to pass the entrance examination.**

부사구의 의미적 역할

(1) 시간

1. She was born **in 1980.**
2. We have been waiting **since one o'clock.**

(2) 장소

1. The dog was asleep **on the grass.**

(3) 원인

1. She died **of cancer.**
2. I was sorry **to hear the bad news.**

(4) 이유 · 판단의 근거

1. He must be a fool **to believe such a thing.**
2. He cannot be a fool **to solve the problem.**

(5) 조건 '~한다면'

1. **To hear him talk**, you would take him for an American.

(6) 양보 '~한다할 지라도'

1. Though he read the book carefully, he couldn't understand it.
2. **To see it**, you will not believe it.
   = Even if you see it, you will not believe it.

(7) 결과 '~해서 결과적으로 ~되다'

1. He worked **only to fail.**
2. He lived **to be a great man**.
3. He didn't live **to see the work finished.**
   (그는 그 일이 끝나는 것을 볼 수 있을 정도로 오래 살지 못했다.)

무의지 동사 live, awake, grow, grow up 등 다음의 부정사는 '결과

(8) 양태(樣態): '~하는 것과 같이, ~와 마찬가지로'

1. He did it **as** he had been told.

2. You may dance **as** you please.
3. **As** food nourishes our body, so books nourish our mind.
as만 쓸 경우보다 so를 같이 쓸 경우가 더 문어적임

(9) 도구
1. I have difficulty eating **with chopsticks.**

(10) 제한
1. **As for me**, I know nothing about the accident.

❷ 절(節, clause)

절: 주어와 동사를 갖추고 있는 온전한 문장. 하나의 절이 다른 절에 종속되어 있을 때, 본 절을 주절(主節, main clause), 종속된 절을 종속절(從屬節, subordinate clause)이라 한다.

종속절은 그 기능에 따라 세 종류로 나뉜다.
(1) 명사절
I think **that he is honest.**
(2) 형용사절
Heaven helps those **who help themselves**.
(3) 부사절
If it is fine tomorrow, we will go on a picnic.

E 문장의 종류

구조로 본 문장의 종류

(1) 단문(短文, simple sentence): 하나의 주부와 하나의 술부로 구성된 문장
1. She heard an explosion.
2. She phoned the police.

(2) 중문(重文, compound sentence): 두 개 이상의 단문으로 구성되며, and, or, but 같은 대등 접속사로 연결되어 있다.

1. Life is short, but art is long.

(3) 복문(複文, complex sentence): 주절과 종속절로 구성되어 있다.

1. When she heard an explosion, she phoned the police.

용법으로 본 문장의 종류

1. 평서문(Declarative Sentence)
2. 의문문(Interrogative Sentence)
3. 명령문(Imperative Sentence)
4. 감탄문(Exclamatory Sentence)

Basic Reading 1

1 Words **are** not the only means of communication. Gestures also communicate. Some gestures **are used** in more than one culture. Others **differ** from culture to culture.

- means[mi:nz] n. 수단
- communication[kəmjù:nəkeʃiən] n. 의사전달
- gesture[dʒéstʃər] n. 몸짓, 손짓

2 **In the development of civilization** the use of tools grew and multiplied. Later the use of steam power revolutionized the whole industrial organization and transportation.

- civilization[sivəlizéiʃən] n. 문명
- multiply[mʌ́ltəplài] v. 증가하다, 증식시키다
- revolutionize[révəlú:ʃənàiz] vt. 혁명을 일으키다
- industrial[indʌ́striəl] a. 산업의, 공업의
- organization[ɔ̀:rgənizeiʃən] n. 조직, 구성, 단체

3 The Englishman is always ready to learn by mistakes. Repeated mistakes and failures **make him wiser and stronger**. It has been said that the English lose all the battles and win all the wars.

- be ready to ~할 준비가 되어 있다
- learn by mistakes 실수를 함으로써 배우다
- battle[bǽtl] n. 전투, 싸움

4 **It is** very difficult **to select** a book of value to you from among the large number of books available today. Yet, the harder the selection is, the greater will be the joy when you have come across the very book you are after. Look for a book as if you were looking for your sweetheart. Never make do with one which is easy of access. Don't spare yourself any trouble for the purpose.

- select[silékt] v. 고르다, 선택하다
- a book of value = a valuable book
- the large number of books (which are) available today
- the harder~ , the greater will be the joy
- come across 우연히 마주치다
- the very book (that) you are after
- make do 임시 변통하다, 때우다, [최소한에] 만족하다 (with)
  We hadn't time for lunch, but we made do with sandwiches.
- be easy of access 접근하기 쉬운
- be swift[slow] of foot 발걸음이 빠른[느린]
- be hard of hearing 귀가 먼
- spare oneself to do (재귀적으로) 몸을 사리다, ~을 아끼다, 절약하다
  He spares no pains to please her.
  그는 그녀의 비위를 맞추기 위해 온갖 노력을 다한다
- the purpose = to select a book of value

5 I find **it** wholesome **to be alone** the greater part of time. To be in company, even with the best, is soon wearisome and dissipating. I love to be alone. I never found the companion that was so companionable as solitude.

H. D. Thoreau

- wholesome[hóulsəm] a. 건전한, 유익한
- to be in company 사람과 어울리는 것

- wearisome[wíərisəm] a. 지치게 하는
- dissipate[dísəpèit] v.(시간 · 재산 등을) 낭비하다
- companionable[kəmpǽnjənəbəl] a. 동무로 사귈만한
- solitude[sálitù:d] n. 고독, 독거(獨居)
- Henry David Thoreau(1817~62) 미국의 초절주의자, 작가, walden(1854)의 저자

6 The choice was his alone. **If he opened one door**, there came out of it a hungry tiger which immediately jumped on him and tore him to pieces as punishment for his guilt. But **if the accused person opened the other door**, there came from it a lady about his own age whom the king had selected from among the most beautiful in the land. As a reward for his innocence, this lady would become his wife.

- immediately[imí:diitli] ad. 즉시
- jump on him 그에게 달려들다
- tear A to pieces : A를 갈기갈기 찢다
- punishment[pʌ́niʃmənt] n. 형벌
- guilt[gilt] n. 유죄
- the accused person 고발된 사람
- reward[riwɔ́:rd] n. 보수, 사례
- innocence[inəsns] n. 순결, 결백, 무죄

7 Your mind, like your body, is a thing whereof the powers are developed by effort. That is a principal use of hard work in studies. **Unless you train your body** you cannot be an athlete, and **unless you train your mind** you cannot be much of a scholar. The four miles an oarsman covers at top speed is in itself nothing to the good, but the physical capacity to hold out over the course is thought to be of some worth.

- whereof = of which(whose)의 뜻을 갖는 관계부사
- a thing whereof the powers are developed by efforts
  그 힘이 노력에 의해서 개발되는 일
- principal[prínsəpəl] a. 주요한
- You cannot be much of a scholar. 대단한 학자는 될 수 없다.
- oarsman[ɔ́:rzmən](－men [mən]) n. 노 젓는 사람
- hold out 견디다, 지속하다

8 There is no doubt that adults, and even highly educated adults, vary greatly in the speed and efficiency of their reading. **Some** proceed very slowly throughout; **others** dash along too quickly and then have to regress. Poor readers in particular may lack the ability to vary their manner of reading according to the type of reading matter and to their intentions in reading it.

- adult[ədʌ́lt, ǽdʌlt] n. 성인
- vary[vέəri] v. 변경하다, 다양하게 하다
- efficiency[ifiʃənsi] n. 능력, 효율
- proceed[prousí:d] vi. 나아가다
- dash[dæʃ] = rush
- regress[rigrés] 되돌아가다(⇔ progress 전진하다), 복귀하다, 퇴보하다
- in particular 특히
- lack[læk] n. 결핍되다, 부족
- according to ~에 따라, 에 의하여
- reading matter 신문, 잡지 등의 읽을 거리
- intention[inténʃən] n. 의지, 의향, 취지

9 Language is one of man's precious possessions. Without it he would be unable to exchange ideas with his fellow men. In the modern world, however, it is not enough to speak only the language of one's own country. **It is said that the**

man who speaks two languages has two minds, for in learning a foreign language, we acquire, to a certain extent, the mentality of a foreign people. Language study, accordingly, is one of the best means of enabling us to understand our fellow men. It is difficult, to be sure, but rich in rewards. **It makes us better citizens** of the international world in which we live.

- precious[préʃəs] a. 고귀한(= invaluable, priceless)
- possession[pəzéʃən] n. 소유, 소유물
- acquire[əkwáiər] vt. 획득하다(come by, obtain)
- mentality[mentǽləti] n. 사고방식, 정신
- accordingly[əkɔ́:rdiŋli] ad. 따라서(therefore)
- means[mi:nz] n. 수단
- rewards[riwɔ́:rd] n. 보상

10 Education is one of the key words of our time. A man without an education, many of us believe, is an unfortunate victim of adverse circumstances deprived of one of the greatest twentieth-century opportunities. Convinced of the importance of education, modern states 'invest' in institutions of learning **to get back 'interest' in the form of a large group of enlightened young men and women who are potential leaders**. Education, with its cycles of instruction so carefully worked out, punctuated by text-books — those purchasable wells of wisdom — what would civilization be like without its benefits?

- victim[víktim] n. 희생자
- adverse[ædvə́:rs] a. 불리한, 반대의
- circumstance[sə́:rkəmstæ̀ns / -stəns] n. 환경, 상황
- deprive A of B : A에게서 B를 빼앗다
- convince A of B : A에게 B를 확신시키다

- **invest**[invést] v. 투자하다
- **institution of learning** 교육기관
- **to get back~** <목적> 부정사의 부사적 용법
- **enlighten**[enláitn] vt. 계몽하다, 설명하다
- **instruction**[instrʌ́kʃən] n. 교육, 교훈
- **punctuate**[pʌ́ŋktʃuéit] v. 구두점을 찍다, 강조하다
- **purchase**[pə́ːrtʃəs] v. 구입하다, 획득하다

Advanced Reading 1

A. Preparing to Read

Having been told by her doctor that she was overweight, she's eating all the fibre and fruit she can.

An autopsy eventually **ascribed** the baby's death **to** sudden infant death syndrome, according to the news.

The great miracle is **at hand**.

B. Approaching to the Topic

Less than fifty years after his death, the door of nature was unlocked and we were offered the dreadful burden of choice. We have usurped many of the powers we once ascribed to God. Fearful and unprepared, we have assumed the lordship over the life and death of the whole world of all living things. The danger and the glory and the choice rest finally in man. The test of his perfectibility is at hand.

Having taken God-like power, we must seek in ourselves for the responsibility and the wisdom we once prayed some deity might have. Man himself has become our greatest hazard and our only hope. So that today, St. John the Apostle may well be paraphrased: In the end is the word, and the word is man, and the word is with man.

from Nobel Prize Acceptance Speech (1962) by John Steinbeck

Vocabularies & Expressions for Comprehension

- 스타인벡의 노벨상 수락 연설이므로 his death의 his는 노벨상을 만든 Alfred Nobel를 지칭함.
- usurp[ju:sə́:rp, -zə́:rp] (권력, 지위 등을) 빼앗다, 약탈하다
- ascribe ~ to (=attribute ~ to) : ~에 돌리다, ~에 기인하는 것으로 하다

His mother ascribed her success to good luck.(그의 어머니는 성공의 원인을 행운에 돌렸다.)

• assume(태도, 임무, 책임 따위를) 취하다, 떠맡다

He assumed the responsibility.(그가 책임을 졌다.)

• lordship over 주권, 영주의 권력, 지배(over)

• at hand ~ 바로 가까이, 가까운 장래에, 곧

• deity[dí:əti] 신(god), 신위, 신성, 신격

• so that=therefore

• St. John the apostle 사도 성 요한

• may well ~해도 당연하다
She may well be proud of her daughter.(그녀는 자신의 딸을 자랑할 만하다.)

• paraphrase[pǽrəfrèiz] 바꿔 쓰다, 말을 바꿔서 설명하다

• In the end is the word, and the world is man, and the world is with man.

이 문장은 존 스타인벡이 성서 요한복음 제1장 제1절에 나오는 In the beginning was the Word, and the Word was with God, and the Word was God. 즉 "태초에 말씀이 계셨고, 그 말씀이 하나님과 함께 있었으며, 그 말씀이 곧 하나님이셨다.
"를 바꿔 표현한 것임.

Sentence Pattern analysis

• We have usurped many of the powers we once ascribed to God.

ascribe to ~ [~에 속한다고 생각했던]의 구문

• Having taken God-like power, we must seek in ourselves for the responsibility and the wisdom we once prayed some deity might have.

Having taken ~ 완료형 분사구분 (As we have take~), **seek ~ for**의 구문. Wisdom we once에서는 wisdom과 we 사이에 that을 보충하여 이해함, 즉 하나님과 다름없는 능력을 이미 가졌으므로 우리는 어떤 신성이 가지고 있기를 한때 기도했던 그 책임과 지혜를 우리들 자신에게서 찾아야 한다.

John Ernst Steinbeck 은 미국의 소설가로 1902년 2월 27일 캘리포니아에서 태어났다. 1962년에 *The Winter of Discontent*로 노벨 문학상을 받았으며, 1939년 *The Grapes of Wrath*로 퓨리쳐상을 받았다. 그의 주요 작품으로는 *Cup of Gold* (1929), *The Pastures of Heaven* (1932), *Tortilla Flat* (1935), *Of Mice and Men* (1937), *The Long Valley* (1938), *Wayward Bus* (1947), *The Perl* (1947), *East of Eden* (1952) 등이 있다.

Wisdom

Genius is one percent inspiration and ninety-nine percent perspiration.

천재란 1퍼센트의 영감과 99퍼센트의 땀으로 이루어진다.

Thomas Edison: Newspaper Interview

Advanced Reading 2

A. Preparing to Read

Nature herself **brought forth** on earth new forms of life in spring.

Dr. Jung has **dedicated** his life **to** caring for others.

Many animal rights activists have **been engaged in** an increasingly bitter war of words with many of the nation's zoos.

B. Approaching to the Topic

Four score and seven years ago our fathers brought forth on this continent, a new nation, conceived in Liberty, and dedicated to the proposition that all men are created equal.

Now we are engaged in a great civil war, testing whether that nation, or any nation so conceived and so dedicated, can long endure. We are met on a great battle-field of that war. We have come to dedicate a portion of that field, as a final resting place for those who here gave their lives that that nation might live. It is altogether fitting and proper that we should do this.

But, in a larger sense, we can not dedicate—we can not consecrate—we can not hallow—this ground. The brave men, living and dead, who struggled here, have consecrated it, far above our poor power to add or detract. The world will little note, nor long remember what we say here, but it can never forget what they did here. It is for us the living, rather, to be dedicated here to the unfinished work which they who fought here have thus far so nobly advanced. It is rather for us to be here dedicated to the great task remaining before us—that from these honored dead we take increased devotion to that cause for which they gave the last full measure of devotion—that we here highly resolve that these dead shall not have died in vain—that this nation, under God, shall have a new birth of freedom—and that government of the people, by the people, for the people, shall not perish from the earth.

Gettysburg Address by Abraham Lincoln

Vocabularies & Expressions for Comprehension

- fourscore 80(score는 20)
- fathers 조상(forefathers, ancestors와 같은 의미)
- bring forth 이룩하다, 낳다
- continent[kάntənənt] 대륙
- conceive[kənsíːv] 구상하다
- dedicated to ~에 봉헌된, 헌신된
- proposition[prὰpəzíʃən / prɔ̀] 명제
- be engaged in ~에 종사하다
- a civil was 내란 (대문자 Civil War는 미국 남북전쟁)
- come to (do)~ ~하게 되다
- portion[pɔ́ːrʃən] 일부, 부분
- final resting-place 마지막 안식처
- give one's life 생명을 바치다
- in a larger sense 더 넓은 의미에서
- consecrate[kάnsəkrèit / kɔ́] 신성하게 하다
- hallow[hǽlou] 성화하다 = make holy
- above one's power to ~ 누군가의 능력을 넘어/능력 밖에
- the living 살아 있는 자
- these honoured dead 이 명예로운 전사자들
- cause[kɔːz] 대의, 큰 목적
- measure[méʒəːr] 분량, 한도
- highly resolve[rizάlv/ zɔ́lv] 굳게 결심하다
- in vain 헛되이
- perish[périʃ] 사라지다 사멸하다

Sentence Pattern Analysis

• Fourscore and seven years ago our fathers brought forth upon this continent a new nation, conceived in liberty and dedicated to the proposition that all men are created equal.

분사구문인 conceived~ and dedicated는 a new nation을 수식함.

• ~ those who here gave their lives that that nation might live.

that 앞에 So를 보충하여 이해함, 즉 (so) that ~may(~하도록)의 구문이며, that nation의 that는 지시형용사, 따라서 '그 나라가 살도록 하기 위해서 생명을 바친 분들'로 옮김.

• It is altogether fitting and proper that we should do this.

It is ~ that should 구문임. 물론 이 때의 should는 말하는 사람의 놀람, 당연, 의무 또는 유감 등의 분위기를 나타낸다.

• The brave men, living and dead, who struggled here, have consecrated it far above our power to add or detract.

living and dead는 the brave men을 수식, who의 선행사는 brave men

• It is for us, the living, rather, to be dedicated, here, to the unfinished work.

It ~ for ~ to 구문

• that government of the people, by the people and for the people

"국민의, 국민에 의한, 그리고 국민을 위한 정부"

Abraham Lincoln 은 미국 켄터키(Kentucky)주에서 출생하여 일리노이(Illinois)주에서 정치에 입문했으며, 남북전쟁을 승리로 이끈 미국 대통령이다. 특히, "국민의, 국민에 의한, 그리고 국민을 위한 정부"란 말은 링컨이 1863년 11월 19일 펜실바니아주 게티스버그에서, 그 곳 전투에서 생명을 바친 이들을 추모한 위 연설에서 나온 것이다. 물론 이 말은 민주주의의 지고한 이상을 응축해서 역설한 것으로 유명하다.

Wisdom

Idleness is only the refuge of weak minds.

심약한 마음의 유일한 피난처는 게으름이다.

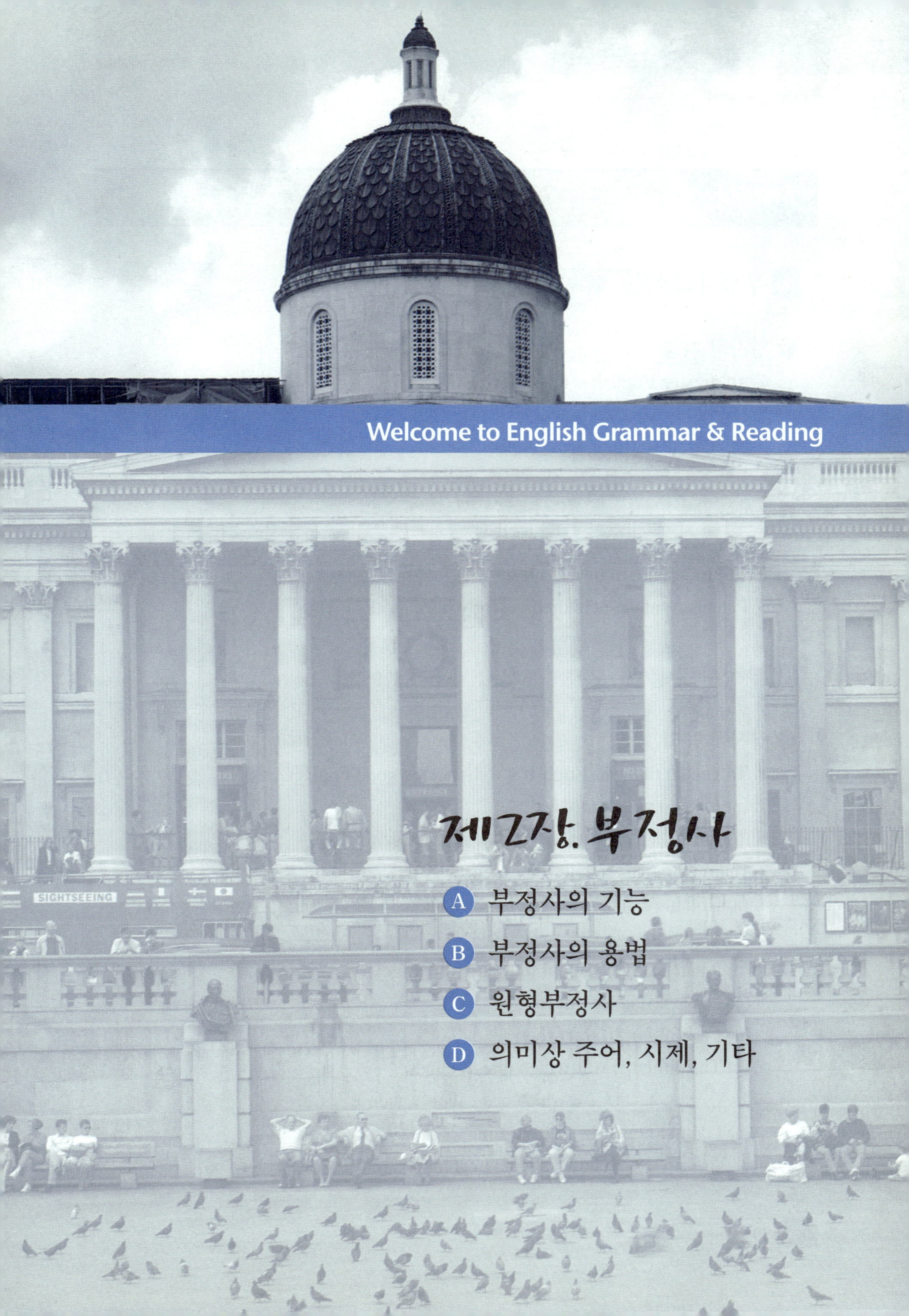

제2장. 부정사

제2장 부정사 *Infinitive*

A 부정사의 기능

❶ 명사적 기능

1. **To master English** is difficult. <주어>
2. I want **to read that book**. <목적어>
3. My task is **to teach oral English**. <보어>

❷ 동사적 기능

1. Our wish is **to unify our divided country**. <목적어 동반>
2. I consider him **to be a genius**. <보어 동반>
3. Parents want their children **to study hard**. <부사 동반>

B 부정사의 용법

❶ 명사적 용법

1. **To keep a diary in English** is a shortcut to good English. <주어>
2. (a) I like **to watch movies**. <목적어>

   (b) I make it a rule **to take a walk every morning**.
3. Her only fault is **to talk too much**. <보어>
4. (a) Nothing can be done **but to go to bed**. <전치사의 목적어>

   부정사 앞에는 전치사를 쓸 수 없는 것이 원칙이나 예외가 있다.

   (b) It had no effect **except to make him angry**.

   (c) I have no choice **but to cry**.

   (d) I was **about to start then**.
5. (a) The difficulty was **which one to choose**. <의문사 + to 부정사 = 명사구>

   = which one I should choose

   (b) I don't know **how to treat him**.

   = how I should treat him

❷ 형용사적 용법

(1) 한정적(限定的) 용법 수식 관계

1. He is not **a person to break his promise.** 〈명사가 의미상 주어〉
2. (a) I have **nothing to say**. 〈명사가 의미상 목적어〉
   (b) I bought **a book to read** on the plane.
   (c) Give me **a chair to sit on.**
3. **The quickest way to travel** is by air. 〈수식 관계〉

(2) 서술적 용법 수식 관계(be to 용법)

to 부정사가 형용사 보어일 경우이다.

Grammar Tip 예의가 운의(다)

1. We **are to meet** him here. 〈예정(be scheduled to = be going to)〉
2. He is **to pay** his debt. 〈의무(should = ought to)〉
3. Happiness **is not to be bought** with money. 〈가능(can) 주로 수동형으로 쓰임〉
4. She said goodbye, little knowing that we **were never to meet** again. 〈운명(be doomed to = be destined to)〉
5. Work hard if you **are to pass** the exam. 〈의도(intend to)〉

(3) 관계대명사 + 부정사

1. I have no house **in which I can live**. = I have no house **in which to live**.

   in과 to 부정사의 충돌을 막기 위해 관계대명사가 필요하다.

   = I have no house **to live in**. (○)

   = I have no house **in to live**. (×)

   = I have no house **which to live in**. (×)

❸ 부사적 용법

Grammar Tip 목이양원조결정

1. He came here**(in order = so as) to meet me**. 〈목적〉

= He came here so that he might(could) meet me.

2. (a) He must be a fool **to believe such a thing**. <이유(판단의 근거)>
   (b) He cannot be a fool **to solve the problem**.
3. **To do his best**, He could not finish it in a week. <양보>
4. (a) I was sorry **to hear the bad news**. <감정의 원인>
   (b) They rejoiced **to know that he would come soon**.
5. **To hear him talk**, you would take him for an American. <조건>
6. (a) He grew up **to be a fine gentleman**. <결과>
   (b) He worked hard **only to fail**.
   (c) He didn't live **to see the work finished**.
   (그는 그 일이 끝나는 것을 볼 정도로 오래 살지 못했다.)
   동사가 부정일 때 '~할 정도로' 로 번역
   live, awake, grow, grow up의 무의지 동사 다음의 부정사는 '결과' 의 용법이 된다.
7. (a) French is difficult **to learn**. <정도(형용사 · 부사에 대한 수식의 정도)>
   (b) You are old enough **to know better**.
   (c) He was so fortunate **as to pass the examination**.

C 원형부정사

❶ 지각(知覺)동사

5형식 본동사가 see, hear, feel, watch, look at, notice, observe, listen to의 지각동사이고, 목적보어가 동사형이 될 경우 그 목적보어는 원형동사가 된다.

1. I **saw** him **enter** the house. <지각동사>
2. I **heard** him **play** the guitar at the concert.

❷ 사역(使役)동사

5형식 본동사가 make, bid, have, let, help(to도 가능)의 사역동사이고 목적보어가 동사형이 될 경우 그 목적보어는 원형동사가 된다.

1. I **made** him **write** a letter of apology. <사역동사>
   = He was made **to** write a letter of apology by me.
   본동사가 사역동사, 지각동사인 5형식 문장이 수동태로 바뀌면 목적보어였던 원형부정사는 to부정사가 된다.
2. **Let** me **know** your address.
3. He **bade** me **clean** his shoes.
4. I will **help** you **(to) do** the work.
5. (a) I will **have** him **repair** it. <'시키다' 의 의미>
   (나는 그가 그것을 수선하도록 시킬 것이다.)
   (b) He **had** his wife **die** last year. <'당하다' 의 의미>
   (그는 작년에 상처(喪妻)를 당했다.)

❸ 관용적 용법

1. (a) You **had better go** at once.
   (b) I think you **had better take** a rest.
   • had better(best) + 동사 원형
2. (a) I **cannot but feel** sorry for the old man.
   (나는 그 노인에게 유감을 느끼지 않을 수 없다.)
   (b) I **cannot help feeling** sorry for the old man.
   • cannot but + 동사 원형 = cannot help ~ing
3. My mother **did nothing but** weep.
   • do nothing but + 동사 원형
4. (a) I **would rather stay** at home than **go out**.
   (b) I **would rather die** than **live** in dishonor.
   (나는 불명예스럽게 사느니 차라리 죽겠다.)
   • would rather A than B = would sooner A than B = would as soon A as B
5. He **may well be** proud of his son.
   (그는 그의 아들을 자랑스럽게 여길만한 이유가 있다.)
   • may well + 동사 원형 = have a good reason to

6. You **may as well go** at once.
(즉시 가는 편이 좋겠다.)
▪may as well 원형 = had better 원형

7. You **may as well** not **know** a thing at all **as know** it imperfectly.
(무엇을 불완전하게 아느니 차라리 모르는 편이 낫다.)

D 의미상 주어, 시제, 기타

❶ 의미상 주어

1. It is difficult **for him** to solve the problem. <의미상 주어: **for + 목적격**>
= It is difficult that he should solve the problem.

2. It is very kind **of you** to say so. <의미상 주어: **of + 목적격**>
= You are very kind to say so.
사람의 성질이나 특징을 나타내는 형용사 nice, good, careless, kind, wise, thoughtful, considerate 다음에 의미상의 주어는 「of + 목적격」으로 표시한다.

3. It is **easy** for Tom to master English.
= Tom is easy to master English. (×)
= English is easy for Tom to master. (◯) <타동사의 목적어>
hard, easy, dangerous, difficult, impossible, pleasant 등의 형용사는 사람이 주어가 될 수 없으나, 주어가 동사의 목적어에서 온 경우에는 가능하다.

❷ 부정사의 시제

1. (a) He seems **to be** ill. <**단순 부정사** : 본동사 시제와 일치>
= It seems that he is ill.
(b) He thought her **to be** honest.
= He thought that she was honest.
(c) The theater happened **to be** crowded yesterday.
= It happened that the theater was crowded yesterday.

2. (a) He seems **to have been** ill. <**완료 부정사** : 본동사보다 한 시제 더 과거>

   = It seems that he was(has been) ill.

   (b) He appears **to have been** rich.

   = It appears that he was rich.

❸ 부정사의 부정

부정어를 to 앞에 놓는다.

1. He did not try to smile. <try를 부정>
2. (a) He tried **not to smile**. <to smile을 부정>

   (b) I told him **not to go** there. <to go 부정>

❹ 분리 부정사

부사의 부정사 수식을 분명히 하기 위해, 부사를 to와 동사원형 사이에 놓는다.

1. He **entirely** failed **to understand** it. <entirely가 failed를 수식, 완전부정>
2. He failed **to entirely understand** it. <entirely가 understand를 수식, 부분부정>

❺ 독립부정사

To tell the truth, I have not read the novel yet. <문장 전체 수식>

ex. To be honest	정직하게 말하면
So to speak	말하자면
To begin with	우선
To be sure	확실히
not to speak of = to say nothing of	~ 은 말할 것도 없이
= not to mention = let alone	
To conclude	결론적으로

Basic Reading 2

1 **The capacity** to endure a more or less monotonous life is one which should be acquired in childhood.

- capacity[kəpǽsəti] n. 능력
- endure[endjúər] v. 견디다, 참다
- more or less 다소
- monotonous[mənɑ́tənəs/ -nɔ́t-] a. 단조로운

2 When you come across a strange word, **never fail to** look it up in your dictionary.

- come across = meet by chance
- look up in the dictionary = find a word in the dictionary

3 "Love" says one writer, "is necessary food for the young; **one has only to** watch **the efforts** of children who are starved of love to gain attentions somehow by any method, **to realize** how desperate is their need."

- to gain 부정사의 형용사적 용법, the efforts를 수식
- somehow adv. 어떻게든지
  I must get it finished somehow(or other).
- to realize 부정사의 부사적 용법「목적」내지는「결과」
- desperate[déspərit] a. 필사적인

4 He **intended to have gone abroad**. He would have gone, if he had not been taken ill.

• go abroad 외국으로 여행하다
• He would have gone, if he had not been taken ill. 가정법 과거완료

5 A lady who was having dinner in a country hotel, turned round and asked a man, who was sitting at the table behind her, to pass the mustard to her. "You **seem to have mistaken** me for a waiter," he answered rudely. "No, not at all," replied the lady coolly, "I merely mistook you for a gentleman."

• pass[pæs] v. (식탁 등에서 물건을) 돌리다, 건네주다
Please pass me the salt.
• mistake A for B : A를 B로 오해하다

6 I carried what luggage I immediately needed with me from lodging, and the rest **was to be sent** by the carrier.

• what luggage = all the luggage that 관계형용사
• lodgings[lɑ́dʒiŋ] n. 하숙
• carrier[kǽriər] 운반인, 운송업자

7 The thought of all the things he has to learn sometimes fills a student with a despair. The mere sight of the thousands of strange words in an English dictionary sometimes paralyses the mind. Yet if we **are to be** students, we must patiently start to learn one thing and then another, step by step.

• despair[dispέər] n. 절망, 자포자기
• paralyse[pǽrəlàiz] vt. 마비시키다 무력하게 만들다
• patiently[péiʃəntli] ad. 끈기 있게, 참을성 있게
• step by step 한 걸음 한 걸음, 착실히

8 He informed us of the times of arrival and departure at various places on the route, **where to change trains**, the times of connections and so on.

- inform A of B : A에게 B를 알리다
- connection[kənékʃən] n. 연결, 관계(= relation)
- and so on = and so forth ~등

9 There is no human society, however primitive, which has not discovered the use of tools, even if these consist of nothing more than **sharpened pieces** of stone and wood **with which to kill** animals for food, or **to dig** the soil for crops.

- however primitive(it may be) 복합관계부사가 이끄는 양보의 부사절
- these = tools
- nothing more than = only
- soil[sɔil] a. 토양
- crop[krɑp] n. 작물
- to kill과 to dig은 sharpened pieces를 수식하는 형용사 용법의 부정사

10 Many public speakers are tempted to rely too heavily on written drafts or note cards to remind themselves of what they are going to speak about. This shows lack of preparation, lack of interest in the audience, and nervousness. Many speakers are so dependent on their notes that if their notes get lost somewhere, they become miserably nervous and unsure of **what to say** or **do** next, and even forget what they have just said.

- be tempted to ~하도록 부추기다
- rely on (depend on) ~에 의존하다

- draft[dræft, drɑːft] n. 초안, 설계도
- remind A of B : A에게 B를 상기시키다
- audience[ɔ́ːdiəns] n. 청중, 관객
- miserably[mízərəbəli] ad. 비참하게, 초라하게
- unsure[ʌnʃúər] a. 불확실한, 믿을 수 없는

11 **To do their leader justice**, he was the last man to shrink from his responsibilities, and he coached his men carefully as to their respective duties.

- the last, He is the last man to tell a lie.
- shrink from 겁내다, 피하다
- responsibility 책임
- coach[koutʃ] v. 지도하다, 가르치다
- as to = concerning = regarding ~에 관하여
- respective[rispéktiv] a. 각각의

12 Work offers social satisfaction, comradeship and contacts with clients, customers or pupils. It **makes** us **feel** needed and recognized and may give a man status of which he is proud.

- offer[ɔ́(ː)fər, ɑ́f-] v. 제공하다
- comradeship[kɑ́mrædʃip] n. 동료 관계
- contact[kɑ́ntækt] n. 접촉, 교제
- client[kláiənt] n. (의사, 변호사 등의 서비스를 받는) 고객, 의뢰인
- customer[kʌ́stəmər] n. (상점 등에서 정기적으로 물건을 사는) 단골, 고객
- recognize[rékəgnàiz] v. 인식하다(acknowledge)
- status[stéitəs] n. 지위, 신분

13 When we get a machine to understand oral language as well as a native speaker does, we can proceed to numerous other practical applications. We will for example be able to talk to a typewriter and **have** it **type** our sentences.

- does = understands
- proceed[prousíːd] vi. 나아가다
- application[æ̀plikéiʃən] n. 적용, 응용

14 When we read the lives of great men we **cannot but be** struck by the manner in which all kinds of experiences that might in themselves seem to be random, or even disastrous, are turned to account in the long run.

- cannot but be struck = cannot help being struck
- manner[mǽnəːr] n. 방법
- random[rǽndəm] a. 닥치는 대로의, 임의의
- disastrous[dizǽstrəs] a. 재난의, 비참한
- turn ~ to (good) account ~을 이용[활용]하다
- in the long run = finally = in the end

15 Charles Dickens, the English novelist, had described the Mississippi river as a "horrible ditch". With Twain, however, it became "all existence" and an important symbol of "the human journey". He had grown up on the river in Hannibal, Missouri. Although the little town was far from the centers of East Coast culture, it was **the perfect place** for the young Twain **to grow up**. There, he could hear many Indian legends and listen to the stories of the black slaves. But the life of the river itself influenced him the most. The arrival of the big steamboats excited his boyhood dreams of adventure.

- horrible[hɔ́:rəbəl] a. 끔찍한, 무서운
- ditch[ditʃ] n. 수로, 도랑

16 Though the Romans became masters of all the world, they were **not too** proud **to learn** useful lessons from the people whom they conquered. similarly, no matter what your position is in life it is never too late to gain experience from others.

- conquer[kάŋkər] v. 정복하다
- no matter what your position is in life 인생에서 네가 어떤 위치에 있든지
- They were not too proud to learn useful lessons ~
  = They were not so proud that they could not learn useful lessons ~

17 The study of words is not merely something that **has to do with** literature. Words are your tools of thought. You can't even think without them.

- have to do with ~와 관계가 있다
- merely[míərli] ad. 단지(only)
- literature[lítərətʃər] n. 문학
- tool[tu:l] n. 도구

18 Without this liberal spirit, social progress would be slow — perhaps **too** slow **to** meet the rapidly expanding demands of a world in which technological capacities are accelerating at a frightening rate. The liberal approach, I feel, is the only hope for preserving the kind of free, democratic society we believe in. Perhaps it is the only hope for preserving any form of human society.

- Without this liberal spirit, social progress would be slow.
  = If it were not for this liberal spirit, <가정법 과거 구문>
- ~ too slow to meet = ~ so slow that it cannot meet ~
- liberal spirit 자유 정신
- progress[prágrəs] v. 진보, 진보하다
- technological[téknəládʒikəl] a. 과학기술의
- capacity[kəpǽsəti] n. 능력, 용량
- preserve[prizə́:rv] v. 보존하다, 보호하다

Advanced Reading 3

A. Preparing to Read

On her right was a thriving vegetable garden and **beyond** it a small orchard of apple trees.

The situation was **beyond** his control.

The guerrillas shot down one aeroplane and **captured** the pilot.

She has her place in the Asian team **not** because she is white **but** because she is good.

B. Approaching to the Topic

The next year there were many victories. The mountain that was beyond the valley and the hillside where the chestnut forest grew was captured and there were victories beyond the plain on the plateau to the south and we crossed the river in August and lived in a house in Gorizia that had a fountain and many thick shady trees in a walled garden and a wistaria vine purple on the side of the house. Now the fighting was in the next mountains beyond and was not mile away. The town was very nice and our house was very fine. The river ran behind us and the town had been captured very handsomely but the mountains beyond it could not be taken and I was very glad the Austrians seemed to want to come back to the town some time, if the war should end, because they did not bombard it to destroy it but only a little in a military way.

from Farewell to Arms by E. Hemingway

Vocabularies & Expressions for Comprehension

- Gorizia 이태리 북동부에 있는 전략적 요충도시
- chestnut[tʃésnʌ̀t, -nət] 너도밤나무

- plain 평원
- fountain[fáuntin] 분수
- a walled garden 담이 쳐진 정원
- handsomely = skillfully
- bombard[bɑmbɑ́ːrd/ bɔm] 폭격하다
- destroy 파괴하다
- in a military way 군사적인 방식으로

Sentence Pattern Analysis

- the town had been captured very handsomely

  그 도시는 솜씨 있게 점령되었다.

- but the mountains beyond it could not be taken에서 it는 town을 가리킨다.

- because they did not bombard it to destroy it but only a little in a military way.

  not ~ but(~이 아니라 ~이다)의 구문

Ernest Miller Hemingway 는 미국의 소설가로 1899년 일리노이주에서 태어났다. 그의 주요 장편 소설로는 *In Our Time* (1925), *The Sun Also Rises* (1926), *Men Without Women* (1927), *A Farewell to Arms* (1929), *For Whom the Bell Tolls* (1940) 등이 있으며, 단편소설로는 *"Soldier's Home"*, *"Indian Camp"*, *" "Killer"*, *"A Very Short Story"*, *"My Old Man"*, *"Big Two-Hearted River"* 등이 있다. 특히 그의 문체는 일명 'hard-boiled style'로 유명하다.

Wisdom

For a man house is his castle.

인간에게 집이란 자신의 성이다.

sir Edward Coke: Institutes

Advanced Reading 4

A. Preparing to Read

He also denied that he would **seek to** annex the country.

He is also **looking forward to** getting more acquainted with social law.

Professor Yun said they were fighting for freedom of speech, freedom of worship, and freedom from **want**.

B. Approaching to the Topic

In the future days, which we seek to make secure, we look forward to a world founded upon four essential human freedoms.

The first is freedom of speech and expression — everywhere in the world.

The second is freedom of every person to worship God in his own way, everywhere in the world.

The third is freedom from want — which, translated into world terms, means economic understandings which will secure to every nation a healthy peace life time for its inhabitants — everywhere in the world.

The fourth is freedom from fear — which, translated into world terms, means a world-wide reduction of armament to such a point and in such a thorough fashion that no nation will be in a position to commit an act of physical aggression against any neighbour — anywhere in the word.

That is no vision of a distant millennium. It is a definite basis for a kind of world attainable in our own time and generation. That kind of world is the very antithesis of the so-called new order of tyranny which the dictators seek to create with the crash of a bomb

Four Freedoms by Franklin D. Roosevelt

Vocabularies & Expressions for Comprehension

- seek to 구하다, 찾다
- look forward to 고대하다
- founded upon ~에 입각한
- freedom of speech and expression 언론과 표현의 자유
- in his own way 그 자신의 방식대로
- freedom from want 결핍으로부터의 자유
- world terms 세계적인 의미
- freedom from fear 두려움으로부터의 자유
- world-wide reduction of armament 전 세계적인 군비 축소
- fashion은 way의 뜻
- aggression[əgréʃən] 침략
- millennium[miléniəm] 천년
- attainable 도달할 수 있는
- generation 세대
- antithesis[æntíθəsis] 정반대
- tyranny[tírəni] 폭정
- dictators[díkteitərs] 독재자들

Sentence Pattern Analysis

- The third is freedom from want — which, translated into world terms, means economic understandings which will secure to everywhere in the world.

  which, translated 사이에 if it is를 보충하여 이해. means의 주어는 물론 which이며 그 선행사는 freedom from want이다.

- The fourth is freedom from fear — which, translated into world terms, means a world-wide reduction of armament to such a point and in such a thorough fashion that no nation will be in a position to commit an act of physical aggression against any neighbour—anywhere in the world.

  이 문장의 means의 주어도 which이다. such~ and such ~that 구문. 따라서, '두려움으로부터의 자유란 어떤 국가도 세계 어느 곳에서든지 이웃 국가를 물리적으로 침략하는 행위를 범할 위치에 있지 않을 만큼 그리고 철저한 방식으로 세계적으로 군비를 감축하는 것을 의미합니다.'

Firanklin D. Roosevelt 는 제32대 미국 대통령을 지냈다. 1882년 1월 30일 뉴욕에서 태어났으며, 하바드대학교에서 역사학을 전공하여 3년만에 학사학위를 받고 이어서 뉴욕 콜롬비아대학교에서 법학을 공부했다. 제2차 세계대전시에는 미국을 승전국으로 이끌기도 했다.

Wisdom

Lazy hands makes a man poor, but diligent hands bring wealth.

손을 게으르게 놀리는 자는 가난하게 되고 손이 부지런한 자는 부하게 된다.

Proverb 10: 4

Welcome to English Grammar & Reading

제3장. 분사

A 분사의 성질

B 분사의 용법

C 분사구문

D 분사의 확장

제3장 분사 *Participle*

A 분사의 성질

❶ 분사의 기능

1. I **am writing** a novel. 〈be + 현재분사〉
2. This book **was written** by my uncle. 〈be + 과거분사〉
3. Winter **has gone**. 〈have + 과거분사〉
4. **Being tired**, I went to bed early. 〈분사구문〉

❷ 현재분사

현재분사는

① 문장 1에서 **진행**(~하고 있는)

② 문장 2에서 **능동**(~하는)의 의미를 갖는다.

1. (a) The **barking** ***dog*** does not bite. 〈진행〉
   (b) ***The girl*** (who is) **reading** a newspaper is my sister.
2. (a) We can buy ***a paper*** **containing** the news for a dime. 〈능동〉
   (b) There are a few ***animals*** **living** under water.
   (c) ***The game*** was very **exciting**.
   (d) An **exciting** ***game***. (= a game which excites onlookers)

❸ 과거분사

과거분사는

① 문장 1에서 **완료**(자동사의 PP)

② 문장 2에서 **수동**(타동사의 PP)의 의미를 갖는다.

1. **fallen** *leaves*, **rotten** *eggs*, **a retired** *general* 〈완료〉
2. (a) ***We*** were much **excited** over the game. 〈수동〉
   (b) **excited** ***onlookers*** (= onlookers who are excited by players)
   (c) I received ***a letter*** **written** in English.

B 분사의 용법

국어에서는 관형어가 명사를 앞에서 수식하는 데에 반하여 영어에서는 앞에서 뿐만 아니라 뒤에서도 수식한다. 영어의 경우, 형용사의 전위수식 관계는 국어의 구조에도 존재하는 구조이기 때문에 한국 학생들이 이해를 하는 데 별 문제가 없다. 하지만, 후위수식 관계는 한국어의 구조에는 존재하지 않기 때문에 그 구조의 습득에 어려움을 겪는 학생들이 많다. 한편으로 생각하면 당연한 결과이기도 하다. 따라서 이에 대한 정확한 이해와 연습이 필요하다.

❶ 한정용법(Attributive use)

분사는 형용사처럼 명사상당어구를 수식할 수 있다.

① 문장 1에서는 전위(前位)수식(명사 앞에서 수식)하고,

② 문장 2에서는 후위(後位)수식(명사 뒤에서 수식)한다.

1. (a) They were awakened by an **approaching** ***train***. <전위수식>
   (b) The **irritated** ***child*** started to cry at last.
2. (a) Don't disturb ***the man*** **remaining** calm. (= who remains ~) <후위수식>
   (b) ***The roads*** **leading** into the country are full of cars. (= which lead ~)
   (c) I will introduce ***a girl*** **called** Nancy to him. (= who is called ~)
   (d) ***The goods*** **ordered** last month have not arrived yet. (= which were ordered ~)
   (e) ***The book*** **read** most in the world is the Bible. (= which has been read ~)

❷ 서술용법(Predicative use)

1. ***He*** sat **reading** a newspaper. <주격 보어>
2. (a) I saw ***her*** **running** across the street. <목적격 보어>
   (b) I had ***my hair*** **cut**.

C 분사구문

「접속사 + 주어 + 동사」로 형성된 종속절(부사절)을 포함하는 복문을 분사를 이용하여 부사구로 줄여서 단문이 되도록 만든 문장이다. 분사구문은 **콤마(,)로 분리되는 형태가 되며 부사적 수식어로써 주절을 수식**한다.

❶ 분사구문의 의미

분사구문의 부사절을 주절과 연관하여 해석하면, 그 의미관계를 **동시동작(부대상황), 양보, 이유, 조건, 시간, 계속**으로 분류할 수 있다.

Grammar Tip 동양(의) 이조시계

1. I was reading a book, **my wife sewing by my side**. <부대상황(동시동작, as, while)>
   = I was reading a book, while my wife was sewing by my side.
2. **Admitting what you say**, I still think you are in the wrong. <양보(though, even if)>
   = Though I admit what you say, I still think you are in the wrong.
3. **Feeling tired**, he went to bed early. <이유(as, since, because)>
   = As he felt tired, he went to bed early.
4. **Turning to the left**, you will find the post office. <조건(if)>
   = If you turn to the left, you will find the post office.
5. **Walking along the street**, I met an old friend of mine.<시간(while, when, after)>
   = While I was walking along the street, I met an old friend of mine.
6. Our train left Pusan at 8:00 a.m., **arriving at Seoul at 12:00**. <계속(and)>
   (= ~ and it arrived at Seoul at 12:00.) <(and + 동사 ; 그리고 ~ 하다)>

❷ 분사구문의 시제

분사구문의 시제는 두 가지가 있다.

① 문장 1의 단순분사구문: 술어동사의 시제와 일치

② 문장 2의 완료분사구문: 술어동사의 시제보다 한 시제 과거로 앞선다 <having + PP>

1. **Being poor**, he couldn't afford to buy a car. <단순분사구문>
   = As he was poor, he couldn't afford to buy a car.
2. **Having finished my homework**, I met her. <완료분사구문>
   = After I had finished my homework, I met her.

❸ 무인칭 독립분사구문

의미상의 주어가 일반인(we, you, they, people 등)일 때 의미상의 주어가 생략되는 분사구문이다.

Generally speaking, boys are fond of girls.

= If we speak generally, boys are fond of girls.

ex. Strictly speaking 엄격히 말하면
Frankly speaking 솔직히 말하면
Talking of ~에 관해 말하자면
Judging from ~ 판단하건대
Seeing[Considering] that ~을 고려하면

❹ 분사구문의 강조

① 현재분사를 강조하기 위해서 「현재분사 + as + 주어 + do 동사」의 형태를
② 과거분사를 강조하기 위해서 「과거분사 + as + 주어 + be 동사」의 형태를 각각 취한다.

1. Standing **as it does** on the hill, the villa commands a fine view.
<현재분사 + as + 주어 + do 동사>
2. Written **as it is** in plain English, the book is fit for beginners.
<과거분사 + as + 주어 + be 동사 >

D 분사의 확장

❶ 분사의 관용적 용법

1. I **go fishing** tomorrow morning. <go ~ ing>
2. It **kept raining** for a week. <keep(on) ~ ing>
3. He **was busy sowing** seeds. <be busy (in) ~ ing>
4. He **had a hard time supporting** his family. <have a hard time (in) ~ ing>
5. He **had no trouble operating** a computer. <have no trouble(difficulty) (in) ~ ing>
6. He **spends his time reading** a novel. <spend(waste) one's time (in) ~ ing>

❷ with + 목적어 + 보어

전치사 with는 다른 전치사와 다르게 목적어와 보어를 동시에 취할 수 있다.

1. It was a calm morning, **with little wind blowing**.
2. **With an eye bandaged**, I could not write properly.
3. He was standing, **with his eyes open**.
4. He lay on a straw, **with his eyes closed and his mouth open**.

Basic Reading 3

1 Fact and fiction are so intermingled in my work that now, **looking** back on it, I can hardly distinguish one from the other.

- fiction[fíkʃən] n. 소설, 허구
- intermingle[ìntərmíŋgəl] v. 섞다, 섞이다; intermingle A with B : A와 B를 혼합하다.
- distinguish A from B = distinguish between A and B 구별하다, 구분하다

2 There is nothing that helps a man in his conduct through life more than a knowledge of his own characteristic weakness, which, **guarded** against, become his strength.

- no ~ more ~ than; Nothing is more important than time.
- conduct[kɑ́ndʌkt] n. 행위, 품행
- characteristic[kæ̀riktərístik] a. 특징적인, 성격상의
- guarded against = if they are guarded against 분사구문
- guard[gɑ:rd] v. 지키다, 삼가다; ~ a person against(from) temptation

3 One of the habits important for the best physical well-being has to do with avoiding excesses. The idea of moderation in all things is no new thought, **having been expressed** by writers several thousand years ago.

- well-being 행복, 안녕
- have to do with ~와 관계가 있다
  A doctor has to do with all sorts of people.
- having been expressed
  = as it(the idea of moderation in all things) was expressed
  중용의 개념은 제시된 것인 바
- moderation[mɑ̀dəréiʃən] n. 알맞음, 중용, 절제

4 **Left to himself**, Henry fell into a day-dream. He thought of his toys and tried to decide which of them he should give to his sister; he had been told he must part with some of them, and indeed it would not make much difference if they were hers by right, since she already treated them as such.

- Left to himself = When he was left to himself
- day-dream 공상, 백일몽
- be told = hear
- part with 내어주다
- by right 정당하게
- as such 그러한 것(사람)으로서

He was a foreigner and was treated as such.

5 **Granting that** we have both the will and the sense to choose our friends well, how few of us have the power! or at least, how limited, for most, is the sphere of choice! Nearly all our associations are determined by chance, or necessity; and restricted within a narrow circle.

- grant(granted) that = even if 설사 ~이라 할지라도
- sense[sens] n. 감각, 분별 판단력
- the power (to choose our friends well)
- association[əsòusiéiʃən, -ʃi-] n. 교제, 연합, 협회
- restrict[ristríkt] vt. 제한(limit, confine), 속박(restrain)

6 By the end of the present century there may well be over **six billion people living on this globe**, an increase of about seventy percent on today's figure. In order to keep pace with this increase in mankind the farmers of the world would have to step up their production of food by at least two per cent every year.

- may well = have a good reason to R
- may as well A as B : B하느니 차라리 A하다
  You may as well not know a thing at all as know it imperfectly.
  (무엇을 불완전하게 아느니 차라리 모르는 편이 낫다.)
- billion[bíljən] n. 10억
- an increase of = which is an increase of
- figure[figjər / -gər] n. 숫자, 꼴(shape), 인물
- keep pace with = keep up with ~와 보조를 맞추다
- set up 촉진(促進)하다, 세우다, 시작하다
- production[prədʌ́kʃən] n. 생산(produce 생산하다, 제조하다)

7 We can see there is **a change taking place** in the U.S.A. It appears that the goal now is to have a pleasant relationship with members of the opposite sex, **with manners being** appropriate to each situation rather than traditional **courtesies applying** in all cases.

- It appears that = It seems that
- relationship[riléiʃənʃip] n. 관계
- manner[mǽnəːr] n. 방법, 태도
- appropriate[əpróuprit] a. (suitable)적절한
- A rather than B : B보다는 오히려 A이다.
- He is a writer rather than a scholar.
- courtesy[kɔ́ːrtəsi] n. 예의(禮儀), 친절

8 I remember that on first venturing out by myself a little distance from home I got lost. In despair of ever finding my way back I began to cry, **hiding my face** against a post at a street corner, and was there soon surrounded by quite a number of passers-by; then a policeman came up, **with brass buttons on his blue coat and a sword at his side**, taking me by the arm he asked me in a

commanding voice where I lived.

- on ~ ing ~ 하자마자
- venture[véntʃər] v. 모험, 감행하다
- ever [긍정문에서] 언제나, 항상, 줄곧, 시종(始終)
- hiding my face against a post = while I was hiding my face against a post
- post[poust] n. 기둥
- take A by the arm; 동사 + 사람 + 전치사(by, on, in) + the + 신체 일부분

  (a) He took me **by** the arm. <by, 붙잡다 계통>

  (b) She struck him **on** the head. <on, 때리다 계통>

  (c) His mother stared him **in** the face. <in, 보다 계통>

9 When the doctor prescribes medicine for a patient, the patient takes the prescription to the chemist's to **have** the medicine **made up**.

- I could not make myself heard on account of the noise.

  = I could not make them hear me account of the noise.
- Please keep the door closed.

10 To read a great novel is to get **the dying battery** of the imagination recharged, and that is what most of us, out of a kind of self-defence, are refusing to do.

- recharge[riːtʃάːrdʒ] vt. 재충전하다
- that = to read a great novel
- self-defence[self-diféns] n. 자기 방위

11 'Please' and 'Thank you' are the small change with which we pay our way as social beings. They are the little courtesies by which we keep the machine of life **oiled** and **running** sweetly. They put our intercourse upon the basis of a friendly cooperation, an easy give-and-take, instead of on the basis of superiors dictating to inferiors. It is a very vulgar mind that would wish to command where he can have the service for asking, and have it with willingness and good feeling instead of resentment.

- courtesy[kɔ́:rtəsi] n. 예의, 호의
- intercourse[íntərkɔ̀rs] n. 교제, 영적 교통
- cooperation[kouάpəréiʃən] n. 협력, 협동
- dictate[díkteít] v. 명령하다, 지배하다
- vulgar[vʌ́lgər] a. 천(賤)한, 야비한
- resentment[rizéntmənt] n. 원한, 분개

12 Among **the many problems facing** our modern civilization, the fate of the aged is certainly one of those foremost in the public mind, **judging** by the number of articles on **this subject carried** by magazines and newspapers. Over the past century, in fact, the average life span in industrialized countries has increased by leaps and bounds until it has now reached 73 years.

- one of those foremost (problems) 가장 중요한 문제점들 중의 하나
- judging by ~ = when we judge by ~
- the aged 노인들
- foremost[fɔ́:rmòust] a. 맨 먼저의, 처음의
- average life span 평균 수명
- by leaps and bounds 급속도로, 비약적으로

13 Recently, I narrowly escaped a head-on collision when a driver who was using his car phone became distracted and crossed the center line. A police officer told me that he knows of several accidents **involving** drivers who were using phones, fax machines or computers and that this is happening more and more.

- head-on collision 정면 충돌
- distract[distrǽkt] vt. 주의를 분산시키다

14 Daisy Miller (1879) is another novel about American innocence **defeated** by the stiff, traditional values of Europe. Daisy brings her "free" American spirit to Europe. She looks at people as individuals, rather than as members of a social class. Despite her goodness, she is completely misunderstood by the European characters. She meets a young American, who has lived in Europe a long time and has taken on the same kind of coldness. The coldness of these people finally leads Daisy to her death.

- innocence[ínəsns] n. 순진함
- defeat[difíːt] vt. 패배시키다, 물리치다
- stiff[stif] a. 경직된, 완고한
- character[kǽriktər] n. (등장) 인물
- take on 띠다, 몸에 지니다

Advanced Reading 5

A. Preparing to Read

A couple of revellers **dropped** their trousers.

She has to go to the men's department to find trousers that **fit** at the waist.

The talks took place **in the presence of** a diplomatic observer.

B. Approaching to the Topic

It is said that the world is in a state of bankruptcy, that the world owes the world more than the world can pay, and ought to go into chancery, and be sold. I do not think this general insolvency, which involves in some sort all the population, to be the reason of the difficulty experienced at Christmas and New Year, and other times, in bestowing gifts; since it is always so pleasant to be generous, though very vexatious to pay debts. But the impediment lies in the choosing. If, at any time, it comes into my head, that a present is due from me to somebody, I am puzzled what to give, until the opportunity is gone. Flowers and fruits are always fit presents; flowers, because they are a proud assertion that a ray of beauty outvalues all the utilities of the world. These gay natures contrast with the somewhat stern countenance of ordinary nature: they are like music heard out of a work-house. Nature does not cocker us: we are children, not pets: she is not fond: everything is dealt to us without fear or favor, after severe universal laws. Yet these delicate flowers look like the frolic and interference of love and beauty. Men use to tell us that we love flattery, even though we are not deceived by it, because it shows that we are of importance enough to be courted. Something like that pleasure, the flowers give us: what am I to whom these sweet hints are addressed? Fruits are acceptable gifts, because they are the flower of commodities, and admit of fantastic values being attached to them. If a man should send to me to come a hundred miles to visit him, and should set before me a basket of fine summerfruit, I should think there was some proportion between the labor and the reward.

Gifts by Ralph Waldo Emerson
from Essays: Second Series (1844)

Vocabularies & Expressions for Comprehension

- bankruptcy[bǽŋkrʌptsi, -rəpsi] n. 파산, 도산(倒産);
- owe[ou] v. 빚지고 있다, −의 은혜를 입고 있다
- chancery[tʃǽnsəri, tʃɑ́:n-] n. 형평법(衡平法) 재판소, 형평법
- insolvency[insɑ́:lvənsi/ -sɔ́l-] n. 『법률』 (빚의) 반제(返濟)불능, 채무초과
- population[pɑ̀pjəléiʃən/ pɔ́p-] n. 인구, (the ~) 주민; 특정 계급의 사람들
- experienced[ikspíəriənst] a. 경험 있는[많은], 숙련된, 노련한; 체험된
- in some sort ~ 어느 정도(까지), 약간
- bestow[bistóu] vt. 주다, 수여[부여]하다
- generous[ʒénərəs] a. 후한, 푸짐한, 풍부한(plentiful), 관대한, 아량 있는
- vexatious[vekséiʃəs] a. 귀찮은, 성가신, 곤란한, 난처한;
- debt[det] n. U,C 빚, 부채. C 의리, 은혜
- impediment[impédəmənt] n. 방해(물), 장애(to); 신체 장애; 언어 장애
- puzzle[pʌ́zl] v. 당혹게 하다, 어리둥절해지다, 어쩔 줄 모르다(about; over)
- opportunity[ɑ̀pərtjú:nəti/ ɔ̀pər-] n. 기회, 호기; 행운
- assertion[əsə́:rʃən] n. 단언, 주장
- outvalue[ɑ̀utvǽlju:] vt. −보다도 가치가 있다
- utility[ju:tíləti] n. 쓸모가 있음(usefulness), 유용, 유익; 실용, (보통 pl.) 실용품
- gay[gei] a. (~er; ~est) 명랑한(merry), 즐거운, 화미(華美)한, 동성애자의
- countenance[kɑ̀untənəns] n. 생김새, 용모, 안색, 표정
- cocker vt. 응석을 받아 주다; (병자를) 소중히 하다
- fond[fɑnd/ fɔnd] a. 애정 있는, 다정한(affectionate), (눈치 · 표정 따위가) 호의에 넘치는
- severe[sivíə:r] a. (severer; -est) 엄한, 호된, 모진, 통렬한,(벌 따위가) 가혹한(harsh)
- frolic[frɑ̀lik/ frɔ̀l-] n. 장난(침), 야단 법석; 유쾌한 모임

- interference[ìntərfíərəns] n. 방해, 훼방; 저촉(抵觸); 충돌; 간섭
- flattery[flǽtəri] n. 아첨, 치렛말, 빌붙음
- commodity[kəmɑ̀dəti/ -mɔ̀d-] n. (pl. -ties) (흔히 pl.) 일용품, 필수품, (pl.) 상품;
  prices of commodities 물가
  staple commodities 중요 상품
- proportion[prəpɔ́ːrʃən] n. 비(比), 비율, 조화, 균형, (일정 비율의) 부분; 몫
- reward[riwɔ́ːrd] n. 보수, 포상; 현상금; 사례금(for). 보답, 응보
  No ~ without toil (격언) 고생 끝에 낙(樂)
- labor ~ 【영국】 −bour [léibər] n. 노동, 근로. 「집합적」 노동자, 애씀, 노력.
  고역; (pl.) 세상사, 속세의 일. 산고, 진통

Sentence Pattern Analysis

- It is said that the world is in a state of bankruptcy, that the world owes the world more than the world can pay, and ought to go into chancery, and be sold.
  It ~ that 의 구문. 세상이 파산상태에 있고, 세상이 갚을 수 있는 이상으로 빚을 지고 있어서 형평법 재판소에 가야만 하고 매각되어야 한다고 말한다.

- a present is due from me to somebody,
  내가 다른 누군가에게 응당 주어야할 선물

- I am puzzled what to give.
  나는 무엇을 줄까 고민한다.

- Nature does not cocker us:
  자연은 우리의 응석을 받아주지 않는다.

- Flowers and fruits are always fit presents
  꽃과 과일은 항상 선물로는 안성맞춤이다.

- after severe universal laws
  엄한 우주법칙을 따라서

• even though we are not deceived by it

우리가 아첨에 현혹되지 않는다 할지라도

• because it shows that we are of importance enough to be courted.

아첨을 받는다는 것은 우리가 구애를 받을 만큼 중요하다는 것을 보여주기 때문에.

• Something like that pleasure, the flowers give us

그런 즐거움과 같은 무엇인가를 꽃은 우리에게 준다.

• what am I to whom these sweet hints are addressed?

이런 달콤한 말들을 듣는 나는 누구란 말인가?

Ralph waldo Emerson (1803-1882) 은 미국의 시인이자 초절주의적 사상가이기도 하다. 그의 주요 저서로는 *Nature* (1836), *The American Scholar* (1837), *Cambridge* (1838), *Poems* (1847) 등이 있다. 특히 에머슨은 동양사상의 영향을 많이 받은 작가로서 최근 그에 대한 연구가 활발하게 진행되고 있기도 하다.

Wisdom

Man is no more than a reed, the weakest in nature. But he is a thinking reed.

인간은 자연 가운데 가장 연약한 갈대에 불과하다. 그러나 인간은 생각하는 갈대이다.

Blaise Pascal: Pensees

Advanced Reading 6

A. Preparing to Read

It is a common saying that time is money.

You may stay here today **so long as** you keep quiet.

Further investigation **was hindered** by the loss of all documentation on the case.

B. Approaching to the Topic

It is a common saying that thought is free. A man can never be hindered from thinking whatever he chooses so long as he conceals what he thinks. The working of his mind is limited only by the bounds of his experience and the power of his imagination. But this natural liberty of private thinking is of little value. It is unsatisfactory and even painful to the thinker himself, if he is not permitted to communicate his thoughts to others, and it is obviously of no value to his neighbours. Moreover it is extremely difficult to hide thoughts that have any power over the mind.

If a man's thinking leads him to call in question ideas and customs which regulate the behaviour of those about him, to reject beliefs which they hold, to see better ways of life than those they follow, it is almost impossible for him, if he is convinced of the truth of his own reasoning, not to betray by silence, chance words, or general attitude that he is different from them and does not share their opinions. Some have preferred, like Socrates, some would prefer today, to face death rather than conceal their thoughts. Thus freedom of thought, in any valuable sense, includes freedom of speech.

A History of Freedom of Thought by John Bagnell Bury

Vocabularies & Expressions for Comprehension

- It is a common saying that ~흔히 말해지고 있다
- be hindered from ~ ing ~을 방해받다
- whatever he chooses 그 가 선택한 어떤 것이든지
- so long as ~하기만 한다면
- conceals 감추다
- of little value 거의 가치가 없다
- bounds 범위, 한계
- communicate[kəmjú:nəkèit] 전달하다, 소통하다
- have any power over ~에 지배력을 행사하다, 맘대로 할 수 있다
- call~ in question 의심하다.
- regulate[régjəlèit] 규율하다, 제한하다
- is convinced of ~을 확신하다.
- is different from ~다르다
- share[ʃεə:r] 공유하다
- prefer to ~을 더 좋아하다

Sentence Pattern Analysis

- If a man's thinking leads him to call in question ideas and customs which regulate the behaviour of those about him, to reject beliefs which they hold, to see better ways of life than those they follow,

  If a man's ~ they follow는 종속절임. leads him은 to call~, to reject, to see와 바로 연결된다. ideas and customs는 call의 목적어임. those they follow에 나오는 those는 ways of life를 가리킴.

- it is almost impossible for him, if he is convinced of the truth of his own reasoning, not to betray by silence, chance words, or general attitude that he is different from them and does not share their opinions.

  it is for him~ to betray의 구문임. 타동사 betray의 목적은 that 이하 절이다. 그리고 by silence, chance words or general attitude는 부사구이다.

- Some have preferred, like Socrates, some would prefer today, to face death rather than conceal their thoughts.

have preferred와 would prefer는 모두 to face death와 연결된다. would prefer today에 나오는 would는 가정법 과거형이다.

John Bagnell Bury (1861-1927) 는 아일랜드 출신의 고전주의자이며 역사학자이다. 그의 주요 저서로는 *History of the Later Roman Empire* (1899), *History of Greece* (1900), *A History of Freedom of Thought* (1913) 등이 있으며, 특히, 열 두 나라의 언어를 구사한 것으로 유명하다.

Wisdom

I think, therefore I am. (Cogito, ergo sum.)

나는 생각한다. 그러므로 나는 존재한다.

Rene Descartes: Le Discours de la Methode

제4장. 동명사

A 동명사의 기능

B 동명사의 용법

C 동명사의 관용적 표현 I

D 동명사의 관용적 표현 II

E 문장전환과 전치사

제4장 동명사 *Gerund*

A 동명사의 기능

1. (a) **Seeing** is believing. <주어>
   (b) **Making** much money is not the aim of life.
2. (a) Her first job had been **selling** cars. <보어>
   (b) I found it unpleasant **walking** in the rain.
3. (a) Most women enjoy **chattering**. <목적어>
   (b) He is sure of **my succeeding**.

B 동명사의 용법

❶ 동명사의 부정

동명사 바로 앞에 not[never]를 둔다.

1. I am sure of the statement **not being** true.
2. Excuse me for **not coming** on time.

❷ 의미상의 주어

1. I don't like **his speaking** ill of others. <동명사 의미상 주어: 소유격>
2. They were glad of **the war being over**. <무생물 주어>
3. He succeeded in **passing** the examination. <주절의 주어와 동일시 생략>
4. **Drinking** too much is not good for health. <일반인 주어>

❸ 동명사의 시제

동명사의 시제는
① 술어동사와 같은 시제를 나타내는 ing 형태의 단순동명사와,
② 술어동사보다 이전 시제를 나타내는 having PP 형태의 완료동명사의 시제가 있다.

1. He was proud **of his father's being rich** <단순동명사>
   = that his father was rich.

2. I am sure **of his coming on time**.
= that he will come on time

3. I am ashamed **of having been idle**. <완료동명사>
= that I was(has been) idle

C 동명사의 관용적 표현 1

1. **It is no use trying** to persuade her.: ~ 하는 것은 소용없다
   ▶ It is no use(good) ~ ing = It is of no use to = It is useless to
   = There is no use (in) ~ ing
2. **There is no knowing** how old she is.: ~하는 것은 불가능하다
   ▶ There is no ~ ing = It is impossible to = We cannot
3. I **cannot help respecting** him.: ~ 하지 않을 수 없다
   ▶ cannot help(avoid) ~ing = cannot choose but 원형 = cannot but 원형
4. He **was on the point of leaving** the room.: 막 ~하려는 참이다
   ▶ be on the point(edge) of ~ing
5. **It goes without saying that** he will help me with the work.: ~은 말할 필요가 없다
   ▶ It goes without saying that ~ = It is needless to say that ~
   = It is a matter of course that ~
6. I never see you **without thinking of** your father.: ~하면 반드시 ~ 하다
   = I never see you but I think of your father.
   = When I see you, I always think of your father.
   = Whenever I see you, I think of your father.
   ▶ not(never) without ~ ing = not(never) but + S + V
   = when S + V, S + always = whenever S + V, S + V
7. He **came near being** drowned.: 거의 ~할 뻔하다
   = He nearly escaped being drowned.
   ▶ come(go) near ~ ing
8. I **feel like sleeping** now.: ~ 하고 싶은 기분이다
   ▶ feel like ~ ing = feel inclined to = have a mind to = be disposed to

9. **I make a point of getting up** at six.: ~ 하는 것을 규칙으로 삼다

▶ make a point of ~ ing = make it a rule to = be in the habit of ~ ing

10. This picture is **of my own painting**.: 자신이 손수 ~ 한

= This is a picture painted by myself.

▶ of one's own ~ ing

11. **Instead of waiting**, she went away.: ~ 하는 대신에

= She did not wait but went away.

▶ instead of ~ ing = not A but B

12. **In spite of being** injured, he attended the class.: ~에도 불구하고

▶ in spite of ~ ing = despite(with all = for all = after all) ~ ing

13. He **is above telling** a lie.: ~ 할 리가 없는

= He is the last man to tell a lie.

▶ be above ~ ing

14. **What do you think about having** lunch together?: ~ 하는 게 어때?

▶ What do you think about(of) ~ ing = Why don't you ~? = How(What) about ~ ing?

= What do you say to ~ ing?

15. I **am far from being** satisfied.: 결코 ~이 아닌

▶ be far from ~ ing

16. **Besides teaching** English, he is studying at graduate school.: ~뿐만 아니라

▶ Besides(In addition to) ~ ing = not only ~ but also ~

17. **On seeing** me, he ran away.: ~하자마자

▶ On(upon) ~ ing = as soon as + S + V = The moment + S + V

18. **In driving** a car, do not fall asleep.: ~할 때

▶ In ~ ing = when + S +V

D 동명사의 관용적 표현 2

보통 전치사 to와 동사원형이 합하여 부정사가 된다. 그런데 전치사 to 다음에 반드시 ~ing형의 동명사가 오는 경우가 있다. 이 「to + ~ing」 경우는 암기해서 구별해야 한다.

전치사 to + ~ing형

1. Do you **object to eating** out?: ~에 반대하다
   ▶ object to ~ ing = be opposed to ~ ing = have an abjection to ~ ing
2. You must **attend to taking care of** the baby.: ~에 주의하다
   ▶ attend to ~ ing = heed to ~ ing = pay attention to ~ ing
3. He **contributed to achieving** our aim.: ~에 공헌하다
   ▶ contribute to ~ ing
4. I **am** not **equal to doing** the task.: ~에 필적하다, ~을 감당할 능력이 있다
   ▶ be equal to ~ ing
5. He **took to gambling**.: ~에 탐닉하다
   ▶ take to ~ ing = be addicted to ~ ing
6. They **fell to drinking**.: ~을 시작하다
   ▶ fall to ~ ing
7. I **look forward to meeting** you in a few days.: ~을 학수고대하다
   ▶ look forward to ~ ing
8. He **devoted himself to painting** a portrait.: ~에 몰두하다
   ▶ devote (apply) oneself to ~ ing
9. He **confessed to having** told a lie.: ~한 것을 고백하다
   ▶ confess to ~ ing
10. **See to buying** the ticket please.: 꼭 ~하다
    ▶ see to ~ ing
11. **What do you say to going** to the movies?: ~하는 것이 어때?
    ▶ What do you say to ~ ing
12. He went to China **with a view to buying** a medicine.: ~할 목적으로
    ▶ with a view to ~ ing
13. The taxi driver **is used to facing** a danger.: ~에 익숙하다
    ▶ be(get) used to ~ ing = be accustomed to ~ ing

E 문장전환과 전치사

1. I insisted **on his going to school**.

   = that he should go to school

   insist on + 동명사

2. She always complains **of his smoking in the room**.

   = that he smokes in the room

   complain[hear, dream, know, admit] of + 동명사

3. Father suggested **our going on a picnic**.

   = that we should go on a picnic

   suggest[deny, like, regret] + 전치사 없이 동명사

4. He is proud **of being a doctor**.

   = that he is a doctor

   be 형용사 of + 동명사

   be [proud / afraid / ashamed / ignorant / sure / certain / confident / aware / conscious] of ~ ing

Basic Reading 4

1 Very few can **enjoy traveling** to their heart's content because it requires plenty of time and money.

- very few (people) can ~ 매우 소수의 사람만이 ~ 할 수 있다
- to one's heart's content 만족할 때까지
- require[rikwáiər] v. 요구하다

2 As we lived in the same town, I could hardly **avoid meeting** him from time to time.

- can hardly avoid meeting = can hardly help meeting 만나지 않을 수 없었다
- from time to time (sometimes) 때때로, 이따금

3 He **remembered seeing** the woman in question talking to the stationmaster and the stationmaster seeing her into the train.

- in question 문제의; the person[matter] in question 당사자[본 건(本件)]
- talk to ~에게 말을 걸다
- stationmaster[stéiʃənmæ̀stəːr] 역장
- see her into the train 그녀를 기차로 배웅하다

4 I must sincerely apologize for **not having presented** myself yesterday as I had promised; but an unexpected affair of the greatest importance called me off at the very moment I was on my way to your house.

- apologize (to A) for B : A에게 B에 대하여 사과하다
- present oneself 출석하다

- an unexpected affair 예상하지 못한 일 <무생물주어>
- of great importance 대단히 중요한; of + 명사 ⇒ 형용사구
- call off 취소하다(cancel)
- at the moment (that) I was ~ <관계부사 that(when)이 생략됨>

5 When my husband retired, we decided to buy a smaller house. At first, we **thought of moving** out of town but I didn't really like doing that. I don't **object to living** in the country but after talking it over we realized that we **were** so **used to living** in this area that it seemed silly to go away from the neighborhood **without having** a very good reason.

- retire[ritáiəːr] v. 은퇴(퇴직)하다
- object to ~ing 항의하다, 반대하다
- be used to ~ing ~에 익숙해 있다
- neighborhood[néibərhùd] n. 이웃, 근처

6 Many old customs are gradually dying out in our country year by year, but some of them **are** no doubt **worth being** preserved and handed down to posterity forever.

- gradually[grǽdʒuəli] ad. 차차, 점차로
- die out 죽어 없어지다, 차차 소멸하다
- be worth ~ ing ~할 가치가 있다
- preserve[prizə́ːrv] v. 보존하다, 유지하다(maintain)
- hand down 유산을 물리다
- posterity[pɑːstérəti] n. 후세(future generation), 자손(offspring); (⇔ ancestry 선조)

7 The distinction between "language" and "literature" in the approach to English is clearly artificial as well as quite misleading and harmful. For **there is no separating** the two disciplines or studies.

- distinction[distíŋkʃən] n. 구별(discrimination)
- language[lǽŋgwidʒ] n. 어학(語學)
- literature[lítərətʃər] n. 문학(文學)
- approach[əpróutʃ] n. 접근법, 연구법
- B as well as A = not only A but also B : A뿐만 아니라 B도 역시
- misleading[mislí:diŋ] a. 오도(誤導)하는
- separate[sépərèit] v. 분리하다
- there is no ~ing = we cannot
- discipline[dísəplin] n. 훈련, 학과, 학문분야

8 Many Americans want their public education system to go back **to teaching** young people the basic subjects of English literature and composition, mathematics, and science.

- public[pʌ́blik] a. 공적인
- system[sístəm] n. 제도, 방식
- composition[kɑ́mpəzíʃən] n. 작문

9 Some slow readers may be good readers, and some fast readers poor readers — it is how much you can understand and remember that counts. **It is no good trying** to read faster than you can assimilate ideas.

- it is ~ that counts : it is ~ that 강조구문
- count[kaunt] vi. 가치가 있다, 중요하다

- It is no good ~ ing ~해야 소용없다
- than 접속사
- assimilate[əsíməlèit] v. (지식 등을)흡수하다, 이해하다, 동화하다

10 The greatest achievement in my life in terms of morality is that I can apologize to someone I have wronged. I can bow my head and ask for forgiveness. I think everyone should learn to do this, everyone should realize that, **far from humiliating**, it elevates the soul.

- achievement[ətʃí:vmənt] n. 성취
- in terms of ~의 면에서
- morality[mɔ(:)rǽləti] 도덕, 도의, 덕성
- apologize to A for B 사과하다
- humiliate[hju:mílièit] v. 굴욕감을 느끼게 하다, 창피를 주다
- elevate[éləvèit] vt. 들어올리다(raise), (정신 · 성격 등을) 고상하게 하다

Advanced Reading 7

A. Preparing to Read

They were **substituting** violence **for** dialogue today.

The long-term future of the country **rests on** how we teach our children.

It's **all up** with them.

B. Approaching to the Topic

Liberty is built on peace and can have no other foundation. War and disorder are its two great enemies. Our free government, as we enjoy it, is the substitution of law for force, of argument for physical strife. It is an achievement of many centuries; it rests on the belief that free discussion is the likeliest way of doing justice and reaching sensible conclusions about policy. But it has rules of its own which must be obeyed. It requires tolerance and mutual forbearance. It requires that minorities shall submit for the time being, when they are outvoted in Parliament; and be content to work for a future in which they will have made their views prevail by reason and argument. If any of these assumptions fail, if our feelings become literally too strong for words, if minorities will not submit and fly from words to blows, or majorities so abuse their power as to drive minorities to physical resistance, then it is all up with liberty

Freedom by J. A. Spender

Vocabularies & Expressions for Comprehension

- foundation[fàundéiʃ-ən] 토대
- disorder[disɔ́:rdər] 무질서

- free government 자유주의 정부
- substitution[sʌ̀bstitjúːʃən] 대리, 대용
- argument[áːrgjəmənt] 논의
- physical strife 육체적 투쟁
- achievement[ətʃíːvmənt] 업적, 성취
- rests on ~에 달려 있다
- likeliest way 가장 적합한 방법
- sensible conclusions[kənklúːʒəns] 현명한 결론
- requires[rikwáiəːrs] 요구하다
- tolerance[tálərəns] 아량
- mutual forbearance[fɔːrbέərəns] 상호 자제
- minorities[minɔ́ːrətis, mai-] 소수
- submit 굴복하다
- for the time being 당분간
- outvote[àutvóut] 투표로 이기다
- Parliament[páːrləmənt] 국회
- prevail[privéil] 우세하다
- assumptions[əsʌ́mpʃəns] 가정, 전제
- literally[lítərəli] 문자 그대로, 축자적으로
- blows[blou] 구타, 강타
- abuse 남용하다
- majorities 다수
- physical resistance[rizístəns] 육체적 저항
- all up 모든 일이 끝나다

Sentence Pattern Analysis

- Our free government, as we enjoy it, is the substitution of law for force, of argument for physical strife.

  이 문장은 substitution ~ for force, ~for physical strife의 구문임. 즉 the substitution of law for force, of argument for physical strife은 「힘을 법으로 대치하고, 육체적 투쟁을 논의로 대치한 것」

- it rests on the belief that free discussion is the likeliest way of doing justice and reaching sensible conclusions about policy.

그것은 자유로운 토론은 정의를 실현하고 정책에 대한 가장 현명한 결론에 도달하는 최적의 방식이라는 믿음에 달려있다.

• or majorities so abuse their power as to drive minorities to physical resistance,

~so ~as to 구문임. 따라서「혹은 다수가 그들의 권력을 남용해서 소수로 하여금 육체적 저항을 하게끔 몰고 간다면」

Wisdom

Power tends to corrupt, and absolute power corrupts absolutely. Great men are almost always bad men.

권력은 부패하기 쉽고, 절대 권력은 절대적으로 부패한다. 위대한 인물들은 거의 항상 악인들이다.

Lord Acton: Historical Essays and Studies

Advanced Reading 8

A. Preparing to Read

Their love of life comes **in spite of**, almost in defiance of, considerable hardship.

Did you **manage to** get anything to eat?

Good will **prevail**.

B. Approaching to the Topic

Every generation rewrites the past. In easy times history is more or less of an ornamental art, but in times of danger we are driven to the written record by pressing need to find answers to the riddles of today. We need to know what kind of firm ground other men, belonging to generations before us, have found to stand on. In spite of changing conditions of life they were not very different from ourselves, their thoughts were the grandfathers of our thoughts, they managed to meet situations as difficult as those we have to face, to meet them sometimes lightheartedly, and in some measure to make their hopes prevail. We need to know how they did it.

John Dos Passos: The Theme Is Freedom

Vocabularies & Expressions for Comprehension

- generation[dʒénəreiʃən] 세대, 시대
- rewrites 고쳐 쓰다
- more or less 다소
- ornamental art 장식적인 예술
- pressing 급박한
- riddles 수수께끼, 어려운 문제
- In spite of changing conditions 변화하는 상황에도 불구하고
- lightheartedly 마음 편하게

- in some measure 어느 정도
- prevail[privéil] 우세하다

Sentence Pattern Analysis

- In easy times history is more or less of an ornamental art, but in times of danger we are driven to the written record by pressing need to find answers to the riddles of today,

  이 문장에서 to find answers to the riddles of today는 a pressing need를 수식함. we are driven to the written record 우리는 기록된 역사에로 돌진하여 간다(급하게 달려간다).

- We need to know what kind of firm ground other men, belonging to generations before us, have found to stand on.

  이 문장에서 to know의 목적어는 what kind of firm ground임. belonging to generations before 우리보다 앞선 시대에 속하는

- they managed to meet situations as difficult as those we have to face, to meet them sometimes lightheartedly, and in some measure to make their hopes prevail.

  이 문장에서 managed to meet 는 그럭저럭 ~에 대처하다. 또한 이어서 나오는 to meet, to make도 managed에 걸린다. those는 situation을 받는다.

John Dos Passos(1896-1970) 은 미국의 소설가로 제1차 세계대전 때는 직접 참전하기도 하였다. 그의 주요 작품으로는 *Three Soldiers* (1920), *Manhattan Transfer* (1925), *U.S.A.* (1938), *The 42nd Parallel* (1930), *Nineteen Nineteen* (1932), *The Big Money* (1936), *District of Columbia* (1952), *Midcentury* (1961) 등이 있다.

Wisdom

If a man shuts his ears to the cry of the poor, he too will cry and not be answered.
귀를 막아 가난한 자의 부르짖는 소리를 듣지 아니하면 자기가 부르짖을 때에도 들을 자가 없으리라.

Proverbs 21:13

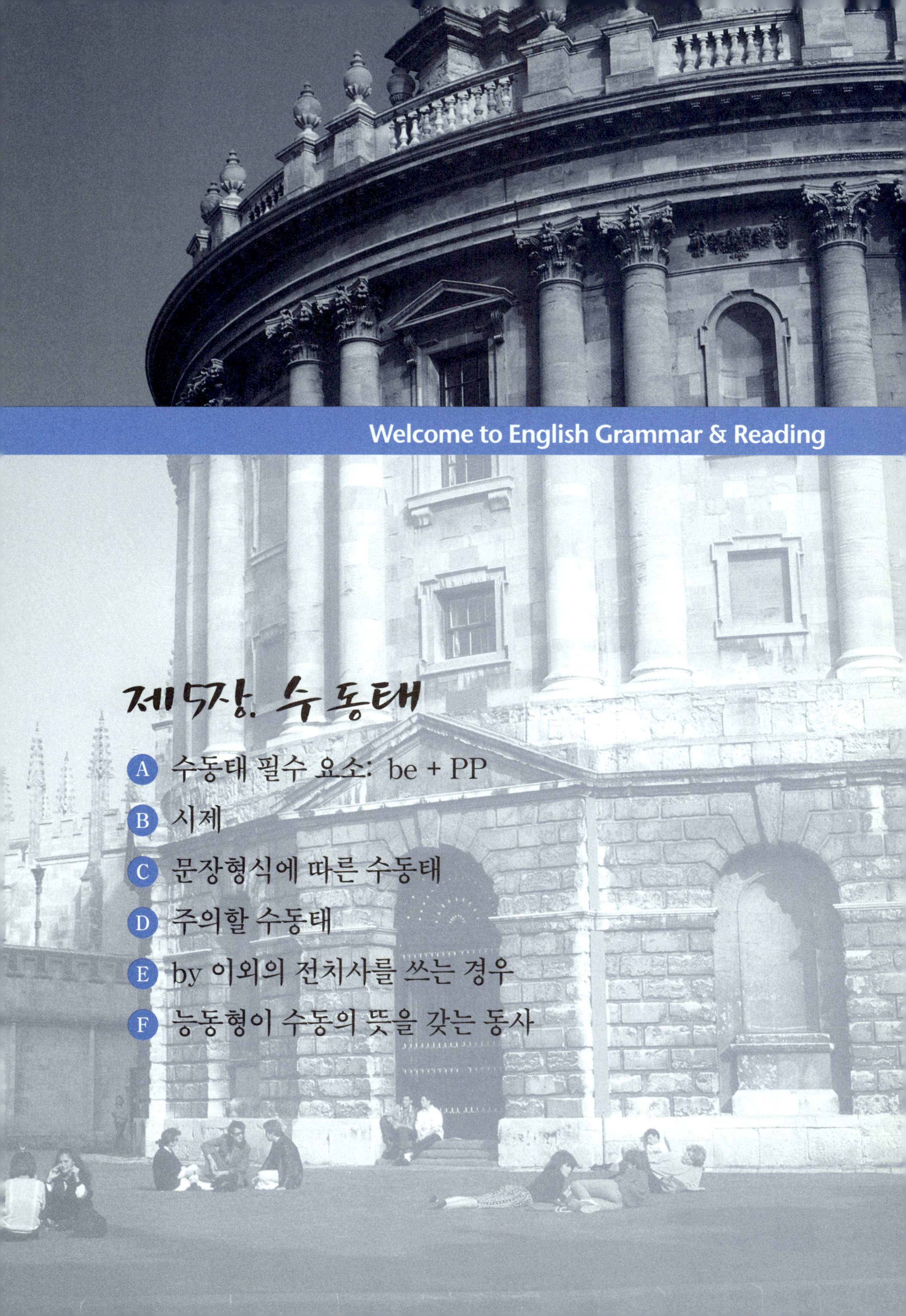

제5장. 수동태

- A 수동태 필수 요소: be + PP
- B 시제
- C 문장형식에 따른 수동태
- D 주의할 수동태
- E by 이외의 전치사를 쓰는 경우
- F 능동형이 수동의 뜻을 갖는 동사

제5장 수동태 Voice

A 수동태 필수 요소: be + PP

수동태의 기본 골격은 be + PP이다. 수동태가 성립하기 위해서는 최소한 '주어 + be PP' 가 필요하다. 'by + 명사' 는 부사구이므로 생략 가능할 뿐만 아니라 by 이외의 '다른 전치사 + 명사' 도 수동태에 자주 등장하기 때문에 수동태에서 절대적으로 필요하다고 할 수 없다.

수동태 기본골격 : [수동태 주어 = 동사의 의미상 목적어] + **be PP** + (**by** 명사)

- 능동태(active voice) : 행위자가 주어일 때
- 수동태(passive voice) : 동사의 의미상 목적어가 주어일 때

1. He made a box yesterday.
2. A box was made by him yesterday.

동사 make의 의미상 주체 he와 의미상 객체 a box는 능동태에서 수동태로 바뀌어도 그 의미관계가 변하지 않는다. 다시 말해서, 1번의 능동태 문장에서 만드는 사람은 he이고 만들어진 대상은 a box인데, 수동태에서도 그 관계(만드는 사람 he, 만들어진 대상은 a box)가 변하지 않는다. 다만 수동태에서는 목적어가 주어가 된다. 이렇게 수동태의 주어는 동사의 의미상 목적어가 되는데, 그러면 그 문장의 동사는 반드시 be + PP의 형태가 되어야 한다.

B 시제

현재수동 is made	과거수동 was made	미래수동 will be made
현재완료수동 have been made	과거완료수동 had been made	미래완료수동 will have been made
현재진행수동 is being made	과거진행수동 was being made	

1. The cake **is made** by Mother. 〈현재 수동〉
2. My window **was broken** by John. 〈과거 수동〉

3. Your voice **will be recorded** on the tape. <미래 수동>
4. This house **has been built** by him. ← He has built this house. <현재완료 수동>
5. This house **is being built** by him. ← He is building this house. <현재진행 수동>

C 문장형식에 따른 수동태

❶ 3형식의 수동태

1. Romeo loves Juliet.
   → Juliet is loved by Romeo.
2. Everybody laughed at me.
   → I was laughed at by everybody.
3. My father never speaks well of my boyfriend.
   → My boyfriend is never spoken well of by my father.

❷ 4형식의 수동태

1. Her friend gave my sister a birthday present.
   → (a) My sister was given a birthday present by her friend.
   → (b) A birthday present was given (to) my sister by her friend.
2. My uncle gave me a watch.
   → (a) I was given a watch by my uncle.
   → (b) A watch was given (to) me by my uncle.

❸ 5형식의 수동태

1. They elected him chairman.
   → He was elected chairman (by them).
2. We heard Mr. Kim scold his students. <지각동사>
   → Mr Kim was heard **to** scold his students.
3. We saw Mr. Kim scold his students. <지각동사>
   → Mr Kim was seen **to** scold his students.

문장 2와 3에서처럼 본동사가 사역동사, 지각동사인 5형식 문장이 수동태로 바뀌면 목적보어였던 원형부정사는 to부정사가 된다.

D 주의할 수동태

❶ 의문문의 수동태

1. What did Watt invent? → What was invented by Watt?
2. Who invented this steam engine? → By whom was this steam engine invented?
   = Who was this steam engine invented by?

❷ 명령문의 수동태

명령문의 수동태 : Let + O + be PP

1. Do it at once.
   → Let it be done at once.
2. Don't touch the bag.
   → (a) **Don't** let the bag be touched.
   → (b) Let the bag **not** be touched.

❸ 목적어가 절인 경우의 수동태

1. They **say** that he **is** honest.
   = It **is said** that he **is** honest.
   = He **is said to be** honest.
2. They **say** that the movie actress **is** still alive.
   = It **is said** that the movie actress **is** still alive.
   = The movie actress **is said to be** still alive.
3. I **believe** that he **was** rich.
   = It **is believed** by me that he **was** rich.
   = He **is believed to have been** rich.

E by 이외의 전치사를 쓰는 경우

1. He is known **to** everybody. <대상>
2. He is known **by** his father. <판단>

3. He is known **for** his novels. <이유>
4. He is known **as** a novelist. <자격>
5. He **is engaged in** writing a novel. <종사하다, 관여하다>
6. He **is engaged to** Nancy. <약혼하다>
7. He **is absorbed in** his business. <몰두하다>
8. I **was pleased with** his work.
9. We **were surprised at** the news.
10. He **was frightened at** the news.
11. He **is** always **worried about** his health. <염려하다>
12. He **is concerned about** her safety. <염려하다>
13. He **was satisfied with** the result.
14. I **am acquainted with** him. < ~와 알고 있는>
15. He **is interested in** this case.
16. He **was occupied in** translating a French novel. <전념하다>
17. She **is occupied with** needlework. <종사하다>
18. The ground **was covered with** snow.
19. I **was caught in** a shower.
20. The room **was filled with** smoke.
21. Wine is made **from** grapes. <화학적 변화>
22. Grapes are made **into** wine. <be made from의 역순>
23. This desk is made **of** wood. <물리적 변화>

F 능동형이 수동의 뜻을 갖는 동사

1. This pen **writes** well.
2. The book **sells** well.
3. The banana **peels** well.
4. This cloth **washes** well.
5. She **photographs** well.
6. This autobiography **reads** like a novel.
7. You **are to blame**.

Basic Reading 5

1 If you love others they will love you. If you speak kindly to them they will speak kindly to you. Love **is repaid** with love, and hatred with hatred.

- repay[riːpéi] v. 갚다, 상환하다
- hatred[héitrid] n. 증오, 미움

2 A weary brain cannot **be made** to perform good work. Often much more **is gained** by a walk through the green fields than could **be acquired** by the study of books.

- weary[wíəri] 피곤한, 기진 맥진한
- perform[pərfɔ́ːrm] (임무 · 일 · 약속 · 명령 등을) 이행하다, 실행하다, 수행하다, (극 · 역을) 연기하다, (음악을) 연주하다
- much more(result)
- gain[gein] 얻다(earn), 획득하다
- than 주격의 유사관계대명사, 선행사가 much more이다
- acquire[əkwáiər] vt. 얻다, 취득하다

3 Tomatoes are originally from the Americas. Potatoes are also originally from the Americas. Both foods **were** first **taken** to Spain and **spread** from there to the rest of Europe.

- originally[əridʒənəli] ad. 원래, 처음부터
- from ~출신의, ~산의
- the Americas 남북 아메리카(the North America and the South America)
- potato[pətéitou] n. 감자
- spread[spred] v. (spread - spread - spread) 퍼지다
- rest[rest] n. 나머지

4 There are rules for introducing people to each other. A younger person **is** generally **introduced** to an older one, a guest to the host or hostess, and one person to a group.

- introduce[intrədjú:s] vt. 소개하다
- host[houst] n. 주인
- hostess[hóustis] n. 안주인
- a guest (is introduced) to the host or hostess, and one person (is introduced) to a group

5 If a man and woman **are being introduced**, they may or may not shake hands.

- shake hands 악수하다

6 In many countries there is a fixed charge for personal services. A certain percentage may **be added** to the bill at a hotel or restaurant for the service. In other places the customer may **be expected** to give a tip whenever services **are performed**.

- fixed charge 정해진 요금
- personal[pə́:rsənəl] a. 개인적인
- service[sə́:rvis] n. 봉사
- percentage[pərséntidʒ] n. 비율, 백분율
- bill[bil] n. 계산서
- customer[kʌ́stəmər] n. 고객, 손님
- perform[pərfɔ́:rm] v. 수행하다

7 The Greeks held the first Olympic Games on the plain of Olympia. In those days Greece **was divided** into many states. The best athletes from these states **were invited** to join the games. Prizes **were given** to the winners in the games. The highest prize was a crown, which **was made** of olive leaves.

- Greek[gri:k] 그리스의; Greece 그리스
- hold[hould] v. (hold - held - held) 개최하다
- plain[plein] n. 평원
- state[steit] n. 국가, 상태
- athlete[ǽθli:t] n. 운동 선수
- crown[kraun] n. 왕관

8 Skeletons and bones of many animals that no longer exist **have been found** preserved in rocks. These remains **are called** fossils. Since most fossils are found in rocks that formed as a result of water action. we know that these early animals lived near or in water.

- skeleton[skélətn] n. 해골, 골격
- that no longer exist : that은 주격관계대명사로서 many animal이 선행사다.
- no longer 이제 ~이 아니다
- preserved는 분사로서 skeleton and bones의 주격보어이다.
- remains[riméin] n. 유물; remain, v. 남다
- fossil[fásl] n. 화석
- as a result of ~의 결과로써

9 It **is** wisely **said** that lost wealth may **be regained** by industry and economy, lost knowledge by study, lost health by temperance and medicine, but lost time **is lost** forever.

• lose[lu:z] v. (lose - lost - lost) 잃다
• wealth[welθ] n. 부(riches); wealthy 부유한
• regain[rigéin] vt. 되찾다, 회복하다
• industry[índəstri] n. 근면, 공업, 산업
• economy[ikánəmi] n. 경제, 경기(business), 절약
• temperance[témpərəns] n. 절제(moderation), 자제(self-restraint)
• lost knowledge (may be gained) by study, lost wealth (may be gained) by temperance and medicine 약, 의약품, 의학

10 Health is a priceless treasure but its value **is** rarely **appreciated** until it is lost. On the basis of personal experience Thomas Carlyle wrote: "The healthy know not of their health but only the sick." Youth especially tend to take good health for granted and squander it thoughtlessly, little realizing that future success and happiness, and even life itself, **are** largely **influenced** and in many instances actually **determined** by the habits of living acquired during one's developmental years.

• priceless[práislis] a. 매우 귀중한
• treasure[tréʒə:r] n. 보물
• rarely 좀처럼 ~않다(seldom)
• appreciate[əprí:ʃièit] v. 올바로 평가하다, 감사하다
• The healthy know not of their health but only the sick(do).
건강한 사람은 그들 건강에 대하여 가치를 모르고 단지 아픈 사람들만이 안다.
• little realizing that ~ ~을 거의 인식하지 못하고서, 분사구문
• squander[skwándə:r] v. 낭비하다
• developmental years 성장기

Advanced Reading 9

A. Preparing to Read

These mountains are so small **that** they aren't shown in maps.

All that money brought was **nothing but** sadness and misery and tragedy.

It did **nothing but** make us ridiculous.

They care for **nothing but** fighting.

He compared how these organisms behaved when left **in contact with** different materials.

B. Approaching to the Topic

There was no answer. The obscurity was now so great that he could see absolutely nothing but a pale nebulousness at his feet, which represented the white muslin figure he had left upon the dead leaves. Everything else was blackness alike. d'Urberville stooped; and heard a gentle regular breathing. He knelt and bent lower, till her breath warmed his face, and in a moment his cheek was in contact with hers. She was sleeping soundly, and upon her eyelashes there lingered tears.

Darkness and silence ruled everywhere around. Above them rose the primeval yews and oaks of The Chase, in which were poised gentle roosting birds in their last nap; and about them stole the hopping rabbits.

Tess of the d'Urbervilles by *Thomas Hardy*

Vocabularies & Expressions for Comprehension

- obscurity[əbskjúərəti] 어둠
- absolutely[ǽbs(ə)lù:tli] 절대적으로

- noting but = only 단지 ~ 에 지나지 않은
- pale[peil] 희미한, 어슴푸레한
- nebulousness[nébjələsnis] 흐릿한 것
- represent[rèprizént] 나타내다
- muslin[mʌ́zlin] 머슬린 천
- dead leaves 낙엽
- stooped 몸을 굽히다
- a gentle regular breathing[bri:ðiŋ] 부드럽고 규칙적인 호흡
- knelt and bent lower 무릎을 꿇고 더 낮게 몸을 구부리다
- in a moment 순간
- cheek 뺨
- soundly 곤하게
- eyelashes 속눈썹
- lingered[líŋgər] 묻어 있다
- tears 눈물
- primeval[praimí:vəl] 원시의, 원시적인
- yews[ju:] 주목나무
- The Chase 소설 「테스」의 유명한 배경 중 하나인 체이스 숲
- nap[næp] 선잠
- hopping 뛰어 다니는

Sentence Pattern Analysis

- The obscurity was now so great that he could see absolutely nothing but a pale nebulousness at his feet,

  so ~ that의 구문 「너무 어두웠기 때문에 그는 발아래 있는 어슴푸레 흐릿한 것만을 겨우 볼 수 있을 뿐이었다.」

- till her breath warmed his face.

  그녀의 숨결이 그의 얼굴을 따뜻하게 할 때까지

- and about them stole the hopping rabbits.

  그들 주변을 깡총거리는 토끼들이 살금살금 오갔다.

Wisdom

The man who makes no mistakes does not usually make anything.

실수를 하지 않은 사람은 대개 아무 것도 하지 않는 사람이다.

Speech by Edward J. Phelps

Advanced Reading 10

A. Preparing to Read

They had absolutely no **compassion** towards any of their victims.

This law is known to hold **true for** galaxies at a distance of at least several billion light years.

Father had **led** me **to** believe the new baby was a kind of present for me.

B. Approaching to the Topic

The decision to forgive is an act of compassion toward oneself. If anger is not released, it perdures and causes the spiritual, emotional and physical damage to self which was discussed earlier. Forgiveness of self in some ways may be the most difficult aspect of forgiveness. Many people set standards of excellence for themselves that are unrealistic and unattainable. This can lead one to be overly demanding and unforgiving of self. This is especially true for people in ministry who are unwilling to forgive themselves for any moral lapses. Ministers are the most compassionate human beings when dealing with others' pain and hurt. Compassion toward themselves, however, is often sadly absent.

Forgiveness: New life

Vocabularies & Expressions for Comprehension

- decision[disíʒən] 결심
- forgive[fəːrgív] 용서하다
- compassion[kəmpǽʃən] 동정, 연민; have compassion on ~을 측은히 여기다
- release[rilíːs] 방출하다
- perdures[pə(ː)rdjúər] 오래 지속하다

- spiritual, emotional and physical damage[dǽmidʒ] 정신적, 정서적 그리고 육체적 피해
- unrealistic[ʌ̀nri:əlístik] 비현실적
- unattainable[ʌ̀nətéinəbəl] 달성할 수 없는
- overly[óuvəli] 명백하게
- true for ~에 유효한
- ministry[mínistri] 성직자들
- unwilling to 마음 내키지 않은
- moral lapses[læps] 도덕적 착오, 실수
- dealing with 다루다
- absent[ǽbsənt] 결핍한, 부재의

Sentence Pattern Analysis

- it perdures and causes the spiritual, emotional and physical damage.
  그것(분노)은 지속되어 정신적, 정서적 그리고 육체적인 피해를 초래한다.

- This can lead one to be overly demanding and unforgiving of self.
  ~lead ~ to 구문. 「이 때문에 우리는 명백하게 지나친 요구를 받을 수 있고 자기를 용서할 수 없게 된다.」

Wisdom

Government, even in its best state, is but a necessary evil; in its worst state, an intolerable one.

정부란 가장 좋은 상태에서조차도 필요악에 불과하며, 최악의 상태에서는 참을 수 없는 악이다.

Thomas Paine: Common Sense

제6장. 시제

제6장 시제 *Tense*

A 현재

1. He **gets up** at six every morning <습관적인 행위>
2. The sun **rises** in the east. <불변의 진리>
3. He **lives** in Seoul, but at present he is living in Pusan. <무제한적 상태의 연속>

B 과거

1. I got up at six this morning. <과거의 시점>
2. Columbus discovered America in 1492. <역사적 사실>
3. My teacher **said** that Columbus **discovered** America in 1492.

C 미래

❶ 단순미래

사람의 의지와 관계없이 미래에 일어나는 사건으로 예상, 추측, 필연을 의미

인칭	평서문	의문문
1인칭	I shall	Shall I
2인칭	You will	Shall you
3인칭	He will	Will he

1. I shall be twenty two next year.
2. Shall I recover soon?
3. Shall you be at home tomorrow afternoon?
4. Will he be in time if he starts now?

※ 단순미래의 경우 현대영어에서 모든 인칭에 will을 쓰는 경향이 있다.

❷ 의지미래

사람의 의지에 따라 미래에 일어날 일이 결정되는 경우

인칭	주어의 의지	speaker(I)의 의지	hearer(You)의 의지
1인칭	I will	I will	Shall I
2인칭	You will	You Shall	Will you
3인칭	He will	He Shall	Shall he

(1) speaker(I)의 의지

1. I will give you my watch.
2. You shall have my watch. = I will give you my watch.
3. He shall have my watch. = I will give him my watch.

(2) hearer(you)의 의지 · 의향을 물어봄

1. Shall I call on you tomorrow? = Do you mind if I call on you tomorrow?
2. Will you do a favor for me?
3. Shall he carry your bag? = What do you think of his carrying your bag?

(3) 주어의 의지

1. If you will play the computer game, do it alone.
2. He will not attend the meeting.

❸ 시간 조건의 부사절

때나 조건의 부사절에서 현재는 미래를 대신한다.

1. **When he arrives here**, I will welcome him. <부사절>
2. **If it rains tomorrow**, I will not start. <부사절>
3. I don't know the time **when he will come back**. <형용사절>
4. I don't know **if it will rain tomorrow**. <명사절>

❹ 현재형 + 미래 표시 부사구

(1) go, come, leave, arrive, begin 등의 동사 현재형이 미래표시 부사구와 올 때 현재는 가까운 미래를 나타낸다.

1. My friends **come** my home next Sunday.
2. We **arrive at** Los Angeles International Airport at 7:00 a.m.
3. The president **leaves** Jerusalem for New York tomorrow.
4. What time **does** the concert **end** this evening?

(2) 확정적인 계획, 약속과 관련되어 현재가 미래를 나타낸다.

1. I **am finishing** my homework soon.
2. He **is getting** married to Nancy this summer.
3. I **am seeing** no one tomorrow.

D 현재완료

have+과거분사의 형태로 과거의 한 시점부터 현재까지의 <완료 · 결과 · 경험 · 계속>을 나타내며, 과거사실과 현재사실을 연관시킨다.

❶ 완료

1. The train has already left.
2. He has finished his homework.
3. I have not finished my homework yet.

❷ 결과

1. My mother has lost her purse.
2. My friend has gone to Brazil.
3. He has become rich.

❸ 경험

1. I have been there four times.
2. My grandmother has never used the Internet.
3. Have you ever been to Egypt? <ever = at any time>

❹ 계속

1. I have lived in this town for fifty years. <①과 ②의 의미를 지님>
   ① I began to live in this town fifty years ago.
   ② Now I live in this town.
2. We have been friends since childhood.

※명백하게 과거를 나타내는 말과 현재완료는 함께 쓸 수 없다.

3. He **finished** his homework yesterday. (◯)
4. He **has finished** his homework yesterday. (×)
5. **When have** you **met** her at the park? (×)

E 과거완료

had+과거분사의 형태로 과거 이전의 시점(대과거)부터 과거시점까지 시간의 경과를 가리키며, 그 기간의 <완료 · 결과 · 경험 · 계속>을 나타낸다.

1. I **had finished** my lunch when you came. <완료>
2. I **had broken** his leg when I visited him. <결과>
3. I **had never met** him until then. <경험>
4. I **had been** ill for two weeks, so I couldn't go there. <계속>
5. He lost the bag he **had bought** two day before. <대과거>
   대과거는 과거에 발생한 두 사건 중에서 먼저 일어났음을 나타낸다.

F 미래완료

will[shall] have+과거분사의 형태로 미래시점까지의 동작이나 상태의 <완료 · 결과 · 경험 · 계속>을 나타낸다.

1. I **will have finished** the work by six o'clock. <완료>
2. I **will have gone** on a trip by the time you come. <결과>

3. If she wins again, she **will have won** three times. <경험>
4. I **will have lived** here for ten years by next May. <계속>

G 시제의 일치와 예외

❶ 시제의 일치

시제의 일치란 종속절의 시제가 주절의 시제에 따라 결정되는 것을 말한다. 주절의 시제가 현재이면 종속절에 모든 시제가 올 수 있으나, 주절의 시제가 과거이면 종속절 시제도 과거나 과거완료가 되어야 한다.

• Tom **thinks** that Mary **loves[has loved]** him.
→ Tom **thought** that Mary **loved[had loved]** him.

❷ 시제의 일치와 예외

1. (a) He **said** that the earth **moves** around the sun. <불변의 진리>
   (b) My father always **said** that time **is** money.
2. (a) I **told** him that I always **go** fishing on weekends. <현재의 습관, 사실>
   (b) She **said** she **lives** in Seoul.
3. He **told** me that Columbus **discovered** America in 1492. <역사적 사실 : 과거>
4. He **says** that he **would write** to her if he **knew** her address. <가정법>
   → He **said** that he **would write** to her if he **knew** her address.
   가정법 시제는 주절의 시제에 영향을 받지 않는다.
5. She **is** happier than she **was** 5 years ago. <비교구문>

H ago/ before

1. He died 10 years ago. <과거시제 + 시간 + ago>
   = He has been dead for 10 years. <현재완료 + for + 시간>
   = 10 years have passed since he died. <시간 + 현재완료 + since + 과거시제>
   = It is 10 years since he died. <It is + 시간 + since + 과거시제>

2. I met her **two days ago**.

ago는 현재를 기준하여 '지금부터 ~ 전의' 뜻으로 명백한 과거를 의미한다

3. I should have met her **two days ago**.

4. I met her **before**.

5. I have met her **before**.

6. He said he had met her two days **before**.

before는 과거를 기준하여 대과거와 결합한다

Basic Reading 6

1 If **you are** sent abroad at an early age, **you will**, by coming in contact with foreign people and their customs and manners, obtain a broader view of life which will be invaluable to you later on.

- abroad[əbrɔ́:d] ad. 해외로
- come(get) in contact with ~와 접촉하다, ~와 연락하다
- custom[kʌ́stəm] n. 풍습, 습관
- manner[mǽnə:r] n. 방법
- obtain[əbtéin] v. 얻다
- view of life 인생관
- invaluable[invǽljuəbl] a. = very valuable
- later on = afterward 나중에

2 Thank you for your letter **which arrived** last week. I'm sorry I **haven't written** to you for two months. I'**ve been** so busy at college that I simply **haven't had** time. Don't be angry with me! Do you like the English family you are staying with? **Have** you **started** your new English course yet? I hope everything goes well with you.

- thank A for B : B에 대하여 A에게 감사하다
- course[kɔ:rs] n. 학과 과목, 강좌
- go well with ~ 잘 지내다, 잘 되다

3 For two decades, the U.S. educational system **has been offering** courses in different subjects such as music, art, cooking, personal money management, and filmmaking. Many people believe that this has led to a lack of attention to the basic skills of writing, calculating, and thinking.

- decade[dékeid] 10년
- educational[èdʒukéiʃənəl] a. 교육의
- system[sístəm] n. 방식
- offer[ɔ́(:)fər] v. 제공하다
- course[kɔ:rs] n. 강좌
- management[mǽnidʒmənt] n. 관리
- filmmaking 영화 제작
- lack[læk] 부족, 결핍
- calculate[kǽlkjəléit] vt. 계산하다

4 Robert was going steady with Susan and was thinking of marrying her. He wanted to know **what kinds of girls her sisters were, what her father was like**, and **how long her mother had been dead**.

- go steady with 정해진 이성과 교제하다, 서로 사랑하는 사이가 되다
- 간접의문 어순 : 의문사 + S + V

what kinds of girls her sister were

what her father was like

how long her mother had been dead

5 Religious faith **is** not a storm cellar to which men and women can flee for refuge from the storms of life. It **is**, instead, an inner spiritual strength that **enables** them to face those storms with hope and serenity. Religious faith **has** the miraculous power to lift ordinary human being to greatness in seasons of stress. Religious faith **is to be** found in the promises of God.

- storm cellar 피난처
- flee[fli:] v. 달아나다
- refuge[réfju:dʒ] n. 피난처

- spiritual strength 영적인 힘
- serenity[sirénəti] n. 마음의 평정
- is to be found = can be found <be to 용법의 가능>

6 During the darkest hours of the Civil War, Lincoln **wrote** to an old friend in Springfield, Illinois, asking him to come to Washington. Lincoln **said** he had some problems he **wanted** to discuss with him. The old neighbor **came** to the White House, and Lincoln **talked** to him about freeing the slaves. After talking for hours, Lincoln **shook** hands with his old neighbor, said good night, and sent him back to Illinois without even asking for his opinion. Lincoln **had done** all the talking himself. That seemed to clear his mind. "He seemed to feel easer after the talk," the old friend said. Lincoln **hadn't wanted** advice. He **had wanted** merely a friendly, warm-hearted listener whom he could talk to. That's what we all **want** when we **are** in trouble.

- the Civil War 남북전쟁
- free[fri:] vt. 자유롭게 하다
- slave[sleiv] n. 노예
- shake hands with ~와 악수하다
- ask for ~을 청하다
- warm-hearted 마음씨가 따뜻한

7 In "Beauty and the Beast," a young girl **meets** a frightening monster. To save her family from his wrath, she **agrees** to live with him. Eventually, by getting to know him, she **overcomes** her loathing and even **grows to** love him. A miracle **occurs**, and he **is restored** to his true, princely self. This **seems** to underscore a cultural assumption that we can change someone for the better through the force of our love, and that if we are female, it is our duty to do so.

• beast[biːst] n. 짐승, 야수
• frightening[fráitniŋ] a. 무서운
• monster[mánstər] n. 괴물
• wrath[ræθ] n. 분노
• eventually[ivéntʃuəli] ad. 결국
• get to ~하게 되다(grow to, come to)
• loathing[lóuðiŋ] n. 혐오감
• princely[prínsli] a. 왕자의
• underscore[ʌndərskɔ́ːr] vt. 강조하다(emphasize), 뒷받침하다
• assumption[əsʌ́mpʃən] n. 가정, 가설

8 If we compare ourselves with other animals, then every organ we possess, except one, **is** totally indistinctive. Other animals **are** stronger, swifter, more sensitive, more sharply acute, more enduring, and so on endlessly. The one exception, of course, **is** our brain. We **have** a brain that can be considered superior to any nonhuman brain in existence. At least, only the human brain **has given rise to** a technological civilization, and it is widely accepted that only the human brain is capable of abstract thought.

• organ[ɔ́ːrgən] n. 기관
• indistinctive[indistíŋktiv] a. 구별되지 않는, 특색이 없는
• swift[swift] a. 빠른
• acute[əkjúːt] a. 예리한
• enduring[indjúəriŋ, en-] a. 참을성이 있는(patient)
• at least 적어도
• give rise to ~을 초래하다, 발생시키다
• technological civilization 기술문명
• abstract thought 추상적인 사고

9 Writing plain English is hard work. No one ever learned literature from a textbook. I **have never taken** a course in writing. I learned to write naturally and on my own. I did not succeed by accident; I succeeded by patient hard work.

- plain[plein] a. 쉬운
- on one's own 스스로
- by accident 우연히

10 He did not go to college a gentleman, but neither did he return one; he went to college as an ass, and returned a prig; to his original folly was superadded a vast quantity of conceit.

- one = a gentleman
- ass[æs] n. 바보(fool)
- prig[prig] n. 학자인 체하는 사람
- folly[fáli] n. 어리석음
- superadd[sù:pərǽd] vt. 추가하다, 덧붙이다
- conceit[kənsí:t] n. 자만심

Advanced Reading 11

A. Preparing to Read

If the trip is a success, a lot of this will be **due to** Mr Kim's efforts.

Hostility towards outsiders **is characteristic of** both human and non-human animals.

It has been claimed **that** wine helps to protect against heart disease.

B. Approaching to the Topic

English and the speech of the United States are one language: but in the more than three centuries that have passed since the first settlements, each has developed in divergent ways. It is not so well known that many older usages of English have been preserved in America which have disappeared from Britain. American has developed new ways of speech, partly through differing conditions of life, partly through its having received many influences from other languages in the process of its absorption of large bodies of immigrants from many lands. The primary difference between English and American is in the rhythm and intonation of speech. It is, however, certain that American English has very considerably influenced British English: and this has been due to a far wider set of circumstances than the mere fact of America's leading position in commerce, the films and finance. Vividness and force in metaphorical expression are characteristic of much American English; and it is natural, therefore, that a selection of these should be taken up into spoken English, especially by the young who are most eager for new linguistic experience.

The English Language *by C. L. Wrenn*

Vocabularies & Expressions for Comprehension

- settlements[sétlmənts] 식민
- divergent[divə́:rdʒənt, dai-] 상이한
- usages[jú:sidʒ, -zidʒ] 관용법
- preserve[prizə́:rv] 보존하다
- disappear[dìsəpíər] 사라지다
- influences[ínflu:əns] 영향
- absorption[æbsɔ́:rpʃən, -zɔ́:rp] 흡수
- immigrants[ímigrənts] (외국으로부터의)이민, 이민자
- primary[práimeri/ -məri] 주요한
- considerably[kənsídərəbli] 꽤, 상당한
- the films and finance[finǽns, fáinæns] 영화와 금융
- vividness 생생함
- metaphorical expression 은유적 표현
- characteristic[kæ̀riktərístik] 특징적인
- selection[siléʃən] 선택
- taken up into 수용하다
- eager for 열망하는
- linguistic experience 언어학적 경험

Sentence Pattern Analysis

- It is not so well known that many older usages of English have been preserved in America which have disappeared from Britain.
  「영국에서는 사라져버린 영어의 더 많은 오래된 관용법이 아메리카에 보존되어 있다는 것은 매우 잘 알려지지 않은 것이다.」 Which의 선행사는 many older usages of English이다.

- partly through its having received many influences from other languages
  「부분적으로는 그것이 다른 언어에서 많은 영향을 받았기 때문에」

- this has been due to a far wider set of circumstances than the mere fact of America's leading position in commerce, the films and finance.
  「이것은 미국이 상업, 영화 그리고 금융에서도 지도적 위치에 있다고 하는 단순한 사실보다는

훨씬 더 넓은 일련의 상황에 기인한 것이다.」 due to ~에 기인한

- Vividness and force in metaphorical expression are characteristic of much American English.
  「은유적 표현 속에 깃든 생생함과 힘은 많은 미국영어의 특징이다.」

- it is natural, therefore, that a selection of these should be taken up into spoken English,
  It ~ that 구문. 「그러므로 이런 것(비유적 표현)의 선택이 구어 영어에 수용된다고 하는 것은 당연한 일이다.」

Wisdom

If the hill will not come to Mahomet, Mahomet will go to the hill.

산이 마호메트에게 오지 않으려 한다면 마호메트가 산으로 가리다.

Francis Bacon: Essays

Advanced Reading 12

A. Preparing to Read

The tears were streaming **so** fast **that** she could not see.

There was snow everywhere **so that** the shape of things was difficult to identify.

A back injury **forced** him **to** withdraw from Wimbledon.

B. Approaching to the Topic

Alice dropped to the ground and lay trembling. She was so frightened at the thought of what she had done that when the man had gone on his way she did not dare get to her feet, but crawled on hands and knees through the grass to the house. When she got her own room she bolted the door and drew her dressing tables across the doorway. Her body shook as with a chill and her hands trembled so that she had difficulty getting into her nightdress. When she got into bed she buried her face in the pillow and wept broken-heartedly. "What is the matter with me?" "I will do something dreadful if I am not careful," she thought, and turning her face to the wall, began trying to force herself to face bravely the fact that many people must live and die alone, even in Winesburg.

Winesburg, Ohio by Sherwood Anderson

Vocabularies & Expressions for Comprehension

- tremble[trémb-əl] 떨다
- fright[frait] 놀라게 하다
- crawl[krɔːl] 기어가다
- knees[niː] 무릎
- bolt[boult] 빗장을 내리다

- doorway 문간, 문쪽
- chill[tʃil] 오한
- nightdress 잠옷
- pillow[pílou] 베개
- broken-heartedly 가슴 저미게
- dreadful[drédfəl] 두려운, 끔찍한
- bravely 용감하게

Sentence Pattern Analysis

- She was so frightened at the thought of what she had done that when the man had gone on his way she did not dare get to her feet,

  so~that 구문. when the man ~his way는 부사절. 「그녀는 자신이 한 일에 너무 놀라서 그 남자가 가버렸을 때 그녀는 감히 일어나질 못했다.」

- her hands trembled so that she had difficulty getting into her nightdress.

  so that 구문. 「그녀의 손은 잠옷을 입지 못할 만큼 떨렸다.」

- began trying to force herself to face bravely the fact that many people must live and die alone,

  force~ to face 구문. the fact와 that 이하는 동격. 「많은 사람들이 홀로 살아야 하고 죽어야 한다는 사실을 용감하게 직면하려고 애쓰기 시작했다.」

Wisdom

Reading makes a full man; conference a ready man; and writing an exact man.

독서는 온전한 인간을 만들며, 상담은 능숙한 인간을 만들며, 필기는 정확한 인간을 만든다.

Francis Bacon: Essays

제7장. 조동사

- A can/could 용법
- B may/might 용법
- C will / would 용법
- D shall / should 용법
- E must / ought to 용법
- F need / dare / used to 용법
- G 추측의 조동사 용법

제7장 조동사 *Auxiliary Verb*

A can / could 용법

1. "**Can** you swim?" "Yes, I can." 〈능력〉
2. "**Can** I go swimming this afternoon?" 〈허가〉
3. **Can** it be true that he has done it? 〈의심〉
4. The news **cannot be** true. 〈추측〉
5. I **cannot but laugh** at the news. 〈관용 표현〉
6. We **cannot** be **too** careful about our health.
7. **Could** you e-mail me his mail address? 〈공손한 표현〉

B may / might 용법

1. "**May** I open the window?" 〈허가〉
2. **May** you have a happy journey! 〈기원〉
3. The train **may** not come on time. 〈추측 가능성〉
4. We eat so that we **may** live. 〈목적〉
5. Whatever you **may** say, I will not believe you. 〈양보〉
6. A man **may** be known by the company he keeps. 〈능력(can)〉
   (사람은 그가 사귀는 사람을 보면 알 수 있다.)
7. You **may well** consult a doctor at once. 〈관용표현〉
   (= have a good reason to R)
   (당신이 즉시 의사에게 진찰을 받는 것은 당연하다.)
8. You **may as well** not know a thing at all **as** know it imperfectly.
   = You **had better** not know a thing at all **than** know it imperfectly.
   (무엇을 불완전하게 아느니 차라리 모르는 편이 낫다.)
9. We **might as well** expect a wolf to be generous **as** ask him for money. 〈가정법과거〉
   (그에게 돈을 구하느니 차라리 이리에게서 관대함을 기대하는 것이 낫다.)

C will / would 용법

❶ will

1. (a) I **will** give you anything you want. 〈의지미래〉
   (b) He **will** have his own way in everything.
2. **Will** you pass me the salt? 〈권유〉
3. He **will** sit for hours without saying a word. 〈불규칙적 습관〉
4. Barking dogs **will** seldom bite. 〈습성〉

❷ would

1. I thought he **would** go with us. 〈will의 과거〉
2. My father **would** take a nap after lunch. 〈불규칙적 습관〉
   cf. There **used to** be a skyscraper here. (규칙적 습관)
3. Dick **would** go despite my warning. 〈의지〉
4. Men who **would** succeed must be abreast of the times. 〈소망(=wish to)〉
   (성공하고자 하는 사람은 시대에 뒤지지 않고 따라가야 한다.)
5. **Would** you please help me? 〈겸손〉

D shall / should 용법

❶ shall

1. Freedom of thought and conscience **shall** not be violated. 〈법률〉
2. (a) You **shall** die. = I will kill you. 〈의지미래〉
   (b) He **shall** die. = I will kill him.

❷ should

(1) 일반용법

1. Children **should** obey their parents. 〈의무〉
2. I said that I **should** be back before dark. 〈시제의 일치〉

(2) 특수용법

1. It is **strange** that he **should** do such a thing. <**감정적 판단** 형용사>

   감정적 판단 형용사(strange, curious, regrettable, odd 등)와 that절이 사용될 때 should는 생략하지 않는다.

2. It is **unfair** that the whole class (**should**) be punished. <**이성적 판단** 형용사>

   이성적 판단 형용사(necessary, important, natural, right, rational, fair 등)와 that절이 사용될 때 should는 생략할 수 있다.

3. (a) I **suggested** that the meeting (**should**) be held again. <주장, 명령, 요구>

   (b) We **demanded** that the mayor (**should**) resign right away.

   주장, 명령, 소망, 요구, 제안 등을 뜻하는 말과 that절이 사용될 때 (should) 원형을 사용한다.

4. He worked hard **lest** he **should** fail. <lest ~ should = so that ~ may not>

   = He worked hard **so that** he **might not** fail.

E must / ought to 용법

❶ must

1. We **must** obey the laws. <① 의무>
2. "**Must** I go at once?"

   "No, you **don't have to [need not].**" <의무의 부정>
3. You **must not** sit on this bench. <금지>
4. That **must be** false. <② 추측>

   (그것은 거짓임에 틀림없다.)
5. It **cannot be** true. <추측의 부정>

   (그것은 사실일 리가 없다.)

must에는 두 가지 의미가 있다.
하나는 ① '해야한다'는 의무의 의미이고,
다른 하나는 ② '~임에 틀림없다'는 추측의 의미이다.
①에 대한 부정의 표현은 don't have to[need not]이고,
②에 대한 부정의 표현은 cannot be이다.
must 조동사에 not을 붙이면 '의무'와 '추측'의 의미가 아닌 '금지'의 의미가 된다.

❷ ought to

1. (a) You **ought to** save your money. <의무>
   (b) We **ought to** love our neighbors.
2. John **ought to** be here by now. <당연한 기대: ~일 것이다>

F need / dare / used to 용법

❶ need

1. (a) **Need** I go to the dentist? <조동사>
   (b) You **need not** worry about your mother.
2. (a) She says she **needs** much money. <일반동사>
   (b) It **needs** to be done carefully.

❷ dare

1. (a) **Dare** you jump from the top of that high wall? <조동사>
   (b) She **dare not** speak a word.
2. (a) He **dares** to insult me. <일반동사>
   (b) Does he **dare** to speak to her?

❸ used to

1. I **used to** take a walk before breakfast. <조동사, 과거의 규칙적 습관>
2. This machine **is used to sharpen** the pencil. <일반동사>
3. He **was used to sitting up** late. <be used to ~ing>

G 추측의 조동사

조동사의 과거형태(could, might, should, ought to)는 그 과거형태가 일부의 경우에서는 과거시제를 표시하는 데 사용되기도 하지만, 또 다른 일부에서는 조동사의 특수의미를 표현하기 위해서 사용되어 현재시제의 성격을 띤다.

Children should obey their parents.

위 문장에서 should는 과거형태의 조동사지만 '과거에 부모에게 순종해야 한다'는 의미가 아니고 '현재'의 의미로 쓰이고 있다. 그래서 정작 과거의 의미로 사용하고자 할 때는 이미 그 조동사의 과거형을 조동사의 특별한 의미로 사용해 버렸기 때문에 다른 형태로 구별해 줄 필요가 생긴다.

이러한 조동사의 과거 의미가 문장에서 필요할 때 완료시제(have + PP)의 도움을 얻어 '과거의 추측' 의미를 만들어 낸다.

- may have + PP　　과거에 ~일지도 모른다
- cannot have + PP　　과거에 ~임은 불가능하다
- must have + PP　　과거에 ~임이 틀림없다
- should have + PP　　과거에 ~했어야 했다
- ought to have + PP　　과거에 ~했어야 했다
- need not + have + PP　　과거에 ~할 필요가 없었다

1. He may be ill. = It is **possible** that he **is** ill.
2. (a) He **may have been** ill. = It is **possible** that he **was** ill.
   (b) The road is muddy. It **may have rained** during the night.
3. He cannot be ill. = It is **impossible** that he **is** ill.
4. (a) He **cannot have been** ill. = It is **impossible** that he **was** ill.
   (b) He **cannot have told** a lie.
5. He must be ill. = It is **certain** that he **is** ill.
6. (a) He **must have been** ill = It is **certain** that he **was** ill.
   (b) I'm afraid we're lost. We **must have taken** the wrong road.
   (c) Something **must have happened** to my sister.
7. (a) You **should have carried** out his plan.
   (b) You **should have seen** the sunrise.
8. (a) The captain of the Titanic **ought to have been** more careful.
   (b) The doctor **ought to have arrived** long ago.
9. He **need not have hurried**. = It was not **necessary** for him to hurry.

Basic Reading 7

1 The first lesson a young man **should** learn is, that he knows nothing; and that the earlier and more thoroughly this lesson is learned, the better it will be for his peace of mind, and his success in life.

- lesson[lésn] n. 교훈
- thoroughly[θə́:rouli] a. 철저히
- peace[pi:s] n. 평화
- success[səksés] n. 성공

2 When I delivered my talk later that day, I told them of this experience, and **suggested** that each man **go** down to the sea, preferably alone, and spend a little time with the sky and vast waters.

- deliver[dilívər] v. (의견을) 말하다
- suggest[səgdʒést] vt. 제안하다
- preferably alone 가급적이면 혼자서
- vast[væst, vɑ:st] a. 광대한
- waters (강 · 호수 · 바다 등의) 물

3 I **would like to** go on a tour now and then for the benefit of my health.

- go on a tour 여행을 떠나다
- (every) now and then = now and again 때때로, 종종
- for the benefit of ~을 위하여

4 She **used to** be an actress, and so she **was used to being** looked at by many people and **to standing** on the stage.

• actress[ǽktris] n. 여배우
• be used to ~ ing ~하는데 익숙하다 (be accustomed to ~ing)

5 Archimedes was the last man to say that anything was impossible. He took great delight in working out hard problems, and when any question puzzled him, he **would** keep studying until he found some sort of answer to it.

• Archimedes 아르키메데스(287-212 B.C.) 그리스 물리학자
• work out 문제를 풀다
• puzzle[pʌ́zl] v. 당황하게 하다
• would 과거의 불규칙적 습관

6 It is obvious that our early human ancestors **cannot have been** acting on a deliberate policy, but **must have been** prompted by an instinctive mechanism — the double mechanism of friendship within the tribe and hostility to all others.

• obvious[ɑ́bviəs] a. 명백한(plain), (⇔ obscure 모호한)
• ancestor[ǽnsestər] n. 선조(⇔ descendant 자손)
• act on (주의 충고 등)을 좇아 행동하다(follow), ~에 작용하다
• deliberate[dilíbərit] a. 신중한, 고의의
• policy[pɑ́ləsi] n. 정책
• prompt[prɑmpt] v. 자극하다
• instinctive[instíŋktiv] a. 본능적인
• mechanism[mékənìzəm] n. 심리과정, 절차, 기계장치
• tribe[traib] n. 부족
• hostility[hɑstíləti] n. 적의, 적개심

7 Don't despise the opinions of the world; you **might as well** say you do not care for the light of the sun, because you can use a candle.

- despise[dispáiz] vt. 경멸하다
- might as well A as B : B하느니 A하는 편이 낫다
- care for 상관하다, 돌보다, 간호하다
- might as well ~ a candle (as despise the opinion of the world)

8 Those with limited time at their disposal **may well** despair of gaining an adequate acquaintance with the many sights and treasures that London holds.

- at one's disposal (command)[dispóuzəl] n. 임으로 할 수 있는
- may well ~하는 것은 당연하다(have a good reason to R)
- despair of[dispɛ́ər] vi. 단념하다
- adequate[ǽdikwit] a. 적절한, 적당한
- acquaintance[əkwéintəns] a. 아는 사이
- the sights 명소, 관광지

9 There is one fact that you **may as well** face now, namely, that the easiest things are rarely the best for you. Trouble has been one of the greatest blessings to mankind.

- may as well ~ 하는 편이 낫다
- face[feis] v. 직면하다
- namely[néimli] ad. 즉, 다시 말해서
- one fact that에서 that은 face의 목적격 관계대명사
- that the easiest things are ~에서 that은 접속사
- blessing[blésiŋ] n. 축복 • mankind[mæ̀nkáind] n. 인류

10 One **might as well** try to stop the progress of a mighty railroad train by throwing his body across the track, **as** try to stop the growth of the world in the direction of giving mankind more intelligence, more prosperity, and more liberty.

- progress[prágrəs] n. 진보
- intelligence[intélədʒəns] n. 지성, 정보
- prosperity[praɑspérəti] n. 번영
- liberty[líbəːrti] n. 자유

Advanced Reading 13

A. Preparing to Read

Many Companies are so busy analysing the financial implications **that** they overlook the effect on workers.

Whether it turns out to be a good idea **or** a bad idea, we'll find out.

By simply planning a route, you can explore at will and stop **whenever and wherever you like**.

B. Approaching to the Topic

All through my boyhood and youth I was known and pointed out as an idle boy; and yet I was always busy following my own private purpose, which was to learn to write. Wherever I went, I took two books with me, one to read, and the other, a notebook to write in. When I read something which particularly pleased me, I sat down at once and tried to imitate that author's style. When I walked in the country, I tried to fit appropriate words to what I saw. Whether I have profited or not, I believe this is the way to learn to write.

Memoirs and Reminiscences by Robert L. Stevenson

Vocabularies & Expressions for Comprehension

- boyhood and youth[juːθ] 청소년시대
- point out 지적하다
- idle[áidl] 게으른
- private[práivit] 사적인, 은밀한
- pleased[pliːzd] 기쁘게 한
- at once 곧, 즉시
- imitate[ímitèit] 모방하다

- fit 맞추다
- appropriate[əpróuprièit] 적절한
- profited or not 유익했든 그렇지 않든

Sentence Pattern Analysis

- I was known and pointed out as an idle boy;
  「나는 게으른 소년으로 알려졌고 지적되었다.」

- yet I was always busy following my own private purpose
  「내 자신의 은밀한 목적을 따르는데 항상 바빴다.」

- I tried to fit appropriate words to what I saw.
  「내가 본 것에 적당한 말을 맞추려고 애썼다.」

- tried to imitate that author's style.
  「그 작가의 문체를 모방하려고 애썼다.」

- Whether I have profited or not
  「내가 유익을 얻든 그렇지 않든」

Wisdom

Examinations are formidable even to the best prepared, for the greatest fool may ask more than the wisest man can answer.

시험이란 최선을 다해 준비한 사람에게도 만만찮은 것이다. 왜냐하면 매우 멍청한 바보라도 가장 현명한 사람이 대답할 수 없는 것을 물을 수 있기 때문이다.

Charles C. Colton: Lacon

Advanced Reading 14

A. Preparing to Read

She has her place in the Asian team **not** because she is white **but** because she is good.

The problem **lay in** the large amounts spent on defence.

Her work as a consultant **consisted in** advising foreign companies on the siting of new factories.

B. Approaching to the Topic

Though we think so much of our body, it is in reality a very small part of us; a man's true life lies not in his body but in that which he does with his body. Before birth we get together our tools; in life we use them, and thus fashion our true life which consists not in our tools and tool-box but in the work we have done with our tools. It is Handel's work, not the body with which he did the work that drags thousands of people on a winter's night from one end of London to another; and this is the true Handel, who is a more living power among us one hundred and twenty-two years after his death than during the time he was amongst us in the body.

Samuel Butler's Notebooks by *Samuel Butler*

Vocabularies & Expressions for Comprehension

- in reality[riːǽləti] 실제로
- lies in ~에 놓여 있다
- fashion[fǽʃən] 형성하다, 만들다
- consists in ~에 존재하다
- drags[dræg] 끌어오다
- amongst[əmʌ́ŋst] ~ 가운데

• infinitely[ínfinitli] (비교급 앞에서) 훨씬

Sentence Pattern Analysis

• a man's true life lies not in his body but in that which he does with his body.

lies not in ~ but in~의 구문.「인간의 진실한 생명은 그의 육체에 있는 것이 아니라 그가 그의 육체를 가지고 행하는 것에 있다.」

• The body changes hourly — the work changes, but infinitely more slowly.

육체는 시시각각 변하며, 작품도 변화지만 무한히 훨씬 더 천천히 변한다.

Wisdom

The business of everybody is the business of nobody.

모든 사람에 관련되는 일은 어떤 사람도 성의를 가지고 하지 않는다.

Thomas Babington Macaulary: Historical Essays

제8장. 접속사·전치사

- A 대등(對等) 접속사
- B 명사절을 이끄는 접속사
- C 종속(從屬) 접속사
- D 접속부사
- E 전치사의 용법
- F 시간과 장소의 전치사
- G 전치사별 의미
- H 군전치사(群前置詞)와 군동사(群動詞)

제8장 접속사 *Conjunction* / 전치사 *Preposition*

A 대등(對等) 접속사

1. He happened to see her **and** came to love her.
2. He is gentle in appearance **but** strong at heart.
3. You **or he is** to blame.
4. It was morning, **for** the birds were singing.
5. This book is **both** interesting **and** instructive.
6. **Not only** my brother **but also** I **am** to go abroad in June.
   = **I as well as** my brother **am** to go abroad in June.
   <not only A but also B = B as well as A: A 뿐만 아니라 B도 역시, **B에 동사 일치**>
7. **Either** you **or he has to** go there.
8. He **cannot** speak **either** English **or** French.
   = He can speak **neither** English **nor** French.
9. **Neither** I **nor he is** going to the movies.

B 명사절을 이끄는 접속사

1. **That** he said so is true.
2. It is true **that** he said so.
3. I heard **the news that** he was dead.
4. Men differ from animals **in that** they can think and speak.
   in that: ~라는 점에서
5. I am quite well **except that** I have a slight cold.
   except[=save =but =only] that: ~라는 점을 제외하면
6. **Whether** he will succeed is doubtful.
   if나 whether는 명사절을 인도한다
7. It is doubtful **whether** he will succeed.
8. I don't know **whether** it will rain or not.

C 종속(從屬) 접속사

❶ 원인

because, since, as, for, now that(= since), in that, seeing that, not that-but that

1. **Because** he was sick, he was absent.
   because: why에 대한 대답, 직접적인 이유
2. **Since** you look tired, you had better take a rest.
   since: 추론의 근거
3. **As** it was very late, I turned back.
   as: since보다 이유 · 원인의 뜻이 약하다.
4. He married her, **for** he loved her. (○)
   For he loved her, he married her. (×)
   for가 이끄는 절은 문장 머리에 오지 않는다.

❷ 조건

if, unless, otherwise, in case, supposing[suppose] that, providing[provided] that, on condition that, so long as

1. I will come **provided** you let me know beforehand.
2. I will do it **on condition that** I am paid.

❸ 양보

though, although, if, even if, even though, whether or, while, as, granting that,no matter, whatever, however, In spite of [despite, in the face of, notwithstanding, after all, for all, with all]+명사

1. **Though** he is rich, he is not happy.
2. Strong **as** the man was, he couldn't remove it.
3. Woman **as** she was, she could not sew.
4. Try **as** you may, you cannot finish it in a week.
   as 양보구문: 형용사[부사, 동사, 무관사 명사] + as + S + V

❹ 시간

when, while, since, till, after, before, by the time, as long as, as soon as, no sooner-than, scarcely-before, hardly-when, the moment, the instant

1. **When** my father died, I was fifteen years old.
2. She sang **as** she washed.
3. It will be long **before** he notices it.
   (오랜 시간이 지나고 나서야 그것을 알아차릴 것이다.)

4. **It will not be long before** spring comes.
   = **Before long** spring will come.
   = **Soon** spring will come.

5 I had gone a mile **before** I got tired.

6. **Scarcely[hardly]** had he seen me **before[when]** he ran away.
   (그는 나를 보자마자 도망쳤다.)
7. He has been interested in flowers **since** he was a little boy.
   (그는 어린 소년 때부터 꽃에 흥미를 가졌다.)
8. I will wait here **until** you come back.
9. We do **not** know the value of health **until** we lose it.
   = **Not until** we lose health **do we know** the value of it.
   = It is **not until** we lose health that we know the value of it.

❺ 장소

where, wherever

1. **Where** there is a will, there is a way.
2. Sit **wherever** you like.

❻ 목적 · 결과

that ~ may, so that ~ may, in order that ~ may

1. Children should go to school **so that** they **may** learn things.

2. He worked hard **in order that** he **might** pass the exam.
3. I worked hard **so that** I **might** not fail.
= I worked hard **lest** I **should** fail.

D 접속부사

문장이나 절을 논리적으로 연결시켜주는 부사로서 접속사와 다르다.

❶ 동격의(Appositive) 접속부사

namely(viz), for example (e.g.), that is(i.e.), in other words

• He started for Paris a week ago, **that is to say**, on the tenth of May.

❷ 양보의(Concessive) 접속부사

however, still, nevertheless, none the less, yet, only, though

• She likes him; he is poor, **though**.

❸ 추정의(Inferential) 접속부사

otherwise, then, in that case

• I went at once; **otherwise** I should have missed the plane.

❹ 결과의(Resultant) 접속부사

therefore, thus, so, hence, of course, consequently, accordingly

• He failed: **therefore** he took the course again.

❺ 부가의(Additive) 접속부사

besides, also, moreover, in addition

• I was tired: **besides** I was very sleepy.

E 전치사의 용법

접속사가 문장을 연결하는 데에 반하여 전치사는 원칙적으로 구를 연결한다. 전치사의 학습은 크게 두 부분으로 나누어 이해할 필요가 있다. 첫째는 전치사 자체적인 의미에 따라서 목적어를 동반하여 개별적인 의미 단위를 만든다. 둘째로는 동사 개별적인 의미에 따라서 그 동사에 적합한 전치사가 필요하다. 이 후자의 경우, 전치사에 대한 이해는 전치사의 범위를 넘어서 모든 동사의 활용에까지 이를 것이므로 단편적인 전치사의 이해가 아닌 동사의 활용 의미와 더불어 전치사를 학습해야 할 것이다.

이 단원에서 전치사의 이해는 첫째 항목의 범주에 해당하는 것으로 기본적인 전치사의 용법에 대한 이해를 도모하는 것이 될 것이다.

❶ 전치사의 기능

(1) 형용사구

1. The flowers **in your garden** are very pretty.
2. The last scene **of the movie** was very impressive.
3. This tool is **of great use** to us.

(2) 부사구

1. He solved it **with ease**.
2. Peter went **into the kitchen** and found her key **under the table**.
3. **On Sundays** I stay **in bed till ten o'clock**.

❷ 전치사의 목적어

전치사는 목적어를 수반하는 것이 원칙이다.

1. I am thankful **to him for his help**. <명사, 대명사>
2. He entered the room **without greeting anybody**. <동명사>
3. I was **about to leave**. <부정사>
4. I will stay **until toward evening**. <구>
5. Men differ from brutes **in that they can think and speak**. <절>
6. His business went **from bad to worse**. <형용사>
7. He returned **from abroad**. <부사>

F 시간과 장소의 전치사

❶ 시간의 전치사

(1) **at, on, in**

1. at : 시간상의 한 점, 시간 · 정오 · 새벽 등의 짧은 시간

   ex. at 7 o'clock, at 11: 40, at night, at dawn, at midnight, at noon, at present, at the same time

2. on : 요일, 날짜, **특정한 날**의 아침 · 점심 · 저녁

   ex. on Saturday, on May 11th, on my birthday, on Saturday afternoon

3. in : 월, 년, 계절 등 비교적 긴 기간, 아침, 점심, 저녁

   ex. in October, in 1945, in summer, in the 21st century, in the morning

(2) **for, during, through, over**

1. I have not seen him **for** three years. 〈for + 수사동반 명사〉
2. I am going to practice Judo every morning **during** summer vacation.〈일정한 기간〉
3. She was ill **through** this winter. 〈전 기간 동안 내내〉
4. The patient won't live **over** today. 〈시간의 계속 · 초과〉

(3) **since, from**

1. She **has been** absent from school **since** Monday. 〈(대)과거의 어느 시점 이후 계속〉
2. He works **from** 9 a.m. **to** 5 p.m. 〈순서의 기점〉

(4) **by, till(until), up to**

1. I'll wait for her here **till(until)** nine. 〈동작 및 상태의 계속〉
2. You must finish writing your report **by** five o'clock. 〈동작의 완료〉
3. He has been ill **up to** now. 〈동작 및 상태의 계속〉

(5) **on time, in time**

1. Please be **on time**. 〈정각에= punctually〉
2. Will you be home **in time** for dinner? 〈시간 안에〉

❷ 장소의 전치사

(1) **at, in**

1. I bought the dress **at a shop** in Seoul. <at: 비교적 좁은 장소>
2. Seoul is the largest city **in Korea**. <in: 넓은 장소>

(2) **above, below; over, under; on, beneath**

1. The sun is rising **above** the horizon. <위치가 높음>
2. The moon has sunk **below** the horizon. <위치가 낮음>
3. The lamps are hanging **over** my head. <바로 위>
4. There were some pretty flowers **under** the tree. <바로 밑>
5. There is a map of Canada **on** the wall. <접촉면 위>
6. **Beneath** the stone, we found a lot of ants. <접촉면 아래>

(3) **across, along, through, throughout, round, around**

1. He went **across** the street. <가로질러>
2. There used to be cherry-trees **along** the river banks. < ~을 따라서>
3. The train passed **through** the tunnel. < ~을 관통하여>
4. He traveled **throughout** the country. < ~의 구석구석까지>
5. The earth moves **round** the sun. < ~의 주위를 도는 운동>
6. The boys sat **around** him. < ~의 주위에 정지한 상태>

(4) **up, down; into, out of**

1. The monkey went **up and down** the tree. <운동의 (위로/아래로) 방향>
2. He ran **into** the room. <밖에서 안으로>
3. He came **out of** the room. <안에서 밖으로>

(5) **to, for, toward**

1. He got **to** London yesterday. <도착지점>
2. The plane is bound **for** Seoul. <목적지, 방향>
3. He stood looking **toward** the rear of the restaurant. <방향>

(6) **between, among**

1. I asked him whether there was much difference **between** British and European law. <둘 사이>
2. She is very popular **among** her classmates. <셋 이상 사이>

G 전치사별 의미

(1) **against**

1. He stood with his back **against** the door. < ~에 기대어>
2. The tower rises high **against** the evening sky. < ~을 배경으로>
3. They sailed **against** the wind <역행하여>
4. The people rose **against** the government < ~에 반대하여>
5. He was elected by a majority of 30 **against** 10. <10표 대 30표>
   (10표 대 30표의 다수의 표 차이로 그는 선출되었다.)

(2) **behind**

1. The train arrived ten minutes **behind** time. <10분 늦게>
2. The child hid **behind** the door. <~뒤에>
3. He is **behind** others in English. <남들 보다 뒤진>

(3) **by**

1. He has a house **by** the river. < ~의 가까이>
2. She missed the train **by** a minute. <분량, 정도: ~만큼>
3. He is paid **by the** hour[day, week, month, year]. <단위>

(4) **beyond**

1. They stayed **beyond** the time limit. <제한시간 이상으로>
2. He lives **beyond** his income. <수입 이상으로>

(5) **for**

1. **for** sale, go **for** a walk <목적>

2. They stood up **for** women's rights. <~에 찬성하여>
3. He left **for** New York. <~을 향하여>
4. substitute A **for** B = replace B with[by] A <A로 B를 대신하다>
   substitute nylon for silk = replace silk with(by) nylon

(6) **of**

1. the works **of** Shakespeare, the love **of** God <주격>
2. a teacher **of** English, the love **of** art <목적격>
3. the master **of** the house, the top **of** the hill <소유격>
4. the city **of** Seoul, the continent **of** Asia <동격>
5. rob[deprive, free, relieve, cure, clear] A **of** B <분리, 제거>
   The man rob me of my purse.
   = The man stole my purse from me.
6. die **of** cancer <원인>

(7) **to**

1. He is on the way **to** school. <운동 방향>
2. She danced **to** the music. <일치>
3. They won the game four **to** three. <비교: 득점이 4 대 3>
4. They went **to** her rescue. <목적>
5. The girl was burn **to** death. <결과>

(8) **with**

1. He walked **with** her. <동반>
2. cut **with** a knife, write **with** a pen <도구>
3. He voted **with** the Socialists. <동의>
4. **With** the best intentions, he failed completely. <양보>
5. He stood **with** a pipe in his mouth. <부대상황>
6. They provided[supplied] sufferers **with** clothing <공급>

H 군전치사(群前置詞)와 군동사(群動詞)

❶ 군전치사(群前置詞)

1. Thoughts are expressed **by means of** words. < ~에 의해서>
2. He came **according to** his promise. < ~에 따라서>
3. The game was called off **because of** rain. < ~ 때문에>
4. He cannot accept your kind invitation **on account of** my illness. < ~때문에>
5. **As for** me, I would rather not go. <문장 머리에 쓰임>
6. There was a heated argument **as to** who should be appointed. <문장 중간에 쓰임>
7. In fact, she loves him. However, she tries to act **to the contrary**.
   <동사 뒤에서; ~에 반대로>
8. A: You look tired.
   B: **On the contrary**, I feel fine. <문장 머리에서; ~에 반대로>

❷ 군동사(群動詞)

(1) 동사 + 전치사

1. Happiness **consists in** contentment.
2. He **takes after** his father.

ex. result from, wait for, consist of, result in, believe in, call on, get over, rely on

(2) 동사 + 부사

1. I couldn't **make out** what he meant.
2. Don't **put off** till tomorrow what you can do today.

ex. break down, come about, drop in, bring up, carry out, give up, take off, turn on

(3) 동사 + 부사 + 전치사

1. We are all **looking forward to** seeing you.
2. Everybody **looks up to** Mr. Smith.

ex. do away with, keep up with, look down on, put up with

Basic Reading 8

1 One should endeavor to utilize all his spare time in **either** work **or** amusement, as time simply idled away is an absolute loss to **both** oneself **and** the public.

- endeavor to[endévər] v. 노력하다
- utilize[jú:tilàiz] vt. 이용하다(make use of)
- amusement[əmjú:zmənt] n. 즐거움
- absolute[ǽbsəlù:t] a. 절대적인
- loss[lɔ(:)s] n. 손실
- the public 대중, 국민, 세상, 사회

2 Reading is valuable just because books are like people. **Just as** a boxer exercises for a real fight with a punching bag or a sparring partner, **so** you can train yourself for relations with real people with a book.

- Just as S + V, so S + V 마치 ~하는 것과 마찬가지로 그렇게 ~한다

3 **No sooner** had I glanced at this letter **than** I concluded it to be that of which I was in search.

- glance[glæns] n. 일견(一見), 흘긋 봄
- conclude[kənklú:d] v. 결론을 내리다
- that = the letter
- in search of ~ ~을 찾아서, ~을 구해서

4 **Nothing** was to be seen but water and sky for five days after the ship left that port, **until** on the sixth day we caught sight of a little island in the distance.

- was to be seen = could be seen
- but = except
- catch sight of ~을 찾아내다
- in the distance 먼 곳에

5 **It was not until** the 18th century **that** the consequence of scientific research work began, for the first time, to provide knowledge of value to technologists.

- consequence[kánsikwèns] n. 결과, 결말
- research[risə́:rtʃ] n. 연구, 학술 조사
- for the first time 처음으로
- provide A with B : A에게 B를 공급하다
- knowledge of value = valuable knowledge
- technologist[teknálədʒist] n. 과학기술자

6 **Whatever** difficulties we may come across, we will help one another to get over.

- whatever difficulties we may come across
  = no matter what difficulties we may come across
  복합관계형용사가 양보의 부사절을 형성한다
- come across = come upon
- get over = overcome

7 **No matter what** business you may be engaged in, you can by no means hope to succeed in it, unless you devote yourself to it body and soul.

- be engaged in ~에 종사하다
- by no means = never
- unless = if ~ not
- devote oneself to ~에 전념하다(apply oneself to)

8 **Whatever** the learned say about a book, **however** unanimous they are in their praise of it, unless it interest you it is no business of yours.

- the learned = men of learning, the + 형용사 = 복수보통명사
- unanimous[ju:nǽnəməs] a. 만장일치의
- interest[íntərèst] vt. 흥미를 주다
- it is no business of yours = it in none of your business

9 Communication is a social activity requiring the combined efforts of two or more individuals. Mere talk to produce sentences, **no matter how** well formed or elegant the outcome, does not by itself constitute communication.

- communication[kəmjù:nəkéiʃən] n. 의사전달, 통신
- require[rikwáiə:r] vt. 요구하다, 명하다
- combined efforts 합동의 노력
- no matter how well formed or elegant the outcome (may be)
- does not constitute의 주어는 Mere talk이다
- by oneself 혼자 힘으로

10 No matter where one may go on this small planet, one will find the same thing. There is no place like home, **be it ever so humble**. **Let a man say what he will**, he will come back to his home at long last.

- No matter where one may go = Wherever one may go
- planet[plǽnət] n. 행성
- be it ever so humble = however humble it may be
- let a man say what he will = whatever a man may say
- at (long) last 마침내(finally)

11 The production of a work of art is not the result of a miracle. It requires preparation. The soil, **be it ever so rich**, must be fed. By taking thought, by deliberate effort, the artist must enlarge, deepen and diversify his personality.

- a work of art 예술작품
- miracle[mírəkəl] n. 기적, 경이
- require[rikwáiəːr] vt. 요구하다, 필요로 하다
- feed[fiːd] v. (feed - fed - fed) 먹이를 주다, 영양분을 주다
- take thought 마음을 쓰다, 걱정하다
- deliberate[dilíbərit] a. 신중한, 사려 깊은
- diversify[divə́ːrsəfai, dai-] v. 다양화하다
- personality[pə̀ːrsənǽləti] 개성(individuality), 인격(character)

12 **With all** this hard task, he learned to write. Above all, he learned to think for himself.

- with all ~에도 불구하고
- task[tæsk] 직무, 과제, 과업
- above all 무엇보다도
- for oneself 혼자 힘으로, 스스로

13 Once John got an idea, he was **so** obstinate **that** nobody could argue him out of it.

- once[wʌ́ns] ad. 일단 ~ 하면 (if[when])
- obstinate[ɑ́bstənit] a. 완고한, 고집센, 집요한
- argue A into[out of] B 설득해서 ~하게[그만두게] 하다

14 They made their way through the trees **only to find** they were still in the greatest forest.

- make one's way 나아가다, 번창하다, 출세하다
- only to 결국 (~ 하는) 것뿐인

15 All at once I saw a human form in the distance, and, **to my surprise**, soon recognized that the traveller was a woman.

- all at once = all of a sudden
- in the distance 멀리서
- to my surprise 놀랍게도; to one's 감정명사, ~ 하게도
- recognize[rékəgnaiz] v. 인정하다. 인지하다, 알아주다

16 **Now that** I have heard your explanation, I am more inclined to agree with you.

- now that = since
- explanation[èksplənéiʃən] n. 설명
- be inclined to ~하고 싶어하는
- agree with 동의하다

Advanced Reading 15

A. Preparing to Read

Because of the popularity of the region, **it** is advisable **to book hotels or camp sites in advance**.

He had done this **without consulting** her.

They told **either** she goes **or** I go.

B. Approaching to the Topic

He was an old man who fished alone in a skiff in the Gulf Stream and he had gone eighty-four days now without taking a fish. In the first forty days a boy had been with him. But after forty days without a fish the boy's parents had told him that the old man was definitely and finally salao, which is the worst form of unlucky, and the boy had gone by their orders in another boat which caught three good fish the first week. It made the boy sad to see the old man come in each day with his skiff empty and he always went down to help him carry either the coiled lines or the gaff and harpoon and the sail that was furled around the mast. The sail was patched with flour sacks and, furled, it looked like the flag of permanent defeat.

The old man and the Sea by E. Hemingway

Vocabularies & Expressions for Comprehension

- the Gulf Stream 멕시코 만류
- definitely 분명하게
- salao 「살라오」, 스페인어로 '아주재수없는 사람' 의미(the worst form of unlucky)
- the worst[wəːrst] 가장 나쁜
- empty[émpti] 텅 빈

- carry 운반하다
- coiled 사린, 돌돌 감긴
- lines 낚시줄
- skiff[skif] 작은 조각배
- gaff[gæf] 갈퀴, 갈고리대
- harpoon[hɑːrpún] 작살
- sail[seil] 돛
- furled[fəːrld] 감아 올린, 말아 올린
- patched 꿰맨
- flour[flauər] 밀가루
- sacks[sæks] 자루, 부대
- flag[flæg] 깃발
- permanent[pə́ːrmənənt] 영원한
- defeat 패배

Sentence Pattern Analysis

- he had gone eighty-four days now without taking a fish.

  「그는 이제껏 한 마리의 고기도 잡지 못한 채 84일을 보냈다.」 had gone은 had been fishing의 의미

- It made the boy sad to see the old man come in each day with his skiff empty.

  It ~ to 구문. 물론 to~ 이하가 진주어. 「노인이 매일 빈 조각배로 돌아오는 것을 볼 때 소년은 슬펐다.」

- the sail that was furled around the mast.

  「돛대에 감겨있는 돛」

- The sail was patched with flour sacks and, furled, it looked like the flag of permanent defeat.

  「그 돛은 밀가루 자루로 꿰매져서 감겨 있었는데, 그것은 마치 영원한 패배의 깃발처럼 보였다.」 이 문장에서 'furled' 는 'when it was furled' 로 바꿔 쓸 수 있음(분사구문).

Wisdom

Without haste, but without rest

서둘지 않지만 쉬지도 않는다.

Johann Wolfgang von Goethe

Advanced Reading 16

A. Preparing to Read

There's a postage and packing fee **in addition to** the repair charge.

They need hostages **in order to** bargain with the government.

It is **not always** dull and raining.

These oils may **cause** irritation to sensitive skins.

B. Approaching to the Topic

The news gives instant coverage of important events. News also provides facts and information. In addition, news is business: a way to make money by selling advertising and/or newspapers and magazines. Sometimes news is propaganda or disinformation: a way to control a population. But whatever news is, it is all around us. You can't escape it. Every day we are bombarded by information: newspapers, magazines, TV, and the computer internet.

'News' does not always mean something that is unquestionably true. Although the news seems to be based on facts, these facts are interpreted and reported the way the media chooses to report them. For example, some information that appears as news is really only speculation or theories formed by the reporters. Futhermore, many journalists and reporters sensationalize or dramatize a news event in order to make a story more interesting. Unfortunately, sensationalism often bends the truth and causes anguish to the people it victimizes. Therefore, as consumers of news we must learn to think critically about the news, the media, and what the truth is.

From North Star

Vocabularies & Expressions for Comprehension

- coverage[kʌ́vəridʒ] 보도
- provides[prəváid] 제공하다
- In addition[ədiʃən] 게다가, 덧붙여서
- advertising[ǽdvərtàiziŋ] 광고하는
- magazines[mæ̀gəzí:n] 잡지
- propaganda[prɑ̀pəgǽndə] 선전
- disinformation[disìnfərméiʃən] 그릇된 정보
- population[pɑ̀pjəléiʃən] 인구, 대중
- escape[iskéip] 탈출하다
- bombard[bɑmbɑ́:rd] 폭격하다, 퍼붓다
- unquestionably[ʌnkwéstʃənəbli] 의심할 바 없이
- interpret[intə́:rprit] 해석하다
- media[mí:diə] 매체
- speculation[spèkjəléiʃən] 추측
- theories[θí:əri] 이론
- Futhermore 더구나
- sensationalize[senséiʃənəlàiz] 선정적으로 보도하다
- dramatize[drǽmətaiz] 극화하다
- in order to ~하기 위해
- Unfortunately[ʌ̀nfɔ́:rtʃənitli] 불행하게도
- bend[bend] 왜곡하다
- anguish[ǽŋgwiʃ] 격통, 고뇌
- victimizes[víktəmàiz] 희생시키다, 속이다
- consumers of news 뉴스를 소비하는 사람들
- critically[krítikəli] 비판적으로

Sentence Pattern Analysis

- a way to a make money by selling advertising and/or newspapers and magazines.
  광고를 팔고/혹은 신문과 잡지를 팔아서 돈을 버는 방법

- a way to control a population. 사람들을 통제하는 방법

- whatever news is,
  어떤 뉴스이든

- You can't escape it.
  이 문장에서 it는 news를 가리킨다. 즉 「뉴스의 홍수에서 벗어날 수 없다.」

- 'News' does not always mean something that is unquestionably true.
  '뉴스'가 의심할 바 없이 진실한 것을 항상 의미하지는 않는다. 'not always'는 부분부정.

- many journalists and reporters sensationalize or dramatize a news event in order to make a story more interesting.
  「수많은 저널리스트와 기자들은 어떤 이야기를 더욱 흥미 있게 만들기 위해서 뉴스 사건을 선정적으로 보도하거나 극화한다.」

- sensationalism often bends the truth and causes anguish to the people it victimizes.
  「선정주의는 종종 진실을 왜곡하고 그것이 희생시키는 사람들에게 격심한 고통을 초래한다.」 여기서 그것(it)은 선정주의를 가리킴.

Wisdom

Remember that time is money.

시간은 돈임을 명심하라.

Benjamin Franklin: Advice to Young Tradesman

Welcome to English Grammar & Reading

제9장. 관계사

- Ⓐ 개 요
- Ⓑ 관계대명사
- Ⓒ 관계형용사
- Ⓓ 관계부사
- Ⓔ 복합관계사
- Ⓕ 유사관계대명사

제9장 관계사 *Relative*

A 개요

관계대명사는 접속사와 대명사의 역할을 하면서 형용사절을 구성한다. 동시에 선행하는 명사나 대명사를 수식한다. 국어는 관형절이 명사를 선행(先行)하면서 수식하는 데에 반해, 영어는 관계사절이 명사를 후위(後衛) 수식한다. 이와 같이 이 부분에서 국어와 영어는 언어 구조상 현저히 다르다.

이러한 원인 때문에 모국어인 국어 구조에 익숙한 우리 학생들이 영어의 관계사 구조 습득에 어려움을 겪는 것은 지극히 당연하다. 따라서 이 부분의 이해와 많은 연습이 필요하다.

- The pen **that I bought yesterday**.
- 내가 어제 구입한 펜

B 관계대명사

❶ 관계대명사 = 접속사 + 대명사

I have a friend. The friend lives in Busan. 〈2문장〉

→ I have a friend **and he** lives in Busan. 〈접속사 +대명사〉

→ I have a friend **who** lives in Busan. 〈관계대명사〉

❷ 관계대명사 who, which, that

관계대명사	who	which	that
선행사	사람	동물·사물	사람·동물·사물

1. I know the man **who** wrote this book.
2. (a) That is ***the riddle*** **which** no one was able to answer 〈선행사가 사물이나 동물〉
   (b) He is ***rich***, **which** she is not 〈선행사가 형용사, rich가 선행사〉
   (c) ***I said nothing***, **which** made her still more angry. 〈선행사가 앞 문장 일부 또는 전체〉
   (d) He spoke in ***French***, **which** language I could not understand. 〈관계형용사〉

(e) **Which** do you prefer, tea or coffee? <의문사, 선택적 의미>

3. (a) This is **the only** car **that** can run like an arrow.
   (b) This is **the best** novel **that** I have read.
   the only, the very, the +서수, 최상급 등으로 선행사가 한정될 때 관계대명사 that을 쓴다.
4. That is the man **whose** house burned down last night. <소유격>

❸ 관계사절과 분사의 후위수식

(1b)와 (2b)의 관계사절에서 「주격관계대명사 + be 동사」를 생략하면 (1a)와 (2a)같이 후위수식관계의 분사가 된다. 관계사절은 형용사절로서 선행사를 수식하고, 분사가 이끄는 구는 형용사구가 되어 명사를 수식한다.

1. (a) ***a skylark*** **singing** high up in the sky
   (b) ***a skylark*** **(which is) singing** high up in the sky
2. (a) I bought ***a book*** **written** in plain English.
   (b) I bought ***a book*** **(which was) written** in plain English.

❹ 관계대명사 소유격, 목적격 whose, whom, which

1. (a) Look at that house **whose** roof is painted red.
   (b) She has a daughter **whose** name is Nancy.
2. John is a boy (**whom**) everyone can depend on.
3. (a) This is the book (**which**) I want to read.
   (b) This is the house **in which** I live.

❺ 목적격 관계대명사

목적격 관계대명사는 생략할 수 있다.

1. This is the house ▼ I live in.
2. Tell me the TV game ▼ you like best.
3. Bob is the only boy ▼ Nancy loves.
4. All the students ▼ Mr. Kim teaches study very hard.
5. This is the girl ▼ I spoke of the other day.

❻ 선행사를 포함하는 관계대명사 what

1. That is not **what** (= **the thing which**) I want.
2. He gave me **what** (= **the thing which**) he had found.
3. **What** (= **the thing which**) Jane said was not right.

❼ what의 관용적 용법

1. He is not **what he was**.
   = He is not what he used to be
   <what one is, 그 사람의 상태>
2. A man should be judged by what he is, not by **what he has**.
   <what one has, 그 사람의 재산>
3. She is beautiful, and **what is better**, very intelligent.
   <what is 비교급, 더욱 ~ 한 것은>
4. **What with hunger** and (**what with**) **cold**, we could not walk any more.
   <what with A, and (what with) B, 한편으로 A로 인하여 또 한편으로 B로 인하여>
5. **What by luck**, and (**what by**) **skill**, he succeeded in business.
   <what by A, and (what by) B, 한편으로 A로 인하여 또 한편으로 B로 인하여>
6. He is **what you call** a medical specialist.
   <what you(we, they, one, people) call = what is called, 소위>

C 관계형용사 = 접속사 + 형용사

관계형용사는 두 문장을 연결하면서 자신은 형용사 역할을 한다. 관계형용사에는 what과 which가 있으며 what은 「all the + 명사 + that」의 의미이고, which는 계속적 용법으로 쓰인다.

1. (a) I gave him **what** money I had. <= **all the** money **that** I had>
   (b) I gave him **what** little money I had. <= **all the** little money **that** I had>
2. (a) He spoke in French, **which** language I couldn't understand.
   (b) I said nothing, **which** fact made him angry.

D 관계부사 = 접속사 + 부사, 전치사 + 관계대명사

관계부사 자신은 부사(=전치사 + 명사) 역할을 하면서, 선행하는 명사를 수식하는 형용사절을 인도한다.

1. I don't know the day. He will come back on the day. 〈2문장〉
   → I don't know the day **and** he will come back on **it**. 〈접속사 +대명사〉
   I don't know the day **on which** he will come back. 〈전치사+ 관계대명사〉
   → I don't know the day **and** he will come back **then**. 〈접속사 + 부사〉
   I don't know the day **when** he will come back. 〈관계부사〉

2. This is (**the place**) (**where**) he worked.
3. Tell me (**the reason**) (**why**) you were absent.
4. Let me know (**the place**) (**where**) you have been.
5. This is **the way in which** I solved the problem.
6. (a) This is **the way how** I solved the problem. (×)
   how는 다른 관계부사와 달리 선행사와 함께 the way how로 쓸 수가 없다.
   (b) This is **the way** I solved the problem. (◯)
   (c) This is **how** I solved the problem. (◯)

E 복합관계사

복합관계사는 「관계사+ever」의 형태로 복합관계대명사, 복합관계형용사, 복합관계부사가 있다. 복합관계대명사와 복합관계형용사는 명사절과 양보의 부사절을 형성하고, 복합관계부사는 시간과 장소의 부사절과 양보의 부사절을 만든다.

종 류	ever가 any의 의미	ever가 no matter의 의미
복합관계대명사	명사절 구성	양보 부사절 구성
복합관계형용사	명사절 구성	양보 부사절 구성
복합관계부사	시간, 장소 부사절 구성	양보 부사절 구성

※ 복합관계사가
① 명사절이나 부사절에서 사용될 경우 ever는 **any** ~로 바꾸어 쓸 수가 있고,
② 양보 부사절에서 사용되면 ever는 **no matter** ~로 바꾸어 쓸 수 있다.

❶ 복합관계대명사

(1) 명사절 구성

1. **Whoever** wishes to succeed must be industrious. <must be의 주어절>
   = Anyone who wishes to succeed
2. He told about the traffic accident to **whomever** he met. <전치사 to의 목적절>
   = anyone whom he met
3. You may choose **whichever** you like. <choose의 목적절>
   = anything that you like

(2) 양보의 부사절 구성

양보의 부사절은 주절과 종속절을 '콤마(,)'로 구분한다.

1. **Whoever** may break this law, he will be punished.
   = No matter who may break this law
2. **Whichever** you may take, you will be satisfied.
   = No matter which you may take
3. **Whatever** you may do, you must do it well.
   = No matter what you may do

❷ 복합관계형용사

(1) 명사절 구성

1. He ate **whatever** food I gave him. <ate의 목적절>
   = any food that I gave him
2. You may take **whichever** course you think the best. <take의 목적절>
   = any course that you think the best
3. You may read **whichever** book you like. <read의 목적절>
   = any book that you like

4. You may take **whichever** hat you like. <take의 목적절>
= any hat that you like

(2) 양보의 부사절 구성

1. **Whichever** hat you may like, I can buy it for you.
= No matter which hat you may like
2. **Whichever** way I turn, I am in a difficult position.
= No matter which way I turn

❸ 복합관계부사

(1) 시간, 장소의 부사절

1. I will see him **whenever** he likes to come. <시간의 부사절>
= at any time when he likes to come
2. You may go **wherever** you like. <장소의 부사절>
= to any place where you like

(2) 양보의 부사절 구성

1. **Wherever** you may go, you first try to make friends.
= No matter where you may go
2. **Whenever** you may call on him, you will not find him in his office.
= No matter when you may call on him
3. **However** difficult it may be, you must finish it.
= No matter how difficult it may be

F 유사관계대명사

유사(類似)관계대명사는 의사(擬似)관계대명사라고도 부른다. as, but, than이 접속사나 전치사로 자주 사용되어 관계대명사라는 것이 의심스러우나, 분명히 접속사와 대명사의 역할을 하는 관계대명사의 역할을 수행한다.

(1) 관계대명사 as

선행사에 as, such, the same이 포함되거나, 앞 문장 전체가 선행사가 된다.

1. He is **as honest a man as** ever lived. <lived의 주어>
2. She is **such a lovely girl as** everyone likes. <likes의 목적어>
3. This is **the same watch as** I lost yesterday <lost의 목적어>
4. **He is an American, as** I knew from his accent. <knew의 목적어>

(2) 관계대명사 than

선행사에 비교급이 있을 때 사용한다.

1. He spends **more money than** he earns. <earns의 목적어>
2. Tom always has **more money than** is necessary. <is의 주어>

(3) 관계대명사 but

선행사에 부정어구가 있을 때 사용하며, 「that + not」로 대체할 수 있다.

1. There is **no one but** loves his own country. <loves의 주어>
   = There is no one that does not love his own country.
2. There is **no rule but** has exceptions. <has의 주어>
   = There is no rule that has no exceptions.

Basic Reading 9

1 It is quite certain that **what a man is** contributes much more to his happiness than **what he has**.

- what a man is = a man's character
- contribute[kəntríbju:t] v. (돈 · 물건을) 기부하다, 기증하다, (원고를) 기고하다
- what he has = his wealth

2 He didn't believe what other people told him of his son, and **what made the matter worse**, he completely lacked **what we called** common sense.

- tell[tel] v. 4형식 동사

  He told me a story.
- what makes the matter worse 설상가상으로
- lack[læk] vt. ~이 없다, 결핍되다, ~을 필요로 하다

  A desert lacks water.

  She lacks common sense.
- common sense 상식

3 **What with** ill health, financial worries, anxiety about her children, **and** the strain of running a business, the poor woman broke down.

- what with A and (what with) B : 한편으로 A하고 한편으로 B해서
- financial[finǽnʃəl, fai-] a. 재정상의, 금융상의
- anxiety[æŋzáiəti] n. 걱정, 근심
- strain[strein] 긴장, 과로, (무리한 사용으로 발 · 등 등을) 아프게 하다
- run a business 사업을 경영하다
- break down 부서지다, 고장나다

4 Reading **is to** the mind, **what** exercise **is to** the body. As by the one, health is preserved, strengthened, and invigorated; by the other, virtue(which is the health of the mind) is kept alive, cherished, and confirmed.

- A is to B, what C is to D : A가 B에 대한 관계는 C가 D에 대한 관계와 같다.
- the one = exercise; the other = reading
- preserve[prizə́:rv] v. 보존하다
- strengthen[stréŋkeən] v. 강하게 하다, 튼튼하게 하다
- invigorate[invígərèit] vt. 기운 나게 하다, 상쾌하게 하다
- virtue[və́:rtʃu:] n. 덕, 미덕, 장점
- cherish[tʃériʃ] vt. 소중히 하다
- confirm[kənfə́:rm] vt. 확실하게 하다(make firm), 확립하다(establish firmly)

5 All that education can do in any case is to teach us to make good use of **what we are**; if we are nothing to begin with, no amount of education can do us any good.

- make use of 이용하다
- what we are 현재의 우리
- nothing 하찮은 것(사람)
- amount[əmáunt] 합계, (금액이) ~이 되다
- do A good = do good to A 착한 일을 하다, 친절을 베풀다, 효력이 있다

6 A man should never be ashamed to own he has been in the wrong, **which** is but saying, in other words, that he is wiser today than he was yesterday.

- be ashamed to ~ 하기를 부끄러워하다
- own[oun] v. 고백하다(confess), 소유하다

- to own he has been in the wrong이 which의 선행사가 된다
- but = only

7 Education alone can conduct us to **that enjoyment of life which** is best in quality and infinite in quantity.

- conduct[kəndʌ́kt] v. 이끌다, 안내하다, 행동하다, 지휘하다(direct)
- conduct a person to[into] a seat ~을 자리로 안내하다
- conduct oneself well 훌륭하게 처신하다
- that enjoyment of life가 which의 선행사
- quality[kwáləti] n. 질, 소질, 특질
- infinite[ínfinit] a. 무한한
- quantity[kwántəti] n. 양

8 From the point of view of the individual, he should do **the work which** makes the best use of his abilities. In fact people are found to choose the jobs which require their abilities and in vocational guidance this is one of the main considerations.

- from the point of view of ~의 견해에 의하면
- the individual 한 개인
- make the best use of ~을 가장 잘 활용하다
- vocational[voukéiʃənəl] a. 직업상의
- guidance[gáidns] n. 안내, 지도, 길잡이
- consideration[kənsidəréiʃən] n. 고려, 숙고

9 To understand any society one must look first at its values. **Those values which** still have the most importance in the United States are freedom,

independence, competition, individualism and equality.

- value[vǽljuː] n. 가치
- freedom[fríːdəm] n. 자유
- independence[ìndipénəns] n. 독립, 자주, 독립심
- competition[kàmpitíʃən] n. 경쟁, 경기
- individualism[ìndəvídʒuəlìzəm] n. 개인주의
- equality[i(ː)kwáləti] n. 평등

10 Population experts project that the world's inhabitants may reach 20 billion in the next century. But they warn that this may be **the maximum population that** the earth can sustain. When we have reached this limit, what will happen to the human species?

- project[prədʒékt] v. 산출하다, 투영하다, 계획, 설계
- inhabitant[inhǽbitənt] n. 주민, 거주자
- billion[bíljən] 10억
- warn[wɔːrn] v. 경고하다, 조심시키다
- the maximum population that the earth can sustain that은 sustain의 목적격 관계대명사
- sustain[səstéin] vt. 떠받치다, (가족 등을)부양하다, (발언 등을)지지하다
- species[spí(ː)ʃiːz] n. (분류상의) 종(種)

11 As he approached the village he met a number of people, but none whom he knew, **which** somewhat surprised him, for he had thought himself acquainted with everyone in the country round. Their dress, too, was of a different fashion from **that to which** he was accustomed.

- approach[əpróutʃ] n. 접근
- a number of = many

- but none ~ = but (he met) none ~
- which 선행사는 앞 절 (he met) none whom he knew이다.
- somewhat[sʌ́mhwɑ̀t] a. 다소, 얼마간
- acquainted with ~와 안면이 있다
- that = the fashion
- be accustomed to 에 익숙하다(be used to)

12 I never met **anyone who** talked to him **who** was not surprised by his ready fund of information on various subjects, his ability to ask intelligent and well-directed question, and his great capacity to listen. <관계대명사의 이중 제한>

- ready[rédi] a. 준비가 되어 있는
- a fund of (지식 등의) 축적
- subject[sʌ́bdʒikt] a. 주제
- intelligent[intélidʒənt] a. 이해력 있는, 지적인
- well-directed 바르게 방향 지워진
- capacity[kəpǽsəti] n. 용적, 용량, 재능

13 The time will surely come **when** my words will come true, but when it actually comes, I shall have been long dead.

- 관계부사 when의 선행사는 the time이다.
- come true 실현되다
- actually[ǽktʃuəli] ad. 실제로, 정말로

14 Every bad habit acquired is a barrier to better habits later; that is **why** first formation of habits in early infancy is so important.

- acquired[əkwáiərd] a. 습득한, 형용사화 한 분사로서 bad habit을 후위 수식한다
- barrier[bǽriər] n. 장벽
- why = (the reason) why
- formation[fɔːrméʃən] n. 형성, 구성
- infancy[ínfənsi] n. 유년, 초기

15 One of the saddest sights in this world is that of a young man who has sacrificed **what** little health and constitution he had on account of the hard struggle for existence.

- that = the sight
- sacrifice[sǽkrəfàis] n. 희생
- what little health and constitution he had
  = all the little health and constitution that he had
  관계형용사 what = all the + 명사 + that
- constitution[kɑ̀nstətjúːʃən] n. (인간의) 체격, 체질
- on account of ~ 때문에
- struggle for existence 생존경쟁

16 Intemperance is one of the most contemptible and loathsome habits into **which** one may fall. It is also one of the most dangerous. It springs from the lack of self-control, and it destroys **what** little self-control may still exist.

- intemperance[intémpərəns] n. 무절제, 방종, 음주벽
- contemptible[kəntémptəbl] a. 경멸할만한, 비열한
- loathsome[lóuðsəm] a. 싫어서 견질 수 없는
- fall into 떨어지다
- spring[spriŋ] v. 튀다, 튀어 오르다
- lack[læk] 결핍, ~이 결핍되다

- self-control 자제심(自制心), 극기심(克己心)
- destroy[distrɔ́i] v. 파괴하다
- what little self-control may still exist
  = all the little self-control that may still exist
  관계형용사 what = all the + 명사 + that
- exist[igzíst] v. 존재하다, 생존하다

17 **Wherever** there is love, there cannot fail to be hatred, malice, jealousy, and rage.

- not fail to do 필연적으로 ~ 하다
- hatred[héitrid] n. 증오
- malice[mǽlis] n. 악의, 앙심
- jealousy[dʒéləsi] n. 질투
- rage[reidʒ] n. 격노, 분노

18 Frau Einstein used to say that her husband liked order in his thinking, but he didn't like it in his living. He does **whatever** he wants to, **whenever** he wants to. And he has only two rules of conduct. The first one is: Don't have any rules whatever. And the second one is: Be independent of the opinion of others.

- Frau 부인(Mrs. 또는 Madam에 상당하는 경칭)
- used to 과거의 습관적인 행동
- whatever he wants to 복합관계대명사가 명사절을 형성하고 있다.
  = anything that he wants to do
- whenever he wants to 복합관계부사가 시간의 부사절을 형성하고 있다.
  = at any time when he wants to do
- whatever [부정구문] 약간의 ~ 도; There is no doubt whatever.
- be independent of ~로부터 독립하여

19 **A banker I know** has his work time under control and now spends more time with his family on his boat. By planning his time carefully he's found it easer to take on new projects and adapt his day-to-day routine to fit his long-term plans.

- a banker (whom) I know know의 목적격 관계대명사가 생략됨.
- take on (일 · 농장 등을) 맡아서 경영하다
- adapt[ədǽpt] v. (언행 · 풍습 등을 환경 · 목적 등에) 적응시키다
- routine[ruːtíːn] n. 정해진 일, 일상의 일

20 Our Asian cultures teach us moderation in **everything we do**, and it is not for us to conquer nature but rather to live in harmony with it. We should refuse to join in the rat race that causes high blood pressure and heart attacks. The quality of a good life seems to me to be made up of living simply, closer to nature.

- moderation[mádəréiʃən] n. 정도에 알맞음, 중용(中庸)
- everything (that) we do do의 목적격관계대명사 that 생략
- conquer[káŋkər] v. 정복하다, 공략하다
- be in[out of] harmony with ~와 조화되어 있다[있지 않다]
- refuse[rifjúːz] v. 거절(거부)하다
- the rat race 생존경쟁
- quality[kwáləti] n. 질, 소질, 특성

21 **The world we live in** is changing fast, and our language is changing along with it. Every living language grows and changes. It changes as the people who use it create new words and find new meanings for old ones.

- the world (which) we live in 전치사 in의 목적어인 which가 생략
- it = the world
- as 접속사, ~함에 따라서

22 Recently, when I asked **Americans I know** why they had had children, they talked about family values, about **the kind of people they want to be**, about **the kind of world they want to leave behind**.

- recently[ríːsəntli] 최근에
- Americans (whom) I know : know의 목적격관계대명사 생략
- about the kind of people (that) they want to be : to be의 보어인 관계대명사 that이 생략
- about the kind of world (that) they want to leave
  behind 타동사 leave의 목적격관계대명사 that 생략
- leave behind (처자 · 재산 · 명성 · 기록 등을) 남기고 죽다, 남기다
  He left debt behind him.

Advanced Reading 17

A. Preparing to Read

This is an era of mass communication.

His lyrics are **as** poignant **as** they ever have been.

Their aim will be to produce **as much** milk **as** possible.

She has her place in the Asian team **not** because she is white **but** because she is good.

B. Approaching to the Topic

This is a delicious evening, when the whole body is one sense, and imbibes delight through every pore. I go and come with a strange liberty in Nature, a part of herself. As I walk along the stony shore of the pond in my shirt-sleeves, though it is cool as well as cloudy and windy, and I see nothing special to attract me, all the elements are unusually congenial to me. . . Though it is now dark, the wind still blows and roars in the wood, the waves still dash, and some creatures lull the rest with their notes. The repose is never complete. The wildest animals do not repose, but seek their prey now; the fox, and skunk, and rabbit, now roam the fields and woods without fear. They are Nature's watchmen, links which connect the days of animated life.

. . . My nearest neighbor is a mile distant, and no house is visible from any place but the hill-tops within half a mile of my own. I have my horizon bounded by woods all to myself; a distant view of the railroad where it touches the pond on the one hand, and of the fence which skirts the woodland road on the other. But for the most part it is as solitary where I live as on the prairies. It is as much Asia or Africa as New England. I have, as it were, my own sun and moon and stars, and a little world all to myself. At night there was never a traveller passed my house, or knocked at my door.

Solitude by Henry David Thoreau

Vocabularies & Expressions for Comprehension

- delicious evening 상쾌한 저녁
- one sense 하나의 감각기관
- imbibe[imbáib] 흡입하다, 섭취하다
- congenial[kəndʒíːnjəl] 마음에 흡족한, 알맞은
- blow[blou] 바람이 불다
- roars[rɔːr] 포효하다, 으르렁거리다
- dash[dæʃ] 철석거리다
- creatures[kríːtʃər] 생물, 피조물
- lull[lʌl] 달래다, 안심시키다
- with their notes 그들의 노래가락으로
- repose[ripóuz] 휴식
- complete[kəmplíːt] 끝내다
- prey[prei] 먹이
- nature's watchmen 자연의 야경꾼, 파수꾼
- links which connect[kənékt] 연결시켜주는 고리
- animated life 활기찬 생명
- visible 볼 수 있는
- hill-tops 언덕 꼭대기
- horizon[həráizən] 지평선
- bounded 한계 지워진
- touches 인접하다, 접촉하다
- the pond[pɑnd/ pɔnd] 연못
- for the most parts 대체로
- solitary[sάlitèri] 외로운, 고독한
- prairies[prέəri] 대평원
- It is as much Asia or Africa as New England

  as much ~ as 구문으로 「~만큼(많이)」

Sentence Pattern Analysis

- The wildest animals do not rest, but seek their prey now.
  - 가장 야성적인 동물들은 휴식을 취하지 않고 이제 먹이 감을 찾아 나선다.

- They are nature's watchmen, links which connect the days of animated life.
  - 그들은 활기찬 생명의 나날을 연결해 주는 고리인 자연의 파수꾼들이다.

- it touches the pond.
  - 연못에 인접한 철도 (it는 철도를 가리킨다)

- it is as solitary where I live as it is on the prairies.
  - as ~ as의 구문, 「내가 사는 곳은 대평원만큼 고독하다.」

Wisdom

It is better that ten guilty persons escape than one innocent suffers.

죄없는 한 사람이 고통을 겪는 것보다는 죄인 열 사람이 도망치는것이 더 낫다.

Sir William Blackstone: Commentary on the Laws of England

Advanced Reading 18

A. Preparing to Read

He **longed for** the winter to be over.

It is generally not advisable **for** expectant mothers **to travel** by air after the 28th week of pregnancy.

Priority will be given to **those who** apply early.

The incident **brings** the total of people wounded **to** five.

B. Approaching to the Topic

Modern European and American history is centered around the effort to gain freedom from the political, economic, and spiritual shackles that have bound men. The battles for freedom were fought by the oppressed, those who wanted new liberties, against those who had privileges to defend. While a class was fighting for its own liberation from domination, it believed itself to be fighting for human freedom as such and thus was able to appeal to an ideal, to the longing for freedom rooted in all who are oppressed. In the long and virtually continuous battle for freedom, however, classes that were fighting against oppression at one stage sided with the enemies of freedom when victory was won and new privileges were to be defended.

Despite many reverses, freedom has won battles. Many died in those battles in the conviction that to die in the struggle against oppression was better than to live without freedom. Such a death was the utmost assertion of their individuality. History seemed to be proving that it was possible for man to govern himself, to make decisions for himself, and to think and feel as he saw fit. The full expression of man's potentialities seemed to be the goal toward which social development was rapidly approaching. The principles of economic liberalism, political democracy, religious autonomy, and individualism in personal life, gave expression to the longing for freedom, and at the same time seemed to bring mankind nearer to its realization.

Freedom: A Psychological Problem? by Erich Fromm

Vocabularies & Expressions for Comprehension

- center[séntər] 집중시키다
- effort[éfərt] 노력
- gain[gein] 획득하다
- spiritual[spíritʃu-əl] 정신적인
- shackles[ʃǽkəl] 족쇄, 차꼬
- bound 속박하다
- oppress[əprés] 억압하다
- privileges[prívəlidʒ] 특권
- defend[difénd] 수호하다, 지키다
- domination[dάmənéiʃən] 지배, 통치
- appeal[əpí:l] 호소하다
- longing for ~에 대한 열망
- rooted in ~에 뿌리박은
- virtually[və́:rtʃuəli] 실제로는
- continuous[kentínjuəs] 계속적인
- reverses[rivə́:rs] 실패, 불운
- conviction[kənvíkʃən] 신념
- utmost[ʌ́tmòust] 최대한의, 극도의
- assertion[əsə́:rʃən] 주장
- individuality[ìndəbidʒuǽləti] 개성
- proving 입증하는
- govern[gʌ́vərn] 지배하다
- decision[disídʒən] 결정
- fit 알맞은, 적합한

- potentialities[poutènʃiǽləti] 잠재력
- rapidly[rǽpidli] 빠르게
- principles[prínsəpəl] 원칙
- liberalism[líb-ərəliz-əm] 자유주의
- democracy[dimákrəsi] 민주주의
- religious[rilídʒəs] 종교적인
- autonomy[ɔːtánəmi] 자율성
- gave expression to ~을 표현하다
- mankind 인류
- realization[ríːələzéiʃ-ən/ -lai-] 실현

Sentence Pattern Analysis

- Modern European and American history is centered around the effort to gain freedom

  근대 유럽과 미국의 역사는 자유를 획득하기 위한 노력에 집중되었다.

- The battles for freedom were fought by the oppressed

  억압받은 사람들이 자유를 위한 전투를 했다. the oppressed는 복수 보통명사

- those who wanted new liberties

  새로운 자유를 원했던 사람들, those who ~ 하는 사람들

- against those who had privileges to defend

  방어할만한 특권들을 지녔던 사람들에 대항하여

- classes that were fighting against oppression at one stage sided with the enemies of freedom.

  억압에 대항하여 싸웠던 계급들이 어느 단계에서는 자유의 적들과 한편이 되었다.
  side with ~에 가담하다, 찬성하다, 한편이 되다

- Many died in those battles in the conviction that to die in the struggle against oppression was better than to live without freedom.

  자유 없이 살기보다는 억압에 대항하여 투쟁하다가 죽는 것이 더 낫다는 신념 아래 수많은 사람들이 그러한 전투 속에서 죽어갔다. better than의 비교급 구분

• History seemed to be proving that it was possible for man to govern himself, to make decisions for himself, and to think and feel as he saw fit.

역사는 인간이 자신을 통제하고, 스스로 결정을 내리고, 생각하고 그가 알맞게 본 바대로 느끼는 것이 가능했다는 것을 입증하는 것처럼 보였다.
물론 이 문장은 that절 이하에서는 it ~ for ~to 구문

Wisdom

I awoke on morning and found myself famous.

아침에 눈을 떠보니 내가 유명해 졌더라.

Lord Byron

제10장. 법

A 법의 종류

B 가정법의 종류

C I wish, as if

D But for [Without], It is high time

E if절 대용

제10장 법 *Mood*

A 법의 종류

• 법(mood)이란 무엇인가?
말하는 사람의 심적(心的) 태도를 표현하는 동사의 형태를 법(法, mood)이라고 한다.

❶ 직설법(indicative mood)
어떤 일을 사실로써 말 할 때 쓰는 동사의 형태

• I think that he is honest.

❷ 가정법(subjunctive mood)
〈상상 · 가정 · 소망〉 등을 말할 때 쓰는 동사의 형태

• I would employ him if he were diligent.

❸ 명령법(Imperative mood)
〈명령 · 요구 · 금지〉 등을 말할 때 쓰는 동사의 형태

• Please speak more slowly.

※ 양보 명령 : 가정법 현재로 볼 수도 있다.

1. **Go where she may**, he will follow her.
   = Wherever she may go
2. **Try as you may**, you cannot finish it in a week.
   = However hard you may try
3. **Be it ever so humble**, there is no place like home.
   = However humble it may be
4. **Be a man rich or poor**, he eats three meals a day.
   = Whether a man is rich or poor

(a) 명령형 + wh + may 형
(b) 명령형 + as + may 형
(c) Be + S + ever so + 형용사 형
(d) 명령형 A or B 형

❹ 조건문과 가정법

조건문과 가정법의 차이

• 단순조건문: 실현 가능성이 반반인 가정
I will employ him if he is diligent.
(실제로 그가 근면하면 나는 그를 고용할 것이다.)

• 가정법(가정법 과거): 실현 가능성이 없는 가정
I would employ him if he were diligent.
(그가 근면하지 않기 때문에 나는 그를 고용하지 않는다.)

B 가정법의 종류

구 분	내 용	조 건 절	귀 결 절
현 재	현재 · 미래의 단순한 일을 가정 · 상상	If S + 원형[현재형]~ If it rain(s) tomorrow	S + will[shall, can, may]~ I will stay at home.
과 거	현재 사실과 반대되는 일을 가정 · 상상	If S + 과거형[were]~ If I were a bird,	S + 조동사의 과거형~ I could fly to her.
과거완료	과거 사실과 반대되는 일을 가정 · 상상	If S + had PP~ If I had been rich,	S + 조동사의 과거형+have PP~ I would have bought that house.
미 래	현재 · 미래의 불확실한 일을 가정 · 상상	If S + should~ If it should rain tomorrow,	S + 조동사의 현재형 [과거형]~ I wouldn't go on a picnic.
		If S + would~ If you would go abroad,	S + 조동사의 현재형[과거형]~ You should study English harder.
		If S + were to~ If I were to be born again,	S + 조동사의 과거형~ I would become an actress

❶ 가정법 과거

현재사실과 반대되는 일을 가정 · 상상

1. If I **were** eighteen, I **could** drive a car.
   = As I am not eighteen, I cannot drive a car.
2. If I **knew** her phone number, I **could** call her right now.
3. If I **were** in the same situation as you, I **would** go mad.

❷ 가정법 과거완료

과거 사실과 반대되는 일을 가정 · 상상

1. If I **had known** your e-mail address, I **would have e-mailed** you.
   = As I did not know your e-mail address, I did not e-mail you.
2. If we **had found** him earlier, we **could have saved** his life.
3. If we **had gone** by car, we **would have saved** time.

❸ 가정법 현재

현재, 미래의 단순한 일을 가정 · 상상 <약한 의심>

1. If he **be**(is) honest, I will employ him.
2. He insisted that she **be** sent to the hospital at once.
3. Long **live** the King!

❹ 가정법 미래

현재나 미래의 불확실한 일을 가정 · 상상 <강한 의심>

1. If it **should** rain tomorrow, I would put off my departure.
2. If you **would** help me, I could finish it by five.
3. If the sun **were to** rise in the west, I would never give it up. <주어의 무의지>

<주어의 의지>

<순수가정>

C I wish, as if

❶ I wish

I wish는 I hope와 달리 가정법과거나 과거완료 문장을 동반할 수 있다.

〈I wish = Would(that) = Would to God = Oh, that = If only〉

1. I wish **I could speak English as fluently as you.**
   = I am sorry that I cannot speak English as fluently as you.
2. I wish **I were a magician like a Harry Portter.**
3. I wish **I had studied harder when I was a high school student.**
   = I am sorry that I did not study harder when I was a high school student.
4. I wished **it were true.**
   = I was sorry that it was not true.
5. I wished **it had been true.**
   = I was sorry that it had not been true.

❷ 직설법 문장 + as if + 가정법

1. He speaks as if **he knew everything on UFOs.**
2. He behaved as if **nothing had happened.**
3. She acts as if **she were a princess.**
4. She treats me as if **I were a child.**
5. He talks as if **he had really been ill.**
6. He talks as if **he knew everything.**
   (그는 마치 모든 것을 알고 있는 듯 말한다.)
7. He talks as if **he had known everything.**
   (그는 마치 모든 것을 알고 있었다는 듯 말한다.)
8. He talked as if **he knew everything.**
   (그는 마치 모든 것을 알고 있는 듯 말했다.)
9. He talked as if **he had known everything.**
   (그는 마치 모든 것을 알고 있었다는 듯 말했다.)

D But for[Without], It is high time

❶ But for[without]

1. **But for[Without]** the snow, we could climb the mountain.
   = **If it were not for** the snow, we could climb the mountain.
   = **Were it not for** the snow, we could climb the mountain.

2. **But for[without]** your advice, we would have hurt his feeling.
   = **If it had not been for** your advice, we would have hurt his feeling.
   = **Had it not been for** your advice, we would have hurt his feeling.

❷ It is high time + 가정법 과거

It is high time **you went to bed**.
= It is high time **you should go to bed**.
= It is high time **for you to go to bed**.

E if절 대용

1. **With** a little more money, I could have bought that computer.
   = If I had had a little more money, I could have bought that computer.
2. I went at once, **otherwise** I should have missed the plane.
   = I went at once, If I had not gone at once I should have missed the plane.
3. **In your place** I wouldn't waste any time and money on such trivial matters.
   = If I were in your place I wouldn't waste any time ~
4. **A wise man** would not do such a thing.
   = If he were a wise man, he would not do such a thing.
5. **During the war**, he would have been put in prison.
   = If it had been during the war, he would have been put in prison.
6. **To hear** her speak English, you would take her for an American.
   = If you heard her speak English, you would take her for an American.

Basic Reading 10

1 If you **should** happen to meet a talkative American, you are by no means obliged to answer all the question you are asked.

- happen to 우연히 ~하다
- talkative[tɔ́:kətiv] a. 수다스런
- by no means = never
- be obliged to = be forced to ~하지 않을 수 없는

2 A well-bred Englishman **would** consider it a bold intrusion on his privacy if a stranger **were to** call on him without an invitation or a letter of introduction. Sunday is not the proper day for making calls; weekends should be chosen for this purpose.

- well-bred 교육을 잘 받은, 예절이 바른
- bold[bould] a. 대담한, 용감한, 과감한
- intrusion[intru:ʒən] n. 침입, 강요
- privacy[práivəsi] n. 사생활, 비밀, 은퇴생활
- call on 방문하다, 요구하다
- invitation[invitéiʃən] n. 초대, 초대장
- a letter of introduction 소개장(to)
- make [pay] a call (on a person) ~을 방문하다
- purpose[pə́:rpəs] n. 목적

3 If we **were** perpetually conscious of the insecurity of life and happiness we **might** easily become morbid, and lose our ardour alike in work and pleasure.

- perpetually[pərpétʃuəl] ad. 영속적으로
- be conscious of 의식[자각]하고 있는

• insecurity[ìnsikjúəriti] n. 불확실성
• morbid[mɔ́:rbid] a. (병적으로) 음울한
• ardo(u)r[ɑ́:rdər] n. 열정, 열심
• alike A and B = Both A and B, young and old alike 노소를 막론하고
• pleasure[pléʒər] n. 즐거움, 쾌감

4 If he **had taken** his customary train that morning, he **would have been** close to the center at the time of the explosion.

• customary[kʌ́stəmèri] a. 습관적인
• close[klouz] vt. (입을) 다물다, (가게 · 관청 · 항구 등을) 닫다
• close[klouz] adj. 가까운(near), 친한 cf. with closed doors 문이 닫혀 있는
• explosion[iksplóuʒən] n. 폭발

5 I think that **If** I **had been** told what it was before I ate, I never **would have eaten** it. But as it was, it turned out to be quite good.

• be told = hear
• as it is [보통 문장 머리에 써서] (그러나) 실상은
• turn out 판명되다(prove)

6 I have never been one of those who sneer at people who give good advice. On the contrary I realized that **if I had followed** all the good advice that has been given to me since my birth, I **should** now be a better man.

• sneer at[sniə:r] v. 비웃다, 냉소하다
• on the contrary (보통 문장 머리에 써서) 이에 반하여
• realize[rí:əlàiz] v. 실감하다

7 Life is not all pain and bitter disillusion. **If** it **were**, life **would be** unbearable, and not worth living. As we grow older, we learn to accept philosophically trials and hardships of life. We learn wisdom from our errors. Sometimes it is only by making mistakes that we can really know how to live correctly.

- pain[pein] n. 고통
- bitter[vítər] a. 쓰라린
- disillusion[disilú:ʒən] n. 환멸
- unbearable[ʌnbέərəbəl] a. 견딜 수 없는
- be worth ~ ing ~의 가치가 있다
  This book is worth reading.
- philosophically[filəsάfikəli] 철학적으로
- trial[tráiəl] n. 시련, 고난; trial and error 시행착오
- hardship[hά:rdʃip] n. 고난
- it is ~ that 강조구문

8 **If it had not been for** the iron armour, he **would have been** killed. As it were, he lost part of his helmet.

- armo(u)r[ɑ:rmwά:r] n. 갑옷, 철갑
- helmet[hélmit] n. 투구
- as it is (과거형은 as it were) [보통 문장 머리에 써서] (그러나) 실상은

9 **But for** his cheerfulness, he **could** never, with so delicate a frame, have got through so vast an amount of self-imposed work.

- cheerful[tʃíərfəl] a. 쾌활한, 명랑한; n. cheerfulness
- delicate[délikit] a. 섬세한, 고운

- frame[freim] n. 뼈대, 체격; a man of fragile frame 체질이 허약한 사람
- get through 마치다, 끝내다
- vast[væst, vɑːst] a. 광대한, 막대한
- self-imposed[self-impóuzd] a. 스스로 부과한

10 Modern technology as a whole, however, **would have been** impossible **but for** the scientist, and the more sophisticated it has grown the more central has been his role.

- technology[teknálədʒi] n. 과학기술
- as a whole 전체로서
- sophisticated[səfístəkèitid] a. 소박한 데가 없는, 닳고닳은, 지나치게 기교적인
- central[séntrəl] a. 중심의, 주요한

11 As soon as he married he took out an insurance policy which **would** guarantee his wife a regular income for the rest of her life, **should** he die.

- as soon as ~하자마자
- take out (전매권 · 면허 등을) 취득하다
- take out an insurance policy 보험증권에 들다
- take out a policy on one's life 생명보험에 들다
- should he die = if he should die

12 **Could we know** all the vicissitudes of our fortunes, life would be too full of hope and fear, exultation or disappointment, to afford us a single hour of true serenity.

- Could we know = if we could know

• vicissitude[visísətjù:d] n. 변화(change)
• fortune[fɔ́:rtʃən] n. 운명
• exultation[ègzʌltéiʃən] n. 환희, 열광
• disappointment[dìsəpɔ́intmənt] n. 실망
• afford[əfɔ́:rd] vt. 할 수가 있다
We can afford to sell cheap
• serenity[sirénəti] n. 평정, 침착

13 I heartily **wish** that in my youth I **had had** someone of good sense to direct my reading. I sigh when I reflect on the amount of time I had wasted on books that were of no great profit to me.

• in my youth = when I was young
• good sense 양식
• direct[dirék, dai-] v. 감독하다, 지휘하다
• sigh[sai] v. 한숨 쉬다
• reflect on[riflékt] v. 숙고하다, 곰곰이 생각하다
• the amount[əmánt] n. 합계
• waste[weist] v. 낭비하다, 허비하다
• of no great profit = not very profitable

14 You may have heard grown-ups say, "**I wish** I **had learned** that at school," or "**I wish** I **had** more education." Why do you suppose they feel that way? Perhaps it's because they think life might be more interesting, or they **might have had** better jobs, **if they had learned** just a little more or **had learned** a little better.

• may have PP ~이었을 지도 모른다
• grown-up 성인 • just = only

15 **The happiest men** I know are those who approach their work **as if it** were their hobby, something to be done for the sheer fun of it, not for the money. These lucky people don't have to escape from their work; they escape into it. Actually, they'd rather be working than not working.

- sheer[ʃiəːr] a. 순수한, 완전한
- for the sheer fun of it 일을 통해서 얻는 순수한 즐거움 때문에
- escape[iskéip] v. 탈출하다
- actually[ǽktʃuəli] ad. 실제로, 정말로
- would[had] rather A than B : B하느니 차라리 A하다

16 **Suppose** you had a sum of money — say, a thousand dollars, what **would** you do with it?

- a large [small] sum of 다액[소액]의
- say 이를 테면(let us say)
- do with ~을 처리하다

17 The human race is the only one that knows it must die, and it knows this only through its experience. **A child** brought up alone and transported to a desert island **would** have no more idea of death than a cat or a plant.

- one = race
- it = the human race
- experience[ikspíəriəns] n. 경험
- bring up 양육하다
- transport[trænspɔ́ːrt] vt. 운송하다
- a desert island 무인도

- A child brought ~ would ~ = If a child were brought ~ he would have ~
- than a cat or a plant (would have idea of death)

18 It is no use trying to run away from difficulties, for they are sure to overtake you. **Face** them boldly, **and** they will often vanish.

- It is no use ~ ing ~해도 소용없다
- be sure to do 틀림없이 ~하는
- overtake[òuvərtéik] v. 따라잡다
- face[feis] n. 직면하다
- boldly[bóuldli] ad. 대담하게
- vanish[vǽniʃ] v. 사라지다, 없어지다

19 Some people say that they cannot spare time for exercise. They cannot be told too soon that they **must find** time for exercise, **or** they will have to find time for being ill in bed.

- spare[spɛəːr] v. 시간을 할애하다
- exercise[éksərsàiz] n. 운동
- be told = hear
- cannot ~ too 아무리 ~하여도 지나치지 않다
  You cannot be too diligent.
- they cannot be told too soon ~ = we cannot tell them too soon ~

Advanced Reading 19

A. Preparing to Read

She **paid tribute to** the university committee.

Somehow, he had **managed to** persuade Mr. Kim to buy one for him.

We are interested in assessing **not only** what the children have learnt **but** how they have learnt it.

B. Approaching to the Topic

Another popular food animal is the pig. How men ever managed to domesticate the pig is a mystery, because in the wild state he is an extremely fierce beast. Hunters who have stalked the wild pig in Asia and Africa say he is more dangerous than the tiger. Not only can he inflict a worse bite, but he's also smarter, ranking just below the great apes in I. Q. George Orwell paid tribute to the pig's intelligence when he made him the hero—or villain—of his satiric novel *Animal Farm*. In that story, as you may remember, the pigs are so much cleverer than the other animals that they take over the farm (after first outwitting their human owners) and rule it as dictators.

We — The Other Animals

Vocabularies & Expressions for Comprehension

- popular[pάpjələr] 인기 있는
- managed to 그럭저럭 해내다
- domesticate[douméstəkèit] 길들이다
- mystery[místəri] 신비
- fierce beast 사나운 짐승
- stalk[stɔːk] 사냥감에 몰래 접근하다

- inflict[inflíkt] 상처를 입히다
- paid tribute to ~찬사를 바치다
- satiric novel 풍자소설
- take over 접수하다
- outwitting 보다 나은 꾀로 속이다, ~ 보다 지혜가 낫다
- dictators[díkteitər] 독재자

Sentence Pattern Analysis

- How men ever managed to domesticate the pig is a mystery,

  어떻게 인간들이 이제껏 돼지를 길들이게 되었는가는 신비스러운 일이다.

- Not only can he inflict a worse bite, but he's also smarter.

  not only ~but의 구문

- ranking just below the great apes in I. Q.

  지능지수가 위대한 원숭이 바로 밑에 위치하는

- the pigs are so much cleverer than the other animals that they take over the farm (after first outwitting their human owners) and rule it as dictators.

  돼지들은 다른 어떤 동물들보다 훨씬 더 영악하여 (자신들의 인간 주인을 최초로 더 나은 꾀로 속인 후) 농장을 접수하며 독재자들로서 농장을 통치한다.
  (cleverer 앞의 much는 비교급을 강조한다.)

Wisdom

Some books are to be tasted, others to be swallowed, and some few to be chewed and digested.

맛만 보아야 할 책이 있고, 그냥 삼켜야 할 책이 있는가 하면 꼭꼭 씹어서 소화해야 할 책도 더러 있다.

Francis Bacon: Essays

Advanced Reading 20

A. Preparing to Read

He loves her **not because** she is rich **but because** she is good.

This **reminds** me **of** Christmas parties.

It is often very hard **to compare** all-male and all-female jobs.

B. Approaching to the Topic

I believe that man will not merely endure: he will prevail. He is immortal, not because he alone among creatures has an inexhaustible voice but because he has a soul, a spirit capable of compassion and sacrifice and endurance. The poet's, the writer's, duty is to write about these things. It is his privilege to help man endure by lifting his heart, by reminding him of the courage and honor and hope and pride and compassion and pity and sacrifice which have been the glory of his past. The poet's voice need not merely be the record of man, it can be one of the props, the pillars to help him endure and prevail.

from Nobel Prize Award Speech by William Faulkner

Vocabularies & Expressions for Comprehension

- endure[endjúər] 참다
- prevail[privéil] 이기다, 우세하다
- immortal[imɔ́:rtl] 불멸의
- inexhaustible voice 고갈되지 않은 목소리
- compassion[kəmpǽʃən] 연민, 동정
- sacrifice[sǽkrəfàis] 희생
- privilege[prívəlidʒ] 특권
- reminding ~of ~을 ~에게 상기시키다

- courage[kə́:ridʒ, kʌ́r-] 용기
- glory[glɔ́:ri] 영광
- the props = property man 재산가
- pillars[pílər] 기둥

Sentence Pattern Analysis

- He is immortal, not because he alone among creatures has an inexhaustible voice but because he has a soul, a spirit capable of compassion and sacrifice and endurance.

  (이 구문은 not because ~ but because 구문임. 즉 ~때문이 아니라 ~때문이다.)
  인간만이 모든 생물들 가운데서 고갈되지 않은 자신의 목소리를 낼 수 있다는 이유에서가 아니라 인간은 영혼, 즉 연민과 희생과 인내를 가능하게 하는 정신을 가지고 있다는 이유에서 불멸입니다.

- It is his privilege to help man endure by lifting his heart, by reminding him of the courage and honor and hope and pride and compassion and pity and sacrifice which have been the glory of his past.

  그의 특권은 마음을 격려함으로써, 인류의 과거 영광이었던 용기와 명예와 희망과 자긍심과 동정과 측은지심과 희생을 상기시킴으로써 인간으로 하여금 인내하게 돕는 것입니다.
  It ~ to 구문임. 뒤의 which의 선행사는 courage, honor, hope, pride ··· sacrifice 등이다.

William Faulkner (1897-1962) 는 노벨 문학상 (1949), 퓰리처상 (1954, 1962)을 수상한 미국의 작가이다. 그는 1897년 9월 2일 미시시피주의 뉴올버니에서 출생했다. 주요 작품으로는 *Sartoris* (1929), *The sound and the Fury* (1929), *As I Lay Dying* (1930), *Sanctuary* (1931), *Light in August* (1932), *Absalom, Absalom!* (1936), *The wild palms* (1939) 등이 있다. 특히 그는 '요크나파토파(Yoknapatawpha)'라는 가공적인 지역을 소설의 주요 무대로 설정하고 미국 남부사회의 변천상을 주로 다루었다.

Wisdom

If you have done foolishly in lifting up yourself, or if you have thought evil, Put your hand over your mouth.

네가 미련하여 스스로 높은 체 하거나 혹 악한 일을 도모하였거든 네 손으로 입을 막으라.

Proverbs 30: 32

제11장. 일치·화법

- A 일치
- B 화법(話法)

제11장 일치 *Agreement* / 화법 *Narration*

A 일치

❶ 시제의 일치

복문에서 주절 동사는 종속절의 동사에 영향을 끼친다.

- 주절의 시제가 현재, 현재완료, 미래일 때 종속절에는 12시제가 모두 올 수 있다.
- 주절의 동사가 과거이면 종속절에는 과거와 과거완료시제가 온다.

이와 같이 주절의 동사에 따라서 종속절의 시제가 변하는 것을 시제의 일치(the Sequence of Tenses)라 한다.

1. (a) I **think** that he is a teacher.
   (b) I **thought** that he **was** a teacher.
2. (a) I **know** that he **was**[**has been**] injured.
   (b) I **knew** that he **had been** injured.
3. (a) I **hope** that he **will** succeed.
   (b) I **hoped** that he **would** succeed.

❷ 시제의 일치 예외

1. They **did not know** that the earth **goes** round the sun. 〈불변의 진리〉
2. He **told** me that he **goes** to bed at ten every day. 〈습관〉
3. He **said** that Columbus **discovered** America in 1492. 〈역사적 사실〉
4. He **says** that he **would** fly to her if he **were** a bird. 〈가정법〉
5. He **said** that he **would** fly to her if he **were** a bird. 〈가정법〉

❸ 주어와 술어동사의 일치

1. **Either** my friend **or I have to** go there. 〈Either A or B〉
   근자일치(近者 一致), the principle of Proximity
2. You or **I am** to blame. 〈A or B〉

3. **Not only** she **but also I am** interested in politics.
   = **I** as well as she **am** interested in politics.
   <not only A but also B = B as well as A: B에 동사의 수 일치>
4. Both you and I **are** good friends.
5. Three years **is** a long time to wait. <시간의 총량: 단수>
6. Three years **have** passed since he died. <시간의 경과: 복수>

❹ 부분을 나타내는 말

부분을 나타내는 말의 바로 뒤에 있는 명사에 따라 단수, 복수가 결정된다.

1. Two-thirds of my books **are** novels.
2. Three-fourths of the earth's surface **is** water.
3. **Many a boy was** playing in the garden. <many + a + 단수명사 + 단수동사>
4. **Many boys were** playing in the garden. <many + 복수명사 + 복수동사>
5. **The number of** patients **is** increasing. <the number of ~, ~의 수 : 단수취급>
6. **A number of** patients **are** dying. <a number of ~, 많은 : 복수취급>

분수, most of, the rest of, part of 등의 부분을 나타내는 말은 of 다음에
① 셀 수 있는 명사가 오면 복수동사를,
② 셀 수 없는 명사가 오면 단수 동사를 쓴다.

B 화법(話法, Narration)

화법(話法)은 다른 사람의 말을 전달하는 표현 방법을 말하는데,
직접화법(直接話法)과 간접화법(間接話法)이 있다.

• 직접화법: 화자(話者)의 말을 말한 그대로 인용부호(" ")에 담아서 전달하는 방법
• 간접화법: 화자(話者)의 말을 전달자의 말로 바꾸어 그 내용을 전달하는 방법

• Mary said to Sam, "I love you." <직접화법>
• Mary told sam that she loved him. <간접화법>

❶ 평서문

① say[said] ⇔ say[said] to
② 피전달문 ⇔ that로 시작하는 문장
③ 시제 일치
④ 인칭대명사 변화

1. (a) He says, "You are honest."
   (b) He says that I am honest.
2. (a) He said, "You are kind to me."
   (b) He said that I was kind to him.
3. (a) He said, "I will meet her here today."
   (b) He said that he would meet her there that day.

화법 전환에 따른 대명사, 부사의 변화

this → that	these → those
now → then	here → there
ago → before	today → that day
next → the next~	last → the previous
tonight → that night	tomorrow → the next[following] day

yesterday → the day before / the previous day
last night → the night before / the previous night

❷ 의문문

① say[said] to ⇔ ask[asked]~
② 의문사가 있는 의문문 ⇔ 의문사+ 주어 + 동사
③ 의문사가 없는 의문문 ⇔ if[whether] +주어+ 동사

1. (a) Nancy said to me, "Where do you want to live?"
   (b) Nancy **asked**[**inquired of**] me where I wanted to live.

2. (a) He said to me, "Why did you strike me?"
   (b) He **asked** me why I had struck him.
3. (a) I said to her, "Have you been to Paris?"
   (b) I **asked** her **if**[**whether**] she had been to Paris.
4. (a) He said to his father, "May I go out now?"
   (b) He **asked** his father **if**[**whether**] he might go out then.

❸ 명령문

① say to ⇔ tell[order, advise, ask, beg]~
② 긍정명령문 ⇔ to 부정사
③ 부정명령문 ⇔ not[never] +to 부정사

명령문 화법전환에서 핵심은 명령문의 직접화법 어조(명령문의 분위기)를 간접화법에서는 전달동사를 통하여 나타내는 것이다.

1. (a) He said to me, "Do your best."
   (b) He **told** me **to do** my best.
2. (a) "Please don't make a noise, Sally." she said.
   (b) She **asked** Sally **not to make** a noise.
3. (a) The doctor said to me, "Don't work too hard."
   (b) The doctor **advised** me **not to work** too hard.
4. (a) He said to me, "Please close the door."
   (b) He **asked**[**begged**] me **to close** the door.
5. (a) The commanding officer said to his men, "Fight off the enemy."
   (b) The commanding officer **ordered** his men to fight off the enemy.
6. (a) Father said to me, "Let's go fishing."
   (b) Father **suggested**[**proposed**] to me that **we** (**should**) **go** fishing.

❹ 감탄문

① say ⇔ cry(out)[exclaim, shout, sigh]~
② 감탄의 의미 ⇔ with delight(기뻐서), with regret(후회하여), with a sigh(한숨을 쉬며)

1. (a) He said, "Hurrah! I've passed the exam."
   (b) He **exclaimed with delight** that he had passed the exam.
2. (a) She said, "How beautiful the cherry blossoms are!"
   (b) She said **how beautiful the cherry blossoms were**.
   (c) She **exclaimed** that the cherry blossoms were very beautiful.

❺ 기원문

① say ⇔ prey[express one's wish]~
② 하나님께 기도 : pray that God may
③ 소망의 표현 : express one's wish that 주어 + may ~

1. (a) He said, "God save my son!"
   (b) He **prayed that God might** save his son.
2. (a) She said, "May my dream come true!"
   (b) She **expressed her wish that** her dream **might** come true.

❻ 중문, 복문

① and, but, or, nor로 연결된 중문의 절 앞에 ⇔ that을 쓴다
② for, as, because 등의 접속사 다음 ⇔ that 쓸 필요없다

1. (a) He said, "The watch is very expensive, and I cannot buy it."
   (b) He said that the watch was very expensive, and that he could not buy it.
2. (a) She said, "I am rich, but I am not contented."
   (b) She said that she was rich, but that she was not contented.
3. (a) He said, "It is morning, for the birds are singing."
   (b) He said that it was morning, for the birds were singing.

Basic Reading 11

1 After I left college, I found it very difficult to get a full-time job. So I decided to take a part-time job as a waitress just to earn spending money. Then, while I was serving meals one day, I overheard two customers talking. One explained that his secretary had left suddenly, and said he didn't know what to do. I stopped serving at once and **asked the man if he would consider me for the job**. He was very surprised but agreed to interview me the next day. To make a long story short, my courage to interrupt the conversation made it possible for me to get the job.

- spending money 용돈
- overheard[óuvərhə:rd] v. 무심코 듣다
- customer[kʌ́stəmər] n. 손님
- secretary[sékrətèri] n. 비서
- interrupt[ìntərʌ́pt] v. 중단시키다

2 There are few people who don't realize the importance of exercise. But many people don't practice it in their daily lives. Their most common excuse is "**I don't have time.**" My answer to such people is "**That's a poor excuse.**" Just as you brush your teeth every day, eat every day, and sleep everyday, you can exercise everyday. With regular exercise, you will feel more rested with less sleep and you will work much more efficiently, As a result, you will actually gain more time than you've given up to exercise.

- realize[ri:əlàiz] v. 인식하다
- practice[prǽktis] n. 연습하다
- excuse[ikskju:z] n. 변명
- rested[restid] a. 기운이 나는
- efficiently[ifiʃəntli] ad. 효율적으로

3 Language never stands still. Every language, until it dies, that is, until it ceases to be spoken at all, is in a state of continual change. The English which we speak and write is **not** the same English that was spoken and written by our grandfathers, **nor** was their English precisely like that of Queen Elizabeth's time. The farther back we go, the less familiar we find ourselves with the speech of our ancestors, until finally we reach a kind of English which is quite as strange to us as if it were a foreign tongue.

- cease[siːs] v. 중지하다, 그만두다
- continual[kəntínjuəl] a. 계속적인
- nor = and neither; nor는 접속사, neither는 부사
- their English = grandfathers' English
- precisely[prisáisli] ad. 정확히, 바로
- farther[fáːrðər] ad. 더 멀리
- ancestor[ǽnsestər] n. 조상, 선조
- foreign tongue 외국어

4 The feeling of individual independence and self-sufficiency is so strong in the United States that often **either** parents **or** their grown children choose not to live together.

- individual[ìndəvídʒuəl] a. 개인적인
- independence[ìndipéndəns] n. 독립
- self-sufficiency[self-səfíʃənsi] n. 자급자족

5 I am happy if my wife and children live in harmony. When all members of my family share good and sad times, and communicate with **each other**, I am happy.

- harmony[há:rməni] n. 조화
- share[ʃεə:r] v. 공유하다
- communicate[kəmjú:nəkèit] v. 의사 전달하다

6 Some scientist discovered that a small amount of red wine might have at least one good effect on our health. **The result of the study suggests** that red wine may lower the level of cholesterol in the blood. However, a recent study proves that it is not the alcohol that lowers the level of cholesterol. In other words, doctors have learned that it is **grapes** that **reduce** cholesterol. As a result of this, people with high level of cholesterol can get the same result by eating grapes.

- effect[ifékt] n. 영향, 결과
- affect[əfékt] vt. 영향을 끼치다
  = have an effect on = have an influence on = influence = affect
- lower[lóuər] v. 낮추다, 줄이다
- cholesterol[kəléstəròl] n. 콜레스테롤
- it is grapes that reduce cholesterol ✚ grapes를 강조한 it is ~ that 강조구문

7 The best equipment a young man can have for the battle of life is a conscience, common sense and good health. There is no friend so good as a good conscience. There is no enemy so dangerous as a bad conscience. Conscience makes us **either** kings **or** slaves.

- be equipped with ~을 갖추고 있다
- equipment[ikwípmənt] n. 준비, 설비, 장비
- no friend so good as a good conscience 좋은 양심처럼 그렇게 훌륭한 친구는 없다.
- conscience[kánʃəns] 양심 (the sense of verifying right and wrong)
- common sense 상식

8 There are many factors involved in job satisfaction. Even though there are individual differences, most people agree that jobs have to offer workers a mental challenge. People have to feel their jobs are meaningful and interesting. And, of course, pay has greatest importance, especially for individuals who cannot gain other satisfactions from their jobs. Jobs which offer a pleasing work environment, good pay, and a mental challenge are sought by most people. **Each person wants** a feeling of fulfillment.

- factor[fǽktər] n. 요인
- involve[inválv] vt. 포함하다
- mental[méntl] a. 정신적인
- challenge[tʃǽlindʒ] n. 도전
- especially[ispéʃəli] ad. 특히
- gain[gein] v. 얻다
- satisfaction[sæ̀tisfǽkʃən] n. 만족
- environment[inváiərənmənt] n. 환경
- seek[si:k] (seek - sought - sought) 찾다, 추구하다
- fulfillment[fulfílmənt] n. 성취, 실현

9 Before the twentieth century, millions of people died needlessly in hospitals. Back then, doctors didn't wash their hands between tasks. They knew little about germs and **how they were spread**. Doctors would finish one operation, then immediately start on another operation. Then they would examine patients, never realizing that they were carrying germs from one person to another. In many cases, they seriously infected the people they were trying to cure.

- needlessly[ní:dlisli] a. 쓸데없이, 불필요하게
- task[tæsk] n. 과업, 직무

- germ[dʒəːrm] n. 세균
- spread[spred] v. 펴다
- operation[àpəréiʃən] n. 수술
- immediately[imíːdiitli] ad. 즉시
- examine[igzǽmin] v. 조사하다
- patient[péiʃənt] n. 환자
- cure[kjuər] v. 치료하다
- seriously[siəriəsli] ad. 심각하게
- infect[infékt] vt. 감염시키다

10 Dear Nicole,

My son is going to marry a girl we'll call Mary. Mary has been eating dinner at our house every Sunday for the last seven months. I always prepare very good food. Mary eats a lot and I believe she likes the food. However, she has never once offered **to help me with the dishes**, or even take her plate into the kitchen. My son thinks that because Mary is a guest she doesn't have to help. I say he's wrong. What do you say?

Joan from Chicago

- marry[mǽri] vt. ~와 결혼하다
- offer[ɔ́(ː)fər] 제공하다
- help + 사람 + with + 일 : 돕다
- plate[pleit] n. 접시

Advanced Reading 21

A. Preparing to Read

For all his failure, he was doing it by himself.

The Queen has **bestowed** a knighthood **on** him.

The weather **bids fair to** improve tomorrow.

Some banks make **it** difficult **to open an account**.

B. Approaching to the Topic

What is the point of teaching a child to solve a quadratic equation? There is a traditional answer to this question. It runs thus: The mind is an instruments, you first sharpen it, and then use it; the acquisition of the power of solving a quadratic equation is part of the process of sharpening the mind. Now there is just enough truth in this answer to have made it live through the ages. But for all its half truth, it embodies a radical error which bids fair to stifle the genius of the modern world. I do not know who was first responsible for this analogy of the mind to a dead instrument. For aught I know, it may have been one of the seven wise men of Greece, or a committee of the whole lot of them. Whoever was the originator, there can be no doubt of the authority which it has acquired by the continuous approval bestowed upon it by eminent persons.

The Aims of Education by *Alfred N. Whitehead*

Vocabularies & Expressions for Comprehension

- quadratic[kwɑdrǽtik] equation[i(:)kwéiʒən] 이차방정식
- runs ~와 같다
- traditional[trədíʃən-əl] 전통적인

- instruments[ínstrəmənt] 도구
- sharpen[ʃɑːrpən] 연마하다
- acquisition[ӕkwəzíʃən] 획득
- for all ~에도 불구하고, ~이지만
- embodies 포함하다.
- radical error 근본적인 실수
- stifle[stáifəl] 숨을 막다, 질식사시키다
- responsible for ~에 책임이 있다
- analogy[ənӕlədʒi] 유사, 유추
- aught[ɔːt] = anything
- seven wise men of Greece 그리스의 현자 7인,
(즉 Thales, chilo, Solon, Perander, Pittacus, Cleobulos, Bias)
- committee[kəmíti] 위원회
- originator[ərídʒənéitər] 창설자, 창시자
- no doubt 의심 없이
- authority[əθɔ́ːriti] 권위 권능
- eminent persons 저명한 사람들
- continuous approval[əprúːvəl] 계속적인 찬성
- bestowed upon 주다, 수여하다

Sentence Pattern Analysis

- Now there is just enough truth in this answer to have made it live through the ages.
  지금 보면, 이 대답 속에는 그것을 수 세대에 걸쳐 생명을 얻게 한 충분한 진리가 있다.

- But for all its half truth, it embodies a radical error which bids fair to stifle the genius of the modern world.
  그러나 그 절반의 진리에도 불구하고, 그것은 근대세계의 천재를 숨막히게 할 가능성이 충분히 있는 근본적인 실수를 포함하고 있다. bid fair to (do) ~할 가망이 충분히 있다.

- For aught I know, it may have been one of the seven wise men of Greece, or a committee of the whole lot of them.
  내가 아는 범위에서는, 그것은 그리스의 현자 7인 중 한사람이었을 지도 모르고, 아니면 그들

전체로 구성된 위원회였을 지도 모른다. aught는 anything과 같은 의미임.

- there can be no doubt of the authority which it has acquired by the continuous approval bestowed upon it by eminent persons.

  그 대답을 저명한 사람들이 끊임없이 승인하여 줌으로써 그것이(그 대답이) 획득한 권위에 대하여 의심할 수가 없다. 앞에 나온 it와 뒤에 나온 it는 answer를 가리킨다.

Afred North Whitehead 은 영국출신의 수학자이자 철학자이다. 그의 주요 저서로는 *Principia Mathe-matica* (1910), *Science and the Modern World* (1925) 등이 있다.

Wisdom

We shall not flag or fail. We shall go on to the end, we shall fight in France, we shall fight on the seas and oceans, we shall fight with growing confidence and growing strength in the air, we shall defend our island, whatever the cost may be, we shall fight on the beaches, we shall fight on the landing grounds, we shall fight in the fields and in the streets, we shall fight in the hills; we shall never surrender.

우리는 쇠퇴하거나 실패하지 않을 것입니다. 우리는 최후까지 싸울 것입니다. 우리는 프랑스에서 싸울 것입니다. 우리는 바다나 대양에서 싸울 것입니다. 우리는 점점 증대하는 자신감과 강화되는 공군력으로 싸울 것입니다. 우리들은 어떤 대가를 치르더라도 우리의 섬을 방어할 것입니다. 우리는 해변에서 싸울 것입니다. 우리는 상륙지에서 싸울 것입니다. 우리는 들판이나 언덕에서도 싸울 것입니다. 우리는 결코 항복하지 않을 것입니다.

Sir Winston Churchill: Speech in the House of Commons

Advanced Reading 22

A. Preparing to Read

We must not **shrink from** the legitimate use of force if we are to remain credible.

Many company is **exchanging** goods **with** foreign countries.

Only a few came to help him.

B. Approaching to the Topic

In the long history of the world, only a few generations have been granted the role of defending freedom in its hour of maximum danger. I do not shrink from this responsibility — I welcome it. I do not believe that any of us would exchange places with any other people or any other generation. The energy, the faith, the devotion which we bring to this endeavor will light our country and all who serve it — and the glow from that fire can truly light the world.

And so, my fellow Americans: Ask not what your country can do for you — ask what you can do for your country.

My fellow citizens of the world: Ask not what America will do for you, but what together we can do for the freedom of man.

Finally, whether you are citizens of America or citizens of the world, ask of us here the same high standards of strength and sacrifice which we ask of you. With a good conscience our only sure reward, with history the final judge of our deeds, let us go forth to lead the land we love, asking His blessing and His help, but knowing that here on earth God's work must truly be our own.

John F. Kennedy

Vocabularies & Expressions for Comprehension

- only a few 소수만이, 극소수의 (=but few, very few)
- grant[grænt, grɑ:nt] 부여하다
- in its hour of maximum danger 자유가 최대 위험에 빠져있을 시간에 (its는 freedom을 가리킨다)
- shrink from ~ ~을 회피하다
- devotion[divóuʃən] 헌신
- endeavor[endévər] 노력
- glow[glou] 백열광
- light 밝히다
- sacrifice[sǽkrəfàis] 희생
- the same high standards of strength[streŋkθ] ~ 동일한 수준의 ~
- good conscience[kɑ́nʃəns/ kɔ́n] 양심
- reward[riwɔ́:rd] 보상, 보답
- on earth 지상에서
- His blessing과 His help에서 His는 God's를 의미함. our own은 그 바로 뒤에 work를 보충하여 이해함, 즉 '우리 자신의 일'

Sentence Pattern Analysis

- only a few generations have been granted the role of defending freedom
  극소수의 세대만이 자유를 수호하는 역할을 부여받았습니다.

- in its hour of maximum danger
  자유가 최대 위험에 빠져있을 시기에 (its는 freedom을 받음.)

- The energy, the faith, the devotion which we bring to this endeavor will light our country and all who serve it.
  우리가 이런 노력에 기울인 힘과 믿음 그리고 헌신은 우리의 조국을 밝혀 줄 것이며, 조국에 봉사한 모든 사람들을 밝혀줄 것입니다. (it는 our country를 받음.)

- and the glow from that fire can truly light the world.
  그 불에서 나온 불빛은 세계를 참으로 밝혀 줄 것입니다. (물론 여기 that fire의 that은 fire를 수식하는 지시형용사)

- Ask not what America will do for you, but what together we can do for the freedom of man.
  - 이 문장은 not ~ but의 구문.
- with a good conscience our only sure reward, with history the final judge of our deeds.
  - 우리의 유일하고 확실한 보상인 양심을 가지고, 우리 행위들에 대한 최후 심판인 역사와 더불어.
- God's work must truly be our own.
  - 하나님의 일이 참으로 우리 자신의 일임에 틀림없다. (our own 다음에 work를 보충하여 이해.)

Wisdom

A man should know something of his own country, too, before he goes abroad.

해외여행을 가기 전에 자신의 나라에 대해 중요한 것을 알아야 한다.

Laurence Sterne: Tristram Shandy

제12장. 형용사·부사

제12장 형용사 *Adjective* / 부사 *Adverb*

A 형용사 용법

❶ 한정용법(Attributive use)

형용사가 명사를 ① 전위(前位)수식(앞에서 수식)하거나,
② 후위(後位)수식(뒤에서 수식)한다.

(1) 전위(前位)수식(Premodification)

1. She has a **beautiful** ***voice***.
2. **Broken** ***bottle*** lay on the floor.

(2) 후위(後位)수식(postmodification)

1. Please give me ***something*** **cold** to drink.
2. This is ***a custom*** **peculiar** to Korea.
3. I met ***a man*** seventy-five years **old**.
4. We have ***a rule*** **similar** to that of Germany.
5. I have answered ***the letter*** (which was) **received** (by me).

❷ 서술용법(Predicative use)

문장에서 주격보어나 목적격보어가 되어 주어나 목적어를 수식하는 형용사를 말한다.

1. ***The moon*** was **beautiful** last night.
2. You must keep ***your room*** **clean**.

❸ 형용사 어순

지시(指示), 수량(數量), 대소(大小), 성상(性狀), 신구(新舊), 재료(材料)와 관련된 형용사의 순서대로 명사를 수식한다.

1. Look at **those two large old stone building**.
2. Look at **the second white wooden house**.

관사 · 소유격 지시어 (this, that)	수량 서수 → 수량		성질 · 상태관련 형용사 대소 → 색 · 신구 → 재료 · 소속			명사
these		two	big	silver	metal	medals
the	first	six				weeks
a			tall	strong	Korean	boy

❹ 목적어 취하는 형용사

보통 전치사가 명사를 목적어로 취하지만, like, near, opposite, worth 등의 형용사는 보어 역할을 하면서 목적어를 동반한다.

1. John looks **like his father**.
2. She is **near twenty years of age**.
3. I live **opposite the post office**.
4. It is not **worth a straw**.

❺ 혼동하기 쉬운 형용사

1. • industrious 근면한 • industrial 산업의
2. • sensible 분별 있는 • sensitive 민감한
3. • considerable 많은, 상당한 • considerate 사려 깊은 • considering ~을 고려하면
4. • momentous 중요한 • momentary 순간적인
5. • successive 계속적인 • successful 성공한
6. • imaginative 상상력이 풍부한 • imaginary 가상적인 • imaginable 상상할 수 있는
7. • respectable 존경할만한 • respectful 공손한 • respective 각자의
8. • desirable 바람직한 • desirous 원하는
9. • economic 경제의 • economical 검소한
10. • historic 역사상 중요성을 갖는 • historical 역사에 관계된
11. • practical 실용적인 • practicable 실행할 수 있는
12. • comparative 비교의 • comparable ~에 필적하는
13. • literal 문자 그대로 • literary 문학의 • literate 학식 있는

14. • special 특별한 • specific 구체적인

15. • healthy 건강한 • healthful 건강에 좋은

16. • uninterested 무관심한(indifferent) • disinterested 공평한(impartial)

B 수량형용사

- 수 : a lot of, lots of, plenty of, a number of = many
- 양 : a lot of, lots of, plenty of, a good (= great) deal of = much

1. He has a lot of(= many) friends.
2. We had a lot of (= much) rain last year.
3. There were plenty of passengers in the bus.
4. There is plenty of money in his purse.
5. **Not a few**(= many) students are learning English.
6. He drinks **not a little**(= **much**) wine every day.

- as many ~ : 같은 수의
- as much ~ : 같은 양의
- like so many ~ : 같은 수의 ~처럼
- like so much ~ : 같은 양의 ~처럼

7. He keeps three dogs and **as many cats**.

   <as many는 three를 지칭한다>
8. The boys worked **like so many ants**.
9. He drank two bottles of beer and **as much wine**.

   <an much는 two bottles를 지칭한다>
10. The white snow on the ground looked **like so much sugar**.
11. He is **not so much** a teacher **as** a scholar.

    <not so much A as B = not A so much as B = A less than B = less A than B

    more[rather] B than A = B more[rather] than A : A라기보다는 차라리 B이다>

C 수사(數詞) 용법

❶ 기수사(基數詞) 서수사(序數詞)

기 수		서 수		기 수		서 수	
1	one	1st	first	11	eleven	11th	eleventh
2	two	2nd	second	12	twelve	12th	twelfth
3	three	3rd	third	13	thirteen	13th	thirteenth
4	four	4th	fourth	14	fifteen	14th	fifteenth
5	five	5th	fifth	20	twenty	20th	twentieth
6	six	6th	sixth	21	twenty-one	21st	twenty-first
7	seven	7th	seventh	22	twenty-two	22nd	twenty-second
8	eight	8th	eighth	30	thirty	30th	thirtieth
9	nine	9th	ninth	40	forty	40th	fortieth
10	ten	10th	tenth	50	fifty	50th	fiftieth

❷ 수(數) 읽기

(1) 정수

253 = two hundred and fifty-three <hundred 다음에 and를 넣는다>

1,469,562 = one million, four hundred and sixty-nine thousand, five hundred and sixty-two

(2) 분수

1/2 a half　　1/3 one[a] third

1/4 one[a] quarter　　3/4 three-quarters

2/3 two-thirds

분자: 기수 / 분모: 서수

(3) 소수점

67.209 = sixty-seven **point** two zero nine

소수점은 point로 읽고 소수점 이하의 숫자는 숫자 하나씩 차례대로 읽는다.

(4) 전화번호

269-8041 = two six nine eight o[ou] four one

(5) 연도, 날짜, 시간

2006 = twenty o[ou] six

1995 = nineteen ninety-five

World war II = World war two (the second world war)

August 31 = August thirty-one (August the thirty-first, the thirty-first of August)

8:25 = eight twenty-five

D 부사의 위치

❶ 부사의 위치

1. My mother **danced** a waltz **cheerfully**. <danced 수식>
2. Mrs. Simpson is a **very beautiful** lady. <beautiful 수식>
3. He **almost always** carries a guitar with him. <always 수식>
4. I arrived **soon after the train left**. <after the train left 수식>

❷ 빈도부사

1. She **sometimes takes** a walk with her dog. <일반동사 앞>
2. I **am always** at home on Sundays. <be 동사 뒤>
3. Tom **will never** quarrel with you again. <조동사 뒤>

4. John meets Susan **every other day**. <2일에 한 번씩>
5. He sends an e-mail to her **every three days** [= **every third day**]. <3일에 한 번씩>

   every +기수+복수명사 = every+서수+단수명사: ~ 마다 한 번씩

❸ 기타 부사 위치

1. Tom was **kind enough** to help me. <enough는 뒤에서 형용사 수식>
2. The president arrived **here safely yesterday**. <장소+방법+시간>

3. Put **on** that cap. <동사+부사+명사>
 = Put that cap **on** <동사+명사+부사>
 = Put it **on**. <동사+대명사+부사>
 = Put on it. (×) <동사+부사+대명사(×)>

❹ 문장수식 부사

• **Fortunately** John passed the entrance exam.
 → **It was fortunate** that John passed the entrance exam.

E 주의할 부사

❶ ago/before/since

1. I met him **two years ago**. <ago: 시간+ago, 현재를 기준하여 얼마 전>
2. I should have met him **two years ago**.
3. I met him **before**.
4. I have met him **before**. <before: 이미(already), 이전에(previously)>
5. She said she had met him **two years before**. <과거를 기준하여 얼마전>
6. I have not seen her **since**. <현재완료시제 + since + 과거시제>

❷ very/much

(1) very: 형용사, 부사, 원급, 현재분사 수식

1. He is a **very good** teacher. <형용사 수식>
2. He works **very hard**. <부사 수식>
3. This is a **very interesting** story. <현재분사 수식>
4. He was **very surprised**. <형용사화된 과거분사 수식>

(2) much : 동사, 과거분사, 비교급, 최상급, 서술용법 형용사 수식

1. I like wine **very much**. <부사 수식>
2. I am **much interested in** this novel. <과거분사 수식>

3. This is **much the better**. 〈비교급 수식〉
4. He is **much the best** student in his class. 〈최상급 수식〉
5. I am **much afraid** of it. 〈서술용법 형용사 수식〉

❸ already/yet

1. John has **already** finished his homework. 〈(긍정문에서)에서 이미〉
2. My father has not read the newspaper **yet**. 〈(부정문에서)에서 아직〉
3. Have you finished lunch **already**? 〈(의문문)에서 벌써〉

❹ too/either

1. I like Bill, and my parents like him, **too**. 〈긍정문〉
2. If she doesn't go, I won't go, **either**. 〈부정문〉

F 부사의 도치

부사가 문장 앞으로 도치되면 동사가 주어 앞으로 이동한다.
① 일반동사의 경우에 do 동사가 이동하고,
② be 동사나 조동사의 경우에 be 동사나 조동사가 이동한다.

1. **Well do** I remember the scene.
2. **Inside of the box were** many books.
3. **Up the hill ran** Mary.
4. **Here comes** the bus. 〈부사+동사+명사〉
5. **Here** it **comes**. 〈부사+대명사+동사〉
6. **Little did** I dream that he could succeed.
   → I **little** dreamed that he could succeed.
7. **Not until we lose health do** we know the value of it.
   → We do **not** know the value of health **until** we lose it.

G 의문 부사

• 의문부사 : when, where, why, how

1. **When** and **where** were you born?
2. **Why** was he absent from school yesterday?
3. **How** did you come here?
4. **How old** is your bike?
5. **How often** a week do you take a bath?
6. "**How much** is it?" "Ten dollars"

• 간접의문 : 의문사+S+V가 명사절로 사용된다.

7. I don't know **when and where you were born**.
8. **How old** do you think **she is**? (◯)
9. Do you think **how old she is**? (×)

8번 문장의 경우 주절의 동사에 guess, imagine, believe, suppose, think 등의 주관적인 대답을 원하는 동사가 오면, 의문사는 문두로 나간다.

Basic Reading 12

1 We are apt to overlook the fact that the source of air pollution is **not always** limited to factories.

- be apt to ~하는 경향이 있는
- overlook[òuvərlúk] vt. 간과하다
- the fact that : the 명사와 that ~ 은 동격 관계
- source[sɔːrs] n. 원천, 근원
- air pollution 대기오염, noise pollution 소음공해, water pollution 수질오염

2 Different kinds of reading matter call for different kinds of reading. A reader must, first of all, decide what type of reading matter he has in his hand; and he must then read it accordingly. **Every** piece of reading matter that comes before our eyes is **not** equally worth reading, **nor** do **all** make equal claims on our attention.

- reading matter 읽을 거리
- call for 요구하다
- decide[disáid] v. 결심하다, 결정하다
- accordingly[əkɔ́ːrdiŋli] ad. 따라서, 그러므로(therefore)
- equally[íːqwəli] ad. 평등하게, 균일하게
- be worth ~ing ~의 가치가 있는
- nor do all make equal claims on our attention
  = and all do not make equal claims on our attention, either
- claim[kleim] v. 요구
- attention[əténʃən] n. 주의, 주목, 주의력

3 Uncle John takes after my dead father so much that I **never** look at him **but** I think of my father.

• take after 닮다(resemble)
• think of 생각하다

4 It is **impossible** to take a walk in the country by oneself **without** being amazed at the vast continent of one's ignorance.

• by oneself 혼자 힘으로
• be amazed at [əméiz] ~에 대해서 놀라다
• vast [væst] a. 광대한
• continent [kántənənt] n. 대륙, 육지
• ignorance [ígnərəns] n. 무지

5 **A great many** people possess books, but very **few** know how to make use of them.

• a great many 아주 많은
• possess [pəzés] vt. 소유하다, 지니다
• make use of 이용하다(utilize)

6 His early death, **not a few** people think, was due to his habit of drinking, Usually he showed **only a little** self-control.

• not a few 적지 않은(many), 상당한 수의
• be due to ~에 기인하는, 때문인
• only a little 극히 적은, 조금 뿐인
• self-control 자제심

7 A threat to the freedom of Europe is a threat to the freedom of America. That is why no administration in Washington can fail to respond to such a threat — **not merely** from goodwill **but** from necessity.

- threat[θret] n.위협
- administration[ædmìnəstréiʃən, əd-] n. 행정, 운영, 경영
- administer[ædmínistər, əd-] v. 관리하다, 운영하다, 시행하다
- respond to[rispάnd] v. 응수하다, 응하다
- not merely A but (merely) B: A뿐만 아니라 B도
- good will 선의

8 Strange to say, my coming to London was **not** to meet people, **but** for more solitude. For I had become so well known in the little town where I had lived that I could **not** step outside the house **without** being engaged in conversation almost immediately.

- solitude[sάlitjù:d] n. 고독, 외로움
- step outside (밖으로) 나오다
- be engaged in ~에 종사하는
- immediately[imí:diitli] ad. 즉시로

9 **Because** a man happen to be unwise, he should **not** be discouraged, for **not a few** unwise men have succeeded in life by their constant effort.

- happen to 우연히 ~ 하게 되다
- discourage[diskə́:ridʒ] v. 낙담시키다
- not a few = quite a few = many
- succeed in 성공하다
- constant[kάnstənt] a. 불변의

10 You **cannot** be **too** careful in the choice of books. A book may be compared to your neighbor; if it is good, it **cannot** last **too** long, if bad, you **cannot** get rid of it **too** quickly.

- compare A to B : A를 B에 비유하다,
  cf. compare A with B : A를 B에 비교하다
- last[læst, lɑ:st] v. 지속하다
- get rid of 제거하다

11 It is futile to expect a hungry and mean population to be **anything but** violent and gross.

- futile[fjú:tl] a. 무익한(useless), 효과 없는
- mean[mi:n] a. 비열한, 초라한
- population[pàpjəléiʃən] n. 인구, 주민
- violent[váiələnt] a. 격렬한, 난폭한
- gross[grous] a. 거친, 조잡한

12 The whole conviction of my life now rests upon the belief that loneliness, **far from being** a rare and curious phenomenon, peculiar to myself and to a few other solitary men, is the central and inevitable fact of human existence.

- conviction[kənvíkʃən] n. 확신, 신념
- rest upon 의지하다, 믿다
- the belief that 동격관계
- loneliness[lóunlinis] n. 고독
- (being) far from ~ing = never
- rare[rɛəːr] 드문, 진기한

- curious[kjúəriəs] a. 호기심이 강한
- phenomenon[finámənàn] n. 현상
- peculiar[pikjú:ljər] a. 독특한, 특유의(to)
- solitary[sálitèri] a. 외로운, 고독한
- inevitable[inévitəbəl] a. 피할 수 없는
- existence[igzístəns] n. 존재, 실재

Advanced Reading 23

A. Preparing to Read

Now that you're here, why not stay for dinner.

His accent is broad, his face hard **with indignation**.

She **volunteered** as a nurse in a local hospital.

B. Approaching to the Topic

Mandatory volunteering made many members of Maryland's high school class of '97 grumble with indignation.

Future seniors, however, probably won't be as resistant now that the program has been broken in. Some, like John Maloney, already have completed their required hours of approved community service. The Bowie High School sophomore earned his hours in eighth grade by volunteering two nights a week at the Larkin-Chase Nursing and Restorative Center in Bowie.

He played shuffleboard, cards, and other games with the senior citizens. He also helped to plan parties for them and visited their rooms to keep them company.

John, fifteen, is not finished volunteering. Once a week he videotapes animals at the Prince George County animal shelter in Forestville. His footage is shown on the Bowie public access television channel in hopes of finding homes for the animals.

from The Washington Times

Vocabularies & Expressions for Comprehension

• Mandatory[mǽndətɔ̀:ri] volunteering[vɑ̀ləntíriŋ] 의무적인 자원봉사, 강제적인 자원봉사
• grumble[grʌ́mbəl] 불평하다
• with indignation[indignéiʃən] 분개하여, 화가 나서
• senior[sí:njər] 상급자
• resistant[rizístənt] 저항자, 방해자
• broken in 깨다, 파기하다
• complete[kəmplí:t] 마치다 이루다
• approved community service 공인된 지역사회 봉사
• sophomore 고등학교나 대학의 2학년
• eighth grade 제8학년
• Nursing and Restorative Center 간호 및 원기 회복원
• shuffleboard 셔플보드 (일종의 원반 밀어치기 놀이)
• videotapes 비디오 테이프에 촬영하다
• shelter 보호소, 은신처
• footage 영화 필름의 길이

Sentence Pattern Analysis

• Mandatory volunteering made many members of Maryland's high school class of '97 grumble with indignation.

필수로 해야 하는 자원봉사 때문에 97년 매릴랜드 고등학교 학급의 많은 구성원들은 화를 내고 불평했다.

• Future seniors, however, probably won't be as resistant now that the program has been broken in.

미래의 상급생들은 하지만 아마도 그 프로그램이 이제 폐지된 이상 저항자로서 있지는 않을 것이다. (이 문장의 'now that은 이제 ~한 이상, ~하므로'.)

• The Bowie High School sophomore earned his hours in eighth grade by volunteering two nights a week at the Larkin-Chase Nursing and Restorative Center in Bowie.

보위 고등학교 이 학년은 보위 지역에 있는 라킨-세이스 양육 및 원기 회복원에서 일 주일에 이틀 밤을 자원 봉사함으로써 제8학년에서 자신의 시간을 획득했다.

- He also helped to plan parties for them and visited their rooms to keep them company.

  그는 또한 그들을 위해서 파티 계획을 짜는 것을 도왔으며, 그들이 적적하지 않도록 그들의 방을 방문했다. to keep ~company 적적하지 않도록

- Once a week he videotapes animals at the Prince George County animal shelter in Forestville.

  일 주일에 한번 그는 포레스트빌 지역에 있는 프린스 조오지 군 동물보호소에서 동물들을 비디오 테이프로 촬영한다.

Wisdom

There is a great deal of difference between the eager man who wants to read a book, and the tired man who wants a book to read.

책을 읽기 원해서 열심히 읽는 사람과 따분해서 책을 읽는 사람 사이에는 큰 차이가 있다.

Gilbert K. Chesterton: Charles Dickens

Advanced Reading 24

A. Preparing to Read

She **took** it **for granted** that the invitation included his husband.

Not a man, woman **nor** child could be seen there.

Experts have been discussing **how to** improve the fight against crime.

B. Approaching to the Topic

What you do say is that you're very fond of reading; and I'm delighted by that. Do you know the essays of Francis Bacon, who lived about the same time as Shakespeare? They're full of good things about reading. Here are some of them, from the essay 'Of Studies'.

'Some books are to be tasted, others to be swallowed, and some few to be chewed and digested.'

'Read not to contradict and confute; nor to believe and take for granted; nor to find talk and discourse; but to weigh and consider'

I can't give you advice better that. The first quotation tells you how to read books of different kinds. I suppose most travel books are 'to be tasted'; it's enough to dip into them and read bits there and there. If you're fond of crime stories (Agatha Christie, Simeon, and the rest of modern favorites), you will, if you're like me, read them quickly; you'll 'swallow' them. And then there are books that you'll read slowly and carefully. If a book's on an important subject you're interested in, you'll want to chew and digest it. And you'll want to weigh what the author says, and consider his ideas and arguments.

On Reading by A. S. Hornby

Vocabularies & Expressions for Comprehension

- be fond of ~을 좋아하다
- be delighted by ~로 기뻐하다
- essays 수필
- taste[teist] 맛보다
- swallow[swálou/ swɔ́l] 삼키다
- chew[tʃuː] 씹다
- digest[didʒest, dàid-] 소화하다
- contradict[kántrədikt/ kɔ̀n-] 논박하다
- confute[kənfjúːt] 논쟁하다
- take for granted ~을 당연하게 받아들이다
- weigh and consider 생각하고 숙고하다
- quotation[kwoutéiʃən] 인용
- dip into 대충 읽다, 대충 담그다
- crime stories 범죄소설
- arguments[áːrgjəmənt] 논증

Sentence Pattern Analysis

- Do you know the essays of Francis Bacon, who lived about the same time as Shakespeare?
  셰익스피어랑 같은 시대 살았던 사람인데, 프란시스 베이컨의 수필을 알고 있니?

- 'Some books are to be tasted, others to be swallowed, and some few to be chewed and digested.'
  맛만 보아야 할 책도 있으며, 꿀꺽 삼켜야 하는 책도 있으며, 더러는 꼭꼭 씹어서 소화시켜야 하는 책도 있다.

- 'Read not to contradict and confute; nor to believe and take for granted; nor to find talk and discourse; but to weigh and consider.'
  논박하거나 논쟁하기 위해서 책을 읽지 말거라, 믿거나 당연하게 받아들이지도 말거라, 재담과 담론을 찾지도 말거라, 오로지 생각하고 숙고하기 위해서 책을 읽어라

- it's enough to dip into them and read bits there and there.
  - 'them' 은 여행서 등을 의미한다. (여행서는 대충 읽는 것으로 충분하고 여기저기 조금씩 읽는 것으로 충분하다.)

- And you'll want to weigh what the author says,
  - 그리고 너는 저자가 말하는 것을 숙고하기 원할 거야

Wisdom

History; which is, indeed, little more than the register of the crimes, follies, and misfortunes of mankind.

역사란, 그것은 정말, 인류의 범죄와 어리석은 짓과 불행의 기록에 불과하다.

Edward Gibbon: Decline and Fall of the Roman Empire

Welcome to English Grammar & Reading

제13장. 비교

제13장 비교 *Comparison*

A 비교 변화

❶ 기본문형

1. Tom is tall. John is tall, too.
2. Tom is **taller than** John.
3. Tom is **the tallest** in the class.
4. John is **not so(as)** tall **as** Tom.

❷ 규칙변화

① 1음절의 형용사, 일부 2음절의 형용사는 원급에 -er, -est를 붙여서 비교급과 최상급을 만든다.

원 급	비교급	최상급
warm	warmer	warmest
large	larger	largest

② 어미 <자음+y>일 때는 y를 i로 고친다.

- busy — busier — busiest
- happy — happier — happiest

③ 어미 <단모음+자음>일 때는 그 자음자를 겹친다.

- hot — hotter — hottest
- sad — sadder — saddest

④ 2음절 이상의 형용사 및 3음절 이상의 형용사는 more, most를 원급 앞에 붙여서 비교급과 최상급을 만든다.

❸ 불규칙 변화

(1) 불규칙 변화 I

원 급	비교급	최상급	원 급	비교급	최상급
good, well	better	best	many(수),much(양)	more	most
bad, ill	worse	worst	little	less	least

(2) 불규칙 변화 II

원급	비교급	최상급	비 고
old	older	oldest	나이, 신구(新舊)
	elder	eldest	장유(長幼), 순서
far	farther	farthest	거리
	further	furthest	정도
late	later	latest	시간
	latter	last	순서

1. (a) He is my **eldest** son. <장유(長幼) 순서>
   (b) He is the **oldest** man in my hometown. <나이>
2. (a) I can go no **farther**. <거리>
   (b) I will inquire **further** into the problem. <정도>
3. (a) He arrived **later** than Jim. <시간>
   (b) I did not read the **latter** part of the book. <순서>

❹ 비교급과 최상급의 강조

1. This lesson is **much** easier than the last.
2. This is **far** the better of the two.

   much, far, by far, even, still, a lot, yet, a great deal: 비교급을 강조할 수 있다.

   much, far, by far, even은 비교급과 최상급 모두를 강조할 수 있다.

❺ 라틴어 비교급

접속사 than 대신에 전치사 to를 쓴다.

1. He is two years **senior to** me.
   = He is two years older than I.
   = He is my senior by two years.
   = He is older than I by two years.
2. I **prefer** staying at home **to** going out.
   = I **prefer to** stay at home rather than (to) go out.

ex. superior (=better)　senior (=older)
exterior (=outer)　major (=more)
anterior (=earlier)　inferior (=worse)
junior (=younger)　interior (=inner)
minor (=less)　posterior (=later)

B 원급의 비교

❶ 동등 비교 A=B

1. Mike can run **as** fast **as** you.
2. New York State is almost **as** large **as** Greece.

❷ 열등 비교 A<B

1. Mary is **not so** tall **as** Tom.
   = Mary is less tall than Tom.
2. She does **not** have **as** much interest in music **as** you.

❸ 배수 비교: times as ~ as

1. This is two **times as** large **as** that.
2. I have three **times as** many books **as** you have.
3. This is **half as large as** that. <반 배>
4. This is **half as large again as** that. <1배 반>
5. Tom has **twice as** much money **as** I (have). <2배>

❹ as ~ as 포함 관용표현

1. Please come back **as** soon **as you can**. <as ~ as one can = as ~ as possible>
   = Please come back **as** soon **as possible**.
2. Our teacher wrote **as many as** ten books. <as many as = 동수의>
3. He earns **as much as** a million won a month. <as much as = 동량의>
4. He is **not so much** a scholar **as** a writer.
   <not so much A as B = A가 아니라 차라리 B이다>

C 비교급의 비교

1. **The climate of Korea** is milder than **that of** Russia.
   반복되는 부분을 that로 받는다.
2. He drove **faster and faster** till we told him to stop. 〈점진 비교급〉
2. Tom is **the taller of the two.** 〈the 비교급 of the two〉
3. He worked **the harder because(as)** he was praised. 〈the 비교급 because〉
4. I like her **none the less for** her faults.
5. (a) **The higher** we climbed, **the colder** it got. 〈The 비교급 S+V, the 비교급 S+V〉
   = As we climbed higher, it got colder. 〈As S+V 비교급, S+V 비교급〉
   (b) **As** my father grew **older**, he grew more obstinate.
6. He is **more** clever **than** wise. 〈동일인이나 동일물에 대한 비교〉

D 주의할 비교구문

❶ 비교구문 I

1. He paid **no more than**(= only) one thousand dollars for the sports car.
   (그는 그 스포츠 카를 구입하면서 단지 1,000달러만 지불했다.)
2. **No less than**(= as many as) one hundred houses were burnt down.
   (100채 이상의 주택이 불에 탔다.)
3. He has **not more than**(= at most = less than) 10 dollars.
   (그는 기껏해야 10달러를 가지고 있다.)
4. He has **not less than**(= at least = more than) 1000 dollars.
   (그는 적어도 1,000달러는 가지고 있다.)

- no more than = only 〈단지: 적다는 의미〉
- no less than = as many(much) as 〈 ~만큼이나: 많다는 의미〉
- not more than = at most 〈기껏해야: 많지 않다는 의미〉
- not less than = at least 〈적어도: 적지 않다는 의미〉

❷ 비교구문 II

1. (a) A whale is **no more** a fish **than** a horse is (a fish).
   = A whale is not a fish any more than a horse is.
   (말이 생선이 아닌 것처럼 고래는 생선이 아니다.)

   (b) He knows **no more** of the world **than** a baby does.
   (아이가 세상을 모르는 것처럼 그는 세상에 대해 알지 못한다.)

2. She is **no less** beautiful **than** my sister (is beautiful).
   = She is as beautiful as my sister.
   (그녀는 내 누이가 아름다운 만큼 아름답다)

3. He is **not more** diligent **than** his brother (is diligent). 〈he ≤ his brother〉
   (그는 그의 동생이 근면한 것보다 더 많이 근면하지 않다.)

4. He is **not less** diligent **than** his brother (is diligent). 〈he ≥ his brother〉
   (그는 그의 동생이 근면한 것보다 더 적게 근면하지 않다.)

- A is no more B than C is D (= B) : 양자부정
  C가 D가 아닌 것처럼 A는 B가 아니다.
- A is no less B than C is D (= B) : 양자긍정
  C가 D인 것처럼 A는 B이다.
- A is not more B than C is D (= B) : 문장 그대로 해석 〈A ≤ C〉
- A is not less B than C is D (= B) : 문장 그대로 해석 〈A ≥ C〉

❸ no 비교급 than = as 반대말 원급 as

1. (a) He is **no better than**(= **as bad as**) a beggar.
   (그는 거지나 다름없다.)

   (b) He is **no taller than** I = He is **as short as** I.
   (그는 나처럼 키가 작다.)

2. He is **not** taller than I = He is shorter than I
   (그는 나보다 키가 크지 않다.)

❹ much (still) more, much (still) less

1. He **can** speak French, **much more** English. 〈긍정문 다음에서〉
2. He **cannot** speak English, **much less** French. 〈부정문 다음에서〉

E 최상급

❶ 최상급을 표현할 수 있는 구조

No (other) boy is **so** tall **as** he. <부정주어 so ~ as>
(그는 키가 가장 크다.)
= He is **as** tall **as any** boy. <as ~ as any 명사>
= He is **as** tall **as ever** lived. <as ~ as ever 동사>
= **No** (other) boy is **taller than** he. <부정주어 비교급 than>
= He is **taller than any other** boy. <비교급 than any other 단수명사>
taller than all the other boys. <비교급 than all the other 복수명사>
taller than anyone else <anything else : 사물일 때>
= He is **the tallest of all** his friends. <수>
the tallest in his class <장소>
the tallest that I have ever seen. <절>

❷ the를 붙이지 않는 최상급

1. This lake is **deepest** at this point. <동일인이나 동일물의 성질 상태 비교>
   cf. This lake is **the** deepest in Canada.
2. He was **happiest** when he was young. <서술적으로 쓰인 최상급>
   cf. He was **the** happiest of those men.
3. He ran **fastest** of all. <부사의 최상급>

❸ 최상급을 사용한 양보

1. **The wisest man** sometimes makes a mistake.
   = Even the wisest man sometimes makes a mistake.
2. **The tallest boy** could not reach the branch.
   = Even the tallest boy could not reach the branch.

Basic Reading 13

1 This rise in impulse buying has coincided with the growth in self-service shopping. Other studies show that in groceries where there are clerks to wait on customers there is about **half as** much impulse buying **as** in self-service stores.

- impulse buying 충동구매
- coincide[kòuinsáid] vi. 동시에 일어나다, (둘 이상의 일이) 부합하다
- grocery[gróusəri] n. 식료 및 잡화점
- clerk[kləːrk] n. 사무원, 점원
- wait on[upon] 시중들다
- This is half as large as that. <반 배>

2 Medical evidence indicates that women on the average, though **not so** strong **as** men in muscular development, are less prone to disease, and though they may complain more frequently of minor ailments, they live longer.

- medical[médikəl] a. 의학의; medicine 약, 의학
- evidence[évidəns] n. 증거, 물증
- indicate[índikèit] v. 가리키다, 나타내다
- on an[the] average 평균하여, 대략
- though not so strong as men in ~
  = though they(women) are not so strong as men in ~
- muscular[mʌ́skjələːr] a. 근육의
- be prone to (좋지 않은 방향으로) 경향이 있는
- complain of[about] 불평하다
- frequently[fríːkwəntli] ad. 자주, 빈번히
- ailment[éilmənt] n. 병

3 It is **not so much** talent **as** character that really counts in life.

- It is ~ that 강조구문
- talent[tǽlənt] n. 재능
- character[kǽriktər] n. 성격, 인격
- count[kaunt] v. 중요하다, 가치가 있다

4 In the study of nature, an explanation must be not only consistent with the facts but also **as** simple and direct **as possible**.

- explanation[èkspləneiʃən] n. 설명
- not only A but also B = B as well as A : A뿐만 아니라 B도 역시
- consistent[kənsístənt] a. 일관된, 모순이 없는(with)
- as ~ as possible 가능한 ~

5 The steamer leaves nothing to be desired **so far as** comfort and luxury **are concerned**.

- steamer[stí:mə:r] n. 기선
- leaves nothing to be desired 미진한 점이 전혀 없다
  cf. leaves much to be desired 미진한 점이 많다
- comfort[kʌ́mfərt] n. 편안함, 위로, 위안하다
- luxury[lʌ́kʃəri] n. 사치, 사치품
- so far as A is concerned: A에 관한 한

6 As for the slaves themselves, **so long as** they were content to obey their master's orders, they seemed to be fairly well off on the plantations.

- as for (보통 문두에 써서) ~에 관한 한
- slave[sleiv] n. 노예

- be content to do ~에 만족하다
- fairly[fέərli] ad. 공정히, 꽤, 어지간히(moderately)
- be well off 유복한 (⇔ be badly off)
- plantation[plæntéiʃən] n. 대규모 농원

7 The most beautiful and profound emotion we can experience is the mysterious. It is the source of all true art and science. He to whom this emotion is a stranger, who can no longer pause to wonder and stand rapt in awe, is **as good as** dead; his eyes are closed.

- profound[prəfáund] a. 깊은, 심원한
- emotion[imóuʃən] n. 감동, 강렬한 감정
- experience[ikspíəriəns] n. 경험, 체험
- the mysterious[misti-əriəs] 신비감(神秘感)
- source[sɔ:rs] n. 원천, 근원, 출처
- He to whom this emotion is a stranger
  = He this emotion is a stranger to whom
- stranger[stréindʒə:r] n. 무경험자(to), 낯선 사람
- pause[pɔ:z] n. 중단하다, 잠시 멈추다
- wonder[wʌ́ndə:r] n. 경이, 놀라움
- stand rapt in[ræpt] ~에 몰두한, 넋을 빼앗긴
- awe[ɔ́:] n. 경외(敬畏), 두려움

8 **The more** I read, **the more** complicated the subject seemed to me, and **the more** conscious I grew of my ignorance.

- complicated[kámplikèitid] a. 복잡한
- subject[sʌ́bdʒikt] n. 주제, 문제, 주어
- grow conscious of (고통 · 감정 · 추위 등을) 의식하고 있는
- ignorance[ígnərəns] n. 무지

9 To escape from nervous fatigue in modern life is a very difficult thing. In the first place, all through working hours, and still more in the time spent between work and home, the urban worker is exposed to noise, most of which, it is true, he learns not to hear consciously, but which none the less wears him out, **all the more owing to** the subconscious effort involved in not hearing it.

- escape[iskéip] v. 달아나다
- nervous[nə́:rvəs] 신경질의; nervousness 신경 과민
- fatigue[fəti:g] n. 피로, 피곤
- in the first place (to begin with) 우선, 첫째로
- urban[ə́:rbən] a. 도시의 (⇔ rural 시골의)
  cf. suburb 교외; the suburbs (상업지구와 구별하여 도시의) 근교
- most of which, ~ , but which ~ : 관계대명사 which의 선행사는 noise이다
- consciously[kánʃəsli] ad. 의식적으로
- none the less 그럼에도 불구하고
- wear out 지치게 하다
- owing to ~ 때문에, 덕택에
- subconscious[sʌbkánʃəs] a. 잠재의식의
- involve[inválv] vt. 수반하다, 포함하다

10 If a man writes a diary which he feels sure that nobody will ever see except himself, he is probably perfectly truthful. There is no motive for being otherwise. He is **no more** ashamed of recording his actions, good and bad, just as they happened, **than** of seeing himself in the bath.

- diary[dáiəri] n. 일기
- There is no motive ~ otherwise 달리 행동해야 할 동기가 없다
- just as they happened 그가 행동한 대로
- than (ashamed) of seeing himself in the bath 목욕하면서 자신을 부끄러워하지 않는 것처럼

11 Resignation, however, has also its part to play in the conquest of happiness, and it is a part **no less** essential **than** that played by effort. The wise man, though he will not sit down under preventable misfortunes, will not waste time and emotion upon such as are unavoidable.

- resignation[rèzignéiʃən] n. 단념, 포기, 체념
- it is a part no less essential than ~ ~만큼 필수적인 역할이다
- no less ~ than = as ~ as
- than that played by effort 노력이 행하는 역할 (that = the part)
- such as are unavoidable 피할 수 없는 것들 (as는 유사관계대명사)
- such = such misfortunes

12 Thinking is as unnatural and laborious an activity for human beings as walking on two legs is for monkeys. We seldom do more of it than we have to; and our disinclination to think is generally greatest at the times when we are feeling the most comfortable. Since this human antipathy to the labor of thought is **no less** manifest in public life **than** it is in private affairs, mankind does not do very much of its historical thinking in easy and prosperous times.

- laborious[ləbɔ́:riəs] a. 힘드는, 어려운, 성가신
- seldom[séldəm] ad. 좀처럼 ~ 않다
- disinclination[disinklinéiʃən] n. 싫증, 마음이 하기 싫어함
- comfortable[kʌ́mfərtəbəl] a. 마음 편한
- antipathy[æntípəəi] n. 반감, 혐오(⇔ sympathy 공감, 동정심), cf. apathy 냉담, 무관심
- manifest[mǽnəfèst] adj. 명백한
- than it is (manifest) in private affairs
- prosperous[práspərəs] a. 번영하는

13 **Nothing** in the world seems **easier than** to get happiness out of money, but the richest in the world testify to the contrary.

- the richest = even the richest people
- testify[téstəfài] v. 증언하다
- to the contrary 그와 반대로 <본동사 뒤에서 수식>

  She may have a kind heart, but her behavior points to the contrary.

  cf. on the contrary <보통 본동사 앞에서, 앞에서 언급한 것과 반대로>

  "You look tired."

  "On the contrary, I feel fine."

14 He doctored **more** people **than any other** doctor around, but he made less money because he was always taking care of the poor.

- doctor[dáktər] v. (사람 · 병을) 치료하다
- less money (than any other doctor around)
- take care of 돌보다(look after)
- the poor = poor people

15 As long as our people cling to the illusion that **nothing** is **as** important **as** making money, our colleges and universities will continue to try to teach young people how to make money.

- as long as ~하는 한
- people[píːpl] 국민
- cling to 집착하다, 매달리다
- illusion[ilúːʒən] 환상, 환각, 오해
- college[kálidʒ] 단과대학; university 종합대학

16 **No** experience is **more** culturally broadening **than** the learning of a foreign language. Nothing proves more convincingly that there are people in the world who do things differently from us

- experience[ikspíəriəns] n. 경험
- culturally broadening 문화적으로 시야를 넓히는
- Nothing proves more convincingly (than the learning of a foreign language) that ~
- convincingly[kənvínsiŋli] ad. 설득력 있게
- prove[pru:v] v. 입증하다

17 Manners are not a demonstration of weakness, but a sign of common sense. Manners are mankind's way of saying, "Let's not fight unless we have to"— and there may be **no higher** wisdom **than** that, in business, in love and marriage, in the transactions of everyday life.

- manners[mǽnə:rs] n. 예의 범절
- demonstration[dèmənstréiʃən] n. 증명, 실연(實演), (감정의) 표명
- common sense 상식
- transactions[trænsǽkʃən] [복수로] 업무, 거래, 매매; cf. transaction 처치, 취급

18 He was, so far as I could judge, **as** free from ambition in the ordinary sense of the word **as any** man who ever lived. If he rose from position to position, it was not because he thrust himself on the attention of his employers, but because his employers insisted on promoting him.

- so far as = as far as ~하는 한
- free from ~을 면한, ~이 없는
- ambition[æmbíʃən] n. 야망

- ordinary[ɔ́:rdənèri] a. 평상의, 보통의
- not because A but because B : A 때문이 아니라 B 때문이다
- thrust[θrʌst] v. 찌르다
- thrust oneself 뛰어들다, 억지로 끼어들다
- employer[emplɔ́iər] n. 고용주 (⇔ employee 피고용인, 종업원)
- insist[insíst] v. 주장하다(on)
- promote[prəmóut] vt. 승진하다, 촉진하다

19 The shy man usually finds that he has been shy without a cause, and that, in practice, no one takes **the slightest** notice of him.

- shy[ʃai] a. 수줍은, 숫기 없는
- cause[kɔ:z] n. 원인, (⇔ effect 결과)
- in practice[prǽktis] 실제로
- take notice of 주의를 기울이다(pay attention to)

20 At present, in **the most** civilized countries, freedom of speech is taken as a matter of course and seems a perfectly simple thing. We are so accustomed to it that we look on it as a natural right. But this right has been acquired only in quite recent times, and the way to its attainment has lain through lakes of blood. It has taken centuries to persuade **the most** enlightened peoples that liberty to publish one's opinions and discuss all questions is a good and not a bad thing.

- civilized[sívəlàizd] a. 교화된, 문명화한
- freedom of speech 언론의 자유
- take ~ as a matter of course ~을 당연한 것으로 여기다
- perfectly[pə:fiktli] ad. 완전히
- be accustomed to[əkʌ́stəmd] ~에 익숙하다(be used to ~)

- look on A as B : A를 B로 간주하다
- a natural right 천부적인 권리
- acquire[əkwáiər] vt. 얻다, 취득하다
- attainment[ətéinmənt] n. 달성, 도달, 학식
- lie - lied - lied - lying vi. 거짓말하다
  lie - lay - lain - lying vi. 눕다
  lay - laid - laid - laying vt. 눕히다
- lie through 펼쳐져 있다(stretch)
- It take + 시간 + to do ~하는 데 시간이 걸리다
- persuade[pə:rswéid] vt. 설득하다
- enlighten[enláitn] vt. 계몽하다, 교화하다
- liberty[líbə:rti] n. 자유

21 The first subject that attracted my attention was religion. For it seemed to me of the greatest importance to decide whether this world I lived in was the only one I had to think about or whether I must look upon it as **no more than** a place of trial which was to prepare me for a life to come.

- religion[rilídʒ-ən] n. 종교, 신앙생활
- this world I lived in = this world (which) I lived in
- look upon A as B : A를 B로 간주하다
- no more than = only
- trial[tráiəl] n. 시련, 시험

Advanced Reading 25

A. Preparing to Read

Mrs. Kang **was enchanted by** the house.

Many companies are expecting flat sales **at most**.

The president has **described** the meeting **as** making a new stage between the military super-powers.

B. Approaching to the Topic

For three thousand years, poets have been enchanted and moved and perplexed by the power of their own imagination. In a short and summary essay I can hope at most to lift one small corner of that mystery; and yet it is a critical corner. I shall ask, What goes on in the mind when we imagine? You will hear from me that one answer to this question is fairly specific: which is to say, that we can describe the working of the imagination. And when we describe it as I shall do, it becomes plain that imagination is a specifically human gift. To imagine is the characteristic act, not of the poet's mind, or the painter's, or the scientist's, but of the mind of man.

The Reach of Imagination by Jacob Bronowski

Vocabularies & Expressions for Comprehension

- be enchanted[entʃǽnt, -tʃɑ́:ntid] by ~에 매혹당하다, 황홀해지다
- be moved by ~에 감동하다
- be perplexed[pərplékst] by ~에 당황하다, 난처하다
- imagination[imæ̀dʒənéiʃən] 상상력
- describe[diskráib] 기술하다 서술하다
- at most 기껏해야, 많아야

- critical corner[kɔ́ːrnər] 비판적인 코너
- fairly[fɛ́ərli] 꽤, 상당한
- specific[spisífik] 명료한
- plain 명백한
- be characteristic of 의 특징을 나타낸다.

Sentence Pattern Analysis

- poets have been enchanted and moved and perplexed by the power of their own imagination.
  시인들은 자신들의 상상력에 매혹당하고 감동받고 당황했다.

- What goes on in the mind when we imagine?
  우리가 상상할 때 마음속에서는 무슨 일이 일어날까?

- To imagine is the characteristic act, not of the poet's mind, or the painter's, or the scientist's, but of the mind of man.
  상상하는 일이란 시인의 마음이나 화가의 마음이나 과학자의 마음을 특징짓는 행위가 아니라 인간의 마음을 특징짓는 행위이다. (not of ~ but of의 구조)

Wisdom

Well-timed silence has more eloquence than speech.

적절한 때의 침묵은 연설보다 더 설득력이 있다.

Marin Farquhar Tupper: Proverbial Philosophy

Advanced Reading 26

A. Preparing to Read

I don't want to **make the wrong decision** and regret it later.

The two countries **merged into** one.

The Frenchman **held his own against** the challenger.

She never **cease to** amaze me.

B. Approaching to the Topic

Should all individuals be free, as far as possible, to formulate and express their own beliefs and make their own decisions, or should they be merged into a social organism directed and controlled by some kind of ruling group? Does government exist in order to protect the rights and welfare of individuals, or should individuals be wholly subordinated to the state?

This conflict between the open and the closed society is by no means peculiar to the twentieth century, though it has now assumed new and more intense forms.

Believers in a closed society assert that the future belongs to them: but in actuality this is not a new institution but a very old one.

Primitive men lived in closed societies. Belonging to tightly-knit tribal groups, they had no sense of individual rights or independence. Under primitive conditions such an attitude was necessary for survival, since it was only through the maintenance of unity and the unquestioning obedience of all its members that the tribe could cope with natural obstacles and hold its own against its enemies.

But as mankind began to reach levels of development, tribalistic unity gradually ceased to be a necessity of survival and became instead an obstacle to further development. Progress now could best be promoted by making individuals free to explore new ideas and new ways of living.

Rights of Individuals in the Open Society by Henry Bamford Pakers

Vocabularies & Expressions for Comprehension

- individuals[ìndəvídʒuəls] 개인들
- as far as possible[pásəbəl] 가능한 멀리까지
- formulate[fɔ́:rmjəlèit] 공식화하다
- beliefs[bilí:f] 믿음
- make their own decisions 자신의 결정을 내리다
- be merged into 합병하다
- a social organism[ɔ́:rgənizəm] 사회적 유기체
- ruling group[gru:p] 통치집단
- directed and controlled 지시 받고 통제 받는
- in order to ~하기 위해
- welfare[wélfɛə:r] 안녕, 복지
- subordinate[səbɔ́:rdənit] ~종속되다
- the state 국가
- conflict[kánflikt/ kɔ́n-] 갈등
- by no means 결코 ~이 아니다
- peculiar[pikjú:ljər] to ~에 특이한, 고유한
- assumed[əsjú:md] ~인 체 하다
- assert[əsə́:rt] 주장하다
- belongs to~에 속하다
- institution[ìnstətjú:ʃən] 제도
- primitive men 원시인들
- tightly-knit[nit] 꽉 짜여진
- tribal[tráibəl] 부족의
- sense 의식
- attitude[ǽtitjù:d] 태도, 자세
- survival[sərváivəl] 생존의
- cope with ~에 대처하다
- obstacles[ábstəkəl/ ɔ́b-] 장애물
- hold one's own against[əgénst, əgéinst] ~ 굴하지 않다, 물러서지 않다
- cease[si:s] 그치다, 그만두다

Sentence Pattern Analysis

- Should all individuals be free, as far as possible, to formulate and express their own beliefs and make their own decisions, or should they be merged into a social organism directed and controlled by some kind of ruling group?
  - 모든 개인은 자신들의 믿음을 공식화하고 표현하고 자신의 결정을 하는데 가능한 최대한 자유로워야 하는가 아니면 어떤 종류의 통치 집단으로부터 지시 받고 통제 받는 사회의 유기적 조직체에 합병되어야 하는가?

- Does government exist in order to protect the rights and welfare of individuals, or should individuals be wholly subordinated to the state?
  - 정부는 개인들의 권리와 행복을 보호하기 위해서 존재하는가 아니면 개인들이 전적으로 국가에 존속되어야 하는가?

- This conflict between the open and the closed society is by no means peculiar to the twentieth century, though it has now assumed new and more intense forms.
  - 열린 사회와 폐쇄된 사회 사이에서 벌어지는 이런 갈등은, 그것이 이제 새롭고 더 강력한 형식인체 가장하더라도, 결코 20세기에만 있는 특유한 것은 아니다.

- Believers in a closed society assert that the future belongs to them: but in actuality this is not a new institution but a very old one.
  - 패쇄된 사회 신봉자들은 미래가 자신들에게 알맞다고 주장하지만, 실제로 이것은 새로운 제도가 아니라 매우 오래된 제도이다. this is not ~ but a very 구문

- since it was only through the maintenance of unity and the unquestioning obedience of all its members that the tribe could cope with natural obstacles and hold its own against its enemies.
  - it~ that의 강조 구문, 즉 「그 부족이 자연의 장애물들을 극복하고 자신들의 적에게 굴복하지 않은 것은 그 구성원 모두의 확실한 복종과 지속적인 일치단결을 통할 때 뿐이었다.」

- tribalistic unity gradually ceased to be a necessity of survival and became instead an obstacle to further development.
  - 부족의 일치단결은 점차 생존에 불필요하게 되었으며, 대신에, 더 많은 발전에 장애가 되었다.

Wisdom

No man is a hero to his valet.

제 아무리 영웅이라해도 시종의 눈에는 보통사람이다.

Anne Bigot

Welcome to English Grammar & Reading

제14장. 명사 · 관사 · 대명사

제14장 명사 *Noun* / 관사 *Article* / 대명사 *Pronoun*

A 명사의 종류

명사의 종류에는 보통명사, 집합명사, 물질명사, 고유명사, 추상명사가 있다.

❶ 가산명사(可算名詞, countable noun)

셀 수 있는 명사를 말하며 보통명사와 집합명사가 있다.

(1) 보통명사(普通名詞)
보통명사는 일정한 형태가 있으며, 하나씩 개체화된다.
보통명사는 반드시 관사를 취하거나, 복수형의 형태를 가져야 한다.

1. He ate **an egg** and **some sandwiches** for lunch.
2. I have **four brothers**.
3. **A sweater** is made of wool.

(2) 집합명사(集合名詞)
① 집합명사는 하나 하나의 개체가 구성하는 집합체를 중점으로 볼 때 단수 취급한다.
② 군집명사(群集名詞)는 그 집합체를 구성하는 하나 하나의 개체를 중심으로 보아 복수 취급한다.

1. (a) John has **a large family**. <집합명사: 단수 취급>
   (b) The audience was **a large one**.
2. (a) **His family are** all early risers. <군집명사: 복수 취급>
   (b) **The audience were** all deeply moved.

(3) 집합명사의 분류
1) The police형 군집명사: the를 수반하여 특정한 계층을 의미하며, **복수 취급**한다.
ex. police, clergy(성직자), gentry(신사), aristocracy(귀족), nobility(고귀한 태생),

1. The police are on the murderer's track.

2) **cattle형 군집명사**: 무리를 나타내는 명사로, 관사를 붙이지 않은 상태로 **복수 취급**한다.
ex. people(사람), cattle, livestock, fish

1. **Cattle** feed on grass
2. There are **many people** in the park.

3) **people형 집합명사**:
① 집합의 한계가 명료하며, 집합체가 하나일 때는 **단수 취급**하며,
② 구성원 내지는 개체들에 중점을 둘 때는 **복수 취급**한다.
ex. a people(민족), family(가족)

1. The English are **an** energetic **people**. <민족>
2. There are **many peoples** in the United States. <여러 민족>
3. There are **four people** in the street. <네 사람>

❷ 불가산명사 (不可算名詞, uncountable noun)

물질명사, 고유명사, 추상명사가 있으며, 불가산명사에는 부정관사를 쓸 수 없고 복수형이 없다.

(1) 물질명사

일정한 형태가 없고 부정관사나 복수형을 쓸 수 없으나, much, little, some, any, no, a lot of 등의 수식은 가능하다.

1. We have **a lot of snow** about this time of the year.
2. Bring me **a glass of water**.
   ex. a cup of coffee, a piece of chalk, a slice of bread, a glass of water, a bottle of wine, a sheet of paper
3. **The water** in this well is good to drink. <한정되는 물질명사: the 사용>

(2) 고유명사

1. **John** is a graduate of University of Beijin.
2. **Seoul** is the capital city of Korea.

(3) 추상명사

1. **Health** is better than **wealth**.
2. Peter is interested in Korean **art**.
3. (a) He is a man **of wisdom**. <of + 추상명사 = 형용사구>
   (b) The matter is **of much importance**.
4. (a) He did it **with ease**. <전치사 + 추상명사 = 부사구>
   (b) He spoke English **with fluency**.
5. He is **all kindness**. <all + 추상명사 = 추상명사 + itself = very + 형용사>
   = He is **kindness itself**.
   = He is **very kind**.

B 명사의 전용

a, the, (e)s는 원칙적으로 가산명사에 사용하나, **불가산명사인 물질명사, 고유명사, 추상명사도 보통명사로 전용되면 관사를 붙여 사용한다.**

❶ 물질명사의 보통명사화

종류, 제품, 개체, 구체적인 사건과 같이 하나씩 개체화되어 보통명사와 같은 의미가 된다.

1. They sell various **wines** at that store. <종류>
2. He has **a glass** in his hand. <제품>
3. He threw **a stone** onto the pond. <개체>
4. There broke out **a fire** last night. <구체적인 사건>

❷ 고유명사의 보통명사화

집안 사람, 제품, 작품 등으로 개체화되어 보통명사화 된다.

1. He is **a Kennedy**. <케네디 집안의 한 사람>
2. **The Stuarts** love to help others. <~ 집 사람들>
3. **A newton** cannot be **a Beethoven** <~ 와 같은 사람>
4. He bought **a Ford** yesterday. <제품 · 작품>

❸ 추상명사의 보통명사화

구체적인 행위, 사람, 사건으로 개체화되어 보통명사화 된다.

1. He showed me many **kindness**. <행위>
2. (a) He is **a success** as a scholar. <사람>
   (b) He was **a failure** as a novelist.
3. The concert was **a great success**. <사건>

❹ the + 단수보통명사 = 추상명사

1. **The pen** is mightier than **the sword**.
   (문(文)은 무(武)보다 강하다.)
2. Both **the mother** and **the father** are necessary to the sound education of children.
   (모성애와 부성애는 두 가지 모두 자녀의 건전한 교육에 필요하다.)

❺ the + 형용사(분사)

1. **The young** should respect **the old**. <the + 형용사 = 복수보통명사>
2. **The beautiful** is higher than **the true**. <the + 형용사 = 추상명사>

C 명사의 수(數)

❶ 복수형 만들기

(1) 규칙변화

1. 단수형에 -S를 붙이고, 「유성음 + S」는 [z]로, 「무성음 + S」는 [s]로 발음한다.
   ex. jobs[z], beds[z], dogs[z], boys[z], caps[s], books[s]

2. 어미가 [s], [z], [ʃ], [tʃ]로 발음될 때, es를 붙이고 [iz]로 발음한다.
   ex. buses[iz], breezes[iz], boxes[iz], dishes[iz], benches[iz]

3. 「자음 + y」일 경우 -ies로 고친다.
   ex. families, countries, ladies, cities, babies

4.「모음 + y」인 경우 -s를 붙인다.
ex. boys, keys

5. 어미가「자음 + o」인 경우 es를 붙인다.
ex. potatoes, heroes, volcanoes, Negroes

6. f, fe로 끝나는 경우 ves를 붙인다.
ex. wolves, leaves, halves, wives

(2) 불규칙변화

1. 모음변화
ex. foot - feet, man - men, woman - women, mouse - mice, tooth - teeth, goose - geese

2. 어미변화
ex. ox - oxen, child - children, brother - brethren(동포)

3. 단 · 복수 동형(同形)
ex. sheep(양), deer(사슴), salmon(연어), trout(송어), series(연속물), Japanese, species(종)

4. 외래어
(a) um - a : datum(data)
(b) us - i : stimulus (stimuli), focus (foci)
(c) a - ae : antenna(antennae, antennas), formula(formulae, formulas)
(d) is - es : crisis(crises), synthesis(syntheses)
(e) on - a : phenomenon(phenomena, phenomenons)
(f) eau - eaux : bureau(bureaux, bureaus)

5. 복합명사의 복수형
ex. fathers-in-law(장인, 시아버지), lookers-on(구경꾼), passers-by(통행인), men-servants(남자 하인), forget-me-nots(물망초)

❷ 복수형 용법

1. 상호복수
   ex. make friends with, exchange seats, change planes, be on good terms with

2. 상시복수
   ex. gloves(장갑), glasses(안경), spectacles(안경), shoes(신발)

3. 학과명: 형태는 복수형이지만 단수취급
   ex. mathematics(수학), economics(경제학), politics(정치학), physics(물리학), statistics(통계학)

D 관사(冠詞)

① 부정관사 a는 문장에서 처음 출현하는 가산명사의 단수형에 사용하고,
② 정관사 the는 문맥상 특정하게 한정될 때 사용한다.

• Once there was **an** old man, and **the** old man had three sons.

❶ 부정관사(不定冠詞, indefinite article)

Grammar Tip 약간의 하마와 같은 어종

1. 약간의(some) : for **a** time, at **a** distance
2. 하나의(one) : Rome was not built in **a** day.
3. 마다(per) : I water the flowers once **a** day.
4. 같은(the same) : John and I are of **an** age.
5. 어떤(a certain) : **A** Mr. Park was looking for you.
6. 종족 대표(any) : **A** dog[The dog] is a faithful animal.
   = Dogs are faithful animals.

❷ 정관사(定冠詞, definite article)

(1) 정관사의 기본용법

1. 앞에서 언급된 명사 앞 : I bought a book, and **the** book was interesting.
2. 서로 알고 있는 경우 : Open **the** door (of the room).
3. 유일무이한 것 : **the** sun, **the** moon, **the** world, **the** Bible
4. 최상급 앞 : Autumn is **the** best season for reading books.
5. 한정되는 명사 앞 : **the** water in this well, **the** milk in this bottle
6. 종족 대표 : **The** dog is a faithful animal.

(2) 정관사의 관용용법

Grammar Tip 강산악 육해공군 공공건물 나라말 시수단신

1. 강, 바다, 대양 앞 : **the** Han river, **the** Yellow sea, **the** Atlantic
2. 산맥 앞 : **the** Alps, **the** Rockies(cf, Mt. Everest, Mt. Baekdu)
3. 악기이름 앞 : He is playing **the** piano.
4. 육로, 기차이름 앞 : **the** Saemaeul, **the** Gyeongbu line, **the** Honam line
5. 해, 배이름 앞 : **the** Mayflower, **the** Titanic
6. 공, 비행기 : **the** Arrow
7. 군도 : **the** Philippines, **the** West indies
8. 공공건물 : **the** White house, **the** Ministry of Education
9. 나라말 : **the** Korean language, **the** English language
10. 시간 : He is hired by **the** day.
11. 수량 : They sell salt by **the** pound.
12. 단위 : Students board by **the** month.
13. 신문 : **the** Dong-A Ilbo, **the** New York times
14. 신체의 일부분 앞 : He took me by **the** hand.

❸ 관사의 생략과 위치

(1) 무관사

the는 명사를 한정하는 기능을 가지고 있는데, 문맥에서 그 한정이 이루어져 관사가 생략되는 경우도 있다.

1. 호격 : Waiter, bring me a cup of coffee.
2. 신분 : President Bush, Minister Kim
3. 질병 : He died of lung cancer.
4. 식사 : Let's have dinner.
5. 운동 : He plays tennis every Sunday.
6. 교통수단 : He went there by train.
7. 공공건물의 본래 추상적 목적
   (a) School begins at eight o'clock.
   (b) He goes to church every Sunday.

(2) 관사의 위치

1. so[as, too how, how(ever)] + 형 + 부정관사 + 명사 : He is **so good a boy**.
2. such[many, what, quite, rather, what(ever)] + 부정관 + 형 + 명사
   : He is **such a good boy**.
3. all[both, half, double] + the + 명사 : **All the boys** were present.

E 대명사(代名詞)

❶ 인칭대명사(人稱代名詞)

(1) 인칭대명사

1. **We** had much snow last year. 〈주격〉
2. **You** should not speak ill of others.
3. We will keep this matter between **you** and **me**. 〈목적격〉
   (비밀로 해두자)

(2) 재귀대명사(再歸代名詞)

대명사(소유격, 목적격)에 self를 첨가한 형태를 재귀대명사라 하며,
(A)강조용법 (B)재귀적 용법 (C)전치사 + 재귀대명사의 관용표현이 있다.

(A) 강조적 용법

명사, 대명사와 동격으로 그 명사, 대명사를 강조한다.

1. **He himself** did it.
2. **I** did it **myself**.
3. **You** must take care of it **yourself**.
4. **The mayor himself** got a brilliant idea.

(B) 재귀적 용법
재귀대명사가 타동사의 목적어로 쓰이는 경우로, 주어의 동작이 다시 주어에게 미친다.

1. He killed **himself** by taking poison.
2. He overslept **himself**.
3. He absented **himself** from school.
4. She prides **herself** on her skill in cooking.
5. He overworked **himself** last night.
6. Please seat **yourself** in a chair.
7. He indulged **himself** in gambling.

(C) 전치사 + 재귀대명사
1. **for oneself** = without other's help : 자기 힘으로
2. **by oneself** = alone : 홀로
3. **of oneself** = automatically = spontaneously : 저절로
4. **in itself** = naturally = by nature : 본래
5. **beside oneself** = insane : 제정신이 아닌
6. **in spite of oneself** = unconsciously : 무의식중에
7. **between ourselves** = in confidence : 우리끼리 얘기지만

(3) 소유대명사(所有代名詞)
1. **A friend of mine** passed the examination.
2. Peter is **a friend of his.**

※ 이중 소유격의 어순: 아래에 나열한 어휘와 소유격은 나란히 사용할 수 없다.
my a friend (×)
a friend of mine (◯)
a[the, this, that, some, any, no, such, what, another] + 명사 +of + 소유대명사

❷ 지시대명사(指示代名詞)

(1) it용법

1. He gave me a watch, but I have lost it. 〈앞에 나온 어구〉
2. It is ten miles to Boston. 〈비인칭 'it' : 거리〉
3. It is spring now. 〈비인칭 'it' : 계절〉
4. It is all over with him. 〈비인칭 'it' : 막연한 상황〉
5. It is important to study English hard. 〈가주어〉
6. I made it a rule to get up early in the morning. 〈가목적어〉
7. It was I that met her there yesterday. 〈It ~ that 강조구문〉

(2) this와 that

1. I want to tell you **this**: we have no time to lose. 〈뒤 문장 지시〉
2. He kept silence, and **this**[=**that**] made her all the more angry. 〈앞 문장 지시〉
3. Health is above wealth, for **this** cannot give so much happiness as **that**.
   〈that = the former(전자), this = the latter(후자)〉
4. What do you think of **this** plan? 〈형용사〉
5. I have learned **that** much. 〈부사〉
6. The climate here is like **that** of Italy. 〈한정된 명사의 반복〉

(3) such

1. I may have offended him, but **such** was not my intention. 〈지시대명사〉
2. He is a child and must be treated as **such**. 〈반복의 대명사〉
3. His behavior was **such** that everyone disliked him.
4. Autumn gives us **such** fruits **as** apples, pears and persimmons. 〈지시형용사〉
   = Autumn gives us fruits **such as** apples, pears and persimmons.
5. He is **such** an honest man **as** everyone trusts. 〈as는 유사관계대명사〉

(4) so

1. A: He is rich. B: **So** he is. : So + S + V (예, 그는 부자다.)
   B: **So** is she. : So + V + S (그녀도 역시 부자다.)

2. A: He is not rich. B: **Neither** is she. : Neither + V + S (그녀 역시 부자가 아니다.)

3. He is not rich, **nor** is she.
   =He is not rich, and neither is she. <nor는 접속사, neither는 부사>

(5) the same

1. This is **the same** watch **as** I gave her. <동일 종류>
2. This is **the same** watch **that** I lost. <동일물>

❸ 부정대명사(不定代名詞, Indefinite Pronoun)

(1) one

1. I lost my umbrella, so I want to buy **one(= an umbrella)**. <a+명사>
   cf. I had lost umbrella, and I found **it** yesterday(= **the umbrella**).
2. One should keep one's promise. <일반인>
3. I have three dogs; a black one, and two white ones. <명사의 반복을 피해서>
4. I received a letter from one Mr. Peter. <one = a certain>
5. **one을 쓸 수 없는 경우**
   (a) 불가산명사를 대신할 수 없다.
   I like red wine better than white.
   (b) 소유격 다음
   My watch is smaller than Peter's
   (c) 기수 다음
   He has three cars and I have two.
   (d) 비교급과 최상급 다음에 of로 한정될 때
   Jane is taller of the two.

(2) one과 another

1. one, the other <둘 중에서 하나는 , 나머지 하나는>
   I have two dogs; **one** is white and **the other** black.
2. the one, the other <전자, 후자>
   I have a brother and a sister; **the one** is a doctor and **the other** a teacher.

3. one, the others[= the rest] <하나는, 나머지 전체는>

He has five sons; **one** is in London and **the others** in Boston.

4. some, others, others <일부는 , 일부는 , 일부는 >

Some were dressed in blue, **others** yellow, **others** red.

5. some, the others[= the rest] <일부는 , 나머지 전체는 >

Some of them like it; **the others** do not.

6. one, another [=a second], a third, ··· , the other <하나씩 열거할 때>

She has five hats; **one** is red, **a second** blue,··· , **the fifth**[**the other**] white.

7. another의 일반적 용법

(a) one more의 의미

He will return in **another** week.

Give me **another** cup of coffee.

(b) different의 의미

To know is one thing and to teach is **another**.

(c) also의 의미

If he is a fool, you are **another**.

(3) all

1. **All** men are mortal. <형용사>
2. He did it **all** by myself. <부사>
3. **All** is not gold that glitters. <대명사>

(4) each와 every

1. **Each** book **has** a different color. <each + 단수명사 + 단수동사>
2. **Every** book **has** an author. <every + 단수명사 + 단수동사>
3. He sends an e-mail to her **every three days**[=**every third day** (3일에 한번씩)].

<every + 기수 + 복수명사 = every + 서수 + 단수명사 : ~ 마다 한번씩>

(5) both, neither, either

1. **Both** restaurants are very good.
2. **Both** of them failed in the exam.
3. **Neither** answer is correct. <둘 다 아니다>

4. **Neither** of his parents is living.
5. Do you know **either** of the two sisters? <둘 중의 하나>
6. Do you know **any** of the sisters? <셋 이상 중의 하나>
7. If you do not go, I will **not**, **either**. <부정문에서 too를 쓰지 않고, either를 쓴다>

(6) some과 any

some은 긍정문에서 쓰고, any는 부정문과 의문문에서 쓰는 것이 원칙이나, 3의 문장에서처럼 some이 '권유'의 뜻을 가질 때 의문문에서 사용되고, 6의 문장에서처럼 any가 '모든'의 뜻을 가질 때 긍정문에서 사용된다.

1. **Some** of the novels are interesting. <긍정문>
2. Ask **some** boys to help us. <긍정문>
3. Will you have **some** more coffee? <'권유'의 의미>
4. I don't have **any** money <부정문>
5. Do you have **any** sugar? <의문문>
6. **Any** child can do such a thing. <'모든'의 의미>

❹ 의문대명사

1. **Who** is your best friend?
2. **What** is he?
3. **Which** do you like better: tea or coffee? <선택적 의미: Which>
4. Do you know **what he is**? <간접의문 = 의문사 + 주어 +동사>
5. I don't know **what he is**.
6. **What** do you think **he is**? <주관적인 답을 원하는 동사>

4번 문장에서 의문문이 종속절이 되면 「의문사 + 주어 + 동사」의 평서문 어순이 된다. 6번 문장의 경우 주절의 동사에 guess, imagine, believe, suppose, think 등의 주관적인 대답을 원하는 동사가 오면, 의문사는 문두로 나간다.

Basic Reading 14

1 If you are ready to learn, all the world is your teacher. Even from a piece of wood, a cloud in the sky, a bird in a tree, or a little baby, you can learn something. **A piece of advice** from a younger boy, or a line in a book may help you to be a good and wise man.

- be ready to ~ ~할 준비가 되어 있다.
- Even from (a piece of wood, a cloud in the sky, a bird in a tree, or a little baby)

2 Knowing another language offers many advantages. It's a window into another culture, since **how a society thinks and views the world** is expressed through its language. To know another language provides different ways of dealing with problems common to us all. Furthermore, since it's common nowadays to have foreign partners, whether you know another language or not makes a difference in the business world. Finally, understanding a different language enables you to look at your own culture from a fresh point of view.

- offer[ɔ́(:)fər, ɑ́f-] v. 제공하다, 제출하다
- advantage[ædvǽntidʒ, əd-] n. 장점
- provide[prəváid] v. 공급하다, 제공하다
- deal with 다루다, 취급하다
- furthermore[fə́:rðərmɔ̀:r] ad. 더욱이, 게다가
- enable 목적어 + to 부정사; enables you to look at ~

3 Certain bacteria in the wrong areas of your body would do you harm. However, many **bacteria are** important to your life. But for the bacteria that help break down the food in your body, you would be in big trouble. In fact, if you could somehow rid your body of all its bacteria, you would probably starve to death because you could not digest your food.

- bacterium(단수) – bacteria(복수)
- do A harm : A에게 해를 끼치다
- rid A of B : A에게서 B를 제거하다
- starve to death 굶주려 죽다

4 Maybe the cheapest way of understanding the United States is travelling in a bus. The Greyhound buses go across the country and **all the big cities** of the United States. The buses travel both days and nights with drivers changing at the various stops. This way of traveling will give you the chance to discover real America and to meet interesting people.

- Greyhound bus 미국의 장거리 버스
- go across 횡단하다
- with drivers changing at the various stops : with + O + OC의 구조이다.
- the chance to discover ~ and to meet ~
  - A and B의 등위접속사 형태에서 A와 B의 성격이 같아야 한다.

5 As a matter of fact, every book worth reading ought to be read in precisely the same way that a scientific book is read — not simply for amusement; and every book worth reading should have **the same** amount of value in it **that** a scientific book has, though the value may be **of a totally different kind**.

- every book (that is) worth reading 읽을 가치가 있는 모든 책
- precisely[prisáisli] ad. 정확히
- amusement[əmjú:zmənt] n. 즐거움, 오락
- amount[əmáunt] n. 양
- of totally different kind : of + 명사 = 형용사구, 전혀 다른 종류인

6 The two coins looked so alike that it was difficult to tell **one** from **the other**.

- so ~ that 너무 ~해서 ~하다
- alike[əláik] a. 서로 같은
- tell A from B : A를 B와 구분하다

7 To know is **one thing**, to act is **another**. Many people know that it is good for the health to keep early hours, but very few put it into practice.

- keep early hours 일찍 자고 일찍 일어나다
- very few 아주 소수의 사람들
- put(bring) it into practice 실행하다

8 If you find **yourself** bored by a book that well-informed people regard as important and readable, be honest with **yourself** and confess that probably the difficulty is **not** in the book **but** in you. Often a book which now seems dull or difficult will prove easy to grasp and fascinating to read when you are more mature intellectually.

- a book that well-informed people regard as ~
  - that은 regard의 목적격 관계대명사, 많이 배운 사람들이 중요하고 읽을만하다고 여기는 책
- (prove) fascinating to read 읽기에 흥미진진한 것으로 판명되다
- be bored by ~에 싫증나다
- well-informed people 박식한 사람들
- confess[kənfés] v. 고백하다, 실토하다
- grasp[græsp] v. 이해하다, 포착하다
- fascinating[fǽsənèitiŋ] a. 매혹적인
- mature[mətjúə:r] a. 성숙한
- intellectually[intəléktʃuəli] ad. 지적으로

9 **No** book will teach you how to write. **No** amount of reading will teach you how to write. Reading is essential, and a practical book can help; but **unless** you have the gem of the writer in you, the unbreakable will to write, you will get nowhere. What is more, if you are to make a success of writing, you will have to work.

- the gem of the writer 작가로서의 싹, 소질
- gem[dʒem] n. 보석, 꽃봉오리
- what is more = moreover 더군다나, 게다가
- the unbreakable will to write 글을 쓰려는 막을 수 없는 의지

10 Washington was **discretion itself** in the use of speech, never taking advantage of an opponent, or seeking a short lived triumph in a debate.

- discretion[diskréʃən] n. 분별, 신중
- take advantage of = utilize 이용하다
- triumph[tráiəmf] n. 승리
- debate[dibéit] n. 논쟁

11 The methodology of social science is inevitably different from **that of natural science**. It is different and must be different for one basic reason — the investigator is inside instead of outside his material. Man cannot investigate man by the same methods by which he investigates external nature.

- methodology[mèθədálədʒi] n. 방법론
- inevitably[inévitəbli] ad. 필연적으로
- natural science 자연과학
- investigate[invéstəgèit] 연구하다
- the investigator is inside instead of outside his material
  조사원은 그가 다루는 자료가 외부가 아닌 내부에 있다

Advanced Reading 27

A. Preparing to Read

They told that the disintegration of the Soviet Union **deprived** western intelligence agencies **of** their main enemies today.

Optimism was gradually **taking the place of** pessimism in the world.

Professor Youn told a disastrous world trade war must be avoided **at all costs**.

B. Approaching to the Topic

A college is a community, and a community consists of people who are bound together by personal ties. The relation between teacher and student is personal relation. There must be a mutual interest, a mutual helpfulness. No mechanical device can take the place of this personal connection. No TV screen can respond to your responses, or share your joys and sorrows, or chat with you over a coke or coffee in the Commodore Room. To mechanize education, to depersonalize it, is to deprive it of its most precious ingredient. Let us cherish this personal element at all costs. Vanderbilt, fortunately, is not too big for us to know one another, and take an interest in one another. Vanderbilt is not too big for us to be friends.

What are We at College for? by Randall Stewart

Vocabularies & Expressions for Comprehension

- community[kəmjúːnəti] 공동체
- consists of ~로 구성되다
- bound ~에 묶여 있는
- personal ties 개인적인 유대
- relation[riléiʃən] 관계

- mutual[mjúːtʃuəl] interest[íntərist] 상호관심
- mutual helpfulness[hélpfəlnis] 상호도움
- mechanical[məkǽnikəl] device[diváis] 기계적 장치
- take the place of ~을 대신하다
- respond to ~에 반응하다
- share[ʃɛəːr] 공유하다
- chat with ~와 이야기하다
- Commodore[kámədɔːr] Room 대학 휴게실
- depersonalize[diːpə́ːrsənəlàiz] 비인간화하다
- deprive ~ of ~ 에서 ~을 박탈하다
- precious ingredient[ingríːdiənt] 귀중한 구성요소
- cherish[tʃériʃ] 소중하게 하다
- at all costs 어떤 대가를 치르더라도

Sentence Pattern Analysis

- a community consists of people who are bound together by personal ties.

  개인적인 유대로 묶여진 사람들로 구성된 공동체

- To mechanize education, to depersonalize it, is to deprive it of its most precious ingredient.

  「교육을 기계화 하는 것, 교육을 비인간화하는 것은 교육의 가장 귀중한 요소를 박탈해버리는 것이다.」 물론 it가 가리키는 것은 education이다.

Wisdom

People ask you for criticism, but they only want praise.

사람들이 비평을 요청하지만 칭찬만을 원하는 것이다.

Somerset Maugham: Of Human Bondage

Advanced Reading 28

A. Preparing to Read

If she had studied at all, she wouldn't have failed.

The big news was quickly **passed on from mouth to mouth**.

Without water, there could not exist any living thing.

B. Approaching to the Topic

Language is so much a part of our daily activities that some of us may come to look upon it as a more or less automatic and natural act like breathing or winking. Of course, if we give the matter any thought at all, we must realize that there is nothing automatic about language. Children must be taught their native tongue and the necessary training takes a long time. Laguage is not something that is inherited; it is art that can be passed on from one generation to the next only by intensive education.

It is difficult to realize the enormously important role that language plays in our social behavior. What would a society without language be like? It would, of course, have no writing or other means of communication by words, for all these are ultimately dependent on spoken speech. Our means of learning would therefore be greatly restricted. We should be obliged, like the animals, to learn by doing or by observing the actions of others. All of history would vanish, for without language there would be no way of re-creating past experiences and communicating them to others.

Laguage and Culture by Harry Hoijer

Vocabularies & Expressions for Comprehension

- is so much a part of our daily activities that ~ 우리의 일상적인 활동 가운데서 많은 부분을 차지하고 있기 때문에. so ~ that 구문으로 이해
- come~ ~하게 되다
- look upon A as B : A를 B로 간주하다
- more or less 다소
- automatic and natural 자동적이고 자연발생적인
- breathing[brí:ðiŋ] and winking 호흡하거나 눈을 깜박거리기
- realize[rí:əlàiz] 깨닫다
- native tongue[tʌŋ] 모국어
- take a long time 오랜 시간이 걸리다
- inherited[inhéritid] 유전되는, 선천적으로 물려받은
- art 기술
- pass 전해지다
- generation[dʒènəreiʃən] 세대
- intensive[inténsiv] 집중적인
- enormously[inɔ́:rməsli] 엄청나게
- play an important role in ~에서 중요한 역할을 하다
- social behavior[bihéivjər] 사회활동
- what would ~ like? ~이 어떤 모습을 할 것인가?
- means of communication[kəmjù:nəkéiʃən] 의사소통의 수단
- ultimately[ʌ́ltəmitli] 궁극적으로
- dependent on spoken speech 구어에 의존하는
- means of learning 학문의 수단
- be restricted[ristriktid] 한정되다
- should be obliged to ~ ~하지 않을 수 없을 것이다
- observe[əbzə́:rv] 관찰하다
- vanish[vǽniʃ] 사라지다
- without language[lǽŋgwidʒ] 언어가 없다면
- re-creat 재창조하다
- communicate[kəmjú:nəkèit] 전달하다

Sentence Pattern Analysis

- Language is so much a part of our daily activities that some of us may come to look upon it as a more or less automatic and natural act like breathing or winking.
  - 언어가 우리들의 일상생활 가운데 많은 부분을 차지하고 있기 때문에 일부 사람들은 호흡이나 눈 깜박거림과 같이 다소 자동적이며 자연발생적인 행위로서 언어를 간주하게 된다. so ~ that 구문

- if we give the matter any thought at all
  - 우리가 그 문제를 조금만 생각해 본다면

- What would a society without language be like?
  - 언어가 없다면 사회는 어떤 모습일까?

- We should be obliged, like the animals, to learn by doing or by observing the actions of others.
  - 우리는 동물처럼 다른 사람들의 행위를 하거나 관찰함으로써 배워야만 할 것이다.

- for without language there would be no way of re-creating past experiences and communicating them to others.
  - 언어가 없다면 과거의 경험을 재창조하여 그것을 다른 사람들에게 전달할 수 있는 길이 없을 것이기 때문이다.

Wisdom

Pride goes before destruction, a haughty spirit before a fall.

교만은 패망의 선봉이요, 거만한 마음은 넘어짐의 앞잡이다.

Proverb 16: 18

제15장. 특수구문

- A 강조를 위한 도치(倒置)
- B 문법상 도치
- C 강조구문
- D 동격(同格)
- E 생략(省略), 삽입(揷入)
- F 무생물 주어

제15장 특수구문 *Miscellany*

A 강조를 위한 도치(倒置)

❶ 부정어

1. **Never have** I seen such a beautiful fish.
2. **Little did** I dream that I would never see him.
3. **Not until** we lose our health **do** we realize its value.
   = We do **not** realize the value of health **until** we lose it.

❷ 부사구

1. **On the top of the hill stood** an old castle.
2. **Well do** I remember the scene.
3. **Here** comes **the bus**. <부사 +자동사 +명사 주어>
4. **Here he** comes. <부사 +대명사 주어+ 자동사>

❸ 보어

1. **Great was** her delight when she heard the news.

B 문법상 도치

❶ So + V + S, So + S + V

A: I'm hungry.
B: So am I. <주어가 다를 때: So + V + S >

A: I'm rich.
B: So you are. <주어가 같을 때: So + S + V>

❷ Neither + V + S

A: He doesn't like coffee.
B: Neither[Nor] do I.

C 강조구문

1. It was **she** that(who) met him at the park yesterday. 〈It is ~ that 강조〉
   = It was **him** that(whom) she met at the park yesterday.
   = It was **at the park** that(where)she met him yesterday.
   = It was **yesterday** that(when) she met him at the park.
2. It was **while I was in America** that I first went to a drive-in restaurant.
3. I **do want** to see her. 〈동사 강조〉
4. This is **the very book** that I have been looking for. 〈명사 강조〉
5. What **on earth(in the world)** are you doing? 〈의문문 강조〉

D 동격(同格)

1. Do you know **Mr. Bush, President of the United States of America**?
2. I cannot bear **the idea of parting from her**.
3. You must not forget **the fact that your father is no longer young**.

E 생략(省略), 삽입(插入)

1. When (**he was**) a boy, he used to swim in the river.
2. Jane went to Greece and Alice (**went**) to Rome.
3. To some life is pleasure, to others (**life is**) suffering.
4. The weather isn't as good as (**it was**) last year.
5. He is, **so to speak**, a walking dictionary.
6. Jack was, **I thought**, very impatient at that time.
7. The castle, **burnt down in 1948**, was never rebuilt.
8. His idea, **it seems to me**, is the best.

F 무생물(無生物) 주어

1. **The heavy rain** prevented them from going out.
   = They could not go out because of the heavy rain.

2. **A thunderstorm** kept the plane from taking off.
   = The plane could not take off because of a thunderstorm.

3. **This medicine** will make you feel better.
   = If you take this medicine, you will feel better.

4. **No amount of wealth** would satisfy Mr. Kim.
   = Even if Mr. Kim had a large amount of wealth, he would not be satisfied.

5. **The next morning** found him sleeping on the bench in the park.
   = He was sleeping on the bench in the park the next morning.

Basic Reading 15

1 Public issues are large and so involved that **it is** only a few **who** can hope to have any adequate comprehension of them.

- public[pʌ́vlik] a. 공공의, 공중의
- issue[íʃuː] n. 문제점, 발행물
- involved[inválvd] a. 복잡한, 뒤얽힌
- only a few = few
- adequate[ǽdikwit] a. 알맞은 적절한
- comprehension[kámprihènʃən] n. 이해력(understanding), 포함(inclusion)

2 He is generally reserved, but if he does talk, he always talks to the point.

- reserved[rizəːrvd] a. 사양하는, 삼가는, 예약한
- to the point 적절한, 딱 들어맞는

3 To write or even to speak English is not a science but an art. There are no reliable rules: there is **only general principle that** concrete words are better than abstract ones, and **that** the shortest way of saying anything is always the best. Mere correctness is no guarantee whatever of good writing.

- reliable[riláiəbəl] a. 믿음직한
- general[dʒénərəl] a. 일반의, 대체적인
- concrete[kánkriːt] a. 구체적인
- mere[miər] a. 단지
- guarantee[gæ̀rəntíː] n. vt. 보증(warrant), 보증하다(affirm)
- no + 명사 + whatever : [부정구문] 약간의 ~ 도

4 I am looked upon as a wealthy person, and **so I am**. I am able to give you every chance to grow wise and good, but I am not, and never shall be, rich enough to have you idle.

- look upon A as B : A를 B로 간주하다
- wealthy[wélθi] a. 부유한, 풍부한
- have you idle 너를 빈둥거리게 내버려두다

5 The hearty handshake, did not in the beginning show friendship but distrust. **Nor did** the customary use of the right hand originate by chance. It was precaution to immobilize the other man's weapon hand.

- hearty[há:rti] a. 마음에서 우러난
- nor 접속사(= and not either)
  cf. neither(= not either) 부사
- Nor did the customary use of the right hand originate by chance.
  = And the customary use of the right hand did not originate by chance, either
- originate[ərídʒənèit] v. 시작하다, 비롯하다
- by chance 우연히
- precaution[prikɔ́:ʃən] n. 조심, 경계, 예방 조치
- immobilize[imóubəlàiz] v. 고정시키다
- weapon[wépən] n. 무기

6 Galileo carried on the construction of telescopes, and all the time he improved their quality and enlarged their power until he built one that magnified thirty times. **What the diameter of the object glass was we do not know**, perhaps two inches or a little more. Whatever its size, the telescope must have seemed like a magician's tool to the people of the time.

- carry on 진행시키다, 운반하다, 지탱하다
- construction[kənstrʌ́kʃən] n. 건조, 건설, 구조
- telescope[téləskòup] n. 망원경
- all the time 그 동안 줄곧
- improve[imprúːv] v. 개선하다
- quality[kwáləti/ kwɔ́l-] n. 질, 특성
- enlarge[enláːrdʒ] v. 크게 하다
- one = a telescope
- magnify[mǽgnəfài] v. 확대하다
- diameter[daiǽmitər] n. 직경
- object glass 대물(對物) 렌즈
- whatever its size (was)
- must have pp ~했음에 틀림없다
- magician[mədʒíʃən] n. 마술사
- the time 당시

7 Advice is like snow in winter: the softer it falls, the longer it stays **upon**, and the deeper it sinks **into**, **the mind**.

- fall[fɔːl] v. 떨어지다
- the longer it stays upon (the mind), and the deeper it sinks into, the mind

8 A sound education does not mean that someone leaves school with his head filled with facts and theories. Education does mean **development**, not only **of the brain**, but **of the whole body**.

- sound[saund] a. 건전한
- leave school 졸업하다
- not only (development) of the brain, but (development) of the whole body
- whole[houl] a. 전체의

9 To some life is pleasure, **to others suffering**. But obedience to duty, at all costs and risks, is the very essence of the highest civilized life.

- some ~ others ~ 일부에게는 ~하고, 나머지에게는 ~ 하다
- to others (life is) suffering
- suffering[sʌ́fəriŋ] n. 고통
- obedience[oubíːdiəns] n. 복종, 순종
- at all costs = at any cost 어떤 비용이 들더라도
- essence[ésəns] n. 본질, 정수
- civilized[sívəlàizd] a. 문명화된

10 Automation can confer marked benefits on mankind, if properly applied, **there is no doubt**, but it will also raise problem of employment and of social life.

- confer[kənfə́ːr] v. 수여하다, 주다(grant)
- marked[mɑːrkt] a. 현저한, 두드러진
- benefit[bénəfit] n. 이익
- it (it is) properly applied 적절히 적용되면
- apply[əplái] v. 사용하다, (규칙을) 적용하다, (원리를) 응용하다

11 The ideal society would **enable** every man and woman **to make** the best of their inborn abilities.

- ideal society 이상적인 사회, 무생물 주어
- enable A to do ~ 할 수 있게 하다
- make the best of 최대한으로 이용하다
- inborn abilities[ínbɔ́ːrn][əbílətis] 타고난 능력들

12 Yet **experience** tells us that indifference to music is a fairly common characteristic of the great and the good.

- experience[ikspíəriəns] n. 경험
- indifference[indífərəns] n. 무관심
- fairly[fέərli] ad. 상당히, 정말로
- characteristic[kæ̀riktərístik] a. 특징적인
- the great 고귀한 사람들, 높은 사람들
- the good 선한 사람들

Advanced Reading 29

A. Preparing to Read

Neither he **nor** she is in the wrong.

Her doctor allows her **neither** to drink **nor** to smoke.

Not only his parents **but also** his wife is against his plan.

B. Approaching to the Topic

It has long been a fashion to say that the East is 'spiritual' and the West is 'material'. But like many things that are carelessly said, it is not true. The East is neither more nor less spiritual than the West, and the West is neither more nor less materialistic than the East. This may be said of all men alike: they prefer to have food rather than to starve, to have shelter than to be homeless, to be healthy rather than diseased, to live long rather than short lives, to be happy rather than sorrowful.

Then where did this myth about the spiritual East and the material West come from? It has its roots in a sort of truth, and this truth can be stated: people in the East like to enjoy life. They will not work so hard that they have no time for simple pleasure in living, in eating, in sleeping, in playing with their children and in talking with their wives and families. They will not take on two jobs if they can pay their bills with one, for two jobs consume their time and distract their minds. They do not want to think constantly about work. But they are not in the least lazy.

East and West by Pearl Buck

Vocabularies & Expressions for Comprehension

- It has long been a fashion to say that ~라고 말하는 것이 오랫동안 유행이 되어 왔다.
- neither more nor less than ~ 보다 더한 것도 덜한 것도 아니다.
- materialistic[mətiəriəlístik] 물질주의적인
- of all men = about all men
- prefer ~ than··· ~보다 차라리 ···을 택한다
- shelter[ʃéltəːr] 오두막
- diseased 병에 걸린
- lives[laivz] 수명
- to be happy, to have shelter, to be healthy, to live long 등은 모두 they prefer에 걸린다.
- myth 신화
- has its roots in ~ 에 근거를 두고 있다 뿌리를 두고 있다
- have no time for ~ 할 시간적 여유가 없다
- take on 떠맡다
- pay one's bills 청구서를 지불하다 생활비를 지불하다
- consume[kənsúːm] 소비하다
- distract[distrǽkt] 산란하게하다
- constantly[kánstəntli/ kɔ́n-] 한결같이
- not in the least[liːst] 전혀 ~이 아니다

Sentence Pattern Analysis

- It has long been a fashion to say that the East is 'spiritual' and the West is 'material'
  - 동양은 정신적이며 서양은 물질주의적이다고 말하는 것이 오랫동안 유행이 되어왔다.

- The East is neither more nor less spiritual than the West, and the West is neither more nor less materialistic than the East.
  - 동양은 서양보다 더 정신적이지도 않고 덜 정신적이지도 않으며, 서양 역시 동양보다 더 물질주의적이지도 않고 덜 물질주의적이지도 않다.

- they prefer to have food rather than to starve
  - 사람들은 굶주리기보다는 음식 먹기를 더 좋아하는 법이다.

• They will not work so hard that they have no time for simple pleasure in living, in eating, in sleeping,

그들은 생활하고, 먹고, 잠자는 소박한 즐거움을 위한 시간적 여유가 없을 정도로 힘들게 일하려 하지 않을 것이다.

• They will not take on two jobs if they can pay their bills with one, for two jobs consume their time and distract their minds.

그들은 하나의 직업으로 자신들의 생활비를 지불할 수 있다면 두개의 직업을 떠맡지 않으려할 것이다. 두 개의 직업은 그들의 시간을 소진시키고 그들의 마음을 산란하게 하니까.

Wisdom

Above all else, guard your heart, for it is the wellspring of life.

무릇 지킬만한 것 보다 더욱 네 마음을 지키라 생명의 근원이 이에서 남이니라.

Proverb 4:23

Advanced Reading 30

A. Preparing to Read

Returned home from the United Kingdom, she went home to see her parents.

Not knowing what to do, he asked his professor for some advice.

This, **we may say**, is an exceptional example.

B. Approaching to the Topic

Let us first consider what science can do and cannot do — its proper scope and function. The sciences study physical and social phenomena in order to arrive at an accurate picture of them. They try to describe how things behave. They may be concerned with the movement of heavenly bodies, the inner workings of the atom, physiological processes, social movements, or human behavior. What is the utility of scientific knowledge? Francis Bacon answers that question by saying that science gives us power. It enables us to exercise a certain degree of mastery or control over the physical and social phenomena of the world in which we live. Another way of answering the question is to say that science enables us to produce things. Applied by the engineer or the physician, it helps him to build bridges or to restore health. But the same knowledge can also be used, as we know, to destroy things and to maim or kill men. In other words, science gives us power which can be used either constructively or destructively. It provides us with means which may facilitate our pursuit of bad ends as well as good. Science itself is not only morally neutral, that is, indifferent to the value of the ends for which the means are used; it is also totally unable to give any moral direction.

Philosophy in an Age of Science by *Mortimer J. Adler*

Vocabularies & Expressions for Comprehension

- its proper scope[skoup] and function 그것(과학)의 고유한 영역과 기능
- phenomena[finάmənə] 현상
- accurate[ǽkjərit] 정확한
- picture[píktʃər] 정황
- them 물리적이고 사회적인 현상을 가리킴
- be concerned with ~을 다루다 ~과 관련되다
- heavenly[hévənli] 천체
- physiological[fiziəlάdʒikəl] 생리학상의
- utility[ju:tíləti] 효용성
- Francis Bacon(1561-1625) 영국의 경험주의 철학자
- enable ~ to do …~에게 …을 할 수 있게 하다
- exercise[éksərsàiz] 행사하다 발휘하다
- a certain degree of ~어느 정도의
- mastery[mǽstəri] 지배
- control[kəntróul] 통제
- applied by ~에 의해서 응용되면
- maim[meim] 불구가 되게 하다
- constructively[kənstrʌ́ktivli] 건설적으로
- destructively[distrʌ́ktəbəli] 파괴적으로
- Provides ~ with … ~에게 …을 제공하다
- means 수단 (이 경우 단수와 복수가 같음)
- facilitate[fəsílətèit] 촉진하다
- pursuit[pərsú:t] 추구
- neutral[njú:trəl] 중립의
- indifferent to~ 에 무관심한
- totally[tóutəli] 전적으로

Sentence Pattern Analysis

- It enables us to exercise a certain degree of mastery or control over the physical and social phenomena of the world in which we live.

  과학은 우리로 하여금 우리가 살고 있는 세계의 물리적이고 사회적인 현상을 어느 정도 지배

하고 통제하게끔 해준다.

• Applied by the engineer or the physician, it helps him to build bridges or to restore health.

엔지니어나 의사에 의해서 응용되면 과학은 다리를 건설하거나 건강을 회복시키는 것을 돕는다.

• It provides us with means which may facilitate our pursuit of bad ends as well as good.

과학은 선한 목적뿐만 아니라 악한 목적을 추구하는 것을 촉진시킬 수도 있는 수단을 제공한다.

• Science itself is not only morally neutral, that is, indifferent to the value of the ends for which the means are used; it is also totally unable to give any moral direction.

과학 그 자체는 도덕적으로 중립적인데, 즉 수단이 사용되어지는 목적의 가치에는 무관심할 뿐만 아니라 전적으로 어떠한 도덕적 방향도 제공할 수가 없다.

Wisdom

Those who sow in tears will reap with songs of joy. He who goes out weeping, carrying seed to sow, will return with songs of joy, carrying sheaves with him.

눈물을 흘리며 씨를 뿌리는 자는 기쁨으로 거둔다. 울며 씨를 뿌리러 나가는 자는 정령 기쁨으로 그 단을 가지고 돌아온다.

Psalm 126: 5~6

Advanced Reading
for making a full man

Part II

Advanced Reading for making a full man

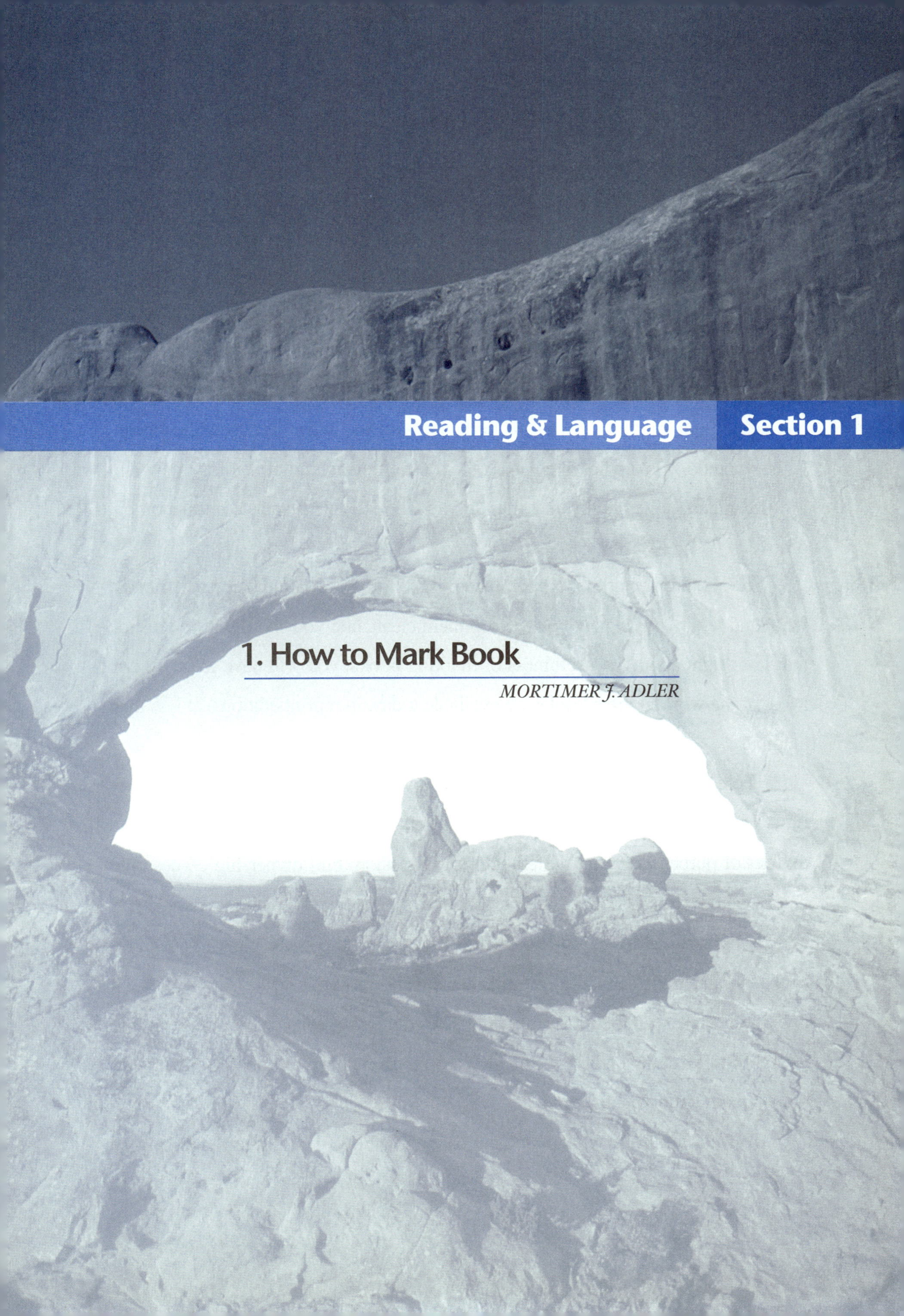

1. How to Mark Book

MORTIMER J. ADLER

1 How to Mark Book

MORTIMER J. ADLER

You know you have to read "between the lines" to get the most important thing out of anything. I want to persuade you to do something equally important in the course of your reading. I want to persuade you to "write between the lines." Unless you do, you are not likely to do the most efficient kind of reading.

I contend, quite bluntly, that marking up a book is not an act of mutilation but of love.

You shouldn't mark up a book which isn't yours. Librarians (or your friends) who lend you books expect you to keep them clean, and you should. If you decide that I am right about the usefulness of marking books, you will have to buy them. Most of the world's great books are available today, in reprint editions, at less than a dollar.

There are two ways in which one can own a book. The first is the property right you establish by paying for it, just as you pay for clothes and furniture. But this act of purchase is only the prelude to possession. Full ownership comes only when you have made it a part of yourself, and the best way to make yourself a part of it is by writing in it. An illustration may make the point clear. You buy a beefsteak and transfer it from the butcher's icebox to your own. But you do not own the beefsteak in the most important sense until you consume it and get it into your blood stream. I am arguing that books, too, must be absorbed in your bloodstream to do you any good.

Confusion about what it means to own a book leads people to a false

Key Words & Phrases 해설

- MORTIMER J. ADLER (1902 ~ 2001) 미국의 철학자, 교육가
- read between the lines 행간을 읽다, 숨은 뜻을 읽어내다.
  ex. If you read between the lines, you understand what someone really means, or what is really happening in a situation, even though it is not said openly.
  행간을 읽어 낸다면, 분명하게 공개적으로 말하지 않더라도 누군가가 정말로 의미하는 것이나 어떤 상황 속에서 실제로 발생하는 것을 안다.
- persuade 설득하다
- write between the lines 행간에 뜻을 넣다, 행간에 숨은 뜻을 써넣다
- contend 주장하다
- quite bluntly 꽤 솔직하게
- marking up a book is not an act of mutilation but of love.
  책에다 표시를 하는 것은 책을 훼손하는 행위가 아니라 책을 사랑하는 행위이다.
  (not ~ but ~ 의 구문)
- librarians 도서관 사서
- and you should 여러분들도 책을 깨끗하게 유지해야 합니다.
  (should 다음에 keep books clean이 생략되어 있음.)
- usefulness 유용성
- Most of the world's great books are available today, in reprint editions, at less than a dollar.
  세계의 위대한 책 중 대부분은 오늘날 재발행판으로 일 달러가 채 안 되는 돈으로 구입할 수 있다.
- The first is the property right you establish by paying for it
  첫 번째 방법은 당신이 책에 돈을 지불하고 갖게 되는 소유권이다.(it = a book)
- act of purchase 구입 행위
- the prelude to possession 소유의 준비(전주곡)
- Full ownership 온전한 소유(권)
- when you have made it a part of yourself

reverence for paper, binding, and type—a respect for the physical thing—the craft of the printer rather than the genius of the author. They forget that it is possible for a man to acquire the idea, to possess the beauty, which a great book contains without staking his claim by pasting his bookplate inside the cover. Having a fine library doesn't prove that its owner has a mind enriched by books, it proves nothing more than that he, his father, or his wife, was rich enough to buy them.

There are three kinds of book owners. The first has all the standard sets and best sellers—unread, untouched. (This deluded individual owns wood pulp and ink, not books.) The second has a great many books—a few of them read through, most of them dipped into, but all of them as clean and shiny as the day they were bought. (This person would probably like to make books his own, but is restrained by a false respect for their physical appearance.) The third has a few books or many—every one of them dog-eared and dilapidated, shaken and loosened by continual use, marked and scribbled in from front to back. (This man owns books.)

Is it false respect, you may ask, to preserve intact and unblemished a beautifully printed book, an elegantly bound edition?

Of course not. I'd no more scribble all over a first edition of *Paradise Lost* than I'd give my baby a set of crayons and an original Rembrandt! I wouldn't mark up a painting or a statue. Its soul, so to speak, is inseparable from its body. And the beauty of a rare edition or of a richly manufactured volume is like that of a painting or a statue.

But the soul of a book can be separated from its body. A book is more like the score of a piece of music than it is like a painting. No great musician confuses a symphony with the printed sheets of music. Arturo Toscanini reveres Brahms, but Toscanini's score of the C-minor Symphony is so thoroughly marked up that no

Key Words & Phrases 해설

당신이 책을 자신의 일부분으로 만들 때

- the best way to make yourself a part of it is by writing in it.
  책을 당신 자신의 일부분으로 만드는 최선의 방법은 책 속에다 글을 써넣는 것이다. (it = book)
- illustration 설명
- a beefsteak 두껍게 저민 쇠고기점 (조각)
- transfer 옮기다
- the butcher's icebox 정육점 냉장고
- your own 당신의 냉장고
- in the most important sense 가장 중요한 의미에서
- until you consume it 당신이 그것을 다 먹기까지는
- books, too, must be absorbed in your bloodstream to do you any good
  책 역시 당신에게 유익하도록 당신의 혈류 속에 흡수되어야만 한다.
- Confusion about what it means to own a book leads people to a false reverence for paper, binding, and type
  책을 소유한다는 것이 무엇을 의미하는가에 대한 혼란 때문에 사람들은 종이와 제본 그리고 타자를 잘못 숭배하게 된다. (lead A to B의 구문)
- the craft of the printer 인쇄업자의 솜씨
- the genius of the author 저자의 천재성
- Having a fine library doesn't prove that its owner has a mind enriched by books
  훌륭한 서재를 갖고 있다고 해서 그 소유자가 책으로 풍요로워진 지성을 가지고 있음을 입증하지는 않는다. (이 문장 ~by book, 다음에 'but'이 생략된 것으로 이해)
- without staking his claim
  그의 권리를 주장하지 않고서도
- by pasting his bookplate inside the cover.
  책 커버 안쪽에다 자신의 장서표를 붙여

one but the maestro himself can read it. The reason why a great conductor makes notations on his musical scores—marks them up again and again each time he returns to study them—is the reason why you should mark your books. If your respect for magnificent binding or typography gets in the way, buy yourself a cheap edition and pay your respects to the author.

Why is marking up a book indispensable to reading? First, it keeps you awake. (and I don't mean merely conscious, I mean wide awake.) In the second place, reading, if it is active, is thinking, and thinking tends to express itself in words, spoken or written. The marked book is usually the thought-through book.

Finally, writing helps you remember the thoughts you had, or the thoughts the author expressed. Let me develop these three points.

If reading is to accomplish anything more than passing time, it must be active. You can't let your eyes glide across the lines of a book and come up with and understanding of what you have read. Now an ordinary piece of light fiction, like, say, *Gone with the wind*, doesn't require the most active kind of reading. The books you read for pleasure can be read in state of relaxation, and nothing is lost. But a great book, rich in ideas and beauty, a book that raises and tries to answer great fundamental questions, demands the most active reading of which you are capable.

If, when you've finished reading a book, the pages are filed with your notes, you know that you read actively. The most famous active reader of great books I know is President Hutchins of the University of Chicago. He also has the hardest schedule of business activities of any man I know. He invariably reads with a pencil, and sometimes, when he picks up a book and pencil in the evening, he finds himself, instead of making intelligent notes, drawing what he calls "caviar

Key Words & Phrases 해설

- nothing more than 단지
- The first has all the standard sets and best sellers—unread, untouched.
  모든 권위 있는 책 세트와 가장 잘 팔리는 책을 읽지 않고 건드리지도 않은 채 가지고 있는 것이 첫 번째 책 소유자의 경우이다.
- delude [dilú:d] 미혹시키다, 속이다, 속이어 ~시키다
  ex. He deluded his wife into belief he is an honest husband.
- a few of them (is) read through, most of them dipped into, but all of them as clean and shiny as the day they were bought.
  그 책 중 몇 권은 통독하고, 그 책 대부분은 띄엄띄엄 대충 읽어서, 그 책 모두는 책을 산 날과 다름없이 깨끗하고 번쩍거린다. (( )속에서와 같이 'is'를 보충하여 이해함.)
- restrain [ristréin] 제지하다, 억제하다
- every one of them (is) dog-eared and dilapidated, shaken and loosened by continual use, marked and scribbled in from front to back.
  그 책 모두는 계속적인 사용으로 책 모서리가 너덜거리고, 남루하고 흔들거리고, 느슨하며, 첫 페이지부터 끝 페이지까지 표시되고 낙서가 되어 있다.
  (괄호 속에서와 같이 is를 보충하여 이해함)
- dog-eared 너무 많이 사용해서 책 페이지의 모서리가 떨어져나가거나 찢어진 상태
  ex. He has many dog-eared copies of ancient history books.
- dilapidated [dilǽpədéitid] 황폐해진, 헐어빠진, 남루한
- Is it false respect, you may ask, to preserve intact and unblemished a beautifully printed book, an elegantly bound edition?
  아름답게 인쇄된 책, 우아하게 제본된 책을 원래대로 흠 없이 보존하는 것이 잘못된 점인가? 라고 당신이 물을 수 있다.
- I'd no more scribble all over a first edition of Paradise Lost than I'd give my baby a set of crayons and an original Rembrandt!
  내가『실락원』의 최초 발행본에다가 온통 휘갈겨 낙서를 하지 않는 것과 마찬가지로 내 아기에게 크레용 세트와 렘브란트의 원본 그림을 주지는 않을 것이다.
  no more ~ than ~의 구문(= not ~ any more than ~)
  ~이 아님은 ~이 그렇지 않음 과 같다, ~이 아닌것과 마찬가지로 ~이 아니다

factories" on the margins. When that happens, he puts the book down. He knows he's too tired to read, and he's just wasting time.

But, you may ask, why is writing necessary? Well, the physical act of writing, with your own hand, brings words and sentences more sharply before your mind and preserves them better in your memory. To set down your reaction to important words and sentences you have read, and the questions they have in your mind, is to preserve those reactions and sharpen those questions.

Even if you wrote on a scratch pad, and threw the paper away when you had finished writing, your grasp of the book would be surer. But you don't have to throw the paper away. The margins (top and bottom, as well as side), the end papers, the very space between the lines, are all available. They aren't sacred.

And, best of all, your marks and notes become an integral part of the book and stay there forever. You can pick up the book the following week or year and there are all your points of agreement, disagreement, doubt, and inquiry. It's like resuming and interrupted conversation with the advantage of being able to pick up where you left off.

And that is exactly what reading a book should be: a conversation between you and the author. Presumably he knows more about the subject than you do, naturally, you'll have the proper humility as you approach him. But don't let anybody tell you that a reader is supposed to be solely on the receiving end. Understanding is a two-way operation; learning doesn't consist in being an empty receptacle. The learner has to question himself and question the teacher. He even has to argue with the teacher, once he understands what the teacher is saying. And marking a book is literally an expression of your differences, or agreements of opinion, with the author.

Key Words & Phrases 해설

ex. Work is not the object of life any more than play is.
일이 삶의 목적이 아님은 놀이가 삶의 목적이 아님과 같다.(part I 239쪽 참조)

- inseparable [insépərəbəl] 분리할 수 없는, 떨어질 수 없는(from)
  ex. Rights are inseparable from duties. 권리는 의무와 분리할 수가 없다.

- the beauty of a rare edition or of a richly manufactured volume is like that of a painting or a statue.
  희귀본이나 화려하게 제작된 책의 아름다움은 그림이나 조각상의 아름다움과 같다.

- Arturo Toscanini [tàskəníː] (1867~1957)
  이탈리아 태생의 미국 관현악 지휘자

- Johannes Brahms [braːmz] (1833~97) 독일의 작곡가

- score [skɔːr] 악보, (둘 이상의 성악 · 기악을 위한) 작품

- Arturo Toscanini reveres Brahms, but Toscanini's score of the C-minor Symphony is so thoroughly marked up that no one but the maestro himself can read it. (but = except)
  토스카니는 브람스를 존경했지만, C-단조 교향곡에 대한 토스카니의 악보는 너무도 철저하게 온통 표시가 돼 있어서 음악거장인 자신을 제외하고 어떤 사람도 그 악보를 읽을 수 없다.

- typography [taipágrəfi] 활판 인쇄, 활판술

- indispensable [indispénsəbəl] 불가결의, 없어서는 안 될, 절대 필요한
  ex. Health is indispensable to everyone. 건강은 모든 사람에게 절대 필요한 것이다.

- accomplish [əkámpliʃ] 이루다, 성취하다, 달성하다.

- glide [glaid] 미끄러지게 하다, 미끄러지듯 나가다
  ex. The swan glided across the lake. 백조는 호수를 미끄러지듯 헤엄쳐 갔다.

- come up with ~을 따라잡다[따라붙다], 찾아내다

- Gone with the wind 『바람과 함께 사라지다』는 미국 여류 작가인 Margaret Munnerlyn Mitchell (1900-1949)의 인기 소설

- in state of relaxation 긴장을 푼 상태에서

There are all kinds of devices for marking a book intelligently and fruitfully. Here's the way I do it:

1. Underlining : of major points, of important or forceful statements.
2. Vertical lines at the margin: to emphasize a statement already underlined.
3. Star, asterisk, or other doodad at the margin: to be used sparingly, to emphasize the ten or twenty most important statements in the book. (You may want to fold the bottom corner of each page on which you use such marks. It won't hurt the sturdy paper on which most modern books are printed, and you will be able to take the book off the shelf at any time and, by opening it at the folded-corner page, refresh your recollection of the book.)
4. Numbers in the margin: to indicate the sequence of points the author makes in developing a single argument.
5. Numbers of other pages in the margin: to indicate where else in the book the author made points relevant to the point marked; to tie up the ideas in a book, which, though they may be separated by many pages, belong together.
6. Circling of key words or phrases.
7. Writing in the margin, or at the top or bottom of the page: recording questions (and perhaps answers) which a passage raised in your mind; reducing a complicated discussion to a simple statement; recording the sequence of major points right through the books. I use the end papers and the back of the book to make a personal index of the author's points in the order of their appearance.

Key Words & Phrases 해설

- fundamental [fʌndəméntl] 기본의, 근본적인, 필수의
- "caviar factories" 철갑 상어알 제조 공장
- on a scratch pad 메모판 위에
- They aren't sacred.
  그것들 (책 페이지의 가장자리, 위, 옆, 아래 여백은)은 신성한 것이 아니다
- integral [íntigrəl] 빠뜨릴 수 없는, 필수의 (essential)
- You can pick up the book the following week or year, and there are all your points of agreement, disagreement, doubt, and inquiry.
  당신은 다음 주나 다음 해에 그 책을 찾아 낼 수 있으며, 거기에는 당신의 동의, 부동의, 의심과 질문의 모든 요지가 있다.
- It's like resuming and interrupted conversation with the advantage of being able to pick up where you left off.
  그것은 마치, 당신이 그만둔 곳을 찾아낼 수 있는 유리함을 갖고서, 다시 계속하거나 중단시킬 수 있는 대화와 같다.
- presumably 추측상, 아마
- humility [hjuːmíləti] 겸손, 겸양, (pl.) 겸손한 행위
- receptacle [riséptək-əl] 그릇, 용기, 피난처 (shelter)
- underlining 밑줄 긋기
- forceful statements 설득력 있는 말
- vertical lines at the margin 가장자리에 수직 선 긋기
- Star, asterisk, or other doodad at the margin
  페이지 가장자리에 별이나 별표, 또는 다른 장식기호 넣기
- to be used sparingly 드물게 사용되는 것
- the sturdy paper 튼튼한 종이
- Numbers in the margin 가장자리에다 숫자 써 넣기
- in the order of their appearance 저자의 요점들이 나타나는 순서대로

The front end papers are, to me, the most important. Some people reserve them for a fancy bookplate. I reserve them for fancy thinking. After I have finished reading the book and making my personal index on the back end papers, I turn to the front and try to outline the book, not page by page, or point by point (I've already done that at the back), but as an integrated structure, with a basic unity and an order of parts. This outline is, to me, the measure of my understanding of the work.

If you're a die-hard anti-book-marker, you may object that the margins, the space between the lines, and the end papers don't give you room enough. All right. How about using a scratch pad slightly smaller than the page size of the book so that the edges of the sheets won't protrude? Make your index, outlines, and even your notes on the pad, then insert these sheets permanently inside the front and back covers of the book.

Or you may say that this business of marking books is going to slow up your reading. It probably will. That's one of the reasons for doing it. Most of us have been taken in by the notion that speed of reading is a measure of our intelligence. There is no such thing as the right speed for intelligent reading. Some things should be read quickly an effortlessly, and some should be read slowly and even laboriously. The sign of intelligence in reading is the ability to read different things differently according to their worth. In the case of good books, the point is not to see how many of them you can get through, but rather how many can get through you—how many you can make your own. A few friends are better than a thousand acquaintances. If this be your aim, as it should be, you will not be impatient if it takes more time and effort to read a great book than it does a newspaper.

You may have one final objection to marking books. You can't lend them to

Key Words & Phrases 해설

- index [índeks] (pl. es, -dices[-disìz]) 색인, 찾아보기
- not page by page, or point by point but as an integrated structure
  페이지마다 혹은 요점 별로가 아니라 하나의 통합된 구조물로서
  (not ~ but ~ 구문)
- If you're a die-hard anti-book-marker
  당신이 책에 표시하는 것을 끝까지 격렬하게 저항하는 사람이라면
- protrude [proutrú:d] (밀어)내다, 내밀다
- inside the front and back covers of the book.
  그 책의 앞표지에서 뒷표지까지 안에 (그 책 속에)
- A few friends are better than a thousand acquaintances.
  얼굴만 아는 천명의 사람보다 몇 안되는 친구가 더 낫다.
- You can't lend them to your friends because nobody else can read them without being distracted by your notes.
  당신이 책에 한 노트(낙서)로 인해서 그 책을 읽을 때 누구나 마음이 산란해지기 때문에 친구에게 책을 빌려줄 수 없다.
- lending it is almost like giving your mind away.
  책을 빌려준다는 것은 마치 당신의 마음을 주어 버리는 것과 같다. (it = book)
- If your friend wishes to read your Plutarch's lives, Shakespeare, or the federalist papers, tell him gently, but firmly, to buy a copy.
  당신의 친구가 당신이 가지고 있는 푸루타크 영웅전이나, 셰익스피어 작품이나 연방주의자 논문을 읽기 원한다면, 그에게 부드러우나 단호하게 책을 사서 보라고 말하라.
- your books are as much a part of you as your head or your heart.
  당신의 책들은 당신의 머리나 심장과 마찬가지로 당신의 한 부분이다.

your friends because nobody else can read them without being distracted by your notes. Furthermore, you won't want to lend them because a marked copy is a kind of intellectual diary, and lending it is almost like giving your mind away.

If your friend wishes to read your Plutarch's lives, Shakespeare, or the federalist papers, tell him gently, but firmly, to buy a copy. You will lend him your car or your coat, but your books are as much a part of you as your head or your heart.

Consider this

1. Does the writer's account of his acquisition of reading skill grip your attention? How much of the writer's advice about reading applies to you? How much of it is to be taken seriously? Or do you have a different perspective of your own about reading?

2. What is the writer's important point? Where is it best stated? Are you as hungry for books, as eager to reading skill as the writer suggested? If not, why not? Have you ever been deeply disturbed, upset, or confused, morally or emotionally, by reading a book? Is it still too close to you? Can you tell about it?

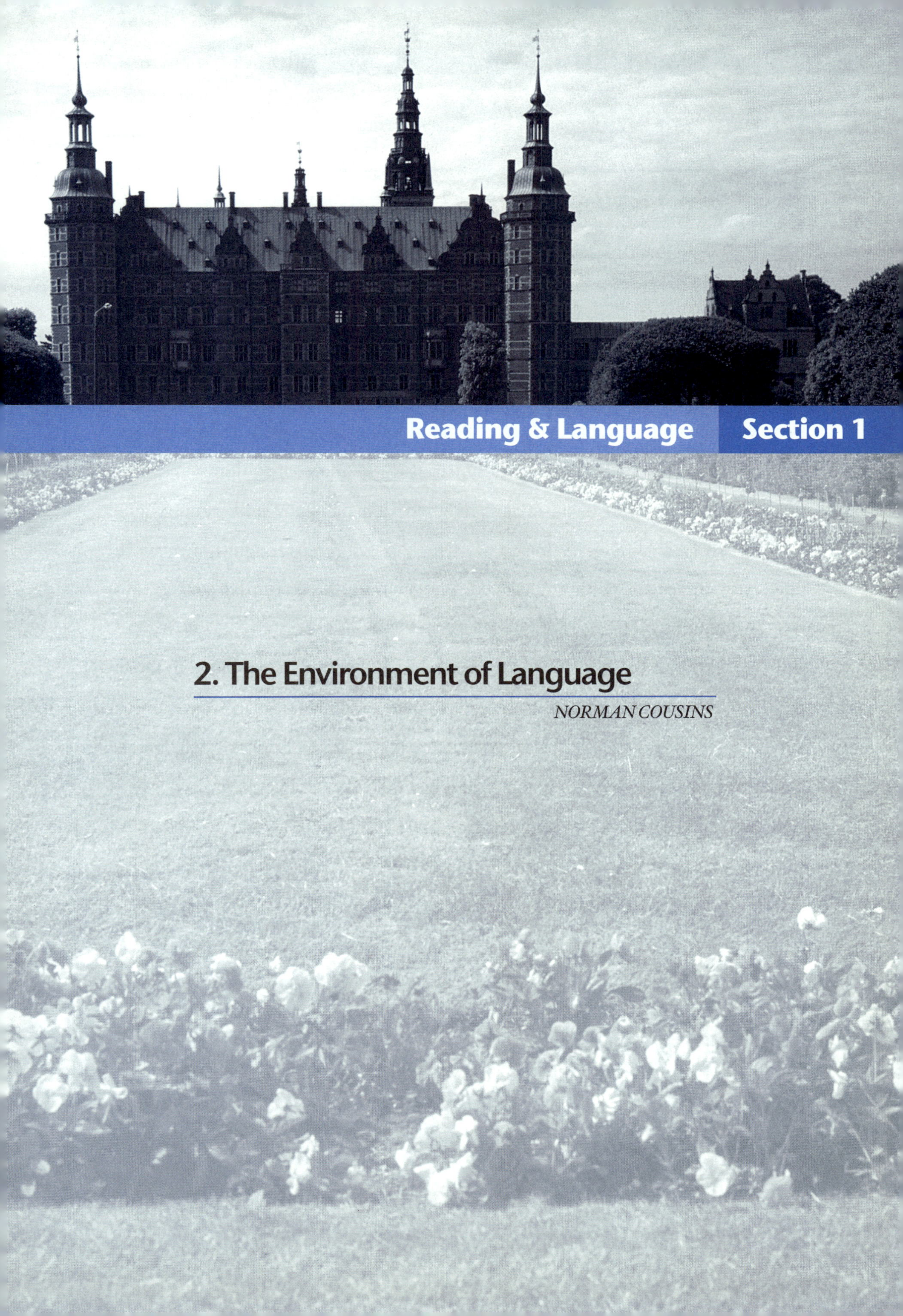

2. The Environment of Language

NORMAN COUSINS

2 The Environment of Language

NORMAN COUSINS

The words men use, Julian Huxley once said, not only express but shape their ideas. Language is an instrument; it is even more an environment. It has as much to do with the philosophical and political conditioning of a society as geography or climate. The role of language in contributing to men's problems and their prospects is the subject of an imaginative and valuable study now getting under way at Pro Deo University in Rome, which is winning recognition in world university circles for putting advanced scholarship to work for the concept of a world community.

One aspect of the Pro Deo study, as might be expected, has to do with the art of conveying precise meaning from one language to another. Stuart Chase, one of America's leading semanticists has pointed out that when an English speaker at the United Nations uses the expression "I assume," the French interpreter may say "I deduced" and the Russian interpreter may say "I consider." When Pope Paul VI sent a cable to Prime Minister Alexei Kosygin and Party Chairman Leonid Brezhnev on their access to office, he expressed the hope that the historic aspirations of the Russian people for a fuller life would be advanced under the new leadership. As translated into Russian by the Vatican's own interpreter, the Pope's expression of hope came out in a way that made it appear that the Pope was making known his endorsement of the new regime. The eventual clarification was inevitably awkward for all concerned.

The Pro Deo study, however, will not be confined to problems of precise

Key Words & Phrases 해설

- NORMAN COUSINS (1912 ~ 1990) 미국의 에세이스트, Saturday Review 편집장
- Huxley [hʌ́ksli] 헉슬리
- The words men use, Julian Huxley once said, not only express but shape their ideas
  인간이 사용하는 언어는 생각을 표현할 뿐만 아니라 생각을 형성하기도 한다고 쥬리안 헉슬리가 한 때 말했다 (not only ~ but (also) 구문)
- have to do with ~과 관련이 있다.
  ex. What do he have to do with you? 자네와 그가 무슨 관계가 있는가?
- geography [dʒiːɑ́grəfi] 지리
- climate [kláimit] 기후
- prospect [prɑ́spekt] 예상, 기대
- getting under way 수행 중에 있는, 진행되고 있는
- in world university circles 세계 대학 사회(계)에서
- scholarship [skɑ́ləːʃip / skɔ́l-] 학문, (특히 고전의) 학식
  ex. advanced scholarship 진보된 학문
- a world community 세계 공동체
- as might be expected 예기되는 바와 같이, 과연
  ex. As might be expected of a gentleman, Dr. Yun was as good as his word.
  과연 신사답게 윤 박사는 약속을 잘 지켰다.
- the art of conveying precise meaning 정확한 의미를 전달하는 기술
- semanticist [simǽntəsist] 의미론 학자
- America's leading semanticists 미국의 주요한 의미론자들
- point out 지적하다
- interpreter [intə́ːrprətər] 통역(자), 해석자
- deduce [didjúːs] 연역(演繹)하다, 추론하다

translation. The major emphasis has to do with something even more fundamental: the dangerous misconceptions and prejudices that take root in language and that undermine human values. The color of a man's skin, for example, is tied to plus-or-minus words that inevitably condition human attitudes. The words "black" and "white," as defined in Western culture, are heavily loaded. "Black" has all sorts of unfavorable connotations, "white" is almost all favorable. One of the more interesting papers being studied by the Pro Deo scholars is by Ossie Davis, the author and actor. Mr. Davis, a Negro, concluded on the basis of a detailed study of dictionaries and *Roget's Thesaurus* that the English language was his enemy. In Roget's, he counted 120 synonyms for "blackness," most of them with unpleasant connotations: blot, blotch, blight, smut, smudge, sully, begrime, soot, becloud, obscure, dingy, murky, threatening, frowning, foreboding, forbidden, sinister, baneful, dismal, evil, wicked, malignant, deadly, secretive, unclean, unwashed, foul, blacklist, black book, black-hearted, etc. Incorporated the same listing were such words as Negro, nigger, and darky.

In the same Roget's Mr. Davis found 124 synonyms for the word "white," almost all of them with favorable connotations: purity, cleanness, bright, shining, fair, blonde, stainless, chaste, unblemished, unsullied, innocent, honorable, upright, just, straightforward, genuine, trustworthy, honest, etc. "White" as a racial designation was, of course, included in this tally of desirable terms.

No less invidious than "black" are some of the words associated with the color yellow: coward, conniver, baseness, fear, effeminacy, funk, soft, spiritless, poltroonery, pusillanimity, timidity, mil-sop, recreant, sneak, lily-livered, etc. Oriental peoples are included in the listing.

As a matter of factual accuracy, "white," "black," and "yellow" as colors are

Key Words & Phrases 해설

- Pope [poup] 로마 교황
- Paul [pɔːl] 폴 (교황이름)
- cable [kéibəl] 해외전보
- Prime Minister 수상
- Aleksei Kosygin [kɔ́siːgin] 코시긴 (1904 ~ 80) : 옛 소련의 수상
- Party Chairman 당 서기장
- Leonid Brezhnev [bréʒnef] 브레즈네프 (1906 ~ 82) : 옛 소련 공산당 서기장
- he expressed the hope that the historic aspirations of the Russian people for a fuller life would be advanced under the new leadership.
  더욱 충만한 삶에 대한 러시아 국민들의 역사적 열망이 새로운 지도력 아래서 증진될 것이라는 희망을 교황은 표현했다.
- As translated into Russian by the Vatican's own interpreter
  바티칸 당국의 통역자에 의해서 (교황의 메시지가) 러시아말로 번역되자 (시간을 나타내는 분사 구문)
- in a way 보기에 따라서는, 다소
- come out (결과가) ~이 되다, 드러나다
- make it appear that ~인 것처럼 보이게 하다
- endorsement [endɔ́ːrsmənt] 승인
- regime, régime [reiʒíːm] 정권
- make known 공표하다 make (~) known ~임을 알리다, 유명해지다
  ex. Professor Yun and Jung are making themselves known in the world.
  윤 교수와 정 교수가 유명해질 것이다.
- clarification [klæ̀rəfikéiʃən] 해명
- eventual [ivéntʃuəl] 종국의, 최후의
- awkwardly [ɔ́ːkwərdli] 거북한, 어색한

not descriptive of races. The coloration range of so-called white people may run from pale olive to mottled pink; so-called colored people run from light beige to mahogany. Absolute color designations—white, black, red, yellow—are not merely inaccurate; they have become symbolic rather than descriptive. What is needed is not so much a change in language as an awareness of the power of words to condition attitudes. If we can at least recognize the underpinning of prejudice we may be in a position to deal with the effect.

To be sure, Western languages have no monopoly on words with connotations that affect judgment. In Chinese, whiteness means cleanliness, but it can also means bloodlessness, coldness, frigidity, absence of feeling, weakness, insensitiviy. Also in Chinese, yellowness is associated with sunshine, openness, beauty, flowering, etc. Similarly, the word "black" in many African tongues has connotations of strength, certainty, recognizability, integrity, while "white" is associated with paleness, anemia, unnaturalness, deviousness, untrust-worthiness.

Consider this

1. What kinds of evidence does the writer use in supporting his argument? Do you think they are equally valid?

2. How do the concrete details, the imagery, and the metaphors that the writer uses contribute to the effectiveness of his argument?

Key Words & Phrases 해설

- for all concerned 관계자 모두에게
- confine [kənfáin] 제한하다
- fundamental [fʌndəméntl] 기초의, 기본의, 근본적인
- misconception [mìskənsépʃən] 오해, 그릇된 생각
- prejudice [prédʒudis] 편견, 선입관
- take root 뿌리박다
- undermine [ʌndərmáin] 음험한 수단으로 훼손하다, 몰래 손상시키다
- inevitably [inévitəbli] 불가피 하게
- condition [kəndíʃən] (사정 따위가) ~을 결정하다, 좌우하다
- be tied to = be connected to 결합되어 있다, 연결되어 있다
- define [difáin] (성격 · 내용 따위를) 규정짓다, 정의 내리다
- as defined in Western culture 서구문화 속에서 규정된 바
- are heavily loaded 잔뜩 실려 있다
- all sorts of unfavorable connotations 온갖 종류의 비우호적인 함축들
- connotation 함축, 언외의 의미
- denotation 명시적 의미, 외연
- One of the more interesting papers being studied by the Pro Deo scholars is by Ossie Davis, the author and actor
  프로 데오 대학의 학자들에 의해서 연구되고 있는 더욱 흥미로운 논문 중 한 편은 저자이자 배우인 오시에 데이비스가 쓴 것이다.
- on the basis of ~을 기초로 하여
- thesaurus [θisɔ́ːrəs] (동의어 · 반의어 등의) 사전
- synonym [sínənim] 동의어
- unpleasant [ʌnplézənt] 불쾌한

Key Words & Phrases 해설

- blot [blɑt / blɔt] (잉크 등의) 얼룩, blotch [blɑtʃ/ blɔtʃ] 부스럼, 반점
- blight [blait] (식물의) 마름병, smut [smʌt] (검댕 · 연기 따위의) 덩어리, 얼룩
- smudge [smʌdʒ] 얼룩

sully [sʌ́li] 더러움, begrime [bigráim] (때 · 검댕으로) 더럽히다,
soot [sut, suːt] 검댕, becloud [bikláud] 흐리게 하다,
obscure [əbskjúər] 어두운, dingy [díndʒi] 거무스름한, murky [mə́ːrki] 어두운,
threatening [θrétniŋ] 험악한, foreboding [fɔːrbóudiŋ] (불길한) 예감,
baneful [béinfəl] 파괴적인, dismal [dízməl] 음울한,
malignancy [məlígnənsi] 적의, secretive [sikriːtiv, siːkrə-] 숨기는,
nigger [nígəːr] (경멸적) 검둥이, darky [dáːrki] (구어 · 경멸적) 검둥이,
purity [pjúərəti] 청정 · 순수, stainless [stéinlis] 흠이 없는,
unblemished [ʌnblémiʃt] 결백한, unsullied [ʌnsʌ́lid] 더럽혀지지 않은,
upright [ʌ́práit, ⌐⌐] 곧은 · 청렴한, genuine [dʒénjuin] 진짜의

- designation 명칭
- tally [tǽli] 장부
- invidious [invídiəs] 비위에 거슬리는, 불쾌한(말 따위) 몹시 차별하는
- no less than ~못지 않게, ~와 같이 [마찬가지로]
  ex. She is no less clever than her elder sister. 그녀는 언니만큼 영리하다.
- No less invidious than "black" are some of the words associated with the color yellow.
  노란색과 관련된 낱말들 중 상당수는 "검정"색 과 마찬가지로 불쾌한 말이다.

- coward [káuərd] 겁쟁이; conniver [kənáivər] 눈감아 주는 사람
- effeminacy [ifémənəsi] 여성적임, 나약; funk [fʌŋk] 움츠림, 두려움

Key Words & Phrases 해설

- pusillanimity [pjù:sələniməti] 무기력, 비겁
- recreant [rékriənt] (시어 · 문어) 겁 많은, 비겁한
- sneak [sni:k] 몰래하기 [하는 사람], factual [fǽktʃuəl] 사실에 입각한

- coloration [kʌləréiʃən] n. 배색, 채색
- not so much ~ as ~라기보다는[도], 오히려
  ex. She is not so much a scholar as a poet. 그녀는 학자라기보다는 오히려 시인이다
  ex. I was not so much angry as disappointed. 나는 성났다기보다는 오히려 실망했다.
- awareness 알아채고 있음, 앎
- underpinning [ʌ́ndərpìniŋ] 받침, 토대
- bloodlessness [blʌ́dlisnis] 핏기 [생기] 없음, 빈혈
- frigidity [fridʒídəti] 냉담, 무기력
- recognizability [rekəgnaiz-əbíləti] 승인, 인식
- integrity [intégrəti] 성실, 정직 (honesty)
- anemia [əní:miə] 빈혈증
- devious [dí:viəs] 우회한, 정도(正道)를 벗어난, 교활한
  ex. take a devious route 우회하다.
  ex. There is something devious about him. 그에겐 어딘가 교활한 데가 있다.

3. Poverty Knows No Color

RODGER HURLEY

3 Poverty Knows No Color

RODGER HURLEY

Poverty is much more than a lack of money. A "Culture of Poverty" is born in the slums and grows with the child from the wrong family, the wrong region of the country, or the wrong ethnic or racial group. This "self-perpetuating" nature of poverty merits careful attention: "Basic to the economics of delinquency is the transmission of poverty across the generations. Today, for the 18-year-old, employment is hard to find. What chance has a slum-dwelling 6-year-old to break out of the cycle of poverty? Individual initiative may be important in determining an individual's destiny, but it is the economic and social forces shaping the way children are brought up, their preparation for adulthood by public institutions, their chances for self-improvement that perpetuate poverty."

This culture of poverty becomes a legacy of psychological distortion, and manifests itself in a profound alienation from the larger society and from other people, an intense feeling of powerlessness, and a belief in the meaninglessness of struggle. The degradation and spiritual depression of poverty are omnipresent; they affect every action that makes up the poor man's "life style." The very contrast between the material life of the poor and that of the affluent society produces an invidious comparison which is psychologically damaging to those who are poverty stricken. Because our national values stress success and high achievement, we applaud efforts at self-improvement and advancement. The world of advertisement stimulates desires for status and material rewards—and shows the splendid benefits afforded those who achieve. This evident wealth, plus the knowledge that

Key Words & Phrases 해설

- Poverty is much more than a lack of money. 가난이란 돈이 없다는 것 그 이상이다.
- in the slums 빈민가에서
- This "self-perpetuating" nature of poverty merits careful attention
가난의 이런 '자기 영속적인' 본성은 주의 깊게 눈 여겨 볼만하다.
- Basic to the economics of delinquency is the transmission of poverty across the generations.
범죄경제학에 대한 근본은 세대를 건너 내려 온 가난의 전이이다.
- What chance has a slum-dwelling 6-year-old to break out of the cycle of poverty?
빈민가에 거주하는 여섯 살짜리가 무슨 기회로 가난의 싸이클에서 벗어날 수 있겠는가?
- Individual initiative may be important in determining an individual's destiny
개인의 진취적 기상도 개인의 운명을 결정짓는데 중요할 수 있다.
- but it is the economic and social forces shaping the way children are brought up, their preparation for adulthood by public institutions, their chances for self-improvement that perpetuate poverty.
그러나 가난을 영속화시키는 것은 어린이들이 자라는 방식을 형성 짓는 경제적 사회적인 힘, 공적인 제도에 의한 성년기 준비 그리고 자기 개발을 위한 기회이다.
- This culture of poverty becomes a legacy of psychological distortion
이런 가난의 문화는 심리학적으로 왜곡의 유산이 된다.
- and manifests itself in a profound alienation from the larger society and from other people, an intense feeling of powerlessness, and a belief in the meaninglessness of struggle
그리고 더 큰 사회와 다른 사람들로부터의 심각한 소외로 나타나며, 무능함에 대한 통렬한 느낌과 투쟁의 무의미성에 대한 믿음으로 나타난다.
- they affect every action that makes up the poor man's life style
그것들은 가난한 사람들의 삶의 양식을 형성하는 모든 행동에 영향을 미친다.
- affluent [ǽflu(:)ənt] 풍부한, 유복한
- invidious [invídiəs] 비위에 거슬리는, 남의 시샘을 받기 쉬운(지위 · 명예 따위)

some people have actually begun at the bottom and reached the top, makes the poor feel guilty for their lack of achievement and even more self-conscious of their deprivation. It is the relativity of their deprivation—the constant contrast they see—that perhaps more than anything else, says Lola Irelan, affects their own life view, and leads them to believe themselves failures.

The general attitude of our society, as expressed either consciously or unconsciously, is a weapon which brutalizes and defeats the poor.

The heritage of slavery, racism—a reiterated, visible, virulent aspect of American life—along with the concomitant economic deprivation, have produced misery for the American Negro on such a scale and in such depth that it is impossible for a white man to comprehend it fully. The pathological impact on a human being of race prejudice alone, ignoring the added evil of poverty, is impossible to overestimate. An American Negro, James Weldon Johnson, declared: "This [segregation and discrimination] is the dwarfing, warping, distorting influence which operates upon each and every colored man in the United States. He is forced to take his outlook on all things, not from the viewpoint of a citizen, or a man, or even a human being, but from the viewpoint of a colored man." J. H. Griffin, who artificially colored his skin black, notes well in *Black Like Me* the "hate stare" which has been a common Negro experience. "It came from a middle-aged, heavy-set, well-dressed white man. He sat a few yards away, fixing his eyes on me. Nothing can describe the withering horror of this. You feel lost, sick at heart before such unmasked hatred."

The impact of racism on the life of the American Negro, especially the poor Negro, cannot be minimized. The utter degradation of Negro experience is central to the problem of poverty and mental retardation. But if the poor Negro has

Key Words & Phrases 해설

- The world of advertisement stimulates desires for status and material rewards—and shows the splendid benefits afforded those who achieve.
  광고계는 지위와 물질적인 보상에 대한 욕망을 자극시키며, 성취한 사람들에게 주어지는 화려한 혜택들을 보여준다.

- This evident wealth, plus the knowledge that some people have actually begun at the bottom and reached the top, makes the poor feel guilty for their lack of achievement and even more self-conscious of their deprivation.
  몇몇 사람이 실제로 밑바닥에서 시작해서 정상에 올랐다는 사실에 덧붙여 이런 분명한 부 때문에 가난한 사람들은 성취하지 못한데서 오는 죄책감을 느끼며, 그들의 궁핍에 대해 훨씬 더 많은 자의식을 느낀다.

- a weapon which brutalizes and defeats the poor
  가난한 사람들을 난폭하게 하고 패배시키는 무기

- The heritage of slavery, racism—a reiterated, visible, virulent aspect of American life—along with the concomitant economic deprivation, have produced misery for the American Negro on such a scale and in such depth that it is impossible for a white man to comprehend it fully.
  반복되고, 명백하게 보이며 악의에 찬 미국 생활의 한 양상인 노예제도와 인종차별주의의 유산 때문에 미국 흑인들은 백인이 온전히 이해하기가 불가능할 정도의 규모와 깊이로 불행을 겪었다.

- This segregation and discrimination is the dwarfing, warping, distorting influence which operates upon each and every colored man in the United States.
  이런 인종차별과 차별대우는 미국에 사는 각각의 유색인 그리고 모든 유색인에게 왜소케하고, 왜곡시키고, 마음을 비뚫어지게 하는 영향력을 미친다.

- hate stare 증오에 찬 시선

- heavy-set 육중한 몸

- if the poor Negro has suffered from the stigma of race, the poor white has suffered from the stigma of not having succeeded in a society which places few racial barriers before him.

suffered from the stigma of race, the poor white has suffered from the stigma of not having succeeded in a society which places few racial barriers before him. A white man's failure in an American society which preaches "upward mobility" is of itself a unique indictment of inferiority. To What else can a white man's poverty be ascribed? The effect of being considered "white trash" at least approximates that of being branded "nigger"; the poor white man, like the poor black man, has his own special burden to bear.

Consider this

1. Trace the steps by which the writer gets from his text to his conclusion about the poverty. Are they all logical?

2. What obstacles stood in the way of the poor man living in the USA? And what do they need in order to overcome them? Are there any new difficulties which derived from the poverty today?

3. "Poverty is much more than a lack of money" according to this article. Do you agree? Why or why not? Do you think that the poor and the rich are raised, from childhood, to read the world differently? How so?

Key Words & Phrases 해설

가난한 흑인이 인종적인 낙인 때문에 고통을 당한다면 가난한 백인은 자신 앞에 인종적인 장애물이 거의 놓여 있지 않은 사회에서 성공하지 못했다는 낙인 때문에 고통을 당한다.

- A white man's failure in an American society which preaches "upward mobility" is of itself a unique indictment of inferiority.

  위로의 이동을 설교하는 미국사회에서 백인이 실패했다는 것은 자연히 열등에 대한 특이한 고발이다.

- The effect of being considered "white trash" at least approximates that of being branded "nigger"

  백인 쓰레기로 여겨지는 결과는 깜둥이로 낙인찍히는 결과와 적어도 비슷하다.

4. The Fabrication of Race

MATTEW FRYE JACOBSON

4 The Fabrication of Race

MATTHEW FRYE JACOBSON

We tend to think of race as being indisputable, real. We see it plainly on one another's faces. It seem a product not of the social imagination but of biology. However, scholars in several disciplines have recently shaken faith in this biological certainty. The conventions by which "race mixing" is understood, they point out, is one site where the unreality of race comes into view. Why is it that in the United States a white woman can have black children but a black woman cannot have white children? Doesn't this bespeak a degree of arbitrariness in this business of affixing racial labels?

The history of racial classification over time is a second such site: entire races have disappeared from view, from public discussion, and from modern memory, though their flesh-and-blood members still walk the earth. What has become of the nineteenth century's Celts and Slavs, for instance? Its Hebrews, Iberics, Mediterraneans, Teutons, and Anglo-Saxons?

인종차별에 항의하는 시위대

In Philip Roth's *Counterlife* (1988) a Gentile woman chances to comment that she seldom repays the attention of Jewish men "because there are enough politics in sex without racial politics coming into it." "We're not race," objects her Jewish listener. The ensuing exchange cuts to the very heart of "difference" and the epistemology of race.

Key Words & Phrases 해설

- indisputable [ìndispjú:təbəl, indíspju-] 논의[반박]의 여지가 없는(unquestionable)
  ex. indisputable evidence

- discipline [dísəplin] (학문의) 분야
  ex. Scholars from various disciplines 여러 학문 분야의 학자들

- Why is it that in the United States a white woman can have black children but a black woman cannot have white children?
  미국에서 백인 여자는 흑인 자녀를 가질 수 있지만, 흑인 여자는 백인 자녀를 가질 수 없는 이유는 무엇일까?
  (▸ 미국에서 백인 어머니와 흑인 아버지 사이에서 태어난 여자아이는 사회 관습상 "흑인"이다. 그러나 그 흑인 여자 아기가 커서 백인 남자와 결혼한다 해도, 그녀의 아이는 여전히 "흑인"이다.)

- Doesn't this bespeak a degree of arbitrariness in this business of affixing racial labels?
  이것은 인종적인 꼬리표를 붙이는 이런 일에서 나타나는 임의성 정도를 보여주는 것은 아닐까?

- The history of racial classification over time is a second such site: entire races have disappeared from view, from public discussion, and from modern memory, though their flesh-and-blood members still walk the earth.
  세월을 뛰어넘는 종족분류의 역사는 제 2의 그런 장소이다. 즉 흠 없는 종족은 시야에서, 대중적인 토론에서 그리고 오늘날의 기억에서 사라졌다. 비록 그들의 살과 피를 물려받은 직계 후손이 여전히 지상을 걸어 다닌다고 해도.

- What has become of the nineteenth century's Celts and Slavs, for instance?
  가령, 19세기 켈트족과 슬라브족은 어찌되었는가?
  (▸오늘날 켈트족(아일랜드인, 스코틀랜드인), 슬라브족(러시아, 폴란드, 체첸인), 아베리아족(스페인, 포르투갈인), 지중해 연안의 코카서스족(이탈리아인, 그리스인 등), 튜튼족(독일과 스칸디나비안인), 그리고 앵글로색슨족은 종족적으로 단일한 종족집단으로 거의 보이지 않는다.)

- Gentile [dʒentail] (유대인 입장에서) 이방인, (특히) 기독교도

"It is a racial matter." she insisted.

"No, we're the same race. You're thinking of Eskimos."

"We are not the same race. Not according to anthropologists, or whoever measures these thing. There's Caucasian, Semitic—there are about five different groups. Don't look at me like that."

"I can't help it. Some nasty superstitions always tend to crop up when people talk about a Jewish 'race'."

"…All I can tell you is that you are a different race. We're supposed to be closer to Indians than to Jews, actually;—I'm talking about Caucasians."

"But I am Caucasian, kiddo. In the U. S. census I am, for good or bad, counted as Caucasian"

"Are you? Am I wrong?"

This passage beautifully conveys the seemingly natural but finally unstable logic of race. The debate over Jews' racial identity begins merely as a matter of conflicting classification: at the outset stable, meaningful categories are assumed, and the question is simply where a particular group belongs—which pigeonhole do jews fit into, Caucasian or Semite? But the question itself points to more profound epistemological crisis; if he is certain that he is a Caucasian, and she is certain that he is not, then what does it mean to call a person a Caucasian in the first place? And where does all this certainty come from?

Once the two characters recognize the slippage in what they had each thought an uncompromising natural fact, both scramble to appeal to some higher authority in order to uphold their initial views. She invokes science ("according to anthropologists …"); he invokes the state "in the U. S. census actors in the

Key Words & Phrases 해설

• chance [tʃæns] 어쩌다가 ~하다, 우연히 일어나다.

ex. She chanced to be out then.= It chanced that she was out then.
　마침 그는 그 때 외출 중이었다.

• "because there are enough politics in sex without racial politics coming into it."

(→ 동일한 인종의 남녀 가운데 있는 성차별만으로 복잡한데, 인종주의와 관련한 논의로 문제를 더 복잡하게 하기를 원치 않는다는 뜻.)

• ensuing [ensú:iŋ] 다음의, 계속되는, 잇따라 일어나는

• cuts to the very heart of

~의 핵심을 붙잡다. 정수를 파악하다 (= captures the essence of~)

• the epistemology of race

인종에 대한 인식론 (우리가 어떻게 한 인종으로부터 다른 인종을 구별해내느냐는 전제적인 문제)

• epistemology 인식론 (앎의 본질에 대한 연구)

• Not according to anthropologists

우리는 인류학자에 따르면 동일한 인종이 아니다

(=We are not the same race according to anthropologists…)

• Caucasian [kɔ:kéiʒən] 백인

• Semitic [simítik] 셈어(헤브라이어 · 아라비아어 따위)

(→ 세계 사람들을 집단으로 분류하는 과학적인 한 방법은 그들의 언어를 비교하는 것이다. 유태인의 히브리어는 아랍어와 더불어 셈어에 속한다.)

• Don't look at me like that. 나를 그렇게 보지 마세요.

(왜 그렇게 의심스럽게 쳐다보나요? 내가 이상한 말을 했다는 건가요?라는 의미)

• nasty [nǽsti]

'불쾌한, 싫은' 의 의미로 disagreeable, unpleasant의 구어적 강의(強意) 표현

• crop up 나타나다

• kiddo [kídou] (미국속어, 친한 사이의 호칭으로서) 자네, 너, 야.

creation and enforcement of these public fictions called races. (Not incidentally, the narratives and images of popular culture, like Roth's best-seller itself, represent another.) Caucasians are not born, these combatants now seem to understand; they are somehow made. It's just a question of who does the making.

The racially inflected caricatures of the Irish in the middle of the nineteenth century are well known, as when Harper's depicted the "Celt" and the "Negro" weighing in identically on the scales of civic merit, but in the 1890s even the Irish novelist John Brennan could write that the Irishness of the emigrants' children showed in their "physiognomy, or the color of their countenances." When in 1891 a Detroit News reporter asked a black whitewasher whether or not he worked with any white men, the laborer answered (in a dialect provided by the journalist), "No, dere's no with men, Dere's some Polacks, but dey ain't white men, you know. Ha! ha! ha!" In his 1908 study Race or Mongrel? Alfred Schultz lamented in unambiguously biological language:

> The opinion is advanced that the public schools change the children of all races into Americans. Put a Scandinavian, a German, and a Magyar boy in at one end, and they will come out Americans at the other end. Which is like saying, let a pointer, a setter, and a pug enter one end of a tunnel and they will come out three greyhounds at the other end.

In her 1910 study of Homestead, Pennsylvania, the sociologist Margaret Byington broke the community down along the "racial" lines of "Slav, English-speaking European, native white, and colored." H. L. Mencken later casually alluded to the volume of literature crossing his desk by "Negro and other non-

Key Words & Phrases 해설

- This passage beautifully conveys the seemingly natural but finally unstable logic of race
  이 구절은 외관상 자연스럽지만 최종적으로는 불안정한 인종의 논리를 멋지게 전달한다
- racial identity 인종적 정체성
- pigeonhole 범주
- recognize the slippage 미끄러짐을 인식하다
  (인종의 개념을 이루고 있는 어떤 든든한 리얼리티가 없다는 것을 이해하게 된다는 의미)
- an uncompromising natural fact 양보할 수 없는 타고난 사실
- scramble 재빨리 또는 필사적으로 움직이다
- invokes 호소하다
- Not incidentally, the narratives and images of popular culture, like Roth's best-seller itself, represent another.
  우연하지 않게도, 대중문화의 내러티브(서사)와 이미지들은 로스의 베스트셀러 자체와 같이 또 다른 타자(他者)를 그린다.
  (가령, 헐리우드 영화들이 중국인, 한국인, 일본인 등 동양인들을 어떻게 그리고 있는가를 생각해 볼 필요가 있다.)
- Caucasians are not born, these combatants now seem to understand; they are somehow made.
  이런 논쟁자들이 이제 이해하는 것 같이, 백인들은 태어나는 것이 아니라 아무래도 만들어진다.
- The racially inflected caricatures of the Irish
  아일랜드인을 인종적으로 왜곡하여 우스꽝스럽게 하기
- Harper's 1850년에 창간된 미국의 장수 잡지
- weighing in identically 동일하게 균형을 맞추어
- civic merit 사회에 대한 유용성

Nordic writers," by which, evidently, he meant people like John Fante and Louis Adamic. In The Sheik (1921), Rudolph Valentino traded on his physiognomical ability to be both the exotic, racial Other and the acceptable, chivalric European—first, as a "savage" Arab, kidnapping Agnes Ayers, an later (safely revealed to be of English and Spanish descent), rescuing her from an even darker African foe. When Porgy and Bess appeared (1935), critics broadly attributed George Gershwin's talent for "American-Negroid music" to the "common Oriental ancestry in both Negro and Jew."

So this history of whiteness and its fluidity is very much a history of power and its disposition. But there is a further point; race is not just a conception; it is also a perception. The problem is not merely how races are comprehended, but how they are seen. In her 1943 obituary of Franz Boas, Ruth Benedict recounted how Boas the physicist having gone to the Arctic to study the properties of water, became Boas the anthropologist upon discovering that his observations did not at all match those of the Eskimos he encountered. Remarked Benedict, "He returned with an abiding conviction that if we are ever to understand human behavior we must know as much about the eye that sees as about the object seen. And he had understood once and for all that the eye that sees is not a mere physical organ but a means of perception conditioned by the tradition in which its possessor has been reared."

If this passage sums up Boas's understanding of the power of culture, it also nicely sums up the properties of race itself. In racial matters above all else, the eye that sees is "a means of perception conditioned by the tradition in which its possessor has been reared." The American eye sees a certain person as black, for

Key Words & Phrases 해설

- even the Irish novelist John Brennan could write that…
  심지어 교육을 잘 받은 아일랜드인조차도 (that 이하 내용을) 믿게끔 되어 있었다라는 의미
- physiognomy [fiziάgnəmi] 인상학, 골상학
- the color of their countenances 그들의 얼굴 색깔
- a Detroit News reporter asked a black whitewasher whether or not he worked with any white men, the laborer answered (in a dialect provided by the journalist), "No, dere's no wite men, Dere's some Polacks, but dey ain't white men, you know. Ha! ha! ha!"
  어떤 디트로이트 신문 기자가 벽 페인트공에게 백인과 함께 일한 적이 있는지 여부를 물었다. 그 노동자가 언론인이 쓰는 특유의 말씨로 말했다. "백인과는 일한 적이 없습죠. 폴란드인 몇 사람과는 일했지만 그들은 백인이 아니잖소, 당신도 알다 싶이. 하! 하! 하!
  (→ 그러나 실제 폴란드인도 백인임)
- dere's no wite men = There are no white men, polacks 폴란드 사람
  (→ 오늘날 폴란드 출신 사람을 "Polack(폴랙)" (경멸적 뉘앙스의 폴란드계인)이라고 부르는 것은 허용될 수 없다. 이것은 마치 유태인을 "a Kike(카이크)" (경멸적 의미의 유대인)라고 부르거나 일본인을 "a Jap(잽)" (경멸적 의미의 일본인)이라고 부르는 것은 오늘날 거의 생각할 수 없는 것과 같다
- mongrel [mʌ́ŋgrəl, mɑŋ-] (동식물의) 잡종, (경멸적) 튀기, 혼혈아.
- lamented 유감을 표명했다
- advance 의견을 제출하다
- Magyar [mǽgjɑːr, mάːg-] 마자르 [헝가리] 사람
- break down 분석하다, 분류하다
  ex. The expenditure is broken down as follows. 지출 명세는 다음과 같이 분류된다.
- native white 미국에서 태어난 백인
  (→ 'colored' 는 대개 African Americans을 지칭 하나, 본문에서는 native American과 Orientals을 포함한 모든 비유럽 인종을 가리킴.)

instance, whom Haitian or Brazilian eyes might see as white. Similarly, an earlier generation of Americans saw Celtic, Hebrew, Anglo-Saxon, or Mediterranean physiognomies where today we see only subtly varying shades of a mostly undifferentiated whiteness. (If pressed, we might come to a consensus on the physiognomical properties of Irishness, Slavicness, or Jewishness, but at a glance these certainly do not strike most Americans with anything like the perceptible force that they did a century ago, or that live racial distinctions do today.)

Thus, it is essential for us to see not only the history of various conceptions of racial "difference," but also the ways in which those conceptions of difference successfully masquerade as nature. The awesome power of race as an ideology resides precisely in its ability to pass as a feature of the natural landscape. Perhaps our most far-reaching ambition should be, then, to help loosen the grip of race by laying bare the moribund, and now quite peculiar, circuitry of an earlier era's racial conceptions and perceptions.

Consider this

1. The author implies that even some of the racial distinctions made today between Caucasians, Asian American, and African Americans could disappear in the future. Do you agree or not? Why? Or why not?

2. The writer shows a deep and sensitive concern for racial experience and awareness. What are the main currents of the essay as revealed here? Do you detect any resemblances of themes in the between "Poverty know no Color" and "The Fabrication of Race"? If so, tell them.

Key Words & Phrases 해설

- H. L. Mencken (1880 ~ 1956)
  1920년대와 1930년대 미국에서 가장 큰 영향력을 행사한 비평가중 한 명
- casually [kǽʒuəli] 우연히, 불쑥,
- Nordic [nɔ́:rdik] 북유럽 사람(의), 백색 인종(의)
- John Fante (1909 ~ 1983) 이탈리아계 미국작가
- Louis Adamic (1899 ~ 1951)
  Slovenia 태생으로 젊은 나이에 미국으로 이주하여 주목받은 작가가 되었다.
- Rudolph Valentino (1895 ~ 1926)
  이탈리아 태생의 미국 배우, 수많은 여성을 매혹시킨 검고 강렬한 눈의 소유자.
- trade on [upon] ~을 이용[악용]하다
  ex. He trades on his past reputation. 자기의 과거의 명성을 이용하고 있다.
- traded on his physiognomical ability
  그의 인상학적인 능력을 사용했다.(인종적으로 모호한 외모를 이용했다는 의미)
- exotic [igzɑ́tik / -zɔ́t-] 이국적인, 이국풍의
- racial Other 인종적인 타자
  (가령 "백인" 영화 관객은 자신들을 그들에게 위협적인 아웃사이더로 남아 있는 아랍의 지도자인 셰이크(Sheik)와 결코 동일시하지 않는다.)
- chivalric European 유럽의 기사 같은 사람
- chivalry 기사도
- an even darker 훨씬 더 피부가 검은(비교급 강조)
- attributed George Gershwin's talent for "American-Negroid music" to the "common Oriental ancestry in both Negro and Jew."
  미국-흑인 음악에 대한 조오지 거쉬윈의 재능을 흑인과 유태인 둘 공통의 동양 조상 덕분으로 생각했다.
  (거쉬윈은 흑인 음악의 요소들을 그의 오페라 작품 속에 통합할 수 있었는데, 유태인과 흑인이 둘 다 원래는 같은 지역(나일강 유역)에서 유래되었기 때문이라고 생각했다.)

Key Words & Phrases 해설

- George Gershwin (1898 ~ 1937) 유명한 유태계 미국작곡가. 그의 걸작인 *Porgy and Bess*는 흑인 영혼을 음악으로 포착한 오페라로서 칭송을 받았다.

- this history of whiteness and its fluidity is very much a history of power and its disposition
  순백(백인)성과 그것의 유동성은 힘과 그 배분의 역사와 다름없다.

- obituary [oubítʃuèri] (약력을 붙여 신문에 싣는) 사망기사, 사망광고(obit)

- Franz Boas (1858 ~ 1942) 근대 인류학의 창시자.
  (그의 중요한 결론 중의 하나는 진정으로 순수한 인종은 존재하지 않는다는 것이며, 어떤 인종도 다른 인종에 비해 천성적으로 우월하지 않다는 것이다.)

- Ruth Benedict (1887 ~ 1948) *The Chrysanthemum and the Sword* (국화와 칼)이란 저서에서 일본문화를 잘 분석한 인물

- recount [rikáunt] 자세히 얘기하다

- how Boas the physicist having gone to the Arctic to study the properties of water, became Boas the anthropologist
  어떻게 물리학자인 보아스가 물의 특성을 연구하기 위해 북극에 갔다가 인류학자 보아스가 되었는지를
  (가령, 보아스는 물과 같이 가장 기본적 것에 대한 기술조차도 문화와 교육에 영향을 받는다는 사실을 발견하고, 결국은 비인간적인 문제 보다는 인간의 문화와 사회를 연구하는데 관심을 갖게 되었다.)

- upon discovering that his observations did not at all match those of the Eskimos he encountered.
  자신의 관찰력이 그가 우연히 만난 에스키모의 관찰력에 필적하지도 못한다는 것을 발견하자

- abiding [əbáidiŋ] 지속[영속]하는, 영속적인
  ex. abiding friendship 변치 않는 우정

- we must know as much about the eye that sees as about the object seen.
  우리는 보여지는 대상에 대해서 알아야 하는 만큼 (대상을) 보는 눈에 대해서도 알아야 한다.

Key Words & Phrases 해설

- once and for all 단호하게, 딱 잘라서(=decisively)
- the eye that sees is not a mere physical organ but a means of perception conditioned by the tradition in which its possessor has been reared.
  보는 눈은 단순히 육체적인 기관이 아니라 그 눈의 소유자가 길러진 전통에 의해서 조건 지워진 인식의 기관이다.
- sums up 요약하다
- Haitian [héiʃən, héitiən] Haiti(사람)의, 하이티의
- subtly varying shades 미묘하게 다채로운 색깔의 농담정도
- live racial distinctions 생생한 인종적인 구별
- live [laiv] 생생한
- the grip of race 인종에 대한 이해력
- awesome [ɔ́:səm] 위엄 있는, 경외케 하는
- laying bare 명확하게 보여 주기 (showing clearly, revealing)
- moribund [mɔ́(:)rəbʌ̀nd, mɑ́r-] 죽어 가는, 소멸해 가는
- circuitry of an earlier era's racial conceptions and perceptions.
  이전 시대의 인종적인 개념과 인식의 전 범주
  (→ 사람들이 받아들이곤 했던 인종적인 믿음과 인식의 전 체계)

5. I Have a Dream

MARTIN LUTHER KING, JR.

5 I Have a Dream

MARTIN LUTHER KING, JR.

연설하는 킹목사

I am happy to join with you today in what will go down in history as the greatest demonstration for freedom in the history of our nation.

Five score years ago, a great American, in whose symbolic shadow we stand today, signed the Emancipation Proclamation. This momentous decree came as a great beacon light of hope to millions of Negro slaves who had been seared in the flames of withering injustice. It came as a joyous daybreak to end the long night of their captivity.

But one hundred years later, the Negro still is not free; one hundred years later, the life of the Negro is still sadly crippled by the manacles of segregation and the chains of discrimination; one hundred years later, the Negro lives on a lonely island of poverty in the midst of a vast ocean of material prosperity; one hundred years later, the Negro is still languished in the corners of American society and finds himself in exile in his own land.

So we've come here today to dramatize a shameful condition. In a sense we've come to our nation's capital to cash a check. When the architects of our republic wrote the magnificent words of our Constitution and the Declaration of Independence, they were signing a promissory note to which every American was to fall heir. This note was the promise that all men, yes, black men as well as white men, would be guaranteed the unalienable rights of life, liberty, and the pursuit of happiness.

Key Words & Phrases 해설

- MARTIN LUTHER KING, JR (1929 ~ 1968)
미국 목사, 시민권리 운동가, 원래 이름은 Michael Luther King, Jr. 임.
- go down in history 역사에 기록되다
- demonstration [dèmənstréiʃən] 데모, 시위 운동
- Five score years ago 백 년 전에, score 이십
- a great American은 노예를 해방시킨 아브람 링컨 대통령을 의미.
- emancipation [imæ̀nsəpéiʃən] (노예) 해방
- proclamation [prɑ̀kləméʃən] 선언[성명]서
- momentous [mouméntəs] 중대한
- decree [dikríː] 법령
- beacon [bíːkən] 횃불
- sear [siəːr] 낙인을 찍다, 시들게[마르게]하다.
- withering [wíð-əriŋ] 생기를 잃게 하는, 괴멸적인
- captivity [kæptívəti] 감금, 속박; in captivity 사로잡히어
- cripple [krípəl] 불구가 되게 하다, 무능케 하다
- manacle [mǽnəkl] 속박
- segregation [sègrigéiʃ-ən] 인종 차별 (대우)
- discrimination [diskrimənéiʃən] 구별, 차별 대우
ex. without discrimination 차별 없이, 평등하게
- the Negro lives on a lonely island of poverty in the midst of a vast ocean of material prosperity
흑인은 물질적 번영의 거대한 대양의 한가운데 있는 가난한 외로운 섬에 살고 있습니다.
- languish [lǽŋgwiʃ] (쇠)약해지다, 초췌해지다, 괴로워하다
- to cash a check 수표를 현금으로 바꾸기 위해

It is obvious today that America has defaulted on this promissory note in so far as her citizens of color are concerned. Instead of honoring this sacred obligation, America has given the Negro people a bad check; a check which has come back marked "insufficient funds." We refuse to believe that there are insufficient funds in the great vaults of opportunity of this nation.

And so we've come to this hallowed spot to remind America of the fierce urgency of now. This is no time to engage in the luxury of cooling off or to take the tranquilizing drug of gradualism. Now is the time to make real the promises of democracy; now is the time to rise from the dark and desolate valley of segregation to the sunlit path of racial justice; now is the time to lift our nation from the quicksands of racial injustice to the solid rock of brotherhood; now is the time to make justice a reality for all God's children. It would be fatal for the nation to overlook the urgency of the moment. This sweltering summer of the Negro's legitimate discontent will not pass until there is an invigorating autumn of freedom and equality.

킹목사 기념비

Nineteen sixty-three is not an end, but a beginning. And those who hope that the Negro needed to blow off steam and will now be content, will have a rude awakening if the nation returns to business as usual.

There will be neither rest nor tranquility in America until the Negro is granted his citizenship rights. The whirlwinds of revolt will continue to shake the foundations of our nation until the bright day of justice emerges.

Key Words & Phrases 해설

- constitution [kὰnstətjúːʃən] 헌법
- Declaration of Independence 독립선언
- a promissory note 약속어음
- to which every American was to fall heir 모든 미국인이 상속받게 되어 있는
- fall heir to 상속받다
- unalienable = inalienable [inéiljənəbəl] (권리 등이) 양도할 [넘겨 줄] 수 없는
  ex. the inalienable rights of man 인간의 절대적 권리
- default [difɔ́ːlt] 채무 불이행
- her citizens of color 미국의 유색 시민 (유색 인종)
- sacred obligation 성스러운 의무
- a bad check 부도수표
- "insufficient funds." 잔고부족
- in the great vaults of opportunity 기회의 커다란 금고 속에
- we've come to this hallowed spot to remind America of the fierce urgency of now
  우리는 미국에게 작금의 맹렬한 긴박함을 상기시키고자 이 신성한 곳에 왔습니다
- to take the tranquilizing drug of gradualism.
  (지금은) 점진주의라는 진정제를 복용할 (때도 아닙니다)
- Now is the time to make real the promises of democracy
  지금은 민주주의의 약속을 실현할 때입니다.
- desolate [désəlit] 황폐한, 황량한
- sunlit [sʌ́nlit] 볕이 드는, 희망에 찬
- quicksand [kwíksæ̀nd] 유사(流砂) (그 위를 걷는 사람 · 짐승을 빨아들임), 방심할 수 없는 위험한 상태[사태]
- brotherhood [brʌ́ðərhùd] 형제애

대중 연설하는 킹목사

But there is something that I must say to my people who stand on the warm threshold which leads into the palace of justice. In the process of gaining our rightful place we must not be guilty of wrongful deeds.

Let us not seek to satisfy our thirst for freedom by drinking from the cup of bitterness and hatred. We must forever conduct our struggle on the high plane of dignity and discipline. We must not allow our creative protest to degenerate into physical violence. Again and again we must rise to the majestic heights of meeting physical force with soul force.

The marvelous new militancy which has engulfed the Negro community must not lead us to distrust of all white people, for many of our white brothers, as evidenced by their presence here today, have come to realize that their destiny is tied up with our destiny and they have come to realize that their freedom is inextricably bound to our freedom. We cannot walk alone.

And as we walk, we must make the pledge that we shall always march ahead. We cannot turn back. There are those who are asking the devotees of civil rights, "When will you be satisfied? We can never be satisfied as long as the Negro is the victim of the unspeakable horrors of police brutality.

We can never be satisfied as long as our bodies, heavy with fatigue of travel, cannot gain lodging in the motels of the highways and the hotels of the cities. We cannot be satisfied as long as the Negro's basic mobility is from a smaller ghetto to

Key Words & Phrases 해설

- overlook [òuvərlúk] 빠뜨리고 보다, (결점 따위를) 눈감아 주다
- sweltering [swéltəriŋ] 찌는 듯이 더운
- legitimate [lidʒítəmit] 합법의, 정당한
- invigorating [invígərèitiŋ] 기운을 돋구는, (공기 · 산들바람 등이)상쾌한
- Nineteen sixty-three is not an end, but a beginning
  1963년은 끝이 아니라 시작입니다 (▸1963년은 킹목사가 연설한 해임.)
- blow off 분출하다
- awakening [əwéikəniŋ] 눈뜸, 각성
- have [get] a rude awakening 갑자기 불쾌한 사실을 알게 되다, 심한 환멸을 느끼다
- citizenship rights 공민권, 시민권
- whirlwind [hwə́:rlwìnd] 회오리 바람, 선풍
- revolt [rivóult] 반란, 폭동
- emerge [imə́rdʒ] 나오다, 나타나다
- threshold [θreʃhould] 문지방, 출발점
- wrongful deeds 불법행위
- the cup of bitterness and hatred 쓰고 증오에 찬 잔
- on the high plane of dignity and discipline 존엄과 자제의 높은 수준에서
- We must not allow our creative protest to degenerate into physical violence.
  우리의 창조적인 항거가 육체적인 폭력으로 타락하게끔 해서는 안 됩니다.
- majestic [mədʒéstik] 장엄한, 위엄 있는 (dignified)
- the marvelous new militancy which has engulfed the Negro community
  흑인 사회를 삼켜버린 불가사의한 새로운 투쟁정신
- for many of our white brothers, as evidenced by their presence here today, have come to realize that their destiny is tied up with our destiny

a larger one.

We can never be satisfied as long as our children are stripped of their selfhood and robbed of their dignity by signs stating "for whites only." We cannot be satisfied as long as a Negro in Mississippi cannot vote and a Negro in New York believes he has nothing for which to vote. No, we are not satisfied, and we will not be satisfied until justice rolls down like waters and righteousness like a mighty stream.

I am not unmindful that some of you have come here out of excessive trials and tribulation. Some of you have come fresh from narrow jail cells. Some of you have come from areas where your quest for freedom left you battered by the storms of persecution and staggered by the winds of police brutality. You have been the veterans of creative suffering. Continue to work with the faith that unearned suffering is redemptive.

Go back to Mississippi; go back to Alabama; go back to Louisiana; go back to the slums and ghettos of the northern cities, knowing that somehow this situation can, and will be changed. Let us not wallow in the valley of despair.

So I say to you, my friends, that even though we must face the difficulties of today and tomorrow, I still have a dream. It is a dream deeply rooted in the American dream that one day this nation will rise up and live out the true meaning of its creed—we hold these truths to be self-evident, that all men are created equal.

I have a dream that one day on the red hills of Georgia, sons of former slaves and sons of former slave-owners will be able to sit down together at the table of brotherhood.

I have a dream that one day, even the state of Mississippi, a state sweltering with the heat of injustice, sweltering with the heat of oppression, will be

Key Words & Phrases 해설

우리의 많은 백인 형제들이, 오늘 여기 그들이 참석한 것으로 입증되듯이, 그들의 운명이 우리의 운명과 묶여 있다는 것을 깨닫기 위해 왔기 때문입니다

- inextricably [inékstrikəbəli] 풀 수 없게, 뒤엉켜
- pledge [pledʒ] 서약
- devotee [dèvoutíː] 열성가
- the unspeakable horrors 이루다 말할 수 없는 공포
- brutality [bruːtǽləti] 무자비, 야만행위
- fatigue [fətíːg] 피로, 피곤
- ghetto [gétou] (흑인 등 소수 민족) 빈민굴, 슬럼(slum)가
- self-hood [sélfhùd] 인격
- "for whites only." 백인전용
- until justice rolls down like waters 정의가 강물처럼 굽이칠 때까지
- excessive trials and tribulation 과도한 시련과 고난
- narrow jail cells 비좁은 감방
- persecution [pə̀ːrsikjúːʃən] (특히 종교상의) 박해
- stagger [stǽgər] 비틀거리다
- unearned suffering 부당한 고통
- redemptive [ridémptiv] 되찾는,
- wallow [wálou / wɔ́l-] 뒹굴다, 허위적거리다
- oppression [əpréʃən] 억압, 탄압, 학대
- crooked [krúkid] 꼬부라진
- all flesh 모든 인간, 인류
- discord [díkɔːrd] 불화
- hamlet [hǽmlit] 작은 마을, 부락

transformed into an oasis of freedom and justice.

I have a dream my four little children will one day live in a nation where they will not be judged by the color of their skin but by the content of their character. I have a dream today!

I have a dream that one day every valley shall be exalted, every hill and mountain shall be made low, the rough places shall be made plain, and the crooked places shall be made straight and the glory of the Lord will be revealed and all flesh shall see it together.

This is our hope. This is the faith that I go back to the South with.

With this faith we will be able to hew out of the mountain of despair a stone of hope. With this faith we will be able to transform the jangling discords of our nation into a beautiful symphony of brotherhood.

With this faith we will be able to work together, to pray together, to go to jail together, knowing that we will be free one day. This will be the day when all of God's children will be able to sing with new meaning—"my country 'tis of thee; sweet land of liberty; of thee I sing; land where my fathers died, land of the pilgrim's pride; from every mountain side, let freedom ring"—and if America is to be a great nation, this must become true.

Let freedom ring from the mighty mountains of New York.

Let freedom ring from the heightening Alleghenies of Pennsylvania.

Let freedom ring from the snow-capped Rockies of Colorado.

Let freedom ring from the curvaceous slopes of California.

But not only that.

Let freedom ring from the Stone Mountain of Georgia.

Key Words & Phrases 해설

- speed up 속도를 내다, 크게 박차를 가하다
  ex. The heart sped up. 가슴이 두근거렸다.
- Negro spiritual [spítʃu-əl] 흑인 영가

Let freedom ring from Lookout Mountain of Tennessee.

Let freedom ring from every hill and molehill of Mississippi, from every mountainside, let freedom ring.

And when we allow freedom to ring, when we let it ring from every village and hamlet, from every state and city, we will be able to speed up that day when all of God's children—black men and white men, Jews and Gentiles, Catholics and Protestants—will be able to join hands and to sing in the words of the old Negro spiritual, "Free at last, free at last; thank God Almighty, we are free at last."

Consider this

1. What are the major indictments Martin Luther King makes and what alternatives does he propose? Do you observe the parallel between King's speech and "The Fabrication of Race" or "Poverty knows No Color". If so, Exlpain them.

2. What function is given to the mind by the title, 'I have a dream? What is the significance of his selecting these words.

3. Does the racial prejudice, segregation and discrimination still exist? If so, what obstacles stood in solving the racial problems today? How does King manage to convince us that racial problem is very serious?

6. John Lock's Political Theory

RICHARD L. AARON

6 John Locke's Political Theory

RICHARD L. AARON

존 로크의 초상화

Locke's political theory is to be found in his *Two Treatises of Civil Government*, particularly in the second of these. The immediate aim of that treatise is apparent: to justify the Revolution of 1688 and to help 'establish the throne of our great restorer, our present King William. But this aim is achieved by securing in turn a great and fundamental political principle, true for the English nation in 1688 and true, in Locke's opinion, for all well regulated communities everywhere and at all times, that government must be with the consent of the governed, that a ruler who has lost the confidence of his people no longer has the right to govern them.

The principle involves a particular view of government and of political community. Locke set himself to refute two theories which were used to justify privilege, oppression, and political slavery. The first was the theory of the divine right of kings as put forward by Robert Filmer, that the king is the divinely ordained father of his people, and that the relation between king and subjects is precisely the same as that between father and child. Locke ridicules the comparison. In the modern state, a large, highly complex organization, parental or patriarchal government is no longer possible, and the claim that it is divinely ordained cannot be substantiated.

The second theory is to be found in its most explicit form in the works of Hobbes, although Locke does not refer to Hobbes by name, at least in the Treatise. Government, in this theory, necessarily involves the complete subjection of the

Key Words & Phrases 해설

- John Locke (1632 ~ 1704) 존 로크, 영국의 17세기 정치 철학자. 주요 저서로는 *Two treatises of government, An Essay Concerning Human Understanding* 등이 있다.
  (Locke 저서는 1689년부터 그의 사망 때까지 익명으로 출판되었다. 물론 *Two treatises of government*란 제목의 이 저서도 익명으로 출판되었다. 이 저서의 서문은 이렇게 시작된다; "Reader, Thou hast here the Beginning and End of a Discourse concerning Government; what Fate has otherwise disposed of the Papers that should have filled up the middle, and were more than all the rest, 'tis not worth while to tell thee.")
- to justify the Revolution of 1688
  1688년의 혁명(명예혁명)을 정당화하기 위해서
- King William
  혁명으로 축출된 King James 2세를 뒤 이어 왕위에 오른 윌리엄 3세를 말함
- in turn 차례로
- a great and fundamental political principle 하나의 큰 근본적인 정치원리
- a ruler who has lost the confidence of his people no longer has the right to govern them
  국민의 신망을 잃은 통치자는 더 이상 그 국민을 다스리는 권리를 갖지 못한다
- government must be with the consent of the governed
  정부는 지배받는 사람들의 동의를 얻어야만 한다
- Locke set himself to refute two theories
  로크는 두 가지 이론을 논박하고자 노력했다
- as put forward by Robert Filmer
  로버트 필머에 의해서 제창된
  (그는 왕권신수설(The theory of the Divine Right of Kings)을 정당화 하는 *Patriarcha*란 저서를 썼다)
- the divinely ordained father 신이 내려준 아버지
- the claim that it is divinely ordained cannot be substantiated

governed to the absolute will of the governor, for without such subjection no civil society is possible. Locke denies this theory categorically. The facts of human experience are against it and reason is against it. A political community is possible in which the governor is limited; in which sovereignty ultimately pertains not to the monarch, as opposed to those whom he governs, but to the people as a whole. Government becomes an instrument for securing the lives, property, and well-being of the governed, and this without enslaving the governed in any way. Government is not their master; it is created by the people voluntarily and maintained by them to secure their own good. Those who, because of their superior talent, have been set to rule by the community, rule not as masters over slaves, or even as fathers over children. They are officers elected by the people to carry out certain tasks. Their powers are to be used in accordance with 'that trust which is put into their hands by their brethren'. For Locke government is a 'trust' and a political community is an organization of equals, of 'brothers', into which men enter voluntarily in order to achieve what they cannot achieve apart.

Such was the view of government which Locke adopted, and the second treatise is an effort to discover a rational justification of this view. Locke might have appealed to experience and to history, or again he might have contented himself with showing the public utility of the theory he advocated. But the late seventeenth century was rationalist and would listen to no arguments other than rationalist ones, and so Locke analysed the notion of political society in order to prove rationally that it was from the first a community of free individuals and that it remained so throughout. He spoke in the language of his day and he made use of the theories of his day. In particular, he borrowed two concepts from earlier political theories, the law of nature and the social contract.

Key Words & Phrases 해설

신이 내린다는 주장은 성립될 수 없다

- Thomas Hobbes (1588 ~ 1679) 토마스 홉스
  영국의 위대한 정치 철학자.
  (저서로는 *Leviathan*은 유명하다. 이 책에서 그는 인간성과 정부와 사회의 필요성을 기술하고 있다. 물론 이것은 Philip Coates가 "Wreaking Hobbes on mankind"에서 설명한 바 있듯이, 그 자신의 시대의 사회적 상황과 정치적 상황을 반영한 염세적인 인간성을 전제로 한 것이다.)

- although Locke does not refer to Hobbes by name
  로크가 홉스의 이름을 언급하지 않는다 해도

- at least 적어도

- the complete subjection of the governed to the absolute will of the governor
  통치자의 절대 의지에 피지배자들의 완전한 복종

- for without such subjection no civil society is possible
  그 같은 복종 없이는 어떠한 시민 사회도 불가능하기 때문이다

- categorically 단언적으로

- as opposed to those whom he governs
  그가 지배하는 사람들과 대립되는 의미에서

- sovereignty ultimately pertains not to the monarch, as opposed to those whom he governs, but to the people as a whole
  주권은 궁극적으로 군주에 속하는 것이 아니라 전체 국민에 속하는 것이다

- and this 그리고 그것을, 더군다나
  (this는 앞문장의 securing the lives~ of the governed 까지를 가리킨다)

- be set to rule 통치하도록 지명을 받다

- that trust which is put into their hands by their brethren
  그들의 동포들에 의해 그들의 손에 맡겨진 그 책임

- what they cannot achieve apart 그들이 흩어져서는 성취할 수 없는 것

Consider this

1. How does the writer construct his argument? Is it convincing? Why, or why not?

2. Does the writer offer any serious solutions for the problems he is describing? Do you believe 'the social contract' from earlier political theories.

Key Words & Phrases 해설

- appealed to~ ~에 호소하다
- or again 또 한편
- content oneself with ~에 만족하다
- the public utility of the theory he advocated
  그가 옹호한 이론의 공적인 효용성
- would listen to no arguments other than rationalist ones
  합리적인 것들 이외의 어떤 주장에도 귀를 기울이려 하지 않았다
- throughout 처음부터 끝까지, 줄 곧
- from earlier political theories 초기 정치이론에서

7. The Nature of Scientific Reasoning

JACOB BROUNOWSKI

7 The Nature of Scientific Reasoning

JACOB BRONOWSKI

태양계 모형도

What is the insight in which the scientist tries to see into nature? Can it indeed be called either imaginative or creative? To the literary man the question may seem merely silly. He has been taught that science is a large collection of facts; and if this is true, then the only seeing which scientists need to do is, he supposes, seeing the facts. He pictures them, the colorless professionals of science, going off to work in the morning into the universe in a neutral, unexposed state. They then expose themselves like a photographic plate. And then in the darkroom or laboratory they develop the image, so that suddenly and startlingly it appears, printed in capital letters, as a new formula for atomic energy.

Men who have read Balzac and Zola are not deceived by the claims of the writers that they do no more than record the facts. The readers of Christopher Isherwood do not take him literally when he writes "I am a camera." Yet the same readers solemnly carry with them from their schooldays this foolish picture of the scientist fixing by some mechanical process the facts of nature. I have had of all people a historian tell me that science is a collection of facts.

It seems impossible that this historian had ever studied the beginnings of a scientific discovery. The Scientific Revolution can be held to begin in the year 1543 when there was brought to Copernicus, perhaps on his deathbed, the first printed copy of the book he had finished about a dozen years earlier. The thesis of

Key Words & Phrases 해설

- JACOB BRONOWSKI (1908 ~ 1974)
  폴란드 태생의 영국 수학자, 과학의 인문학적 특성을 강조함.
- the nature of scientific reasoning 과학적 추론의 본질
- insight [insait] 통찰, 통찰력
- a man of insight 통찰력이 있는 사람
- see into ~을 조사하다,
- imaginative [imǽdʒənətiv, -néitiv] 상상의, 상상적인
- creative [kri:éitiv] 창조적인, 창조력이 있는
- merely [míərli] 단지, 그저
- silly [síli] 어리석은(stupid)
- the only seeing which scientists need to do is, he supposes, seeing the facts
  과학자들이 볼 필요가 있는 유일한 보기는, 문학자가 생각건대, 사실들을 보는 일이다
- go off 떠나다
- picture [píktʃər] 마음에 그리다, 묘사하다
- like a photographic plate 사진 감광판(건판)처럼
- develop (사진)상을 현상하다
- printed in capital letters 대문자로 인화되어
- as a new formula for atomic energy 원자 에너지의 새로운 공식으로서
- no more than 단지
- Honore de Balzac [bǽlzæk, bɔ́:l-] 발자크 (1799 ~ 1850) 프랑스의 소설가
- Émile Zola [zóulə] 졸라 (1840 ~ 1902) 프랑스의 자연주의 소설가
- Christopher Isherwood 현대 영국소설가 겸 극작가
- literally [lítərəli] 글자 뜻 그대로, 축어적으로

this book is that the earth moves around the sun. When did Copernicus go out and record this fact with his camera? What appearance in nature prompted his outrageous guess? And in what odd sense is this guess to be called a neutral record of fact?

Less than a hundred years after Copernicus, Kepler published (between 1609 and 1619) the three laws which describe the paths of the planets. The work of Newton and with it most of our mechanics spring from these laws. They have a solid, matter-of-fact sound. For example, Kepler says that if one squares the year of a planet, one gets a number which is proportional to the cube of its average distance from the sun. Does anyone think that such a law is found by taking enough readings and then squaring and cubing everything in sight? If he does, then, as a scientist, he is doomed to a wasted life, he has as little prospect of making a scientific discovery as an electronic brain has.

It was not this way that Copernicus and Kepler thought, or that scientists think today. Copernicus found that the orbits of the planets would look simpler if they were looked at from the sun and not from the earth. But he did not in the first place find this by routine calculation. His first step was a leap of imagination — to lift himself from the earth, and put himself wildly, speculatively into the sun. "The earth conceives from the sun," he wrote, and "the sun rules the family of stars." We catch in his mind an image, the gesture of the virile man standing in the sun, with arms outstretched, over looking the planets. Perhaps Copernicus took the picture from the drawings of the youth with outstretched arms which the Renaissance teachers put into their books on the proportions of the body. Perhaps he had seen Leonardo's drawings of his loved pupil Salai. I do not know. To me, the gesture of Copernicus, the shining youth looking outward from the sun, is still

Key Words & Phrases 해설

- solemn [sάləm] 엄숙한, solemnly [sάləmli] 엄숙하게
- carry with 기억하다
- by some mechanical process 어떤 기계적인 과정으로
- of all people (구어) (그 많은 사람 중에) 하필이면
  ex. They chose me as a chairman, of all people.
  그들은 하필이면 나를 의장으로 뽑았다.
- The Scientific Revolution 과학혁명
- Nicolaus Copernicus [koupə́ːrnikəs] (1473~1543)
  코페르니쿠스, 지동설을 제창한 폴란드의 천문학자
- perhaps on his deathbed 아마 그의 임종시에
- about a dozen years earlier 대략 십여 년 전에
- prompt [prαmpt / prɔmpt] 자극하다, 격려[고무]하다
- outrageous [autréidʒəs] 터무니없는, (미국속어) 굉장한
- Less than a hundred years 백 년도 채 안 돼서
- Johann Kepler [képlər] (1571~1630)
  케플러, 독일의 천문학자, 행성 운동에 관한 Kepler's law를 발견
- planet [plǽnət] 행성
- path [pæθ, pɑːθ] (천체의) 궤도
- Isaac Newton [njúːtn] (1642~1727)
  뉴턴, 영국의 물리학자, 수학자로 만유인력 법칙 발견
- mechanics [məkǽniks] 역학
- square [skwεəːr] 제곱하다
- cube [kjúːb] 세제곱하다
- one gets a number which is proportional to the cube
  우리는 세제곱에 비례하는 수를 얻는다

vivid in a drawing which William Blake in 1780 based on all these: the drawing which is usually called Glad Day···.

No scientific theory is a collection of facts. It will not even do to call a theory true or false in the simple sense in which every fact is either so or not so. The Epicureans held that matter is made of atoms two thousand years ago and we are now tempted to say that their theory was true. But if we do so we confuse their notion of matter with our own. John Dalton in 1808 first saw the structure of matter as we do today, and what he took from the ancients was not their theory but something richer, their image: the atom. Much of what was in Dalton's mind was as vague as the Greek notion, and quite as mistaken. But he suddenly gave life to the new facts of chemistry and the ancient theory together, by fusing them to give what neither had: a coherent picture of how matter is linked and built up from different kinds of atoms. The act of fusion is the creative act.

All science is the search for unity in hidden likenesses. The search may be on a grand scale, as in the modern theories which try to link the fields of gravitation and electromagnetism. But we do not need to be browbeaten by the scale of science. There are discoveries to be made by snatching a small likeness from the air too, if it is bold enough. In 1935 the Japanese physicist Hideki Yukawa wrote a paper which can still give heart to a young scientist. He took as his starting point the known fact that waves of light can sometimes behave as if they were separate pellets. From this he reasoned that the forces which hold the nucleus of an atom together might sometimes also be observed as if they were solid pellets. A schoolboy can see how thin Yukawa's analogy is, and his teacher would be severe with it. Yet Yukawa without a blush calculated the mass of the pellet he expected to see, and waited. He was right; his meson was found, and a range of other

Key Words & Phrases 해설

- orbit [ɔ́:rbit] 궤도
- in the first place 맨 먼저, 우선 무엇보다도
- by routine calculation 판에 박힌 계산으로는
- a leap of imagination 상상력의 도약, 도약적인 상상력
- speculatively [spékjəléitivli] 사색적으로, 순전히 이론적으로
- "The earth conceives from the sun,"
  지구는 태양에서 생겨났다 (conceive = be made, be created)
- virile [vírəl, vírail] 사나이의, 힘찬
- with arms outstretched [áutstrétʃt] 쭉 뻗쳐진 양팔을 가진
- vivid [vívid] 생생한
- William Blake [bleik] (1757 ~ 1827) 블레이크 영국의 시인 · 화가
- hold (신념 · 신앙 등을) 간직하다, (학설 등을) 신봉하다
- matter is made of atoms 물질은 원자들로 이루어져 있다.
- be tempted ed to do ~하고 싶어지다
  ex. I am tempted to question that. 나는 그것을 의심하고 싶어진다.
- confuse [kənfjú:z] 혼동하다
  ex. She confused liberty with license. 그녀는 자유와 방종을 혼동했다.
- John Dalton [dɔ́:ltən] (1766~1844)
  돌턴, 영국의 화학 · 물리학자, 원자론을 발표하고, 근대화학의 기초를 확립한 과학자
- the ancients [éinʃənts] 고대 문명인
- take from ~에게서 이어받다
  ex. He took his good looks from his mother.
  (그는 자신의 어머니의 미모를 이어받았다.)
- fuse [fjúz] 융합시키다, 융합하다.
- coherent [kouhíərənt] 시종 일관된, 이치가 닿는

mesons, neither the existence nor the nature of which had been suspected before. The likenesses had borne fruit.

The scientist looks for order in the appearances of nature by exploring such likenesses. For order does not display itself of itself; if it can be said to be there at all, it is not there for the mere looking. There is no way of pointing a finger or camera at it; order must be discovered and, in a deep sense, it must be created. What we see, as we see it, is mere disorder···.

Science finds order and meaning in our experience, and sets about this in quite a different way. It sets about it as Newton did in the story which he himself told in his old age, and of which the schoolbooks give only a caricature. In the year 1665, when Newton was twenty-two, the plague broke out in southern England, and the University of Cambridge was closed. Newton therefore spent the next eighteen months at home, removed from traditional learning, at a time when he was impatient for knowledge and, in his own phrase, "I was in the prime of my age for invention." In this eager, boyish mood, sitting one day in the garden of his widowed mother, he saw an apple fall. So far the books have the story right; we think we even know the kind of apple; tradition has it that it was a Flower of Kent. But now they miss the crus of the story. For what struck the young Newton at the sight was not the thought that the apple must be drawn to the earth by gravity; that conception was older than Newton. What struck him was the conjecture that the same force of gravity, which reaches to the top of the tree, might go on reaching out beyond the earth and its air, endlessly into space. Gravity might reach the moon: this was Newton's new thought; and it might be gravity which holds the moon in her orbit. There and then he calculated what force from the earth would hold the moon, and compared it with the known force of gravity at tree height. The

Key Words & Phrases 해설

- All science is the search for unity in hidden likenesses
  모든 과학은 숨겨진 유사함 속에서 통일성을 찾아내는 것이다.
- on a grand scale 웅대한 규모로
- gravitation [grӕvətéiʃən] 인력(작용), 중력
- electromagnetism [ilèktroumǽgnətizəm] 전자기(電磁氣), 전자기학
- browbeat [braubì:t] (얼굴 · 말 따위로) 을러대다, 위협하다
  ex. He browbeat her into agreeing 그는 그녀를 을러대어 승낙케 했다.
- snatch [snӕtʃ] 와락 붙잡다, 잡아채다
- bold [bould] 대담한(daring), 담력이 있는
- a paper which can still give heart to a young scientist
  한 젊은 과학자에게 여전히 마음을 빼앗기게 할 수 있는 논문
- as his starting point 그의 출발점으로서
- pellet [pélit] 탄알, 산탄
- waves of light 빛의 파동
- nucleus [njú:kliəs] 핵
- thin [θin] 빈약한
- severe [sivíə:r] 엄한, 용서 없는
  ex. She is severe with his children. 그녀는 아이들에게 엄하다.
- without a blush 얼굴을 붉히지 않고서
- observe [əbzə:rv] 관찰하다, 관측하다,
- mass [mӕss] 질량
- meson [mízɑn, mésɔn] 종행면(縱行面) : 몸 중앙에서 좌우가 같게 세로로 자른 면
- For order does not display itself of itself
  질서는 저절로 나타나지 않기 때문이다.
  of itself 저절로, 자연히, display oneself 나타나다

forces agreed; Newton says laconically, "I found them answer pretty nearly." Yet they agreed only nearly: the likeness and the approximation go together, for no likeness is exact. In Newton's science modern sciences is full grown.

It grow from a comparison. It has seized a likeness between two unlike appearances; for the apple in the summer garden and the grave moon overhead are surely as unlike in their movements as two things can be. Newton traced in them two expressions of a single concept, gravitation: and the concept (and the unity) are in that sense his free creation. The progress of science is the discovery at each step of a new order which gives unity to what had long seemed unlike.

Consider this

1. In his opening paragraph, Bronowski pictures what the "literary man", or perhaps the ordinary non-scientist, thinks of as the nature of science. Is this a fair representation of the ordinary man's view of science? What features of science or of the presentation of science might contribute to the development of that view?

2. In his fourth paragraph Bronowski indicates that an electronic brain has little or no chance of making a scientific discovery. Do you agree? Why, or why not?

3. Bronowski recounts the famous story of Newton and the apple. What general principle about science is he exemplifying in this story?

Key Words & Phrases 해설

- at all은 <조건절>에서는 '일단 ~이면, ~할 바엔'의 의미로 쓰인다.
  ex. If you do it at all, do it well. 당신이 기왕 할 바에는 잘 해라.
- set about 퍼뜨리다
  ex. She set a rumor about. 그녀는 소문을 퍼뜨렸다.
- caricature [kǽrikətʃúər] (풍자) 만화, 풍자하는 글
- broke out 발생했다
- plague [pleig] 역병(疫病), 전염병, (흔히 the) 페스트
- at a time 동시에
- be impatient for ~탐나서 못 견디다, ~안타깝게 기다리다
- in his own phrase 자신의 말로 표현하면
- widowed mother 미망인이된 어머니, 과부 어머니
- crus [kruːs, krʌs] (해부학) 다리
- what struck the young Newton 젊은 뉴톤의 마음속에 갑자기 떠오른 것
- gravity [grǽvəti] 중력, 지구인력
- conception [kənsépʃən] 개념
- conjecture [kəndʒéktʃər] 추측
- there and then (=then and there) 그 때 그 자리에서, 즉석에서
  ex. She decided to refuse his proposal there and then.
  그녀는 즉석에서 그의 제안을 거절하기로 결심했다.
- laconically [ləkɑ́nikəli] 간결하게
- approximation[´prA@ks´me@iS´n] 근사, 비슷한 것[일]
- in that sense 그런 의미에서
- at each step of a new order 새로운 질서의 각 단계에서

8. The new age of Man

MALCOLM GLADWELL

8 The new age of Man

MALCOLM GLADWELL

Michael R. Rose began his quest to solve the problem of human aging in 1976 with 200 garden-variety, fertilized female fruit flies. He was then a graduate student in genetics at the University of Sussex, testing a new idea known as the evolutionary theory of aging, and he started out by putting his flies in milk bottles with nutrients in the bottom. In the uncertain world of the fruit fly drosophila, where predators and natural hazards abound, the kinds of flies which survive are those which reproduce the fastest, and these were no exception. They were, in Roses words, trailer-park flies: quick to reach sexual maturity, capable of laying a thousand eggs in their five-week period of fertility, and for a few hours, just after they reach maturation, possessed of almost dizzying sexual prowess. Left to their own devices, they would have continued to reproduce at the same breakneck pace. But Rose wasn't interested in the normal rules of fruit-fly life. He wanted to reward not the flies that reproduced the fastest but the ones that lived the longest; and so, once his female flies came of age, he would wash away their eggs and larvae every other day, destroying all the progeny of his most precocious flies. The only eggs he saved were those laid near the very end of the fruit flies five-week fertility cycle in other words, those eggs born to the parent flies who were healthy and sexually active latest in life. Then, with these eggs in hand, he repeated the process. He bred those specially selected fruit flies, and kept only those offspring produced at the very end of the fruit-fly fertility period, once more rewarding the hardiest and longest-lived flies. He stayed in the lab sometimes for 21 hours at a stretch, and

Key Words & Phrases 해설

- aging, age- [éidʒiŋ] n. 나이를 먹음; 노화; (술 등의) 숙성(熟成)
  ex. the ~ process 노화 작용
- variety [vəráiəti] n. 이종(異種); 〖생물〗 변종(subspecies 아래의 구분);
- fertilize [fə́:rtəláiz] v. 〖생물〗 수정[수태]시키다
- genetics [dʒinétiks] n. pl.「단수취급」유전학(遺傳學);「복수취급」유전적 특질
- nutrient [njú:triənt] n. 영양소; 영양제, 자양물; 음식
- drosophila [drousáfilə / -snɔ́f-] n. (pl. ~s, -lae [-li:]) 〖곤충〗 초파리
- predator [prédətər] n. 약탈자; 육식 동물
- maturity [mətjú-ərəti, -tʃú:- / -tʃúərə-] n. U ① 성숙, 숙성; 원숙
- maturation 성숙
- dizzying [díziiŋ] a. 현기증나게 하는, 어지럽게 하는. ~ly -ad
- prowess [práuis] n. ① 용감, 무용(武勇)(valor); 용감한 행위. ② 훌륭한 솜씨. ~d -a.
- breakneck [bréiknèk] a. ① (목이 부러질 정도로) 위험하기 짝이 없는
  ex. at ~ speed 무서운 속력으로
- larva [lá:rvə]
  n. (pl. -vae [-vi:]) 〖곤충〗 애벌레, 유충; 변태 동물의 유생(幼生)(올챙이 따위)
- come [be] of age~ 성년에 달하다(달해 있다)
- every other day [week, year, door, line] 하루[한 주일, 한 해, 한 집, 한 행] 걸러
- progeny [prádʒəni / prɔ́dʒ-]
  n. (pl. ~; 동식물인 경우 -nies) 자손,「집합적」아이; 종족, 일족;
- precocious [prikóuʃəs] a. 조숙한, 일된, 어른다운(아이 · 거동 따위);
- fertility [fə:rtíləti] n. 〖동물〗 번식[생식]력
- offspring [ɔ́:fspríŋ]
  n. (pl. ~(s))「집합적」자식, 자녀; 자손, 후예, (하나의) 자식, 자손
- at a stretch 단숨에, 단번에

when he went home he would see flies in his sleep. He bred generation after generation, eventually conducting his experiment on a scale that no other fruit-fly researcher had ever attempted, and each time he measured the life span of a new round he found that his drosophila offspring lived a little longer than their forebears.

But Rose makes it clear that he expects those efforts to result in fundamental increases in life span. At one point when we were talking, he walked into the hallway outside his office, where a research paper posted on the wall showed, in a bar graph, how long Roses Methuselah flies were now living. Look here, he said, pointing to the graph. This would correspond to a human life span of 200 years.

Ten or fifteen years ago, scientists didn't talk like this. The traditional scientific approach to the problem of aging has been to accept our biological limits and try to rearrange the lives and the care of the elderly to make old age more manageable. Our efforts have been largely palliative to put elevators in buildings, to make public spaces accessible to wheelchairs, to devise better treatments for cataracts, to perform coronary-bypass operations to cut down on chest pain, and even, in the case of one of the more imaginative projects sponsored by the Centers for Disease Control, to try to make fluid-filled pads for elderly hips and thus protect against the fractures that are such a common form of disability in the old. The motto of the Gerontological Society of America has been Add life to years, not years to life, which is a statement not just of intention but of apparent fact. For a long time, no one thought you could add years to life. Mice were thought to live about two years, dogs about 15 years, and human beings at most 100 years all according to some immutable genetic clock and any scientists who made spectacular claims of reversing the aging process were treated with skepticism.

Key Words & Phrases 해설

- forebear, for-[fɔ́:rbɛ̀ə:r] n. (보통 pl.) 선조
- Methuselah [mieju:zələ]
  n. 〚성서〛 므두셀라(969세까지 살았다는 전설상의 사람; 창세기 V: 27); (m–) (종종 우스개) 「일반적」 C (아주) 나이 많은 사람, 시대에 뒤진 사람
- palliative [pǽliéitiv, -liə-] a. 완화하는, 경감하는, 임시적인
- cataract [kǽtərǽkt] n. 〚의학〛 백내장(白內障); (수정체의) 혼탁부(混濁部)
- coronary [kɔ́:rənèri, kár- / kɔ́rənəri] 〚해부학〛 관상(冠狀) (동맥)의; 심장의
- fracture [frǽktʃə:r] n. 〚의학〛 골절, 좌상(挫傷)
- gerontology [dʒèrəntálədʒi / -tɔ́l-]
  n. U 노인학, 노년학(노화 현상 연구).
  [cf.] geriatrics. ㊇-gist —n. ㊇-tologic, -ical [-təládʒik/ -lɔ́dʒ-], [-əl] -a.
- immutable [imjú:təbəl] a. 변경할 수 없는, 불변의

Even the idea of treating aging with hormones like testosterone, melatonin, and DHEA currently being celebrated as the fountain of youth in one breathless magazine article after another does not represent a dramatic departure from this way of thinking. Hormone-replacement therapy is meant to give the aging body a tune up, to delay or lessen certain problems associated with old age. Yet even that modest goal comes with certain caveats. DHEA for example, changes the color of rodent livers from pink to brown; when 16 rats were fed DHEA for a year and a half, in a recent study at Northwestern University, 14 developed liver cancer. Nor is melatonin likely to be any better. Writing in the journal Cell late last year, Steven Reppert and David Weaver, of Harvard Medical Schools Laboratory of Developmental Chronobiology, pointed out that the animal experiments that triggered the melatonin craze were conducted on strains of mice with a genetic defect that made it impossible for them to produce melatonin on their own. When the experiments were done in mice that, like human beings, make the hormone naturally, the authors noted dryly, The treatment actually shortened survival by inducing reproductive tract tumors.

The new field of aging is quite different. It is not a tune-up so much as an engine overhaul. There is Rose, with his Methuselah flies, and behind him, in just the past decade, there has arisen a whole field of scientists using evolutionary and genetic techniques to create entirely new long-lived strains of lower organisms. Last year, two researchers at Montreals McGill University published a paper in the journal Science showing how they genetically altered worms to live almost seven times as long as is normal. Kenyon showed me one of her mutant worms moving across a microscope slide as gracefully and vigorously at 8 weeks as a normal worm moves at 2 weeks. Over the past 5 years, too, an entirely separate field has

Key Words & Phrases 해설

- hormone [hɔ́ːrmoun] n. U 〖생화학〗 호르몬
- testosterone [testástəròun / -tɔ́s-] n. 〖생화학〗 테스토스테론(남성 호르몬의 일종)
- melatonin [mèlətóunin]
  a. 〖생물〗 멜라토닌(망막이 받은 빛의 양에 반비례하여 송과선(松果腺)에서 분비되는 호르몬; 바이오리듬 조절에서 중요함; 양서류에서 흑색소포(素胞)를 퇴색시켜 표피의 빛을 밝게 하는 작용을 함)
- celebrated [séləbrèitid] a. 세상에 알려진(for)
- caveat [kéiviæ̀t] n. 경고, 제지, 억제; 단서(但書)
- rodent [róud-ən-t] a. n. 〖의학〗 (특히 궤양이) 잠식성의
- ract [trækt]
  n. 〖의학 · 해부학〗 관(管), 도(道), 계통; (신경 섬유의) 다발, 삭(索)
- tumor, -mour [tjúːməːr] n. 〖의학〗 종양(腫瘍); 돌출부
- overhaul [óuvərhɔ̀ːl] n. 철저한 조사, 분해 검사[수리], 오버홀; 정밀검사
- strain [strein]
  n. 종족, 혈통, 가계(家系); 계통. 유전질, 소질; 기질, 기풍; 경향.
  변종(變種). 〖유전학〗 균주(菌株), 계통(본래의 세균과 성질이 약간 다른 균)
- organism [ɔ́ːrgənìzəm] n. 유기체[물]; 생물(체)
- mutant [mjúːtənt] a. 변화한; 〖생물〗 돌연변이의[에 의한]. 〖생물〗 돌연변이체
- cellular [séljələr] a. 세포로 된, 세포질[모양]의

arisen that analyzes aging at the cellular level and looks to treat and possibly cure many of the conditions and diseases of old age by focussing on the mysterious role played by the strips of DNA that cap the ends of our chromosomes. There are now serious researchers not just science fiction writers or crackpots who think that we are close to curing cancer and other diseases of old age, and there are some who are convinced that the day is not far off when science may be able to extend the human life span by 20 or 50 or even 100 years. To this new crop of researchers on aging those who look at the extension of life at a cellular or evolutionary level growing old now seems less an immutable fact of human existence than a chronic disease that can be delayed and treated and manipulated as if it were diabetes or high cholesterol. This is what is so extraordinary about looking at Roses flies and seeing them buzz about energetically in their plastic cages weeks after normal flies would be dead. Its not that they are imposing and impressive and bear the marks of some dramatic scientific intervention. Quite the opposite: they look just like normal flies and act like normal flies. Roses flies, by their very ordinariness, make longer life seem eminently possible.

Consider this

1. What is the writer's important point? What kinds of evidence does the writer use in supporting his argument? Do you think they are equally valid?

2. Do you have a different perspective of your own about aging?

Key Words & Phrases 해설

- chromosome [króuməsòum] n. 〖생물〗 염색체
- crackpot [krǽkpàt / -pɔ́t] n. a. (구어) 정신이 돈(사람); 별난 생각을 지닌(사람)
- chronic [kránik / krɔ́n-] a. 〖의학〗 만성의, 고질의. [opp.] acute. 상습적인
- diabetes [dàiəbí:tis, -ti:z] n. U 〖의학〗 당뇨병
- cholesterol, cholesterin [kəléstəròul, -rɔ̀:l / -rɔ̀l], [kəléstərin / kɔ-]
  U. 〖생화학〗 콜레스테롤(지방 · 혈액 · 담즙 따위에 있음)

History & World　Section 4

9. Sarajevo: Survival Guide 1993

FAMA

9 Sarajevo: Survival Guide 1993

FAMA

사라예보 전경

Climate Sarajevo's climate is very continental, with a short hot summer, when nights are still cold due to the constant breeze coming from the surrounding mountains. Winters are rich with snow, from November until April. Snow has been recorded in August and in June—a fact which can be found in old Sarajevo chronicles. War so far hasn't changed the climate. The moon is still shining, the sun rises, rains fall, and it snows, too.

Accommodation Those who were lucky still live in their apartment. Refugees and those whose apartments have been burned or destroyed by grenades are inhabiting the apartments of those who left Sarajevo before or during the war. Temporary leases and bills of sale are being issued. Some entered flats by breaking the doors and changed locks. You can change apartments if one of your friends manages to leave town. Some people have two or three apartments. Depending on what each of them can offer—electricity, gas, water; or minimal security—people move from one apartment to another. Some are living in communes. Old families have disintegrated—new ones are being formed.

Windows are gone, destroyed by perpetual detonations. It was kind of pleasant during the summer—plastic came only with the first rains. People fixed it to the window-frames with the wide tape used in factories for packing, but the glue gave up under the rain and winds. Then they used nails. Whoever had no plastic—a

Key Words & Phrases 해설

- Sarajevo's climate is very continental
  사라예보의 기후는 꽤 대륙성 기후이다
- so far 지금까지
- accommodation [əkɑ̀mədéiʃən]
  (호텔 · 객선 · 여객기 · 병원의) 숙박[수용] 시설, 편의 시설
- refugee [réfjuːdʒi] 피난자, 난민
- grenade [grənéid] 수류탄(handqrenade)
- inhabit [inhǽbit] (~에)살다, 거주하다
  (▸ live와는 달리 타동사로 쓰이며, 통상 개인에게는 쓰지 않고 집단에 씀.)
- before or during the war 전쟁전이나 전쟁기간에
- lease [liːs] (토지 · 건물 따위의) 차용계약, 차용증서
- bills of sale 매도증서
- flat [flæt] 플랫식 주택 (각 층에 1가구가 살게 만든 아파트), pl. 플랫식 공동 주택
- Depending on what each of them can offer
  각 아파트가 제공할 수 있는 것 (가스, 물, 전기, 안전도 등)에 의지하여
- commune [kɑ́mjuːn] 집단 농장, 공동 부락.
- disintegrate [disíntingrèit] 허물어지다, 붕괴하다
- new ones are being formed 새로운 가족들이 형성되었다.
- by perpetual detonations 계속되는 폭발로
- People fixed it to the window-frames with the wide tape used in factories for packing
  사람들은 공장에서 사용하는 포장용 광폭 테이프로 창문틀에다 플라스틱을 고정시켰다.
- glue [gluː] [일반적] 접착제, 풀
- cardboard boxes 마분지 상자

more than precious item on the black market—would cover the windows with cardboard boxes left behind from humanitarian aid. However, the best for the purpose proved to be the smaller sacks for the rice provided by UNPROFOR.

사라예보의 폭격 맞은 건물

Water Water shortages may last for days, or weeks. The reasons are always the same—no electricity, or an act of terror. Then the search starts. First, one checks a basement. Then you may go to Konak (which serves only the privileged), then to Sedam Brace on Bistrik, where long lines form, then in the neighborhood of Pionirska Dolina, where one waits under the snipers. Those who carry water, depending on their strength and the number of canisters, do so several times a day, traveling several kilometers, waiting in each line for at least three hours. The lucky ones are those with bicycles, which are pushed rather than ridden. The same with the owners of baby-carriages or former supermarket carts. Anything that rolls will do, for anything is easier than carrying the water by hand.

People stand in lines, in the rain, waiting with buckets for their portion of rainwater. Day or night—it doesn't really matter. People drink it and use it for doing laundry. It is very good for your hair, which becomes silky and shiny.

The washing machine is a household appliance from some long-gone time. It has no function. The women of Sarajevo are again first-class laundresses. The only thing lacking is a battledore, lye soap and a clean river to wash what they have.

Sarajevo by Night Sarajevo life is dependent on the cycle of the sun. Without

Key Words & Phrases 해설

- humanitarian aid 인도주의적인 원조
- sacks for the rice 쌀자루
- UNPROFOR [ʌ́nproufɔ̀ː] 유엔보호군 (**U**nited **N**ations **Pro**tection **For**ce)
- shortage [ʃɔ́ːrtidʒ] 부족(不足), 결핍(deficiency)
- Konak 숙소를 의미하나 여기서는 고관대작의 저택
- Sedam Brace on Bistrik (지명)
- Pionirska Dolina (계곡명)
- sniper [snáipər] 저격병
- canister [kǽnistər] 양철통
- The lucky ones are those with bicycles, which are pushed rather than ridden
  자전거를 가지고 있는 사람들은 운이 좋은 사람들이었는데, 그 자전거는 타고 다니기보다는 밀고 다녔다.
- The same with the owners of baby-carriages or former supermarket carts
  유모차나 이전에 쓰던 슈퍼마켓용 손수레를 가진 사람들도 똑같이 운이 좋은 사람들이다.
  (The same with~는 It is the same with~의 의미 또는 The same can be said about the owners~ 의 의미)
- will do (아무에게) 도움이 되다, 쓸 만하다 (수동형은 불가능)
- a household appliance 가정 전기 제품
- first-class laundresses 일급 세탁부
- battledore [bǽtldɔːr] 빨랫방망이
- lye [lai] 잿물, (세탁용) 알칼리액
- Nicola Tesla (1857 ~ 1943)
- Sleeping is entirely conditioned by the arrival of water and electricity
  잠자는 것은 전적으로 물과 전기가 공급되느냐에 좌우된다.

civilization based on inventions of two Americans—Tesla, who was born in the neighborhood and who we are proud of, and Edison, who they are proud of—you have to learn to go to sleep early and wake up early. So many evenings are spent in envy of those who have electricity.

Sleeping Sleeping is entirely conditioned by the arrival of water and electricity. If they appear at the same time, the shock is complete. The race against time starts—in order to use both in the best possible way. It doesn't matter that it is two or five O'clock in the morning. We cook, we wash, we clean, we take baths. Sometimes even a loaf of bread can be baked, the most, wonderful gift.

Heating The major problem is fuel. You cannot buy wood or coal.

During the first summer, all dry benches, trees and wooden material were collected. This autumn, in parks, alleys, courtyards and cemeteries trees started to fall—birches, poplars, ash-trees, plum-trees, apple-trees, Cherry-trees, pear-trees, all the way down to brushwood. The wooden backs of benches in parks were taken away, doors and doorframes of ruined apartments, handrails from the hallways, shelves from abandoned stores and kiosks, wooden stools and bars from restaurants, even the crosses and pyramids from the cemeteries. All bombed houses and barracks were dismantled with dismaying speed. But fuel is still scarce. Those who were wise took scrap wood from their garages early in the summer. Then they used paper. Now new kinds of fuel are being manufactured. Plastic bags from US lunch packages—a leftover from the Persian Gulf War—can heat five liters of water.

UNHCR supplied the city with numerous but not sufficient thermal foils for

Key Words & Phrases 해설

- The race against time starts 시간과의 경주가 시작된다.
- alley [ǽli] (미국) 뒷골목 (back-lane), (영국) 좁은 길, 샛길, (정원 · 숲 속 등의) 오솔길
- birches, poplars, ash-trees, plum-trees, apple-trees, Cherry-trees, pear-trees
  자작나무, 포플러나무, 양물푸레나무, 자두나무, 사과나무, 벚나무, 배나무
- brushwood [brʌ́ʃwùd] 베어 낸 작은 나뭇가지
- kiosk, kiosque [kí:ɑsk] (역 · 광장 등에 있는) 신문 매점 · 공중 전화실 · 광고탑 · 지하철도 입구 따위의 간이 건축물
- All bombed houses and barracks were dismantled with dismaying speed.
  모든 폭격 맞은 집과 막사에서는 경악할만한 속도로 설비 등이 제거되었다.
- dismantle [dismǽntl] (건물 · 배에서) 설비를[기구 · 장비 · 방비 등을] 제거하다
- dismay [disméi] 당황, 경악. with dismay 당황하여
- scarce [skə:rs] (음식물·돈·생활 필수품이) 부족한, 적은, 결핍한(of) (서술적으로 쓰임)
  ex. Money is scarce. 돈이 부족하다.
- garage [gərá:ʒ/ gǽra:dʒ] (자동차) 차고
- leftover [léftòuə:r] (종종 pl.) 잔존물
- (plastic bags) can heat five liters of water 5리터의 물을 데울 수 있다.
- UNHCR (Office of the) 유엔 난민 고등 판무관 (사무소)
  United **N**ations **H**igh **C**ommissioner for **R**efugees
- thermal foils 보온용 금속 막
- meteorologist [mì:tiərɑ́lədʒist/ -rɔ́l-] 기상학자
- they were very high 기온이 매우 높았다
- macaroni, macca- [mæ̀kəróuni] 마카로니, 이탈리아 국수

windows. On every window, from the outside, one can read their name: UNHCR—they are the owners of our lives.

November temperatures were very nice last year. Meteorologists have informed us they were very high, in comparison with times no one remembers any more: about 9 degrees Centigrade in the apartment. It was warmer to take a walk than to sit inside. Fortunately, everyone can get warm while searching for water and wood.

Eating The main dishes of 1992 were macaroni and rice. You wouldn't believe how many different ways they can be prepared! They couldn't be bought except on the black market. That was the case during the first months of siege. Now, everyone is saving them, jealously, if they still have any. With additions and a lot of imagination, one US lunch package can feed five people. Rice, macaroni and bread are often eaten together—otherwise it is difficult to survive. For each resident of Sarajevo, during the first seven months of war, you couldn't count more than six packages of humanitarian aid. One had to invent ways to preserve and make last for as long as possible what is normally envisioned for one person, one meal, one use.

In spring, summer and fall, all kinds of leaves it is possible to find were used as ingredients—from parks, gardens, fields and hills which were not dangerous to visit. Combined with rice, and well seasoned, everything becomes edible. Each person in Sarajevo is very close to an ideal macrobiotician, a real role model for the health-conscious, diet-trouble West. People are healthy, in spite of everything, for no one eats animal fat anymore, nor meat nor cheese—meals are made without eggs, without milky onions, vegetables. We eat a precious mix of wild

Key Words & Phrases 해설

- siege [siːdʒ] 포위 공격
- resident [rézid-ənt] 거주자
- make last 오래가게 하다, 오래 쓰게 하다 (여기서 last는 동사)
- envision [invíʒən] 상상[구상]하다, 계획[기대]하다
- One had to invent ways to preserve and make last for as long as possible what is normally envisioned for one person, one meal, one use.
  우리는 평상 상태로는 1인용, 한 끼 식사, 1회 사용할 것으로 기대된 것을 가능한 오래 쓸 수 있고 오래 보존하는 방법을 고안해내야 했다.
- ingredient [ingríːdiənt] (요리의) 재료 (of, for)
  ex. There are many ingredients of making a cake.
  케이크를 만드는 데 필요한 재료가 많다.
- well seasoned 잘 맛을 낸
- edible [édəbəl] 식용에 적합한,
- macrobiotic [mæ̀kroubaiátik] 장수식(長壽食)의, macrobiotic food 장수[건강] 식품
- animal fat 동물성 지방
- with incredible speed 믿을 수 없는 속도로
- often mean more than news transmitted through the official channels.
  (소문은) 종종 (정부의 공식 견해를 밝히는 신문이나 언론매체) 공식적인 통로를 통해서 전달되는 뉴스보다 더 믿을 수 있다.
- "this time for Sure" 이번에는 확실하다
- on military intervention 군사적 개입에 관해서
- on the siege of the city being lifted 도시의 포위 해제에 관해서
- on establishing corridor and safe haven 통행로와 피난처 설치에 관해서
- they are regularly, each time "for sure," wrong
  "확실하다"고 한 매번 정규적으로 틀린다.
- Rumors are spread by all 소문은 모든 종류의 사람들에 의해서 퍼진다.

imagination.

Rumors Rumors are the most important source of information. They spread with incredible speed and often mean more than news transmitted through the official channels. They regularly—"this time for Sure—report on military intervention, on the siege of the city being lifted, on establishing corridor and safe havens. And they are regularly, each time "for sure," wrong. Rumors are spread by all: housewives, univer- sity professors, teenagers, doctors. No one is immune. Rumors travel the city quicker than you can, and they are mostly optimistic. Only later you might hear opinions that they were too optimistic.

Shopping Stores have been broken into, shelled, deserted. This situation lasted for months and then, in October, a few brave owners reopened some of them. There you can find toothpaste, soap, toilet paper(rarely), light bulbs and foil for preserving food—remnants from the pre-war rich Sarajevo. Supermarkets are gone. Some, completely ravaged, since December have been selling just the one and only kind of bread. People got food stamps sometime in June, but they never served their purpose—you could never buy anything with them. Only one card works, the one that appeared in December, for bread. If you manage to wait in a line, you can get 233 grams per person daily. Single men and women are forming trios, so that each of men gets a whole loaf every third day. Business hours are from 8 a. m. to 3 p. m, but most places close at noon.

Key Words & Phrases 해설

- immune [imjúːn] (공격 · 병독 등을) 면한, 면제한
- optimistic [àptəmístik] 낙관적인
- shelled 폭격받은
- light bulbs 전구
- foil for preserving food 식품 보관용 호일
- remnants from the pre-war rich Sarajevo
  전쟁 이전의 부유했던 사라예보의 잔존물
- ravage [rǽvidʒ] 약탈[파괴]하다, 황폐하게 하다
- food stamps 정부가 지급하는 식료품 교환권
- Single men and women are forming trios 독신남녀들은 3인조를 짰다
- it helps you to keep in good shape 걸으면 체형을 좋게 유지시키는데 도움이 된다
- urban [ə́ːrbən] 도시의
- a compulsory sports discipline 필수 체육 교과
- traffic signs 교통신호
- dangerous spots 위험한 장소
- at maximum speed 최대속도로
- pedestrian [pədéstriən] 보행자
- in all directions 사방팔방으로 = in every directions
- recklessly [réklisli] 분별 없게, 무모하게
- negotiate [nigóuʃièit] 협상[협의]하다, 교섭하여 결정하다
- wage [weidʒ] (전쟁 따위를) 수행하다, 하다
- Audis, BMWs, Mercedes [mə́ːrsidiːz] (=MERCEDES-BENZ)
  세계 유명 자동차 이름들
- yuppie [jʌ́pi] 여피족(=Yúppy); 고학력으로 직업상의 전문적인 기술을

Recreation

Walking: Six kilometers a day—that is the average for those who don't need to go far. Some believe it helps you to keep in good shape.

Running: This is the favorite sport practiced by everyone in Sarajevo. All crossroads are run through as are all the dangerous neighborhoods. Running with stolen wood, you run to the line where others are standing. Something is on sale, and you will know what it is only when you join the line.

Rock-climbing: Urban rock-climbing is a compulsory sports discipline. In Stead of adequate ropes, one uses sheets. Climbers calculate the distances between balconies, from higher ones to the lower ones which have not yet been reached by fire.

Transportation Imagine driving through streets with no street lights (they have been torn down or are not working), without any traffic signs (they are gone), without any attention paid to pedestrians, at maximum speed across the crossroads and other dangerous spots. People are driving recklessly in all directions. No one pays any attention to crashes. Broken cars are abandoned easily and damages are negotiated in quick conversations. This is the war with the biggest ever civilian motor pool. The war is being waged in Audis, in BMWs, in Mercedes and VW Golfs, as well as in expensive yuppie jeeps.

General Tips When you come to Sarajevo, be prepared and be mature. It might prove to be the most important decision you have made in your life. Bring: good shoes which allow you to walk long and run fast, pants with many pockets, pills for water, Deutsche Marks (small denominations), batteries, matches, jars of

Key Words & Phrases 해설

지니고, 도시(근교)에 살며, 높은 소득을 올리고 있는 젊은 엘리트 (**y**oung **u**rban **p**rofessionals+-**ie**)

- tip [tip] (유익한) 조언, 묘책.
- mature [mətjúə:r, -tʃúə:r] 심사 숙고한, 신중한.
- pills for water 정수제
- small denominations 소액 지폐
- fussy [fʌ́si] 떠들기 좋아하는, 성가신, 까다로운

vitamins, canned food, drinks and cigarettes.

Everything you bring will be consumed or exchanged for useful information. You should know when to skip a meal, how to turn trouble into a joke and be relaxed in impossible moments. Learn not to show emotions and don't be fussy about anything. Be ready to sleep in basements, be eager to walk and work surrounded by danger. Give up all your former habits. Use the telephone when it works, laugh when it doesn't. You'll laugh a lot. Laugh, don't hate.

Consider this

1. From the title of this article, this report would seem to promise instruction for surviving in war. Do you learn how to survive in the hard times? Do you learn anything else?

2. What is this write's attitude to the reader?

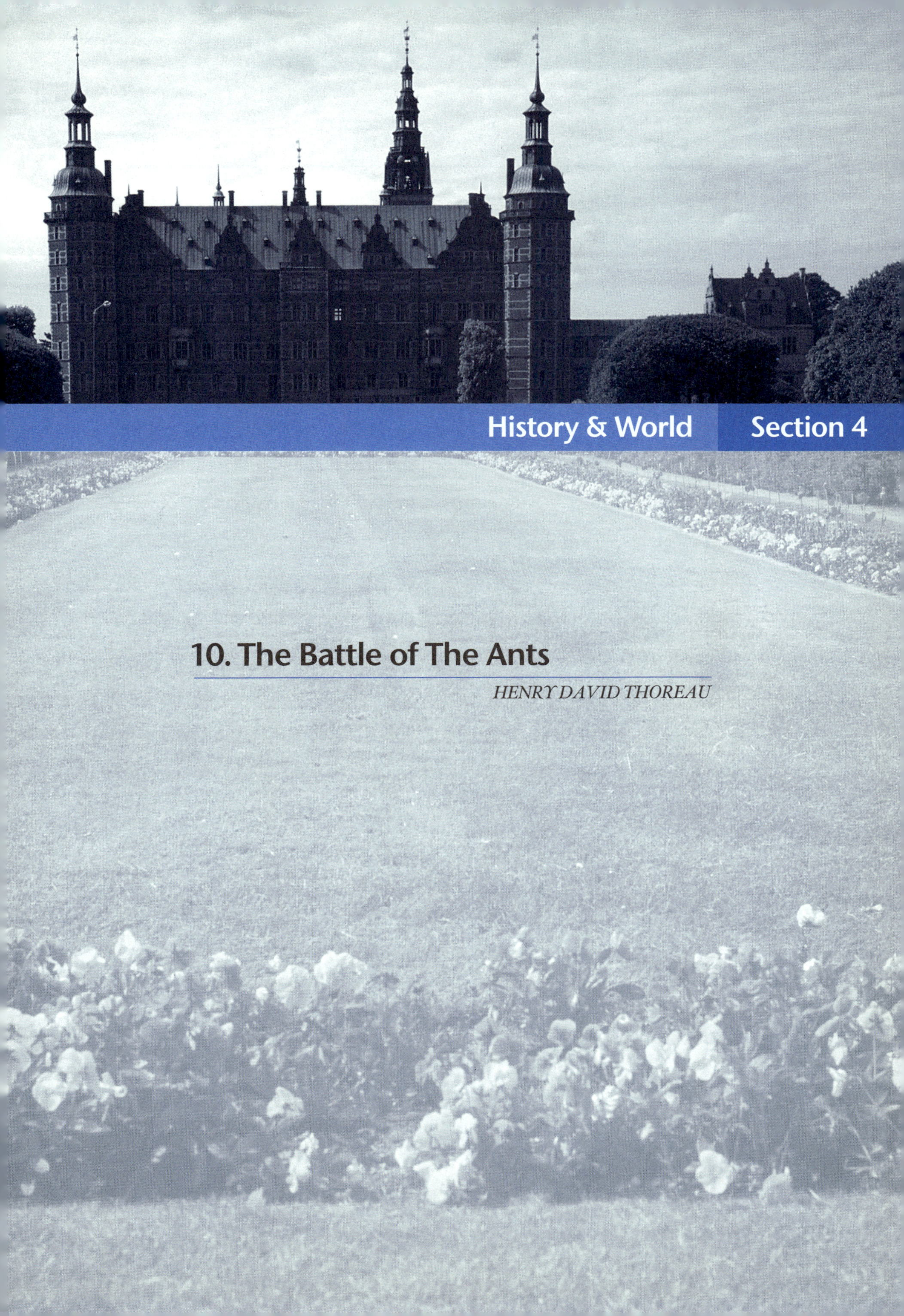

10. The Battle of The Ants

HENRY DAVID THOREAU

10 The Battle of The Ants

HENRY DAVID THOREAU

소로우 초상

One day when I went out to my wood-pile, or rather my pile of stumps, I observed two large ants, the one red, the other much large, nearly half an inch long, and black, fiercely contending with one another. Having once got hold they never let go, but struggled and wrestled and rolled on the chips incessantly. Looking farther, I was surprised to find that the chips were covered with such combatants, that it was not a *duellum*, but a *bellum*, a war between two races of ants, the red always pitted against the black, and frequently two red ones to one black. The legions of these Myrmidons covered all the hills and vales in my wood-yard, and the ground was already strewn with the dead and dying, both red and black. It was the only battle which I have ever witnessed, the only battle-field I ever trod while the battle was raging; internecine war; the red republicans on the one hand, and the black imperialists on the other. On every side they were engaged in deadly combat, yet without any noise that I could hear, and human soldiers never fought so resolutely. I watched a couple that were fast locked in each other's embraces, in a little sunny valley mid the chips, now at noonday prepared to fight till the sun went down, or life went out. The smaller red champion had fastened himself like a vice to his adversary's front, and through all the tumblings on that field never for an instant ceased to gnaw at one of his feelers near the root, having already caused the other to go by the board; while the stronger black one dashed him from side to side, and, as I saw on looking nearer, had already divested him of several of his members. They fought with more pertinacity than bulldogs. Neither

Key Words & Phrases 해설

- HENRY DAVID THOREAU (1817 ~ 1862) 미국의 시인, 에세이스트, 철학자, 그의 주요 저서인 *Walden* (1854)에서는 초절주의를 주창하고, "Civil Disobedience"에서는 시민자유를 옹호한 것으로 유명함.
- wood-pile 장작더미
- stump [stʌmp] (나무의) 그루터기
- or rather 더 정확히 말하면
- observe [əbzə́:rv] 관찰하다, 주시[주목]하다.
- the one red, the other much large, nearly half an inch long, and black 한 마리는 붉은 개미, 다른 한 마리는 매우 커서 대략 반 인치나 되는 검은 개미
- fiercely contending with one another 서로 맹렬하게 싸우는
- Having once got hold 한번 뒤엉키자
- rolled on the chips incessantly 나무토막 위에서 끊임없이 뒹굴었다
- incessant [insésnt] 끊임없는, 간단없는
- *dellum* (라틴어로) 전쟁
- combatant [kəmbǽtənt, kɑ́mbət-, kʌ́m-] 싸우는 사람, 전투원
- the red always pitted against the black 붉은 개미는 항상 검은 개미와 싸웠다
- The legions of these Myrmidons 용맹한 뮈르미돈(개미) 군단
- Myrmidon [mə́:rmədɑ́n, -d-ən / -dɔ́n] 그리스신화에 나오는 Achilles의 충실하고 용맹한 부하 뮈르미돈을 가리킴, '개미'의 뜻의 결합사인 myrmec(o)-을 연상시킴
  ex. the myrmidons of the law 법률의 앞잡이 (집달관 · 순경 등)
- wood-yard 장작마당
- strew [stru:] (~의 표면을) 온통 뒤덮다 (with)
  ex. Her desk is strewn with journals. 그녀 책상 위가 신문잡지로 (뒤덮여) 어수선하다.
- raging [réidʒiŋ] 격노한, 맹렬한
- internecine [intərní:sin, -sain] 서로 죽이는, 다 같이 쓰러지는, 치명적인

manifested the least disposition to retreat. It was evident that their battle-cry was "Conquer or die." In the meanwhile there came along a single red ant on the hillside of this valley, evidently full of excitement, who either had despatched his foe or had not yet taken part in the battle; probably the latter, for he had lost none of his limbs; whose mother had charged him to return with his shield or upon it. Or perchance he was some Achilles, who had nourished his wrath apart, and had now come to avenge or rescue his Patroclus. He saw this unequal combat from afar—for the blacks were nearly twice the size of the red—he drew near with rapid pace till he stood on his guard within half an inch of the combatants; then, watching his opportunity, he sprang upon the black warrior, and commenced his operations near the root of his right fore leg, leaving the foe to select among his own members; and so there were three united for life, as if a new kind of attraction had been invented which put all other locks and cements to shame.

I should not have wondered by this time to find that they had their respective musical bands stationed on some eminent chip, and playing their national airs the while, to excite the slow and cheer the dying combatants. I was myself excited somewhat even as if they had been men. The more you think of it, the less the difference. And certainly there is not the fight recorded in Concord history, at least, if in the history of America, that will bear a moment's comparison with this, whether for the numbers engaged in it, or for the patriotism and heroism displayed. For numbers and for carnage it was an Austerlitz or Dresden. Concord Fight! Two killed on the patriots' side, and Luther Blanchard wounded! Why here every ant was a Buttrick—"Fire! for god's sake fire!"—and thousands shared the fate of Davis and Hosmer. There was not one hireling there. I have no doubt that it was a principle they

소로우의 통나무집

Key Words & Phrases 해설

- republican [ripʌ́blikən] 공화주의의자
- on (the) one hand 한편으로[에서]는
- on the other hand 또 (다른) 한편으로는, 이와 반대로
- imperialist [impíəriəlist] 제국[영토 확장]주의자
- resolutely 단호히, 결연히
- I watched a couple that were fast locked in each other's embraces,
  나는 서로의 포옹으로 단단히 붙어 있는 한 쌍의 개미를 주시했다.
- in a little sunny valley mid the chips
  나무토막들 중간 약간의 햇빛이 드는 골짜기에서
- champion [tʃǽmpiən] (주의 등을 위해 싸우는) 투사, 옹호자
- gnaw [nɔː] 물어 끊다
- from side to side 옆으로, 좌우로
- pertinacity [pə̀ːrtənǽsəti] 끈덕짐, 불요불굴
- Neither manifested the least disposition to retreat
  어느 쪽도 퇴각할 의향을 전혀 표명하지 않았다
- dispatch, des– [dispǽtʃ] 죽이다(kill), (죄수를) 재빨리 '처치하다'
- limb [lim] (사람 · 동물의) 수족, 손발
- Patroclus 호머가 쓴 *일리아드*에 등장하는 그리스 전사
  (아킬레스가 그를 위해 복수를 해 줌)
- they had their respective musical bands stationed on some eminent chip
  그들은 높이 솟은 나무토막 위에 주둔하고 있는 각자의 음악대를 가지고 있었다.
- playing their national airs 그들의 국가 노래를 연주하는
- The more you think of it, the less the difference
  우리가 그 일을 생각할수록 (개미와 인간의) 차이는 더욱 적어진다.
- Concord [kάkərd / kɔ́ŋ-] 콩코드

fought for, as much as our ancestors, and not to avoid a three-peny tax on their tea; and the results of this battle will be as important and memorable to those whom it concerns as those of the battle of Bunker Hill, at least.

I took up the chip on which the three I have particularly described were struggling, carried into my house, and placed it under a tumbler on my window-sill, in order to see the issue. Holding a microscope to the first-mentioned red ant, I saw that, though he was assiduously gnawing at the near fore leg of his enemy, having severed his remaining feeler, his own breast was all torn away, exposing what vitals he had there to the jaws of the black warrior, whose breastplate was apparently too thick for him to pierce; and the dark carbuncles of the sufferer's eyes shone with ferocity such as war only could excite. They struggled half an hour longer under the tumbler, and when I looked again the black soldier had severed the heads of his foes from their bodies, and the still living heads were hanging on either side of him like ghastly trophies at his saddle-bow, still apparently as firmly fastened as ever, and he was endeavoring with feeble struggles, being without feelers, and with only the remnant of a leg, and I know not how many other wounds, to divest himself of them; which at length, after half an hour more, he accomplished. I raised the glass, and he went off over the window-sill in that crippled state. Whether he finally survived that combat, and spent the remainder of his days in some Hotel des Invalides, I do not know; but I thought that his industry would not be worth much thereafter. I never learned which party was victorious, nor the cause of the war, but I felt for the rest of that day as if I had my feelings excited and harrowed by witnessing the struggle, the ferocity and carnage, of a human battle before my door.

Kirby and Spence tell us that the battles of ants have long been celebrated and the date of them recorded, though they say that Huber is the only modern author

Key Words & Phrases 해설

(미국 Massachusetts 주 동부의 마을, 독립 전쟁의 시발이 된 곳)

- whether for the numbers engaged in it, or for the patriotism and heroism displayed.
  그 전쟁에 참전한 숫자로나 거기에서 보여진 애국주의나 영웅적인 행위로나
- Austerlitz [ɔ́sːtərlits] 오스터리츠
  (슬로바키아와 접경에 있는 체코의 도시로 1805년 Napoleon이 러시아 · 오스트리아 연합군을 격파한 곳)
- Dresden [drézdən] 나폴레옹이 승리한 드레스덴 (독일 동부의 도시) 전투
- For numbers and for carnage it was an Austerlitz or Dresden
  (참전한) 숫자나 대량학살로나 그것은 오스터리츠나 드레스덴 전투와 같았다
- There was not one hireling there 거기에서 누구도 돈을 받고 싸우지 않았다
- tumbler [tʌ́mbləːr] (굽 · 손잡이가 없는) 컵, 그 컵 한 잔
- Holding a microscope to the first-mentioned red ant
  첫 번째로 언급한 붉은 개미에다 현미경을 갖다 대고서
- window-sill 창턱
- assiduously [əsídʒuəsli] 주도면밀하게
- though he was assiduously gnawing at the near fore leg of his enemy
  그가 주도면밀하게 그의 적의 앞다리 부근을 물어뜯는다 할지라도
- exposing what vitals he had there to the jaws of the black warrior
  그의 급소가 검은 전사의 턱에 노출되었으므로
- whose breastplate was apparently too thick for him to pierce
  그의 가슴팍은 그가 꿰뚫기에 명백하게 너무도 두꺼웠다
- carbuncle [kάːrbʌŋkəl] 옹(癰), 정, 여드름, 뾰루지
- ferocity [fərάsəti / -rɔ́s-] 사나움, 잔인성 (fierceness)
- sever [sévəːr] 절단하다, 끊다 (from)
- like ghastly trophies 소름끼치는 전리품처럼

who appears to have witnessed them. "Aeneas Sylvius," say they, "after giving a very circumstantial account of one contested with great obstinacy by a great and small species on the trunk of a pear tree," adds that "this action was fought in the pontificate of Eugenius the Fourth, in the presence of Nicholas Pistoriensis, an eminent lawyer, who related the whole history of the battle with the greatest fidelity. A similar engagement between great and small ants is recorded by Olaus Magnus, in which the small ones, being victorious, are said to have buried the bodies of their own soldiers, but left those of their giant enemies a prey to the birds. This event happened previous to the expulsion of the tyrant Christiern the Second from Sweden." The battle which I witnessed took place in the Presidency of Polk, five years before the passage of Webster's Fugitive-Slave Bill.

Consider this

1. Thoreau uses the Latin words to describe the battle of the ants and he quickly follows this with a reference to the Myrmidons of Achilles. What comparison is implicit here? Find further examples of it. This passage comes from a chapter entitled "Brute Neighbors"; how does this comparison amplify the meaning of that title?

2. Describe the life, or part of the life, of an animal so that, while remaining faithful to the facts as you understand them, your description opens outward as does Thoreaus', and speaks not only of the animal but also of man, society, or nature. How many other ant's war do you find in the history books?

Key Words & Phrases 해설

- saddle-bow 안장의 앞머리
- Hotel des Invalides 부상당한 병사와 선원을 위한 유명한 프랑스 병원
- I never learned which party was victorious, nor the cause of the war
  나는 어느 무리가 승리를 거두었는지도 그 전쟁의 대의명분이 무엇이었는지도 알지 못했다
- Kirby and Spence 19세기 미국 곤충학자
- Huber 유명한 스위스 곤충학자
- harrow (정신적으로) 괴롭히다 (torment)
- celebrated [séləbrèitid] 세상에 알려진 (for)
  ex. Namwon is celebrated for its hot springs.
- Aeneas [iːníːəs] 그리스 · 로마신화에 나오는 아에네아스(Troy)의 용사로, Anchises와 Aphrodite의 아들, 서사시 *Aeneid*의 주인공
- obstinacy [ɑ́bstənəsi] n. 완강
  with great obstinacy 매우 완강히, 끈질기게
- who related the whole history of the battle with the greatest fidelity.
  그는 그 전투의 전체적인 역사를 가장 충실하게 이야기 했다.
- expulsion [ikspʌ́lʃən] 추방
- Fugitive-Slave Bill 탈주자 노예 법안으로 1851년에 통과됨.

소로우가 거닐었던 월든 호수

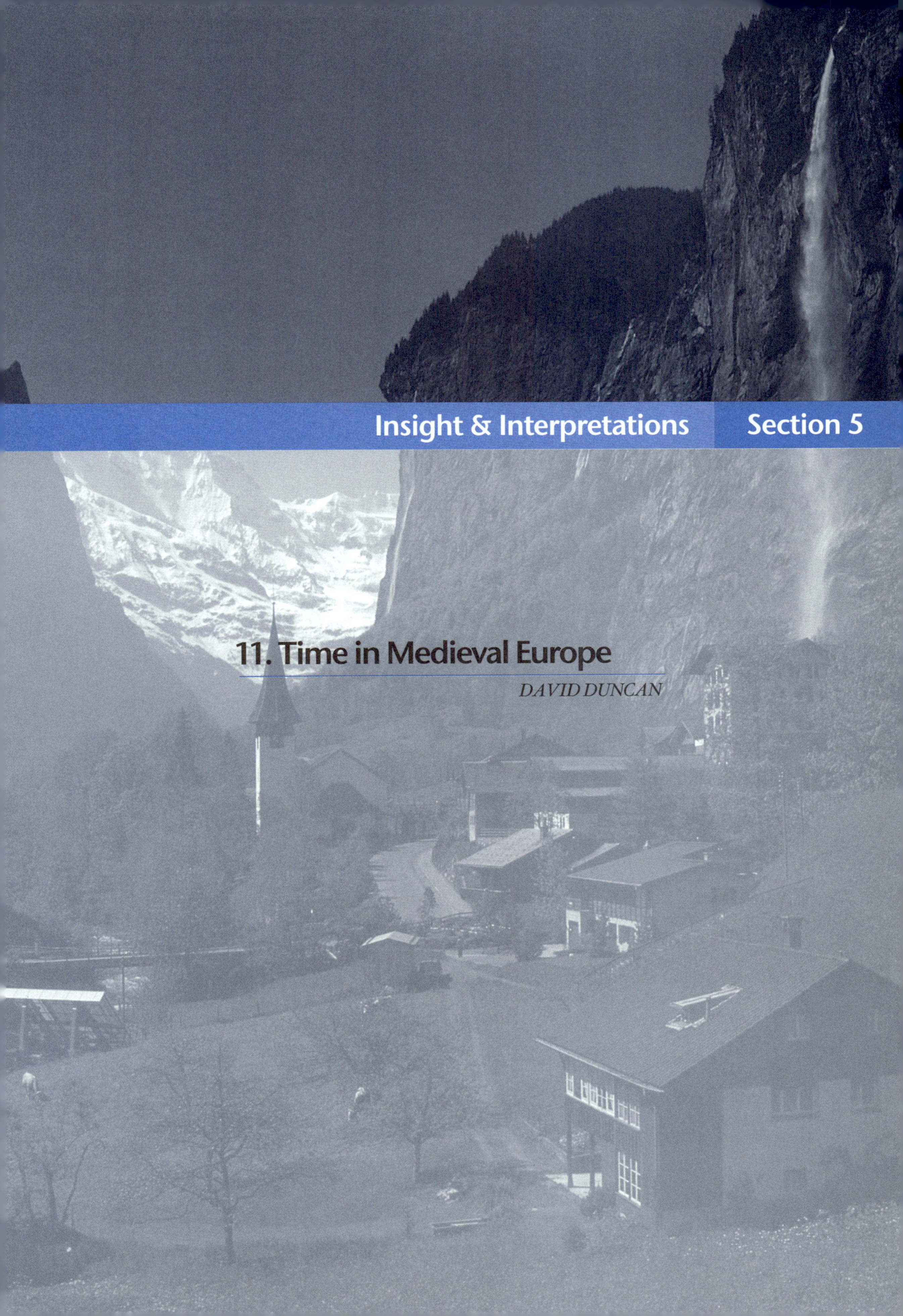

11. Time in Medieval Europe

DAVID DUNCAN

11 Time in Medieval Europe

DAVID DUNCAN

What did time mean to a farmer in the Rhine River valley in the year 800? What sort of calendar did, say, a weaver use in central France? Or a fisherman on the often drizzly coast of Northumbria?

Little is known about commoners during a period when even chronicles and official records of kings and nobles are scarce. On a continent of illiterates barely getting by, most people seem to have spent their days hoeing fields, avoiding wild beasts, worrying about crops and the weather, burying the dead, celebrating marriages and local saint's days, and telling stories around hearth fires during the long, cold, deadly winters. They lived, ate their meager portions, bore children, repaired leaks in their thatch roofs, tried to avoid armies if they came into the area, took an excited peek at the lord or king if he came along their road, grudgingly paid taxes, attended mass, followed the orders of the lord's foreman, and died, all in a continuous cycle of days and years that to them had no discernible past or future.

To farmers on the Rhine or weavers in France, who had little control over their environment or their lives, the whole idea of attempting to calculate and measure something as unfathomable and unremitting as time was either blasphemous or laughable. The few written insights into the mind-set of commoners on the subjects of time, calendars, and science in general suggest a great deal of snickering at monks, scholars, and astrologers bumbling about counting on their fingers and staring at the sky. The Miller in Chaucer's Canterbury Tales pokes fun

Key Words & Phrases 해설

- eaver [wíːvəːr] n. (베)짜는 사람, 직공(織工)
- drizzly [drízli] a. 이슬비의; 이슬비 오는; 보슬비가 올 것 같은
- meager, 【영국】 -gre [míːgəːr] a. 빈약한(poor); 야윈(thin); 불충분한(scanty)
- portion [pɔ́ːrʃən]
  n. 한 조각, 일부, 부분(part)(of), 몫(share)(of); (음식의) 1인분(of)
- thatch [θætʃ] n. U (지붕 따위를 이기 위한) 짚, 억새, 풀. C 초가지붕
- peek [pîːk] n. 엿봄; 흘끗 봄
- grudging [grʌ̀idʒiŋ] n. 엿봄; 흘끗 봄
- mass [mæs] n. (or M-) 미사(보통 가톨릭의 성찬의 의식); 미사곡
- foreman [fɔ́ːrmən]
  n. (노동자의) 십장(什長), 직장(職長), 공장장, 감독; 배심장(陪審長)
- unfathomable [ʌnfǽðəməbəl]
  a. 잴 수 없는, 깊이를 헤아릴 수 없는[알 수 없는]; 불가해한(inexplicable)
- unremitting [ʌnrimítiŋ] a. 간단 없는, 끊임[그칠 새] 없는; 끈질긴
- blasphemous [blǽsfəməs] a. 불경한, 모독적인; 말씨 사나운. ㊕ ~ly -ad
- snicker [sníkəːr] vi. 【미국】 킬킬거리다(snigger) (at; over);
- astrologer [əstrɑ̀lədʒər / -trɔ́l-] n. 점성가(astrologist)
- bumble[1] [bʌ́mbəl] v. 큰 실수를 하다, 실책을 하다; 떠듬거리며 말하다

at an asstronomer-asstrologer, but the verse might also have applied to anyone with their head in the clouds, so to speak:

Men sholde nat knowe of Goddes pryvetee.
Ye, blessed be alwey a lewed man
That noght but oonly his bileve kan!
So ferde another clerk with astromye;
He walked in the feeldes for to prye
Upon the sterres, what ther sholde bifalle,
Til he was in a marle-pit yfalle.

In other words, this "clerk," or scholar of astronomy, did not heed what every "lewed"--unlearned--Christian knew and believed: that "men should not know of God's private affairs." He foolishly studied the moon and stars and was such a dolt, according to the Miller, that he was looking up when he should have been looking down at his feet--and fell in a "marle-pit."

Still, even the simplest Christian presumably had at least a vague knowledge of critical events in Christian history. In fact, for most people this timeline remained far more real than a history of their own ara: the sequence of the Creation and events in the Old Testament; and episodes in Christ's life and the lives of the saints. These events needed to be recorded and dated to become valid, and it was this need that motivated time reckoners such as Dionysius and Bede to devise their year-by-year dating schemes in an age when otherwise few people cared about what year it was beyond year 6 or 10 in the reign of their local king or squire.

Several Chronological schemes were proposed and used besides Dionysius

Key Words & Phrases 해설

- heed [hi:d] vt., vi. (−에) 주의[조심]하다, (−을) 마음에 두다. ke fun at −을 놀리다
- dolt [doult] n. 바보, 멍청이
- marl [ma:rl]
  n. U. 이회(泥灰), 이회토(土)(비료용); U,C 이회토로 만든 벽돌; (시어) 흙(earth).
  ♣ the burning ~ 초열(焦熱) 지옥의 고통. marle-pit 이회토 구덩이
- presumable [prizú:məbəl] a. 추측[가정] 할 수 있는, 있음직한, −bly −ad. 추측상;
- timeline [táimlàin] n. 우주비행 중의 스케줄
- Dionysius [dàiəniʃiəs, -siəs] n. 디오니시오스(Syracuse의 왕; 430?-367 B.C.)
- scheme [ski:m] n. 계획, 기획, 설계. 일람표, 도표(schema), 도식(圖式), 도해

Exiguus's anno Domini, These included the old Roman system of fifteen-year indictions, which had started with the first year of Constantine's reign in 312. Iberians used something called the Era of Spain, which tracked Easter cycles starting with the Roman conquest of Iberia in 38 B.C. Others observed the Era of the Passion, with year 1 dated back to A.D. 33, supposedly the date of Christ's crucifixion and resurrection. But none was more popular as a possible alternative to the year of our Lord than a timeline based on the date of the Creation as year 1. Bede, for instance, carefully studied what he considered the relevant passages in the Bible and somehow came up with a specific day that he believed God began forming the sky, earth, and water: March 18, 3952 B.C. If Europeans had decided to use Bede's calculation of the Creation, our year 2000 would be 5951 A.C.--after the Creation.

And what about predicting the future? Time in Christianity was, of course, heading someplace: to Christ's second coming and eventually to eternity, events that would occur along the same timeline as past events. This made it tempting for medieval chronologists to try to date not only the beginning of the world, but the end. A century before Charlemagne, one scholar in the royal Frankish court calculated, using poor addition, that the world was 5,928 years old in the year 727. Applying this to the notion that the world was moving through six ages of 1,000 years apiece, this computer decided that the world would end in exactly 72 years.

Bede, following the example of Augustine, condemned such predictions. He insisted that future time belonged to God, "who, as the Everlasting, created times whenever he wanted, knows the end of times, and puts an end to the fluctuating processes of time when he wishes." Still, most people who thought about such things believed that however old the earth might be, the end was near. "The world

Key Words & Phrases 해설

- the Passion (십자가 위의) 예수의 수난(기) (마가복음 ?V -X V 등); 예수 수난화[곡]
- Charlemagne [ʃàːrləmèin] n. 샤를마뉴 대제(大帝) (서로마제국 황제; 742-814)
- Frankish [frǽŋkiʃ] a. 프랑크족의; 서유럽인의
- apiece [əpíːs] ad. 하나[한 사람]에 대하여, 각자에게, 각각
- Augustine [ɔ́ːgəstìːn, əgʌ́stin, ɔgʌ́stin]
  n. St. ~성(聖) 아우구스티누스 ① 기독교 초기의 교부(354-430)
- fluctuate [flʌ́ktʃuèit]
  v. (물가 · 열등이) 오르내리다, 변동[동요]하다; -ating [-èitiŋ] —a. 변동이 있는

is growing old," wrote Fredegar, a seventh-century Frankish chronicler who wrote in corrupt Latin. "We live at the end of time."

Medieval chroniclers were constantly looking for portents of the grand finale: plagues, earthquakes, eclipses, battles, and omens of every kind. Mystics looked for signs of the Antichrist's coming, with writers such as the remarkable theologian and poet Hildegard von Bingen offering vivid descriptions of what he would look like: "A beast with monstrous head, black as coal, with flaming eyes, wearing asses' ears and with gaping jaws decorated with iron hooks."

Amidst this official pessimism certain dates took on meaning at least for a few, such as the coming of the year 1000, though the anno Domini system was still not widely followed. Even where it was, Christians did not necessarily fear the end. They expected trials and tribulations and a final, horrific apocalypse, as predicted in the Bible. But they also looked forward to what would come after the current age ended and the calendar truly stopped--when Christ would usher in an age of eternal happiness for the elect, which of course included them.

But despite the "vast indifference to time" that permeated Europe during the reign of Charlemagne, already under way were real changes that centuries later would usher in a revolution in the perception of time. For even though Charlemagne saw clocks as curiosities, his keen interest in them and the idea of telling time made a lasting impression on future generations. At the same time a new invention was spreading slowly across the West: the bell were used to signal hours and other times of the day. By legend, church bells were invented in the fifth century in the town of Nola in Campania-- thus the term "Campanola bells." Another legend credits Pope Sabinianus (pope from 604 to 606) with ordering churches to mark the hours of the day by ringing their bells. Bells probably spread

Key Words & Phrases 해설

• corrupt [kərʌ́pt]

a. (언어가) 사투리화한; 전와(轉訛)된, 틀린; (텍스트 등이) 원형이 훼손된, 틀린 데 투성이인

• portent [pɔ́:rtənt]

n. (불길 · 대사건의) 징조, 전조(omen); 경이적인 사람 [사건, 물건]; U (불길한) 의미

• finale [finá:li, -nǽli-]

a. 【It.】 피날레. ① 〖음악〗 끝악장, 종악장(終樂章), 종곡
② 〖연극〗 최후의 막, 대미(大尾); 종국, 대단원

• mystic [místik] n. 신비가(神秘家), 신비주의자

• theologian [θì:əlóudʒiən] n. 신학자; 〖가톨릭〗 신학생

• gape [geip, gæp]

n. v. 입을 크게 벌림; 하품(yawn); 입을 딱 벌리고 멍하니 봄; 〖동물〗 벌린 입의 크기; 벌어진[갈라진] 틈(새)

• usher [ʌ́ʃər]

v. -vt. 『~+목/ +목+부/ +목+전+명』 안내하다, 전갈하다, 선도(先導)하다(in; out; into)

• permeate [pə́:rmièit] v. -vt. ① 스며들다, 침투하다, 투과하다. 퍼지다

• curiosity [kjùəriásəti / -ɔ́sə-] n. C 진기한 물건

first to monasteries, where monks used hand bells to signal canonical hours. Later tower bells summoned people to mass.

Bells probably had a minimal impact on the average person. Yet they were the first mechanical "clocks" to govern everyday life in Europe, usually rung according to time as measured on a water clock or sundial. Imagine a farmer in a field being told to have an acre plowed by the time the bell tower ring noon, when before he had been told by his lord simply to work until the sun was high. Or think of a clock that signaled the beginning of a mass with an exactitude never before known when hours were measured using the position of the sun in the sky. This was an entirely different way of viewing time, with a measurement of it being assigned a specific value.

The Holy Roman Emperor Charlemagne died on January 28, 814. His empire died soon after, as his heigs argued and fought and divided his realms among them. With it perished the political order that Charlemagne had briefly imposed. So did the emperor's infatuation with learning, manuscripts, and marvelous timepieces, which it turned out was not shared by his immediate successors. They dismissed the scholars from the court and closed the schools for children opened by the emperor. Still, the age of Charlemagne ignited a spark, with the scholar Alcuin of York and others compiling encyclopedias and collecting manuscripts. It also provided an example and a context for quality, taste, humanistic culture, and sound grammar, which laid a foundation for a slow--very slow--evolution toward an era when dates and calendars would begin to matter to more than just a few monks sitting in their cloisters trying to calculate the age of the world and when the end would come.

But Enrope was not where the action was for time reckoning and the calendar

Key Words & Phrases 해설

• canonical [kənánəkəl / -nɔ́n-]

a. 교회법에 의한; 정전(正典)으로 인정된; 정규의, 표준[기본]적인

• canonical [kənánəkəl / -nɔ́n-]

n. (pl.) (성직자의) 제의(祭衣), 성의(聖衣)

♣ ~ hours 『가톨릭』 정시과(定時課), 성무 일도(聖務日禱);

• sundial [sʌ́ndàiəl] n. 해시계

• acre [éikər] n. 에이커(약 4,046.8㎡; 略: a.)

• exactitude [igzǽktətjùːd] n. 정확, 엄밀; 정밀(도); 꼼꼼함, 엄정

ex. -with scientific ~과학적 정밀성으로

• ignite [ignáit]

v. -vt. ① (-에) 불을 붙이다; 작열케 하다; 흥분시키다

② 『화학』 극한까지[세게] 가열하다.

vi. 불이 댕기다, 발화하다; (달아서) 빛나기 시작하다

• cloister [klɔ́istər]

n. 수도원(남자 수도원은 monastery, 여자 수도원은 convent 또는 nunnery); 은둔처; (수도원 따위의 안뜰을 에우는) 회랑(回廊); (the ~) 은둔[수도원] 생활

anyway in Bede's or Charlemagne's era. Indeed, as Europe slept, developments were under way far to the East, where science was not ignored and a long line of brilliant thinkers were making discoveries that centuries later would penetrate at last the darkness of the West to astonish and inspire men like Roger Bacon, and to once again commence the movement of time.

Consider this

1. What is the writer's important point? What kinds of evidence does the writer use in supporting his argument? Do you think they are equally valid?

2. Do you have a different perspective of your own about time?

12. Agriculture's Mixed Blessing

JARED DIAMOND

12 Agriculture's Mixed Blessing

JARED DIAMOND

We are accustomed to assuming that the transition from the hunter-gatherer lifestyle to agriculture brought us health, longevity, security, leisure, and great art. While the case for this view seems overwhelming, it is hard to prove. How do you actually show that the lives of people ten thousand years ago got better when they abandoned hunting for farming?

The question has become answerable only in recent years, through the newly emerging science of "paleopathology": looking for signs of disease in the remains of ancient peoples. In some lucky situation, the paleopathologist has almost as much material to study as does a pathologist. For example, archaeologists in the deserts of Chile found well-preserved mummies whose medical condition at the time of death could be determined by an autopsy, just as one would do on a fresh corpse in a hospital today.

Usually, though, the only human remains available for paleopathologists to study are skeletons, but they still permit a surprising number of deductions about health. To begin with, a skeleton identifies its owner's sex, and his/her weight and approximate age at the time of death. Thus, with enough skeletons, one can construct mortality tables like those used by life insurance companies to calculate expected life span and risk of death at any given age. Paleopathologists can also calculate growth rates by measuring bones of people of different ages, can examine teeth for cavities (signs of a high-carbohydrate diet) or enamel defects (signs of a poor diet in childhood), and can recognize scars that many diseases

Key Words & Phrases 해설

- be accustomed to –에 익숙하다. get [become] ~to –에 익숙해지다
- hunter-gatherer lifestyle 수렵채집 생활 방식
- longevity [landʒévəti / lɔn-] n. U 장수; 수명;
- paleopathology paleopathologist
- pathologist 병리학자, 병리의사
- pathology [pəθáləd͡ʒi / -θɔ́l-] n. U 병리학; 병리; 병상(病狀)
- arch(a)eologist [ɑ́:rkiáləd͡ʒist / -ɔ́l-] n. 고고학자
- mummy [mʌ́mi] n. 미라   mummied [mʌ́mid] a. 미라가 된
- autopsy [ɔ́:tɑpsi, -təp- / -tɔp-] n. 검시(檢屍), 검시(檢視), 시체 해부, 부검(剖檢)
- remain [riméin] n. ① (보통 pl.) 잔존물; 유물, ② (보통 pl.) 유체, 유해(遺骸)
- deduction [didʌ́kʃən] n. 추론
- identify [aidéntəfái] v. (사람의 성명 · 신원, 물건의 명칭 · 분류 · 소속 따위)를 밝히다
- mortality [mɔ:rtǽləti] tables 사망률 표
- cavity [kǽvəti] n. 〖해부학〗 (신체의) 강(腔)
- enamel [inǽməl] n. U 〖치과〗 법랑질(質)

such as anemia, tuberculosis, leprosy, and osteoarthritis leave on bones.

One straightforward example of what paleopathologists have learned from skeletons concerns historical changes in height. Many modern cases illustrate how improved childhood nutrition leads to taller adults: for instance, we stoop to pass through doorways of medieval castles built for a shorter, malnourished population. Paleopathologists studying ancient skeletons from Greece and Turkey found a striking parallel. The average height of hunter-gatherers in that region toward the end of the Ice Age was a generous five feet ten inches for men, five feet six inches for women. With the adoption of agriculture, height crashed, reaching by 4000 B.C. a low value of only five feet three for men, five feet one for women. By classical times, heights were very slowly on the rise again, but modern Greeks and Turks have still not regained the heights of their healthy hunter-gatherer ancestors.

Another example is the study of thousands of American Indian skeletons excavated from burial mounds in the Ilinois and Ohio river valleys. Corn, first domesticated in Central American thousands of years ago, became the basis of intensive farming in those valleys around A.D. 1000. Until then, Indian hunter-gatherers had skeletons "so healthy it is somewhat discouraging to work with them, "as one paleopathologist complained. With the arrival of corn, Indian skeletons suddenly became interesting to study. The number of cavities in an average adult's mouth jumped from less than one to nearly seven, and tooth loss and abscesses became rampant. Enamel defects in children's milk teeth imply the pregnant and nursing mothers were severely undernourished. Anemia quadrupled in frequency; tuberculosis became established as an epidemic disease; half the population suffered from yaws or syphlis; and two-thirds suffered from osteoarthritis and other degenerative diseases. Mortality rates at every age

Key Words & Phrases 해설

- anemia [əníːmiə] n. 〖의학〗 빈혈증; 생기[활력]의 결핍. ㊇-mic -a. 빈혈(증)의
- tuberculosis [tjubə̀ːrkjəlóusis]
  n. (pl. -ses [-siːz]) U,C 〖의학〗 결핵(병)(略: T.B., TB), (특히) 폐결핵(pulmonary ~)
- leprosy [léprəsi] n. U 〖의학〗 나병, 한센병
- osteoarthritis [ástiouaːrəráitis / ɔ̀s-] n. U 〖의학〗 나병, 한센병
- straightforward [strèitfɔ́ːrwəːrd] a. (일이) 간단한
- nutrition [njuːtríʃ-ən] n. U ① 영양; 영양 공급[섭취]
- stoop [stuːp] v. vi. 몸을 꾸부리다[굽히다]
- excavate [ékskəvèit] vt. –에 구멍[굴]을 파다, 발굴하다
- burial [bériəl] n. 매장, 매장식
- mound[1] [maund] n. 흙무덤
- domesticate [douméstəkèit] v. -vt. (식물 · 이민 등을) 토지에 순화(馴化)시키다;
- abscess [ǽbses] n., vi. 종기, 농양(膿瘍)(을 형성하다)
- rampant [rǽmpənt]
  a. (병 · 범죄 · 소문 등이) 만연하는, 대유행의; 마구 퍼지는. ㊇~ly
- quadruple [kwadrúːpəl, kwádru- / kwɔ́drupəl] vt., vi. 4배로 하다[되다]
- epidemic [èpədémik] n. 유행병, 전염병; (사상 · 전염병 따위의) 유행
  ex. There is an ~ of cholera reported. 콜레라가 돈다는 보도가 나왔다.
  ex. an ~ of terrorism 다발(多發)하는 테러 행위
- epidemic [èpədémik] a. 유행성[전염병]의
- yaws [jɔːz] n. pl. 「단수취급」 〖의학〗 인도마마(frambesia)
- syph [sif] n. (속어) =SYPHILIS. syphilis [sífəlis] n. U 〖의학〗 매독
- degenerative [didʒénərèitiv, -rət-] a. 퇴화적인; 타락적인
  ex. a ~ disease 퇴행성(退行性) 질환

increased, with the result that only 1 percent of the population survived past age fifty, as compared to 5 percent in the golden days before corn. Almost one-fifth of the whole population died between the ages of one and four, probably because weaned toddlers succumbed to malnutrition and infectious diseases. Thus corn, usually considered among the New World's blessings, actually proved to be a public-health disaster. Similar conclusions about the transition from hunting to farming emerge from studies of skeletons elsewhere in the world.

There are at least three sets of reasons to explain these things that agriculture was bad for health. First, hunter-gatherers enjoyed a varied diet with adequate amounts of protein, vitamins, and minerals, while farmers obtained most of their food from starchy crops. In effect, the farmers gained cheap calories at the cost of poor nutrition.

Second, because of that dependence on one or a few crops, farmers ran a greater risk of starvation if one food crop failed than did hunters. The Irish potato famine is merely one of many examples.

Finally, most of today's leading infectious diseases and parasites of mankind could not become established until after the transition to agriculture. These killers persist only in societies of crowded, malnourished, sedentary people constantly reinfected by each other and by their own sewage. The cholera bacterium, for example, does not survived for long outside the human body. It spreads from one victim to the next through contamination of drinking water with feces of cholera patients. Measles dies out in small populations once it has either killed or immunized most potential hosts; only in populations numbering at least a few hundred thousand people can it maintain itself indefinitely. Such crowd epidemics could not persists in small, scattered bands of hunters who often shifted camp.

Key Words & Phrases 해설

- succumb [səkʌ́m] vi. 죽다
  ex. ~ to cancer 암으로 죽다
- starch [stɑːrtʃ] n. U ① 녹말, 전분
- in effect (1) 실제에 있어서는, 사실상 (2) 요컨대
- sedentary [séd-əntèri / -t-əri]
  a. 앉은 채 있는; 정주하는; 『동물』 이주하지 않는(새); 착생(着生)의
- bacterium [bæktíəriəm] n. BACTERIA의 단수형
- sewage [suːidʒ] n. BACTERIA의 단수형
- feces, fae- [fíːsiːz] n. pl. 배설물, 똥; 찌끼(dregs), 침전물

Tuberculosis, leprosy, and cholera had to await the rise of farming, while smallpox, bubonic plague, and measles appeared only in the past few thousand years with the rise of even denser populations in cities.

Besides malnutrition, starvation, and epidemic diseases, farming brought another curse to humanity: class divisions. Hunter-gatherers have little or no stored food, and no concentrated food sources like orchards or herds of cows. Instead, they live off the wild plants and animals that they obtain each day. Everybody except for infants, the sick, and the old joins in the search for food. Thus there can be no kings, no full-time professionals, no class of social parasites who grow fat on food seized from others.

Only in a farming population could contrasts between the disease-ridden masses and a healthy, nonproducing, elite develop. Skeletons from Greek tombs at Mycenae around 1500 B.C. suggest that royals enjoyed a better diet than commoners, since the royal skeletons were two or three inches taller and had better teeth (on the average, one instead of six cavities or missing teeth).

These signs of health differentials within local communities of farmers in the past appear on a global scale in the modern world. To most American and European readers, the argument that humanity could no the average be better off as hunter-gatherers than we are today sounds ridiculous, because most people in industrial societies today enjoy better health than most hunter-gatherers. However, Americans and Europeans are an elite in today's world, dependent on oil and other materials imported from countries with large peasant populations and much lower health standards. If you could choose between being a middle-class American, a Bushman hunter, and a peasant farmer in Ethiopia, the first would undoubtedly be the healthiest choice, but the third might be the least healthy.

Key Words & Phrases 해설

- measles [míz-əlz] n. pl.「주로 단수취급」 홍역, 마진(痲疹); 풍진(風疹)
- immunize [ímjənàiz] vt. 면역이 되게 하다, 면역성을 주다(against)
  ㊉ immunization[-nizéiʃən] -n. 면역성 부여
  ex. catch(the) ~ 홍역에 걸리다
- indefinitely [indéfənətli] ad. 막연히, 애매하게; 무기한으로
  ex. put off ~ 무기 연기하다
- bubonic plague 〚의학〛 선(腺) 페스트
- live off –에 의존하여 생활하다

While giving rise to class divisions for the first time, farming may also have exacerbated sexual inequality already in existence. With the advent of agriculture, women often became beasts of burden, were drained by more frequent pregnancies, and thus suffered poorer health. For example, among the Chilean mummies from A.D. 1000, women exceeded men in osteoarthritis and in bone lesions from infectious disease.

Instead of the progressivist party line that we chose agriculture because it was good for us, a cynic might ask how we got trapped by agriculture despite its being such a mixed blessing.

Perhaps the main reason we find it so hard to shake off the traditional view that farming was unequivocally good for us is that there's no doubt that it meant more tons of food per acre. Population densities of hunter-gatherers are typically one person or less per square mile, while densities of farmers average at least ten times higher. This is partly because nomadic hunter-gatherers have to keep their children spaced at four-year intervals by infanticide and other means, since a mother must carry her toddler until it's old enough to keep up with the adults. Because sedentary farmers don't have that problem, a woman can and does have a child every two years. We forget that farming also resulted in more mouths to feed, and that health and quality of life depend on the amount of food per mouth.

As population densities of hunter-gatherers slowly rose at the end of the Ice Age, bands had to "choose," whether consciously or unconsciously, between feeding more mouths by taking the first steps toward agriculture, or else finding ways to limit growth. Some bands adopted the former solution, unable to anticipate the evils of farming, and seduced by the transient abundance they enjoyed until population growth caught up with increased food production. Such

Key Words & Phrases 해설

- exacerbate [igzǽsərbèit, iksǽs-] vt. (고통 · 병 · 노여움 따위를) 악화시키다
  ㉺ exacerbation [-ʃən] -n. 악화, 격화; 〖의학〗 악화
- a beast of burden[draft] 짐나르는 짐승(마소 · 낙타 등)
- lesion [lí:ʒ-ən]
  n. 외상, 손상(injury); 정신적 상해; 〖의학〗 (조직 · 기능의) 장애; 병변; 「일반적」 손해
- nomadic [noumǽdik] a. 유목(생활)의; 유목민의; 방랑(생활)의
  ex. ~ tribes 유목 민족 ㉺ -ically [-kəli] -ad.

bands outbred and then drove off or killed the bands that chose to remain hunter-gatherers, because ten malnourished farmers can still outfight one healthy hunter. It's not that hunter-gatherers abandoned their life-style, but that those sensible enough not to abandon it were forced out of all areas except ones that farmers didn't want. Modern hunter-gatherers persist mainly in scattered areas useless for agriculture, such as the Arctic and deserts.

Consider this

1. What is the writer's important point? What kinds of evidence does the writer use in supporting his argument? Do you think they are equally valid?

2. Do you have a different perspective of your own about Agriculture?

Life and Literature Section 6

13. Multiple Personality

IAN HACKING

13 Multiple Personality

IAN HACKING

There has always been a popular face to the idea of multiple personality. The Romanctic fiction and poetry of the nineteenth century positively reeks of duality. Dr. Jekyll and Mr. Hyde is the best known, Dostoyevsky's Mr. Golyadkin of The Double is the greatest artistic creation, and James Hogg's The private Memoirs and Confessions of a Justified Sinner is the one that scares me the most. The modern movement has thrived not on fiction but on a new genre, the multobiography. This is the book-length story of a multiple, usually packaged as an "as-told-to," and often turned into a movie or TV special.

The book that introduced the movement was Sybi. Published in 1973, it is a fictionalized story of Cornelia Wilbur and her multiple patient Sybil. Wilbur's professional accounts of the case were routinely rejected by scholarly and medical journals, apparently on the grounds that no one could take multiple personality seriously. One crushing insult followed upon a paper she read at the annual meeting of the American Academy of Psychoanalysis. Wilbur believed that the academy published all the papers that were read, but she was telephoned and told there were "space problems." Since Sybil's story would not be received by the experts, it had to be told for the public. It was written up by a journalist, Flora Rheta Schreiber. Schreiber insisted that Sybil be cured before she began work. A book without a happy ending would not sell. When Sybil was cured, Schreiber came to live in what had virtually become the Wilbur-Sybil menage and wrote the book.

Key Words & Phrases 해설

- reek [ríːk] v. 냄새가 나다(of); (비유) –의 낌새가 있다(of; with)
- Jekyll [dʒékəl, dʒíːkəl] n. 지킬 박사(R. L. Stevenson의 소설 중의 인물)
(Dr.) ~ and (Mr.) Hyde 이중 인격자
- ménage [meinάːʒ] n. 【F.】 살림, 가정(家政); 가정(家庭), 세대(household)
- break ground ~ 파다, 갈다; 착수[기공]하다, 새 사업을 시작하다
- perverse [pərvə́ːrs] a. ① 외고집의, 심술궂은, 성미가 비꼬인, 빙퉁그러진

Wilbur's work broke new ground because she actively sought out childhood traumas. She traced Sybil's multiplicity to perverse, vindictive, and usually sexually oriented assaults by Sybil's mother. Wilbur was no orthodox Freudian. She worked on Sybil's memories with both hypnosis (anathema to Freud) and Amytal. She did not believe in the ritualized distancing between patient and analyst demanded by American psychoanalysis. The two women became friends, went for long rides in the country, and lived for a while in the same house. Sybil's treatment involved 2,534 office hours. It took so long, Wilbur was to tell people, only because in the 1960s there was simply no knowledge about multiple personality.

A doctrinaire Freudian would work with Sybil's memories of abuse in order to help the patient understand what they meant to her in the present. It would be of little moment whether these were true memories or fantasies. Wilbur went on to confirm, as best she could, that the events Sybil painfully came to remember really had happened. She went to the family home and saw at least the instruments of torture, the enema bag, the tool for lacing boots that had been stuck into Sybil's orifices. The passive father did not contradict the stories. Of course the existence of the objects of torture--which were also, in those days, common household furnishings--did not prove that they had been perverted for sadistic uses. But Wilbur believed Sybil, and by the time of the book and above all the film, no one could doubt the reality.

Sybil became a prototype for what was to count as a multiple. She was an intelligent young woman, with a promising career, who experienced substantial periods of lost time. She had fugue episodes; she would recover herself in a strange place with no idea how she got there. But other features are more important.

Key Words & Phrases 해설

- vindictive [vindíktiv] a. 복수심이 있는, 원한을 품은, 앙심 깊은;
- hypnosis [hipnóusis] n. (pl. -ses [-siːz]) U, C 최면(상태), 최면술
  ex. under ~ 최면술에 걸려
- nathema [ənǽθəmə]
  ① 교회의 저주, 아나테마; (가톨릭 교회에서의) 파문(破門).
  ② 「일반적」 저주; 증오
- Amytal [ǽmitɔ̀ːl, -tæ̀l] n. 아미탈(진정제; 상표명)
- doctrinaire [dɑ́ktrənέər / dɔ́k-] n. 공론가(空論家), 순이론가, 교조(敎條)주의자
  ㉺ -nairism [-nέərizəm] -n. U 교조주의; 공리공론(空理空論)
- of little [no] moment ~ 그다지 [조금도] 중요하지 않은
- enema [énəmə] n. (pl. ~s, ~ta [-tə]) 〖의학〗 관장제(灌腸劑), 관장기
- orifice [ɔ́ːrəfis , ɑ́rə-/ ɔ́ri-] n. 구멍, 빼끔한 구멍(관(管) · 동굴 · 상처 따위의)
- pervert [pəːrvə́ːrt] vt. ① (상도(常道)에서) 벗어나게 하다 ② 악용하다, 곡해하다
- prototype [próutoutàip] n. 원형(archetype); 표준, 모범, 본(보기)(model)

Patients in the past had tended to have two or three or even four alters. Sybil had sixteen. There were child alters. There were two alters of the opposite sex. Some alters knew about others. They argued, fought, tried to help or destroy each other. This idea of dynamic relationship between different personalities had been glimpsed before, but it was the reports of Sybil that made them prominent. Above all, the etiology of her disorder was writ large. She really had been abused as a child. "Sybil," the main presenting personality, had no memory of those sorry events. But her alters did remember. Indeed they had been created in order to cope with horror. They would be dissociated from the main personality, so that Sybil, herself, did not need to be conscious of those scars. She did not need to hate her other, who had done those things to her. She could even love her mother, while some of the alters were full of hate. Other alters lived out a life that Sybil would like to have lived, had she not been so assaulted when she was growing up.

During the 1970s the public conception of child abuse and neglect was shifted to sexual abuse and incest. The theory of multiple personality followed in train. By 1986 a questionnaire survey of clinicians treating multiple personality produced a sample of one hundred patients, ninety-seven of whom reported experiencing significant trauma in childhood, most often sexual in nature.

There is now no difficulty in summarizing the 1980s prototype for multiple personality: a middle-class white woman with the values and expectations of her social group. She is in her thirties, and she has quite a large number of distinct alters--sixteen, say. She spent a large part of her life denying the very existence of these alters. The alters include children, persecutors, and helpers, and at least one male alter. She was sexually abused on many occasions by a trusted man in her family when she was very young. She has previously been throug parts of the

Key Words & Phrases 해설

- etiology, aeti- [ìːtiálədʒi / -ɔ́l-] n. U 원인론; 『의학』 병인학(病因學)
- writ [written] large 대서 특필하여; 대규모로; 확대[강조]하여
- dissociate [disóuʃièit] v. -vt. 분리하다, 떼어놓다(from); 떼어서 생각하다; 『정신의학』 (의식을) 분열시키다
- clinician [[kliníʃən] n. 임상의(醫) in ~ 사실상:
  ex. There is, in ~, such a thing as hell. 지옥이라는 것은 사실상 있는 것이다.

mental health system and has been diagnosed with many complaints, but her treatments have not helped her in the long run until she came to a clinician sensitive to multiple personality. She has amnesia for parts of her past. She has the experience of "coming to" in a strange situation with no idea of how she got there. She is severely depressed and has quite often thought about suicide.

In 1972, multiple personality had seemed to be a mere curiosity. In 1992, there were hundreds of multiples in treatment in every sizable town in North America. What has happened? Is a new form of madness, hitherto almost unknown, stalking the continent? Or have multiples always been around, unrecognized? Were they classified, when they needed help, as suffering from something else? Perhaps clinicians have only recently learned to make correct diagnoses. Or, as a majority of psychiatrists still contend, is there simply no such thing as multiple personality disorder? Is the epidemic the work of a small but committed band of therapists, unwittingly aided and abetted by sensational stories in the tabloids and afternoon TV talk shows?

We hear moral conviction on all sides. Psychiatrists who reject multiple personality are accused of complacently dismissing the victims, the abused, the momen and children. Is that true? There are doctors who see themselves as scientists, dedicated to objective fact, not social movements. They resent the media hype that surrounds multiple personality. They are dubious about the sheer scope of the epidemic. How can a mental disorder be so at the whim of place and time? How can it disappear and reappear? How can it be everywhere in North America and nonexistent in the rest of the world until it is carried there by missionaries, by clinicians who seem determined to establish beachheads of multiple personality in Europe and Australasia? The only place that multiples flourish overseas is in the

Key Words & Phrases 해설

- amnesia 기억상실
- stalk² [stɔ:k] v. -vi. ① 성큼성큼[천천히] 걷다, 활보하다(stride) (along)
  ② (역병 따위가) 만연하다, 퍼지다(spread)
- epidemic [èpədémik] n. 유행병, 전염병; (사상 · 전염병 따위의) 유행
- therapist [θérəpist] n. =THERAPEUTIST
- abet [əbét] vt. (-tt-) (부)추기다, 선동[충동, 교사]하다
- complacent [kəmpléisənt] ~ly -ad. 만족하여
- hype [haip] n. 과대 광고[선전], 과장
- dubious [djú:biəs] a. 의심스러운, 수상한; 결정키 어려운, (운명 따위가) 미결정의
- sheer¹ [ʃiə:r] a. 섞이지 않은, 물타지 않은, 순수한 [cf.] mere¹, pure
- whim [hwim] n. 잘 변하는 마음, 일시적인 생각, 변덕
- missionary [míʃ-ənèri / -nəri] n. ① 선교사, 전도사
  ② (주의 · 사상의) 주창자, 선전자(propagandist)
- beachhead [bí:tʃhèd] n. 〖군사〗 해안 교두보, 상륙 거점. [cf.] bridgehead 발판

Netherlands, and that florescence, say skeptics, was nourished by intensive visiting by the leading American members of the movement.

Is multiple personality a real disorder as opposed to a product of social circumstances, a culturally permissible way to express distress or unhappiness? That question makes a presupposition that we should reject. It implies that there is an important contrast between being a real disorder and being a product of social circumstances. The fact that a certain type of mental illness appears only in specific historical or geographical contexts does not imply that it is manufactured, artificial, or in any other way not real.

In a 1992 talk Frank Putnam, author of Diagnosis and Treatment of Multiple Personality Disorder(1989), candidly stated that "very little is known about the alter personalities and what they represent." His increasing reservations about alter personalities are shared by an influential group of psychiatrists within the multiple movement who have long held that the emphasis on personalities is wrongheaded. In 1993 David Spiegel, chair of the dissociation disorders committee for the 1994 edition of the Diagnostic and Statistical Manual of Mental Disorders, wrote that "there is a widespread misunderstanding of the essential psychopathology in this dissociative disorder, which is failure of integration of various aspects of dentiey, memory, and consciousness. The problem is not having more than one personality; it is having less than one personality." One is reminded of Alice, 'to pretend to be two people! Why, there is hardly enough of me left to make one respectable person!'"

We shall find over and over again that multiple personality is a moving target. Yet two things are constantly in view, memory and psychic pain. Whether the illness involves more than one personality or less than one, the disorder is

Key Words & Phrases 해설

- florescence [flɔːrésəns] n. U 개화(開花); 한창; 개화[전성]기, 번영기
- as opposed to –에 대립하는 것으로서(의); –과는 대조적으로[전혀 다르게]
- permissible [pəːrmísəbəl] 허용할 수 있는; 지장 없을[무방한] 정도의(잘못 따위)
- candidly [kǽndid] 솔직히
- wrongheaded [rɔ́ːŋhédid] a. (생각이) 비뚤어진, 뒤틀어진; 완미한, 사리에 어두운
- dissociation [disòusiéiʃən] n. 〖정신의학〗 (의식 · 인격의) 분열;
- psychopathology [sàikoupəθálədʒi / -θɔ́l-] n. U 정신 병리(학). ㉺ -gist -n.
- integration [ìntəgréiʃən] n. 통합; 완성, 집성

supposed to be a response to childhood trauma. Memories of the early cruelties are hidden and must be recalled to effect a true integration and cure. Multiple personality and its treatment are grounded upon the supposition that the troubled mind can be understood through increased knowledge about the very nature of memory.

Consider this

1. What is the writer's important point? What kinds of evidence does the writer use in supporting his argument?

2. Do you have a different perspective of your own about multiple personality?

Key Words & Phrases 해설

• supposition [sʌ́pəzíʃən] n. U 상상, 추측, 추찰(推察); C 가정, 가설
ex. on the supposition that ~ -이라 가정하고, -이라 간주하고

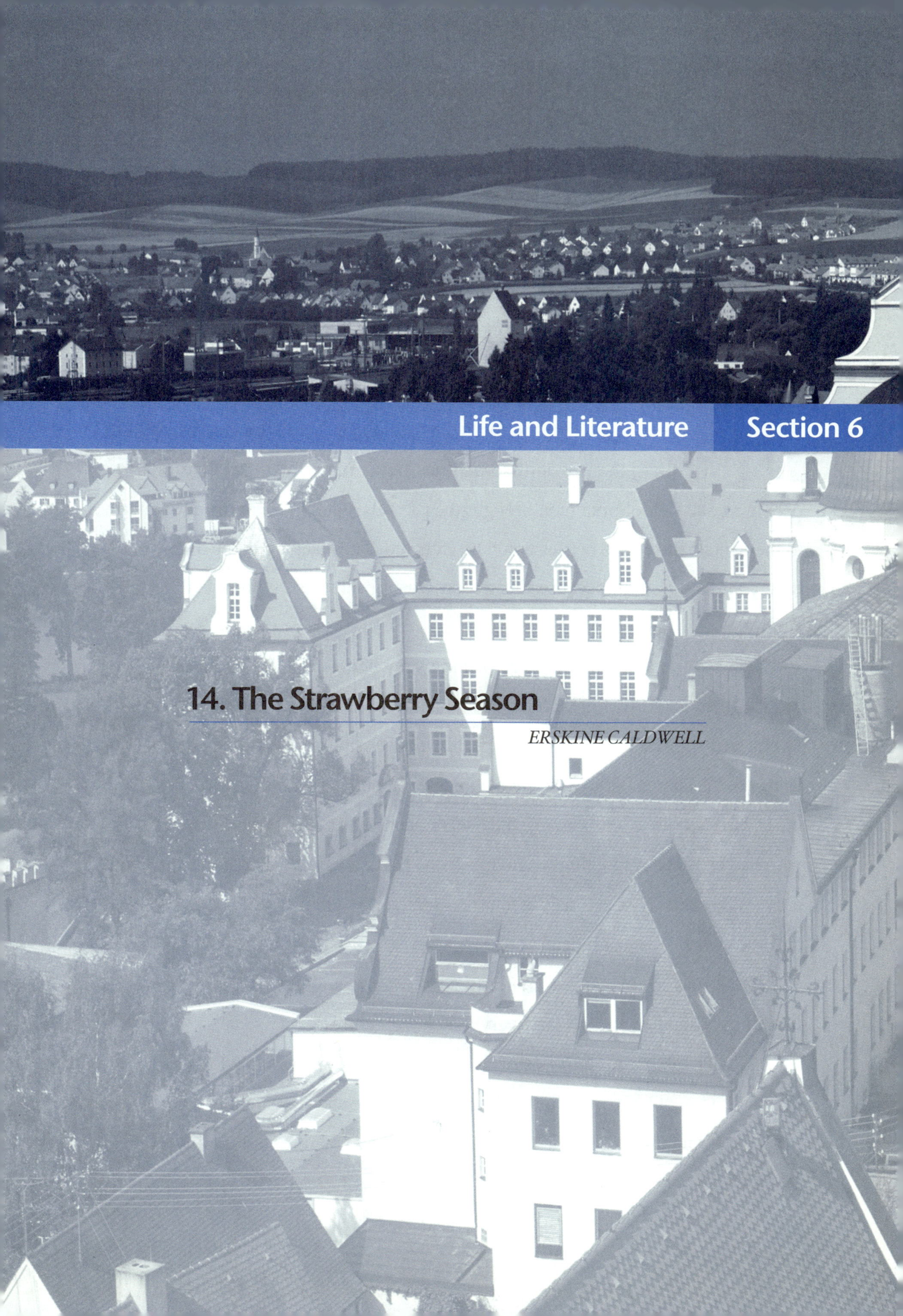

14. The Strawberry Season

ERSKINE CALDWELL

14 The Strawberry Season

ERSKINE CALDWELL

콜드웰 초상

Early in the spring when the strawberries began to ripen, everybody went from place to place helping the farmers gather them. If it had been a good season for the berries and if there were many berries to pick, there would sometimes be as many as thirty-five or forty people in one field. Some men brought their families along, going from one farm to the next as fast as the berries could be gathered. They slept in barns or any place they could find. And, because the season was so short, everybody had to work from sunrise to sunset.

We used to have the best times picking strawberries. There were always a lot of girls there and it was great fun teasing them. If one of them stooped over a little too far and showed the least bit of herself, whoever saw her first shouted as loudly as he could. The rest of us would take up the yell and pass it all over the field. The other girls would giggle among themselves and pull their skirts down. The girl who had caused the shouting would blush and hurry away to the packing shed with a tray of baskets. By the time she returned some other girl had stooped over too far and everybody was laughing at her.

There was a girl named Fanny Forbes who was always showing some of herself by stooping over too far. Everybody liked Fanny.

Another thing we had a lot of fun out of was what we called "strawberry-slapping." One of us would slip up behind a girl while she was stooping over filling her baskets and drop a big juicy ripe strawberry down her dress. It usually stopped

Key Words & Phrases 해설

- ERSKINE CALDWELL (1903 ~ 1987) 미국의 작가
- THE STRAWBERRY SEASON 딸기 수확 철
- Early in the spring 이른 봄
- pick [pik] 따다
- from place to place 이리저리로, 여기저기로
- helping the farmers gather them 딸기 따는 농부들을 도우러
- as many as thirty-five or forty people in one field
  밭 하나에 서른 다섯 명 혹은 마흔 명 쯤의 사람들이
- bring along 데리고 오다
- barn [bɑ:rn] 헛간, 광
- from sunrise to sunset 동틀 무렵에서 해질 녘까지
- teasing [tí:ziŋ] 지분거리는
- If one of them stooped over a little too far and showed the least bit of herself
  처녀 중 한 명이 (딸기 따려고) 몸을 너무 많이 굽혀서 신체의 일부가 조금이라도 보이면
- The rest of us would take up the yell and pass it all over the field
  우리 나머지 사람들은 그 고함소리를 받아들여 온 들판에 퍼지게 하곤 했다
  (it = the yell)
- The other girls would giggle among themselves and pull their skirts down
  다른 처녀들은 자기들끼리 낄낄대고 웃으며 자기들의 (올라간) 치마를 끌어내리곤 했다
- the packing shed (딸기) 포장하는 작업장, shed [ʃed] 헛간, 작업장
- By the time she returned 그 처녀가 돌아올 때 쯤
- everybody was laughing at her 모든 사람이 그녀를 보고 웃었다
- There was a girl named Fanny Forbes who was always showing some of herself by stooping over too far
  (딸기 딸 때) 몸을 너무 많이 굽혀서 자신의 신체 일부를 늘 드러나게 하던 패니 포

midway of her back and there we slapped it good and hard. The mashed strawberry made a mess. The red juice oozed through the cloth and made a big round stain. If the berry was against the skin it was even worse. Very few girls minded that though. Everybody wore his old clothes in the fields and it did not matter about the stain. The worst part was being laughed at. Everybody stopped picking berries to laugh. When that was over, everybody went back to work and forgot it until somebody else got strawberry-slapped. We had a lot of fun picking berries.

Fanny Forbes got more strawberry-slappings than any other girl. All the boys and men liked her and she never became angry. Fanny was good-looking, too.

One day I went to a field where I knew the strawberry crop was good. It was a small field of only two or three acres and few people ever bothered to go there. I decided to go before somebody else did.

When I reached the field, Fanny was finishing the first two rows. She had thought of having the whole field to herself, just as I had thought of doing. We did not mind the other being there as long as no one else came.

"Hello, Fanny," I said, "What made you think of coming over here to Mr. Gunby's place today?"

"The same thing that made you think of it, I guess," she answered, blowing the sand off a handful of berries and putting them into her mouth.

We started off side by side. Fanny was a fast picker and it was all I could do to keep up with her. About an hour before noon the sun came out hot and the sky became cloudless. The berries were ripening almost as fast as we could gather them. Fanny filled a dozen boxes from her next row. She could pick all day and never have a single piece of vine among her berries. She used only the thumb and

Key Words & Phrases 해설

브스라는 처녀가 있었다

- strawberry-slapping 딸기 눌러 으깨기
- It usually stopped midway of her back
  딸기는 대개 처녀의 등 한 가운데에서 걸려 멈췄다
- The mashed strawberry made a mess 짓이겨진 딸기는 엉망이 됐다
- ooze [uːz] (물, 과즙이)스며 나오다
- a big round stain 커다란 둥근 얼룩
- If the berry was against the skin 딸기가 피부에 부딪치는 경우라면
- it was even worse 상태가 훨씬 안 좋았다 (even은 비교급 강조)
- Very few girls minded that though
  하지만 그것 (딸기 으깨기)에 신경을 쓰는 처녀는 거의 없었다. (though 하지만)
- The worst part was being laughed at
  가장 안 좋은 역은 웃음거리가 되는 것이었다
- When that was over 그 일 (웃는 일)이 끝났을 때
- crop [krɑp / krɔp] 수확
- the first two rows 첫 두 줄 (이랑)
- blowing the sand off a handful of berries
  한 움큼의 딸기에서 모래를 불어내면서
- side by side 나란히
- a fast picker 딸기를 빠르게 따는 사람
- keep up with ~에 (뒤떨어) 지지 않다, 따라 잡다
  ex. She could not keep up with her class.
  그녀는 학급의 다른 아이들을 따라가지 못했다.
- The berries were ripening almost as fast as we could gather them
  딸기는 거의 우리가 딸기를 따는 만큼 빠르게 익어가고 있었다

the next two fingers, making a kind of triangle that grasped the berry close to the stem and lifted it off. She never mashed a berry like some people were forever doing.

I had never before noticed it in any other field, but today Fanny was barelegged. In the afternoon it was much cooler without stockings, of course, and it was the best way to keep from wearing them out in the knees. She saw me looking at her bare legs and smiled just a little. I wanted to tell her how nice-looking they were but I did not dare to.

The mid-afternoon was even hotter than it had been at twelve o'clock. The slight breeze we had felt in the morning was gone and the sun hung over us like a burning glass. Fanny's legs were burned brown.

Before I knew what I was doing I stole up behind Fanny and dropped a great big juicy berry down the open neck of her dress. It frightened her at first. Believing that I was several rows away she thought it was a bug or insect of some kind that had fallen down the opening of her dress. When she jumped up and saw me standing behind her however she laughed and reached down into the bosom of her waist for the berry. I was certain I saw it under her dress. Before she could reach it with her hand I slapped it as hard as I could. I thought surely she would laugh as she had always done when somebody strawberry-slapped her, but this time she did not laugh. She sat down quickly, hugging herself tightly. I then realized something was wrong. She looked up at me and there were tears in her eyes. I fell on my knees beside her. I had slapped her breasts.

"What's the matter. Fanny?" I begged. Did I hurt you? I didn't mean to. Honest, I didn't mean to."

"I know you didn't mean to." she said, the tears falling on her lap, "but it did

Key Words & Phrases 해설

- (she) never have a single piece of vine among her berries
  그녀가 딴 딸기 가운데는 단 한 조각의 딸기 덩굴도 없었다.
- thumb [θʌm] 엄지손가락
- a kind of triangle 일종의 삼각형
- stem [stem] (풀 · 나무의) 줄기
- barelegged [bέərlègid, -lègd] 발을[정강이를] 드러낸[내놓고], 양말을 안 신은
- The slight breeze 가벼운 산들바람
- like a burning glass 불타는 유리처럼
- Before I knew what I was doing 내가 무얼 하는지도 모르는 사이에
- a bug or insect 벌레나 곤충
- reach down 손을 내 뻗다
- as hard as I could 내가 할 수 있는 한 세게
- as she had always done 그녀가 늘 그랬던 것 (웃었던 것)처럼
- hug [hʌg] 꽉 껴안다
- She looked up at me and there were tears in her eyes
  그녀는 나를 올려다보았는데 그녀의 눈에는 눈물이 그렁거렸다.
- lap [læp] 무릎
- She wiped the tears from her eyes 그녀는 눈에서 흘러내리는 눈물을 훔쳤다
- plead [pli:d] 간청하다(implore)
- unbutton [ʌnbʌ́tn] (~의) 단추를 끄르다
- The scarlet stain 주홍빛 얼룩
- against the white cloth 흰 천을 배경으로 하여
- unfasten [ʌnfǽsn / -fá:sn] 벗기다, 풀다
- to get the berry out 딸기를 꺼내기 위해서

hurt. You mustn't hit me there."

"I'll never do it again, Fanny. I promise I won't"

"It's all right now." she smiled painfully. "It still hurts a little though."

Her head fell on my shoulder. I put my arms around her. She wiped the tears from her eyes.

"It's all right now." she repeated. "It will stop hurting soon." She lifted her head and smiled at me. Her large round blue eyes were the shade of the sky when the sun has begun to rise.

"I'll never strawberry-slap you again as long as I live, Fanny," I pleaded, hoping she would forgive me.

Fanny unbuttoned the dress down to her waist. The berry was mashed beneath her underclothes. The scarlet stain looked like a morning-glory against the white cloth.

"I'll have to unfasten this too, to get the berry out," she said.

"Let me get it," I urged. "You don't want the juice all over your fingers."

She unfastened the undergarment. The berry lay crushed between her breasts. They were milk-white and the center of each was stained like a mashed strawberry. Hardly knowing what I was doing I hugged her tightly in my arms and kissed her lips for a long time. The crushed strawberry fell to the ground beside us.

When we got up, the sun was setting and the earth was becoming cool. We found our boxes and baskets of berries and walked across the fields to the barn. When we got there, Mr. Gunby counted them and paid us the money we had earned.

We went through the barnyard to the front of the house and stood at the gate looking at each other for several minutes. Neither of us said anything. Fanny had

Key Words & Phrases 해설

- urge [ʌ́rdʒ] 재촉하다, 주장하다
- undergarment [ʌ́ndərgɑrmənt] 속옷
- Hardly knowing what I was doing 내가 무얼 하는지도 거의 모르게
- the sun was setting 태양은 지고 있었다.
- barnyard [bɑ́:rnjɑ́:rd] 헛간의 앞마당
- sweetheart [swí:thɑ̀:rt] 연인, 애인

once said she had never had a sweetheart. I wish she had been mine.

Fanny turned and went down the road in one direction and I went up the road in another. It was the end of the strawberry season.

Consider this

1. What is the theme of the story. What is the author's attitude toward his main character?

2. Why didn't Fanny laugh as usual when the main character strawberry-slapped her. Do you think this is a funny story, or a happy story? Why or why not?

15. Hills Like White Elephants

ERNEST HEMINGWAY

15 Hills Like White Elephants

ERNEST HEMINGWAY

헤밍웨이

The hills across the valley of the Ebro were long and white. On this side there was no shade and no tree and the station was between two lines of rails in the sun. Close against the side of the station there was the warm shadow of the building and a curtain, made of strings of bamboo beads, hung across the open door into the bar, to keep out flies. The American and the girl with him sat at a table in the shade, outside the building. It was very hot and the express from Barcelona would come in forty minutes. It stopped at this junction for two minutes and went on to Madrid.

"What should we drink? the girl asked. She had taken off her hat and put it on the table."

"It's pretty hot," the man said.

"Let's drink beer."

"Dos cervezas," "the man said into the curtain."

"Big ones?" a woman asked from the doorway."

"Yes. Two big ones."

The woman brought two glasses of beer and two felt pads. She put the felt pads and the beer glasses on the table and looked at the man and the girl. The girl was looking off at the line of hills. They were white in the sun and the country was brown and dry.

"They look like white elephants," she said.

"I've never seen one," the man drank his beer.

Key Words & Phrases 해설

- ERNEST HEMINGWAY (1899 ~ 1961) 미국의 작가, 1954년 노벨문학상 수상
- Ebro 스페인 북부에 있는 강
- made of strings of bamboo beads 대나무 구슬을 꿰어 만든
- hung across the open door into the bar
  (커튼은) 술집 안 쪽으로 열린 문을 가로질러 걸려 있었다
- to keep out flies 파리를 쫓기 위해서
- the express from Barcelona (스페인) 바로셀로나에서 오는 급행열차
- junction [dʒʌ́ŋkʃən] 연락역, 갈아타는 역
- and went on to Madrid 그리고는 (스페인) 마드리드로 계속 달렸다
- "It's pretty hot," 꽤 덥군
- "Big ones?" a woman asked from the doorway."
  매주 큰 걸로요? 한 여자가 문간에서 물었다.
- "Yes. Two big ones." 그렇소, 큰 걸로 두 잔 주시오.
- The woman brought two glasses of beer and two felt pads.
  그 여자는 맥주 두 잔과 두개의 펠트 천 잔 받침을 가져왔다.
- look off ~에서 눈을 떼다
- They were white in the sun and the country was brown and dry.
  언덕들은 태양 속에서 하얗게 빛났고, 시골은 다갈색을 띠었으며 메말라 있었다.
- "They look like white elephants," 언덕은 흰 코끼리 같아 보여요.
- "I've never seen one," the man drank his beer.
  "나는 그런 것을 본 적이 없어." 남자는 맥주를 들이켰다.
- "No, you wouldn't have." 그래요, 당신은 보지 않았을 거예요 (seen one 생략)
- "I might have," the man said. 보았는지도 모르겠소, 남자가 말했다 (seen one 생략)
- "Just because you say I wouldn't have doesn't prove anything."
  오로지 내가 보지 않았을 거란 당신의 말은 어떤 것도 입증하지 않으니까 말이오.
  ('you say' 앞에 주어로 'what'을 보충하여 이해하며, 'have' 다음에 'seen one'을

"No, you wouldn't have."

"I might have," the man said. "Just because you say I wouldn't have doesn't prove anything."

The girl looked at the bead curtain. "They've painted something on it," she said. "What does it say?"

"Anis del Toro. It's a drink."

"Could we try it?"

The man called "Listen" through the curtain. The woman came out from the bar.

"Four reales."

"We want two Anis del Toro."

"With water?"

"Do you want it with water?"

"It's all right."

"You want them with water?" asked the woman.

"Yes, with water."

"It tastes like licorice," the girl said and put the glass down.

"That's the way with everything."

"Yes," said the girl. "Everything tastes of licorice, Especially all the things you've waited so long for, like absinthe."

"Oh, cut it out."

"You started it," the girl said. "I was being amused. I was having a fine time."

"Well, let's try and have a fine time."

"All right. I was trying. I said the mountains looked like white elephants. Wasn't that bright?"

Key Words & Phrases 해설

보충하여 이해)

- just because ~ 오로지 ~ 이니까, ~ 인 고로

  ex. She has played the piano just because she was asked to.

  그녀는 부탁을 받고서 피아노를 쳤다.

- "They've painted something on it," 구슬 커튼 위에 뭔가를 그려 (써) 놓았네요.
- "What does it say?" 무슨 말이에요?
- Anis del Toro 술의 일종
- Four reales 사 리얼이오. real [rí:əl, re:al] 스페인 동전, 옛 스페인의 작은 은화
- "Could we try it?" 한번 마셔볼 수 있을까요?
- "With water?" 물과 함께 드릴까요?
- "It tastes like licorice," 감초 같은 맛이 나네요. licorice [líkərəs] 감초(甘草)
- "That's the way with everything" 만사 그런식이군
- absinth(e) [ǽbsinθ] 압생트 (프랑스산의 독주)
- "Oh, cut it out." 오 그만둬요. (말 말아요)
- "You started it," 당신이 먼저 시작했잖아요.
- amused [əmjú:zd] 재미있어 [즐거워] 하는
- "It's really an awfully simple operation, Jig,"

  지그, 그것은 사실 굉장히 간단한 수술이야.

  (※ 수술(operation)은 낙태수술(abortion)을 의미함, 지그(Jig)는 여성등장 인물 이름.)

- "It's not really an operation at all." 그것은 정말로 수술도 아니야.
- The girl looked at the ground the table legs rested on.

  그녀는 테이블 다리가 놓여 있는 땅을 바라보았다.

- "I know you wouldn't mind it, Jig.

  지그, 당신이 수술을 내켜하지 않는다는 걸 난 알아. (it = operation)

- It's really not anything. 그건 (수술) 정말로 아무것도 아니야
- bother [bάðə:r / bɔ́ð-] ~을 괴롭히다

"That was bright."

"I wanted to try this new drink. That's all we do, isn't it — look at things and try new drinks?"

"I guess so."

The girl looked across at the hills.

"They're lovely hills," she said. "They don't really look like white elephants. I just meant the coloring of their skin through the trees."

"Should we have another drink?"

"All right."

The warm wind blew the bead curtain against the table.

"The beer's nice and cool," the man said.

"It's lovely," the girl said.

"It's really an awfully simple operation, Jig," the man said. "It's not really an operation at all."

The girl looked at the ground the table legs rested on.

"I know you wouldn't mind it, Jig. It's really not anything. It's just to let the air in."

The girl did not say anything.

"I'll go with you and I'll stay with you all the time. They just let the air in and then it's all perfectly natural."

"Then what will we do afterward?"

"We'll be fine afterward. Just like we were before."

"What makes you think so?"

"That's the only thing that bothers us. It's the only thing that's made us unhappy."

Key Words & Phrases 해설

- I've known lots of people that have done it."
  그런 일(수술)을 한 많은 사람들을 난 알아.
- "So have I," 나도 그래요 (알아요).
- "if you don't want to you don't have to.
  당신이 원치 않으면 (수술을) 할 필요가 없어.
- Because I don't care about me." 난 어찌돼든 상관 안 하기 때문에.
- "I don't want you to do it if you feel that way."
  당신이 그런 식으로 느낀다면 나는 당신이 그것을 하는 것을 원치 않아
- Far away, beyond the river, were mountains. 멀리 강 너머에는 산들이 있었다.
- And once they take it away, you never get it back."
  그들이 그것을 빼앗아간 이상, 결코 되찾지 못할 거야.
- "Come on back in the shade," 자, 그늘로 되돌아 갑시다.
- Could we have another beer? 맥주 한 잔 더 할 수 있을까요?
- But you've got to realize 하지만 당신은 깨달아야만 해.
- go through with ~을 끝까지 해내다(complete)
  ex. She is determined to go through with the undertaking.
  그녀는 맡은 일을 끝까지 해낼 결심이다.
- But I don't want anybody but you. 하지만 난 당신 외에 어떤 사람도 원하지 않아.
- He did not say anything but looked at the bags against the wall of the station.
  그는 기차역 벽에 기대어 있는 가방을 바라볼 뿐 아무 말도 하지 않았다.
- There were labels on them 가방들에는 꼬리표들이 달려 있었다.
- "But I don't want you to," he said, "I don't care anything about it."
  "난 당신이 실행하기를 원치 않는다면, 난 상관치 않아"라고 그가 말했다.
- "I'll scream," 비명을 지를 거예요.
- "The train comes in five minutes," 오 분 있으면 기차가 들어옵니다.
- "I'd better take the bags over to the other side of the station,"

The girl looked at the bead curtain, put her hand out and took hold of two of the strings of beads.

"And you think then we'll be all right and be happy."

"I know we will. You don't have to be afraid. I've known lots of people that have done it."

"So have I," said the girl. "And afterward they were all so happy."

"Well," the man said, "if you don't want to you don't have to. I wouldn't have you do it if you didn't want to. But I know it's perfectly simple."

"And you really want to?"

"I think it's the best thing to do. But I don't want you to do it if you don't really want to."

"And if I do it you'll be happy and things will be like they were and you'll love me?"

"I love you now. You know I love you."

"I know. But if I do it, then it will be nice again if I say things are like white elephants, and you'll like it?"

"I'll love it. I love it now but I just can't think about it. You know how I get when I worry."

"If I do it you won't ever worry?"

"I won't worry about that because it's perfectly simple."

"Then I'll do it. Because I don't care about me."

"What do you mean?"

"I don't care about me."

"Well, I care about you."

"Oh, yes. But I don't care about me. And I'll do it and then everything will be

Key Words & Phrases 해설

가방들을 역 맞은편에 옮겨 놓은 것이 더 좋겠군.

- He picked up the two heavy bags 그는 무거운 가방 두 개를 집어 들었다.
- we'll finish the beer 맥주를 마저 다 마실 거야
- Coming back 돌아오자
- They were all waiting reasonably for the train
  모두들 이성적으로 기차를 기다리고 있었다

fine."

"I don't want you to do it if you feel that way."

The girl stood up and walked to the end of the station. Across, on the other side, were fields of grain and trees along the banks of the Ebro. Far away, beyond the river, were mountains. The shadow of a cloud moved across the field of grain and she saw the river through the trees.

"And we could have all this," she said. "And we could have everything and every day we make it more impossible."

"What did you say?"

"I said we could have everything."

"We can have everything."

"No, we can't."

"We can have the whole world."

"No, we can't."

"We can go everywhere."

"No, we can't. It isn't ours any more."

"It's ours."

"No, it isn't. And once they take it away, you never get it back."

"But they haven't taken it away."

"We'll wait and see."

"Come on back in the shade," he said. "You mustn't feel that way."

"I don't feel any way," the girl said. "I just know things."

"I don't want you to do anything that you don't want to do—"

"Nor that isn't good for me," she said. "I know. Could we have another beer?"

"All right. But you've got to realize—"

"I realize," the girl said. "Can't we maybe stop talking?"

They sat down at the table and the girl looked across at the hills on the dry side of the valley and the man looked at her and at the table.

"You've got to realize," he said, "that I don't want you to do it if you don't want to. I'm perfectly willing to go through with it if it means anything to you."

"Doesn't it mean anything to you? We could get along."

"Of course it does. But I don't want anybody but you. I don't want any one else. And I know it's perfectly simple."

"It's all right for you to say that, but I do know it."

"Would you do something for me now?"

"I'd do anything for you."

"Would you please please please please please please please stop talking?"

He did not say anything but looked at the bags against the wall of the station. There were labels on them from all the hotels where they had spent nights.

"But I don't want you to," he said, "I don't care anything about it."

"I'll scream," the girl said.

The woman came out through the curtains with two glasses of beer and put them down on the damp felt pads. "The train comes in five minutes," she said.

"What did she say?" asked the girl.

"That the train is coming in five minutes."

The girl smiled brightly at the woman, to thank her.

"I'd better take the bags over to the other side of the station," the man said. She smiled at him.

"All right. Then come back and we'll finish the beer."

He picked up the two heavy bags and carried them around the station to the other tracks. He looked up the tracks but could not see the train. Coming back, he walked through the barroom, where the people waiting for the train were drinking. He drank an Anis at the bar and looked at the people. They were all waiting reasonably for the train. He went out through the bead curtain. She was sitting at the table and smiled at him.

"Do you feel better?" he asked.

"I feel fine," she said. "there's nothing wrong with me. I feel fine."

Consider this

1. In this story, the imagination is liked, to the body of a pregnant woman. Her lover or husband wants the fetus aborted, and she wants to keep him. Ultimately, he will win. If you agree, what make you think so? If not, why not?

2. This short story has been called one of the best examples of hard-boiled style in the English literature. Can we feel the energy of coercion and the weight of despair in the awful white spaces that separate the line, the words, and the paragraphs.

3. "The American" asks if she feels "better," as if the way one viewed the world were an illness, or a misbehavior, from which one recovers. "I feel fine," she lies. Do you agree? Why or why not?

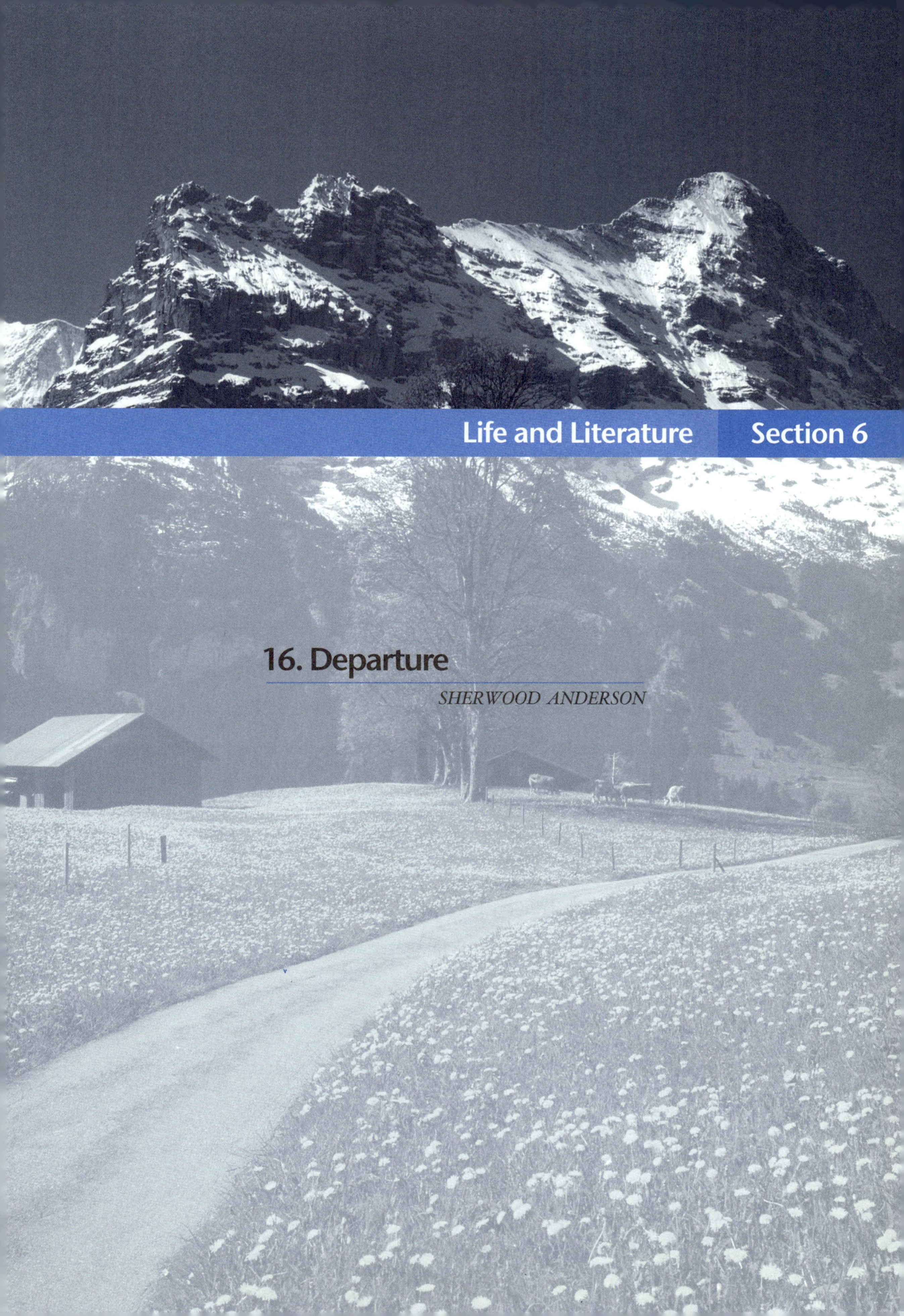

16. Departure

SHERWOOD ANDERSON

16 Departure

SHERWOOD ANDERSON

앤더슨

Young George Willard got out of bed at four in the morning. It was April and the young tree leaves were just coming out of their buds. The trees along the residence streets in Winesburg are maple and the seeds are winged. When the wind blows they whirl crazily about, filling the air and making a carpet underfoot.

George came downstairs into the hotel office carrying a brown leather bag. His trunk was packed for departure. Since two o'clock he had been awake thinking of the journey he was about to take and wondering what he would find at the end of his journey. The boy who slept in the hotel office lay on a cot by the door. His mouth was open and he snored lustily. George crept past the cot and went out into the silent deserted main street. The east was pink with the dawn and long streaks of light climbed into the sky where a few stars still shone.

Beyond the last house on Trunion Pike in Winesburg there is a great stretch of open fields. The fields are owned by farmers who live in town and drive homeward at evening along Trunion Pike in light creaking wagons. In the fields are planted berries and small fruits. In the late afternoon in the hot summers when the road and the fields are covered with dust, a smoky haze lies over the great flat basin of land. To look across it is like looking out across the sea. In the spring when the land is green the effect is somewhat different. The land becomes a wide green billiard table on which tiny human insects toil up and down.

All through his boyhood and young manhood George Willard had been in the

Key Words & Phrases 해설

- Sherwood Anderson (1876 ~ 1941)은 미국 작가이다.
  그는 *Winesburg, Ohio, Poor White, Many Marriages* 그리고 *Dark Laughter*을 포함하여 7권의 소설과 20여권의 책을 썼다. 그는 세계 1차대전과 2차대전 사이의 미국소설에 많은 영향력을 주었다. 특히 그의 글쓰기는 어네스트 헤밍웨이와 윌리엄 포크너와 같은 작가들의 문체에 미친 영향력이 컸다.
- departure 출발
- the young tree leaves were just coming out of their buds
  어린 나무 잎들이 막 싹터 나왔다.
- the residence streets 주택가
- the seeds are winged 씨앗들은 날개가 이었다.
- When the wind blows they whirl crazily about
  바람이 불 때 그 씨앗들은 미친 듯이 여기 저기 맴돌면서 날아다니다
- filling the air and making a carpet underfoot.
  대기를 충만하게 하다가 발아래 양탄자처럼 깔리면서
- thinking of the journey he was about to take
  그가 막 하려는 여행에 대해 생각하면서
- lay on a cot 간이침대에 누었다
- he snored lustily 힘차게 코를 골았다
- the silent deserted main street 조용하고 황량한 중심가
- long streaks of light 길다란 빛 줄기
- Trunion Pike 투루니언 유료도로
- a great stretch of open fields 넓게 펼쳐진 훤히 뜨인 들판
- in light creaking wagons 가볍게 삐걱 거리는 짐차들을 타고
- a smoky haze lies over the great flat basin of land
  연기 같은 자욱한 아지랑이가 광활하고 평평한 분지의 땅에 드리워 있었다.
- be covered with ~ 로 덮여있다

habit of walking on Trunion Pike. He had been in the midst of the great open place on winter nights when it was covered with snow and only the moon looked down at him; he had been there in the fall when bleak winds blew and on summer evenings when the air vibrated with the song of insects. On the April morning he wanted to go there again, to walk again in the silence. He did walk to where the road dipped down by a little stream two miles from town and then turned and walked silently back again. When he got to Main Street clerks were sweeping the sidewalks before the stores. "Hey, you George. How does it feel to be going away?" they asked.

The westbound train leaves Winesburg at seven forty-five in the morning. Tom Little is conductor. His train runs from Cleveland to where it connects with a great trunk line railroad with terminals in Chicago and New York. Tom has what in railroad circles is called an "easy run." Every evening he returns to his family. In the fall and spring he spends his Sundays fishing in Lake Erie. He has a round red face and small blue eyes. He knows the people in the towns along his railroad better than a city man knows the people who live in his apartment building.

George came down the little incline from the New Willard House at seven o' clock. Tom Willard carried his bag. The son had become taller than the father.

On the station platform everyone shook the young man's hand. More than a dozen people waited about. Then they talked of their own affairs. Even Will Henderson, who was lazy and often slept until nine, had got out of bed. George was embarrassed. Gertrude Wilmot, a tall thin woman of fifty who worked in the Winesburg post office, came along the station platform. She had never before paid any attention to George. Now she stopped and put out her hand. In two words she voiced what everyone felt. "Good luck," she said sharply and then turning went on

Key Words & Phrases 해설

- tiny human insects toil up and down
  조그마한 인간 곤충들이 오르락 내리락 땀 흘려 일하고 있었다.
- only the moon looked down at him 달만이 그를 내려다 보았다
- when bleak winds blew 쓸쓸한 바람이 불 때
- when the air vibrated with the song of insects 곤충들의 노래로 공기가 떨릴 때
- the road dipped down 길이 내리막이 되었다,
- clerks were sweeping the sidewalks before the stores
  점원들이 가게 앞 보도를 청소하고 있었다
- The westbound train leaves Winesburg
  서쪽으로 가는 기차가 와이스버그를 떠나다
- great trunk line railroad 큰 간선 철도
- in railroad circles 철도계에서는
- what is called 이른바
- easy run 운행하기에 용이한 길
- the little incline 경사진 길
- everyone shook the young man's hand 모든 사람들이 그 젊은이와 악수를 했다.
- More than a dozen people waited about
  십 여 명 이상의 사람들이 주변에서 기다렸다.
- She had never before paid any attention to George
  그녀는 이전에는 결코 조오지에게 주목하지 않았다.
- went on her way 가버렸다.
- George felt relieved 조오지는 안도감을 느꼈다.
- He scampered hurriedly aboard 그는 재빨리 서둘러서 기차에 올랐다
- hoping to have a parting word with him
  그와 작별인사를 한마디 나누기를 바라면서

her way.

When the train came into the station George felt relieved. He scampered hurriedly aboard. Helen White came running along Main Street hoping to have a parting word with him, but he had found a seat and did not see her. When the train started Tom Little punched his ticket, grinned and, although he knew George well and knew on what adventure he was just setting out, made no comment. Tom had seen a thousand George Willards go out of their towns to the city. It was a commonplace enough incident with him. In the smoking car there was a man who had just invited Tom to go on a fishing trip to Sandusky Bay. He wanted to accept the invitation and talk over details.

George glanced up and down the car to be sure no one was looking, then took out his pocketbook and counted his money. His mind was occupied with a desire not to appear green. Almost the last words his father had said to him concerned the matter of his behavior when he got to the city. "Be a sharp one," Tom Willard had said. "Keep your eyes on your money. Be awake. That's the ticket. Don't let anyone think you're a greenhorn."

After George counted his money he looked out of the window and was surprised to see that the train was still in Winesburg.

The young man, going out of his town to meet the adventure of life, began to think but he did not think of anything very big or dramatic. Things like his mother's death, his departure from Winesburg, the uncertainty of his future life in the city, the serious and larger aspects of his life did not come into his mind.

He thought of little things—Turk Smollet wheeling boards through the main street of his town in the morning, a tall woman, beautifully gowned, who had once stayed overnight at his father's hotel, Butch Wheeler the lamp lighter of Winesburg

Key Words & Phrases 해설

- Tom Little punched his ticket 탐 리틀이 그의 기차표에 구멍을 뚫었다 (개찰 했다)
- on what adventure he was just setting out
  그가 무슨 모험적일 일로 이제 막 길을 떠나고 있는지
- Tom had seen a thousand George Willards go out of their towns to the city
  탐은 수많은 조오지 윌라드같은 사람들이 그들의 고향을 떠나 도시로 가는지를 보았다
- It was a commonplace enough incident with him
  그 일은 그에게는 흔해 빠진 사건에 불과했다
- talk over details 세부적인 것에 관해 이야기 하다.
- George glanced up and down 조오지는 위 아래로 훑어 보았다.
- His mind was occupied with a desire not to appear green
  그의 마음속에는 미숙하지 않게 보이려는 욕망으로 가득차 있었다.
- "Be a sharp one," 예리한 사람이 되거라,
- Keep your eyes on your money 너의 돈을 잘 간수하거라
- a greenhorn 미숙한 사람, 풋내기
- to meet the adventure of life 삶의 모험에 직면하기 위하여
- come into one's mind. 생각이 떠오르다 생각나다
- wheeling boards 판자들을 수레로 운반하는
- beautifully gowned 아름답게 가운을 입은
- the lamp lighter of Winesburg 와인스버그의 가로등을 켜는 사람
- holding a torch in his hand, 그의 손에 횃불을 들고서
- putting a stamp on an envelope 봉투에 소인을 찍으며
- The young man's mind was carried away by his growing passion for dreams
  젊은이의 마음은 불타오르는 꿈에 대한 열정으로 도취되었다.
- One looking at him would not have thought him particularly sharp.

hurrying through the streets on a summer evening and holding a torch in his hand, Helen White standing by a window in the Winesburg post office and putting a stamp on an envelope.

The young man's mind was carried away by his growing passion for dreams. One looking at him would not have thought him particularly sharp. With the recollection of little things occupying his mind he closed his eyes and leaned back in the car seat. He stayed that way for a long time and when he aroused himself and again looked out of the car window the town of Winesburg had disappeared and his life there had become but a background on which to paint the dreams of his manhood.

Consider this

1. In what way does the title describe this short story? What is this story's thesis? Describes what happen to George who try to depart.

2. How do you know that the main character's memories are reliable? Isn't there an almost universal tendency to sentimentalize childhood?

Key Words & Phrases 해설

우리가 그를 바라 봤다면 그가 특별하게 예리하다고 생각지 못했을 것이다.
(= if one had looked at him, one would not have thought him particularly sharp.)

- With the recollection of little things occupying his mind
  그의 마음을 차지하고 있던 사소한 것에 대한 회상으로
- He stayed that way for a long time 그는 그런 식으로 오랫동안 머물러 있었다.
- when he aroused himself 그가 일어났을 때
- his life there 거기(와이스버그 오하이오)에서의 그의 삶은
- a background on which to paint the dreams of his manhood
  그의 성년기의 꿈을 그리기 위한 배경

17. Flower-Myths: Narcissus, Hyacinth

EDITH HAMILTON

17 Flower-Myths: Narcissus, Hyacinth

EDITH HAMILTON

The first story about the creation of the narcissus is told only in an early Homeric Hymn of the seventh or eighth century, the second I have taken from Ovid. There is an immense difference between the two poets, who are separated from each other not only by six or seven hundred years, but also by the fundamental difference between the Greek and the Roman. The Hymn is written objectively, simply, without a touch of affectation. The poet is thinking of his subject. Ovid is as always thinking of his audience. But he tells his story well. The bit about the ghost trying to look at itself in the river of death is a subtle touch which is quite characteristic of him and quite unlike any Greek writer. Euripides gives the best account of the festival of Hyacinthus; Apollodorus and Ovid both tell his story. Whenever there is any vividness in my narrative it may be ascribed securely to Ovid. Apollodorus never deviates into anything like that.

In Greece there are most lovely wild flowers. They would be beautiful anywhere, but Greece is not a rich and fertile country of wide meadows and fruitful fields where flowers seem at home. It is a land of rocky ways and stony hills and rugged mountains, and in such places the exquisite vivid bloom of the wild flowers,

A profusion of delight,
Gay, bewilderingly bright,

Key Words & Phrases 해설

• hyacinth [háiəsìnθ] n. 〖식물〗 히아신스; U 보라색;

• Ovid [ávid / ɔ́vid] n. 오비디우스(로마의 시인; 43 B.C. - 17 A.D.?)

• Hyacinthus [hàiəsínθəs]
n. 〖그리스신화〗 히아킨토스(Apollo가 사랑한 미소년, 죽을 때 그의 피에서 hyacinth 가 났다고 함)

• deviate [dí:vièit] v. (상도 · 규칙 · 원칙 따위에서) 벗어나다, 빗나가다

• profusion [prəfjù:ʒən] n. a. ~ of 풍부한, 다량의, 많은

Comes as a startling surprise. Bleak heights are carpeted in radiant colors; every crack and crevice of a frowning crag blossoms. The contrast of this laughing, luxuriant beauty with the clear-cut, austere grandeur all around arrests the attention sharply. Elsewhere wild flowers may be little noticed-but never in Greece.

That was as true in the days of old as it is now. In the faraway ages when the tales of Greek mythology were taking shape men found the brilliant blossoms of the Greek spring a wonder and a delight. Those people separated from us by thousands of years, and almost completely unknown to us, felt as we do before that miracle of loveliness, each flower so delicate, yet all together covering the land like a rainbow mantle flung over the hills. The first storytellers in Greece told story after story about them, how they had been created and why they were so beautiful.

It was the most natural thing possible to connect them with the gods. All things in heaven and earth were mysteriously linked with the divine powers, but beautiful things most of all. Often an especially exquisite flower was held to be the direct creation of a god for his own purpose. That was true of the narcissus, which was not like ours of that name, but a lovely bloom of glowing purple and silver. Zeus called it into being to help his brother, the lord of the dark underworld, when he wanted to carry away the maiden he had fallen in love with Demeter's daughter, Persephone. She was gathering flowers with her companion in the vale of Enna, in a meadow of soft grass and roses and crocus and lovely violets and iris and hyacinths. Suddenly she caught sight of something quite new to her, a bloom more beautiful by far than any she had ever seen, a strange glory of a flower, a marvel to all, immortal gods and mortal men. A hundred blossoms grew up from the roots, and the fragrance was very sweet. The broad sky above and the whole earth

Key Words & Phrases 해설

- crevice [krévis] n. (벽 · 바위 등의) 갈라진 틈, 균열
- crag [kræg] n. 울퉁불퉁한 바위, 험한 바위산
- austere [ɔːstíər] a. (austerer; -est) 엄(격)한, 준엄한, 가혹한. [SYN.] ⇨ SEVERE
- arrest [ərést] vt. (사람 눈 · 주의 등을) 끌다
  ex. ~ her attention [eyes] 그녀의 주의를 끌다 [눈에 띄다]
- mantle [mǽntl] n. (미국 · 영국고어) 망토, 외투; (비유) (권위 등의 상징으로서의) 옷
- true [truː] of. 해당되는 [하는]
- Demeter [dimíːtər]
  n. 〖그리스신화〗 데메테르(농업 · 풍요(豊饒) · 결혼의 여신) [cf.] Ceres
- Persephone [pəːrséfəni]
  n. ① 〖그리스신화〗 페르세포네(Hades의 아내로 명부(冥府)의 여왕).
  ② 봄(의 여신) (의인화(擬人化))
- crocus [króukəs]
  n. (pl. ~es, -ci [-sai, -kai]) 〖식물〗 크로커스(사프란속(屬); 적황색, 사프란색;
- marvel [máːrv-əl] n. 놀라운 일, 경이, 이상함
- fragrance, -grancy [fréigrəns], [-si] n. U 향기, 방향(芳香)

laughed to see it, and the salt wave of the sea.

Only Persephone among the maidens had spied it. The rest were at the other end of the meadow. She stole toward it, half fearful at being alone, but unable to resist the desire to fill her basket with it, exactly as Zeus had supposed she would feel. Wondering she stretched out her hands to take the lovely plaything, but before she touched it a chasm opened in the earth and out of it coal--black horse sprang, drawing a chariot and driven by one who had a look of dark splendor, majestic and beautiful and terrible. He caught her to him and held her close. The next moment she was being borne away from the radiance of earth in springtime to the world of the dead by the king who rules it.

This was not the only story about the narcissus. There was another, as magical, but quite different. The hero of it was a beautiful lad, whose name was Narcissus. His beauty was so great, all the girls who saw him longed to be his, but he would have none of them. He would pass the loveliest carelessly by, no matter how much she tried to make him look at her. Heartbroken maidens were nothing to him. Even the sad case of the fairest of the nymphs, Echo, did not move him. She was a favorite of Artemis, the goddess of woods and wild creatures, but she came under the displeasure of a still mightier goddess, Hera herself, who was at her usual occupation of trying to discover what Zeus was about. She suspected that he was in love with one of the nymphs and she went to look them over to try to discover which. However, she was immediately diverted from her investigation by Echo's gay chatter. As she listened amused, the others silently stole away and Hera could come to no conclusion as to where Zeus's wandering fancy had alighted. With her usual injustice she turned against Echo. That goddess condemned her never to use her tongue again except to repeat what was said to her. "You will always have the

Key Words & Phrases 해설

• chasm [kǽzəm] n. (지면 · 바위 따위의) 깊게 갈라진 틈; 깊은 구렁; 빈틈(gap), 간격;

last word," Hera said, "but no power to speak first."

This was very hard, but hardest of all when Echo, too, with all the other lovelorn maidens, loved Narcissus. She could follow him, but she could not speak to him. How then could she make a youth who never looked at a girl pay attention to her? One day, however, it seemed her chance had come. He was calling to his companions. "Is anyone here?" and she called back in rapture, "Here--Here." She was still hidden by the trees so that he did not see her, and he shouted, "Come!"--just what she longed to say to him. She answered joyfully, "Come!" and stepped forth from the woods with her arms outstretched. But he turned away in angry disgust. "Not so," he said; "I will die before I give you power over me." All she could say was, humbly, entreatingly, "I give you power over me." but he was gone. She hid her blushes and her shame in a lonely cave, and they say she has so wasted away with longing that only her voice now is left to her.

So Narcissus went on his cruel way, a scorner of love. But at last one of those he wounded prayed a prayer and it was answered by the gods: "May he who loved not others love himself." The great goddess Nemesis, which means righteous anger, undertook to bring this about. As Narcissus bent over a clear pool for a drink and saw there his own reflection, on the moment he fell in love with it. "Now I know," he cried, "what others have suffered from me, for I burn with love of my own self--and yet how can I reach that loveliness I see mirrored in the water? But I cannot leave it. Only death can set me free." And so it happened. He pined away, leaning perpetually over the pool, fixed in one long gaze. Echo was near him, but she could do nothing; only when, dying, he called to his image, "Farewell--farewell," she could repeat the words as a last good-by to him.

They say that when his spirit crossed the river that encircles the world of the

Key Words & Phrases 해설

- Nemesis [néməsis] n. 〖그리스신화〗 인과 응보 · 보복의 여신
- entreat [entríːt]
  v. -에게 탄원하다(for). 간청 [부탁] 하다. entreatingly -ad. 간원 [애원] 하듯이, 간절하게
- humbly [hʌ̀mbli] ad. 겸손하게, 황송하게; 천한 신분으로
- pine[pain] away 『~ / +부』 (슬픔 · 사랑으로) 파리 [수척] 해지다, 한탄하며 지내다
- lean over -에 기대다; -의 위로 구부리다
- bring about 일으키다; 해내다;

dead, it leaned over the boat to catch a final glimpse of itself in the water.

The nymphs he had scorned were kind to him in death and sought his body to give it burial, but they could not find it. Where it had lain there were blooming a new and lovely flower, and they called it by his name, Narcissus.

Another flower that came into being through the death of a beautiful youth was the hyacinth, again not like the flower we call by that name, but lily-shaped and of a deep purple, or, some say, a splendid crimson. That was a tragic death, and each year it was commemorated by

The festival of Hyacinthus
That lasts throughout the tranquil night.
In a contest with Apollo
He was slain.
Discus throwing they competed.
And the god's swift cast
Sped beyond the goal he aimed at
and struck Hyacinthus full in the forehead, a terrible wound.

He had been Apollo's dearest companion. There was no rivalry between them when they tried which could throw the discus farthest; they were only playing a game. The god was horror-struck to see the blood gush forth and the lad, deathly pale, fall to the ground. He turned as pale himself as he caught him up in his arms and tried to staunch the wound. But it was too late. While he held him the boy's head fell back as a flower does when its stem is broken. He was dead and Apollo, kneeling beside him, wept for him, dying so young, so beautiful. He had killed

Key Words & Phrases 해설

- stanch[1] [stɑːntʃ, stɔːntʃ]

  v. (피 · 눈물 따위를) 멈추게 하다; (상처를) 지혈하다; (새는 곳 등을) 막다

- discus [dískəs]

  n. (pl. ~ es, disci [dískai]). (경기용) 원반(原盤); (the ~) =DISCUS THROW; 〖동물 · 식물〗 =DISK

him, although through no fault of his, and he cried, "Oh, if I could give my life for years, or die with you." Even as he spoke, the bloodstained grass turned green again and there bloomed forth the wondrous flower that was to make the lad's name known forever. Apollo himself inscribed the petals--some say with Hyacinth's initial, and others with the two letters of the Greek word that means "Alas"; either way, a memorial of the god's great sorrow.

There is a story, too, that Zephyr, the West Wind, not Apollo, was the direct cause of the death, that he also loved this fairest of youths and in his jealous anger at seeing the god preferred to him he blew upon the discus and made it strike Hyacinth.

Consider this

1. How do the concrete details, the imagery, and the metaphors that the writer uses contribute to the effectiveness of his story. what is the writer's important point?

2. Do you have a different perspective about myth?

Translation into Korean

영문 해석

Translation into Korean

제1장 문장

Basic Reading 1

1. 단어들만이 의사전달의 수단인 것은 아니다. 제스처 또한 의사를 전달한다. 어떤 제스처들은 어떤 특정한 하나의 문화권 이상에서 사용된다. 다른 제스처들은 문화와 문화 사이에서 서로 다르다.

2. 문명의 발달과정에서 도구의 사용은 증가하고 늘어났다. 그 후에 증기 기관의 사용은 전 산업 조직과 운송에 혁명을 일으켰다.

3. 영국인은 항상 실수를 함으로써 배울 준비가 되어 있다. 실수와 실패가 반복되면, 그는 더욱 현명하고 강해진다. 영국 사람들은 전투에서는 모두 지지만 전쟁은 모두 이긴다고 전해져 왔다.

4. 오늘날 이용 가능한 많은 책 가운데서 당신에게 값어치가 있는 책을 고르는 것은 매우 어렵다. 하지만, 그 선택이 힘들면 힘들수록 당신이 찾던 바로 그 책을 얻게 되었을 때 그 기쁨은 더욱 더 클 것이다. 당신이 당신의 애인을 찾는 것처럼 책을 찾아보아라. 결코 접근하기 쉬운 책에 만족하지 마세요. 그 목적을 위해 수고를 아끼지 마세요.

5. 나는 많은 시간동안 혼자 있는 것이 유익하다는 것을 발견한다. 심지어 가장 친한 친구와 더불어서 조차도 함께 있는 것은 얼마 있지 않아 지치게 하고 힘이 빠지게 한다. 나는 혼자 있는 것을 좋아한다. 나는 고독처럼 그렇게 친근한 동료를 결코 발견하지 못한다.

6. 선택은 오직 그가 혼자서 하는 것이었다. 만일 그가 그 중 하나의 문을 열면, 그 안에서 굶주린 호랑이가 나와 그의 유죄에 대한 처벌로 즉시 그에게 달려들어 그를 갈기갈기 찢어 놓을 것이다. 그러나 만일 피고인이 다른 문을 열면, 나이가 피고인과 비슷하며 그 나라에서 가장 아름다운 여인들 중에서 임금이 뽑은 여인이 그 곳에서 나올 것이다. 그의 무죄에 대한 보상으로 그 여인은 그의 아내가 될 것이다.

7. 육체와 마찬가지로 당신의 정신은 그 힘이 노력에 의해서 길러지는 것이다. 그 것이 공부를 함에 있어서 열심히 노력하게 되는 주요한 이유이다. 신체를 단련하지 않으면 운동선수가 될 수 없으며, 정신을 단련하지 않으면 학자로서 상당한 위치에 오를 수가 없다. 뱃사공이 전속력으로 노를 젓는 4마일 그 자체는 이득이 되지 않지만, 그 과정을 견디어 내는 육체적인 능력은 상당한 가치가 있는 것으로 여겨진다.

8. 성인들 그리고 심지어 고도로 교육받은 성인들도 그들의 읽기 능력에 대한 속도와 능력은 매우 다양하다. 어떤 사람들은 매우 느리게 전체적으로 읽어 나간다; 다른 사람들은 너무 빨리 읽어 나가다 다시 돌아와 읽어야 한다. 특히 책을 잘 읽지 못하는 독자는, 읽기 자료의 유형과 그 자료들을 읽는 그들의 의도에 따라서, 읽기의 방법을 다양하게 조절할 능력이 결여되어 있을 수 있다.

9. 언어는 인간의 고귀한 소유물 가운데 하나이다. 언어가 없다면 인간은 동료와 의사를 교환할 수 없을 것이다. 그러나 현대 세계에 있어서는 자신의 모국어 하나만을 말하는 것으로는 충분하지가 않다. 두 개의 언어를 말하는 사람은 두 개의 정신을 소유하고 있다고 말한다. 왜냐하면 외국어를 배우는 과정에서 우리는 어느 정도까지

는 외국인의 사고방식을 획득하기 때문이다. 따라서 언어 공부는 우리로 하여금 우리의 동료 인간들을 이해하도록 하는 가장 훌륭한 수단 중에 하나이다. 그것이(언어를 배우는 것이) 어려운 것은 분명하지만 보상은 크다. 언어 공부는 우리에게 우리가 살고 있는 국제사회의 보다 훌륭한 시민이 되도록 한다.

10. 교육이라는 말은 우리 시대의 중요한 어휘들 중의 하나이다. 교육을 받지 못한 사람들은 20세기가 주는 가장 위대한 기회들 중에 하나를 빼앗긴 역경의 불행한 희생자라고 많은 사람들은 생각한다. 교육의 중요성을 확신하고 있기 때문에, 현대국가들은 교육기관에 투자를 하고 그 이자를 앞으로 지도자가 될 잠재능력을 지닌 개화된 젊은 남녀라는 커다란 집단의 형태로 되돌려 받기를 바란다. 가름침의 주기가 매우 주의 깊게 계획되고 구매 가능한 지식의 샘인 교과서에 의해 강조되는 교육, 그 교육이 가져다주는 이득이 없다면 문명은 어떠한 모습으로 나타나 보일까?

Advanced Reading 1

그 분이 세상을 떠난 지 오 십 년이 채 못 되어 자연의 문이 자물쇠가 열리고 우리는 선택이라는 두려운 짐을 지게 되었습니다. 우리가 일찍이 하나님께 돌렸던 많은 힘들을 우리들이 탈취했습니다. 공포에 떨고 아무런 준비도 안 된 채 우리는 온 세상에 사는 생명체의 삶과 죽음을 좌우할 지배력을 장악하게 되었습니다. 위험과 영광과 선택은 최종적으로 인간에게 달려 있습니다. 인간의 완전무결함에 대한 시험이 가까이 다가오고 있습니다.
하나님과 다름없는 능력을 이미 가졌으므로 우리는 어떤 신성이 가지고 있기를 한 때 기도했던 그 책임과 지혜를 우리들 자신에게서 찾아야 합니다. 인간 자신은 우리의 가장 큰 위험이자 우리의 유일한 희망이 되었습니다. 따라서 오늘날 성 사도 요한의 말씀을 이렇게 바꿔 쓸 만도 하겠습니다. '마지막에 말씀이 있나니, 그 말씀은 인간이요, 그 말씀은 인간과 더불어 있느니라.'

존 스타인 벡: 노벨상 수상 연설에서

Advanced Reading 2

팔십 칠 년 전, 우리의 조상들은 이 대륙에, 자유 가운데 구상되고 모든 사람들은 평등하게 창조되었다는 신조에 바쳐진, 한 새로운 국가를 탄생시켰습니다. 지금 우리는 커다란 내란에 휘말려 있으며, 그 나라 혹은 그렇게 구상되고 그렇게 헌신한 어떤 나라가 계속하여 존속할 수 있을 것인가를 시험하고 있습니다. 우리들은 그 위대한 전쟁터에서 만나고 있습니다. 우리는 그 들판의 일부를 그 나라가 살도록 그들의 생명을 바친 사람들의 최후의 안식처로서 바치기 위해 왔습니다. 우리가 이런 일을 한다는 것은 전적으로 적절하고 타당한 것입니다. 그러나 더 넓은 의미에서, 우리는 이 땅을 바치는 것도 할 수 없으며, 우리는 이 땅을 성스럽게 할 수도 없으며, 우리는 이 땅을 신성하게 할 수도 없습니다. 이곳에서 싸웠던 용감한 사람들 — 생존해 있거나 돌아가셨거나 할 것 없이 — 이 땅을 성스럽게 하고 있습니다. 우리들의 힘이 그것을 더하거나 감하게 할 수 없습니다.
세상 사람들은 우리들이 여기서 말하는 것을 오래 기억하거나 기록하지도 않겠지만, 그 분들이 이곳에서 행한 일은 결코 잊지 않을 것입니다. 살아있는 우리들은 오히려 이 곳에서 싸웠던 분들이 지금까지 그렇게도 고귀하게 진행시켜온 미완성의 사업에, 이 땅에서, 헌신해야합니다. 오히려 우리들은 우리 앞에 남아 있는 위대한 일에 헌신해야 합니다. 즉 명예롭게 돌아가신 분들로부터, 그분들이 충성의 마지막 한 방울 조차 남김없이 바친 그 대의명분에 우리가 더욱 충성을 맹세하는 일, 돌아가신 이들이 헛되이 죽지 않았다는 것을 여기서 굳게 결의하는 일, 이 나라가 하나님 아래서 자유의 새로운 탄생을 맞이하는 일, 그리고 국민의, 국민에 의한, 그리고 국민을 위한 정부가 지상에서 사멸하지 않도록 하는 일에 헌신해야 합니다.

아브라함 린컹의 케티스버그 연설

제2장 부정사

Basic Reading 2

1. 다소 단조로운 삶을 참아내는 능력은 반드시 어린 시절에 획득해야할 능력이다.

2. 낯선 단어를 당신이 접하게 될 때, 당신은 사전을 반드시 찾아봐라.

3. 어떤 작가는 "사랑은 어린이를 위한 필요한 양식이다; 그들의 필요가 얼마나 절실한가 하는 것을 인식하기 위해서는 사랑에 굶주린 아이들이 어떻게든지 관심을 얻기 위해서 힘쓰는 노력들을 우리는 지켜보기만 하면 된다."라고 했다

4. 그는 해외에 가려고 의도했다. 그가 아프지 않았다면 그는 해외에 갔었을 것이다.

5. 시골 호텔에서 저녁 식사를 하고 있었던 한 숙녀가 몸을 돌려서 그녀의 뒤 식탁에서 앉아 있었던 신사에게 겨자를 그녀에게 전달해 달라고 부탁했다. "당신은 나를 시중드는 사람으로 오해한 것으로 보입니다"라고 그는 무례하게 대답했다. "아닙니다, 나는 단지 당신을 신사로 오해했었습니다"라고 그 숙녀는 차갑게 대답했다.

6. 나는 내가 곧바로 필요로 했던 모든 짐을 하숙집에서 운반했고, 나머지는 짐꾼에 의해서 운반될 예정이었다.

7. 학생이 배워야 할 모든 것들에 대한 생각은 때때로 자신을 실망시킨다. 영어 사전에 나와 있는 수천 개의 낯선 단어를 단지 한번 쳐다보는 것만으로도 때때로 마음을 무력하게 만든다. 그러나 만약 우리가 학생이라면 우리는 한 단계 한 단계

씩, 하나씩 또 하나씩 끈기 있게 배우기를 시작해야 한다.

8. 그는 우리에게 노정상의 여러 장소에 대한 도착과 출발시간, 즉 기차를 바꾸어 탈 장소, 연결지점의 시간 등에 대하여 우리에게 알려주었다.

9. 비록 도구가 먹을 것을 위해 동물들을 잡고, 혹은 작물을 위해 토양을 파는 단지 돌과 나무로 된 날카로운 조각에 불과해도 도구의 사용이, 아무리 원시적 사회라 한다고 해도, 발견되지 않는 사회는 없다.

10. 많은 대중 연사들은 그들이 말하려고 하는 것에 대하여 자신들에게 상기시키기 위해서 글로 된 초안이나 노트를 너무 심하게 의존하도록 유혹 받는다. 이것은 준비 부족, 관객에 대한 흥미 부족, 신경과민을 드러낸다. 많은 연사들은 그들의 노트에 너무 의존하게 되어 만약 그들의 노트가 분실되면, 그들은 몹시 신경과민이 되어 무엇을 말해야 될 것인지, 다음에 무엇을 해야 할 것인지 확신하지 못하고, 심지어 그들이 조금 전에 말한 내용을 망각하기도 한다.

11. 그들의 지도자를 올바르게 평가한다면, 그는 자신의 책임감을 회피할 가장 마지막 사람이었고, 그는 그의 부하들이 각자의 임무에 전념하도록 주의 깊게 지도했다.

12. 일은 사회적 만족, 동료 관계, 의뢰인 고객 혹은 학생들과의 접촉을 제공해 준다. 일은 다른 사람이 우리를 필요로 하고 인정하는 존재임을 느끼게 만들어 주며 자신이 자랑스럽게 여기는 지위를 부여해 줄 수 있다.

13. 우리가 모국어 화자가 구어를 이해할 수 있는 것처럼 훌륭하게 구어를 이해할 수 있는 기계를 확보할 수 있다면, 우리는 수많은 다른 실용적인 적용을 수행해 낼 수 있다. 우리는 예를 들어 타자기에게 말하여 타자기로 하여금 우리의 문장을 타이핑하게 할 수 있을 것이다.

14. 우리가 위대한 인물의 삶을 읽을 때면, 우리는 그 자체로는 임의적으로 보일 수 있으며 심지어 재난으로 여겨지는 모든 종류의 경험이 결국에는 삶에 유용하게 활용되는 그 삶의 방법에 감명을 받지 않을 수 없다.

15. 영국의 소설가인 찰스 디킨스는 미시시피강을 “끔찍한 도랑”이라고 묘사했다. 하지만 퉤인에게 미시시피강은 “모든 존재”와 “인간 여행”의 중요한 상징이었다. 그는 미주리주 하니발 강변에서 성장했다. 비록 작은 마을은 동부 해안 문화 중심지로부터 멀리 떨어져 있었지만 어린 퉤인이 성장하기에는 완벽한 장소였다. 거기에서, 그는 많은 인디안 전설을 들을 수 있었고, 흑인 노예에 관한 이야기를 들을 수 있었다. 그러나 강 자체의 삶이 그에게 가장 영향을 끼쳤다. 커다란 증기선의 도착은 그의 소년 시절 모험에 대한 꿈을 흥분시켰다.

16. 비록 로마인들이 모든 세계의 주인이 되었지만, 그들은 결코 교만하지 않아서 그들이 정복한 사람들로부터 유용한 교훈들을 배웠다. 유사하게, 인생에서 당신의 위치가 어떠하던 간에 다른 사람들로부터 경험을 얻기에 너무 늦는 경우는 없다.

17. 단어의 연구는 단지 문학과 연관 있는 어떠한 것만은 아니다. 단어들은 사고의 도구들이다. 당신은 단어가 없이는 생각조차 할 수 없다.

18. 이러한 자유 정신을 소유하지 않는다면 사회적 진보는 늦을 수밖에 없을 것이다. 아마 너무 늦어서 과학 기술 역량이 놀랄만한 속도로 가속화되는 세계의 급속도로 팽창하는 요구를 충족하지 못할 것이다. 자유적 접근은 우리가 믿는 자유롭고 민주적인 사회를 보존하기 위한 유일한 희망이라고 나는 느낀다. 아마 그것이야말로 어떠한 인간 사회 형태를 보존하기 위한 유일한 희망이다.

Advanced Reading 3

다음 해에는 더 많은 승리가 있었다. 너도밤나무 숲이 우거진 골짜기와 언덕배기 너머에 있는 산은 탈환되었고 남쪽의 고원 들판 너머에서도 승리가 있었다. 우리는 팔월에 강을 건넜고, 담이 쳐진 정원에는 분수와 짙은 그늘을 드리우는 많은 나무들이 있고, 집 옆에는 보라색 등덩굴이 드리워져 있는 고리찌아의 어떤 집에 주둔했다. 이제 전투는 다음 산 너머 몇 마일 떨어지지 않은 곳에서 벌어지고 있었다. 그 도시는 매우 훌륭했으며, 우리가 주둔한 집 역시 매우 좋았다. 강이 우리들 뒤로 흘렀고, 도시는 매우 만족스럽게 탈환되어 졌으나 강 너머 산은 탈환되지 않았다. 나는 오스트리아 사람들이 전쟁이 끝난 다음에 언제라도 다시 이 도시로 되돌아오길 원하고 있는 것 같아 매우 기뻤는데, 그들은 이 도시를 파괴하기 위해서 폭격하는 것이 아니라 단지 전략적인 방식으로 조금만 폭격했기 때문이었다.

헤밍웨이의 무기여 잘 있거라에서

Advanced Reading 4

우리가 안전하게 하려는 미래에서, 우리는 세상이 네 가지 기본적인 인간의 자유 위에 세워지기를 고대합니다.
첫째는 세계 도처의 언론과 표현의 자유입니다.
둘째는 세계 도처에서 자신의 방식대로 하나님을 숭배하는 신앙의 자유입니다.
셋째는 결핍으로부터의 자유입니다. 세계적인 의미로 바꿔 말하면, 결핍으로부터의 자유란 세계 모든 곳에서 모든 나라의 국민들에게 건전한 평화로운 삶을 보장해 줄 수 있는 경제적 이해를 의미합니다.
넷째는 공포로부터의 자유입니다. 그것은 세계적인 넓은 의미에서 볼 때 군비를 세계적인 폭의 철저한 방식으로 축소하여 세계 어디에서나 어떤 나라도 다른 나라에게 실제적인 침략을 범할 위치에 놓이지 못하게 하는 것입니다.
그것은 먼 천년 후의 비전이 아닙니다. 그것은 우리 시대와 우리 세대에 달성할 수 있는 세계를 위한 명확한 토대입니다. 이런 세계는 독재자들이 폭탄을 터뜨려 이룩하려는 이른바 새로운 독재 질서와는 정반대의 세계입니다.

루즈벨트의 네 가지 자유

제 3장 분사

Basic Reading 3

1. 사실과 허구는 내 작품 속에 매우 뒤섞여 있어서 이제 그것을 회상해 보면 나는 거의 사실과 허구를 구별할 수가 없다.

2. 인생을 통한 자신의 행위의 측면에서, 자신의 특징적인 결함은 잘 극복이 되면 자신의 강점이 될 수 있는데, 이에 대한 지식보다 한 개인에게 도움이 되는 것은 없다.

3. 최상의 신체적 평안을 위해 중요한 습관중의 하나는 과도함을 피하는 것과 관계가 있다. 모든 것에 있어서 중용의 개념은 수 천년 전 작가들이 제시한 전혀 새로운 생각이 아니다.

4. 헨리는 혼자 남아 있게 되었을 때 백일몽에 빠져들었다. 그는 그의 장난감에 관하여 생각하였고, 그것 중에 어느 것을 그의 누이에게 주어야 할 것인지를 결정하고자 했다; 그는 그들 중에 일부를 내어 주도록 지시 받았으며, 이미 누이가 장난감들을 그렇게 여겼기 때문에 그것들이 정당하게 그녀의 것이 된다고 해도 커다란 차이가 생기지 않을 것이었다.

5. 설령 우리가 우리의 친구들을 잘 선택할 수 있는 의지와 감각을 가지고 있다 할지라도, 우리 가운데서 아주 소수만이 그 힘을 가지고 있을 것이며, 혹은 적어도, 대다수의 사람들에게 그 선택의 영역은 얼마나 제한적이겠는가! 거의 모든 우리의 교제는 우연히 혹은 필요에 의해서 결정이 된다; 그리고 좁은 범위로 제한된다.

6. 금세기(20세기)가 끝날 무렵에 지구에 살고 있는 인구는 오늘날의 숫자에 약 70%의 증가를 이루어 60억을 넘게 될 것이다. 인류의 증가와 보조를 맞추기 위해서 세계의 농부들은 적어도 매년 2%의 식량 증산을 촉진해야 할 것이다.

7. 미국에서 변화가 일어나고 있음을 볼 수 있다. 현재의 목표는 모든 경우에서 적용되는 전통적인 관례에 따르기보다는 각각 상황에 적절한 방법으로 반대의 성과 유쾌한 관계를 유지하는 것으로 보인다.

8. 혼자 힘으로 집으로부터 약간 먼 거리를 처음으로 모험해 갔을 때, 나는 길을 잃었던 것을 기억한다. 줄곧 돌아오는 길을 찾다 낙심하여 거리 모퉁이 기둥에 기대어 내 얼굴을 묻고 울기 시작했다. 그러자 곧 나는 상당히 많은 행인들에 의하여 둘러싸이게 되었다; 그 때 허리에 칼을 차고 놋쇠 단추가 달린 파란 코트를 입은 한 경찰관이 다가와서 내 팔을 붙잡고 명령하는 목소리로 내가 어디에 살고 있는지 물었다.

9. 의사가 환자를 위하여 약을 처방할 때, 환자는 그 처방전을 약사에게 가져가서 그 약이 조제되게 한다.

10. 위대한 소설을 읽은 것은 닳고 있는 상상력 배터리를 충전하는 것이다. 그리고 그것은(위대한 소설을 읽는 것) 우리의 대부분이, 일종의 자기 방위로, 그렇게 하기를 거절한다.

11. 'Please'와 'Thank you'라는 말은 우리가 사회적 존재로서 빚지지 않고 살아나가는 잔돈이라 할 수 있다. 그것들은 우리가 인생이라는 기계에 기름을 쳐서 부드럽게 작동해 나가도록 하는 조그마한 예절이다. 그것들은 윗사람이 아랫

사람에게 명령을 하는 기초가 아니라 친근미가 넘치는 협력과 서로 양보해서 공평하게 주고받는 기초 위에 우리의 교제를 올려놓는다. 부탁을 함으로써 봉사를 받을 수 있고, 그것도 분개하는 마음 대신에 기꺼이 좋은 기분으로 대접받을 수 있는데도 명령을 하고자 하는 사람은 매우 천(賤)한 마음의 소유자이다.

12. 현대 문명이 직면하고 있는 많은 문제 가운데서 노인의 운명이라고 하는 문제는, 이 문제에 관해서 신문, 잡지에 실린 기사의 수로 판단해 볼 때 확실히 일반 사람들의 마음속에 제일 먼저 떠오르는 것 중의 하나이다. 지난 세기에 걸쳐서 사실상 공업국가들의 평균 수명은 비약적으로 연장되어, 마침내 오늘날에는 73세까지 이르게 되었다.

13. 최근에 카폰을 사용하고 있었던 한 운전자가 주위가 분산되어 중앙선을 넘어왔을 때 나는 정면충돌을 아슬아슬하게 모면하였다. 한 경찰관은 전화나 팩시밀리, 또는 컴퓨터를 사용하고 있던 운전자들이 일으킨 여러 건의 사고에 대해 알고 있으며, 이런 일이 더욱더 많이 발생하고 있다고 나에게 말했다.

14. <데이지 밀러>(1879)는 유럽의 경직된 전통적 가치에 패배하는 미국인의 순수함에 대한 또 하나의 소설이다. 데이지는 그녀의 자유로운 미국정신을 유럽으로 가지고 온다. 그녀는 사람들을 사회 계층의 구성원으로보다는 개인으로 바라본다. 그녀의 선량함에도 불구하고 이 소설 속에 등장하는 유럽인들에게 그녀는 완전히 오해를 당한다. 그녀는 한 젊은 미국인을 만나는데, 그는 유럽에서 오래 살아서 유럽인들과 똑같은 차가움을 가지고 있었다. 이 사람들의 차가움이 마침내 데이지를 죽음으로 이끈다.

Advanced Reading 5

세상이 파산상태에 있고, 세상이 갚을 수 있는 이상으로 세상에 빚을 지고 있어서 형평법 재판소에 가야만 하고 매각되어야 한다고 말한다. 이 일반적인 채무초과가–그것은 어느 정도 모든 사람들과 관련이 있다– 성탄절과 새해, 그리고 다른 때에 선물을 주는데서 겪는 어려움의 이유가 된다고 나는 생각하지 않는다. 빚을 갚는데 매우 난처하다고 해도 후해지는 것은 항상 매우 유쾌한 일이니까. 그러나 어려움은 선물을 선택하는데 있다. 만약 어떤 때고 내가 다른 누군가에게 어떤 선물을 응당 주어야한다는 생각이 머릿속에 떠오른다면 나는 그 기회가 다하기까지 무엇을 줄 것인가에 대해 고민한다.
꽃과 과일은 항상 알맞은 선물이다. 꽃은 한줄기 아름다움이 세상의 모든 유용한 것들 보다도 더 가치가 있다는 자랑스러운 주장과 같기 때문이다. 이런 꽃들의 화미한 본성은 보통 자연의 약간 엄격한 모습과 대비된다. 꽃은 작업장에서 들려나오는 음악과 같다. 자연은 우리의 응석을 받아주지 않는다. 우리는 어린애이지 애완동물이 아니다. 자연은 호의적이지 않다. 엄한 우주의 법칙을 따라서 모든 것은 두려움이나 호의 없이 우리에게 주어진다. 그러나 이런 아름다운 꽃은 사랑과 아름다움의 장난과 간섭처럼 보인다. 우리가 구애를 받을 만큼 중요하다는 것을 보여주기 때문에 비록 우리가 그 아첨에 현혹을 당하지 않는다고 해도 사람들은 우리가 아첨을 좋아한다고 말하곤 한다. 그런 즐거움과 같은 무엇인가를 꽃은 우리에게 주는 것이다: 이런 달콤한 말들을 듣는 나는 누구란 말인가? 과일은 마음에 드는 선물이다. 과일은 일용품의 꽃이고, 과일에 덧붙여지는 환상적인 가치를 인정하기 때문이다. 만약 어떤 사람이 일백마일 떨어져 있는 나에게 그를 방문하도록 초청장을 보내고, 내 앞에 좋은 여름 과일 바구니를 차려낸다면 나는 수고와 보람사이에 다소간의 균형이 있었다고 생각할 것이다.

랄프랄도 에머슨: 선물

Advanced Reading 6

사상은 자유라고 흔히 말한다. 인간은 자기가 생각하는 것을 감추는 한 무엇을 선택하여 생각하든지 결코 방해받을 수 없다. 인간의 마음 작용이란 오직 자신의 경험의 폭과 상상력에 제한을 받을 따름이다. 그러나 이렇게 사적으로 누리는 생각의 자연스런 자유는 거의 가치가 없는 것이다. 자신의 사상을 다른 사람들에게 전달하는 것이 허용되지 않는다면 생각하는 사람 그 자신에게는 불만족스러울 뿐만 아니라 고통스럽기까지 하며, 이웃 사람들에게는 아무런 가치가 없다는 것이 분명해 진다. 더구나 마음을 지배하는 사상을 감추어 두기란 극도로 어려운 것이다.

만약 어떤 사람의 생각이 그 주변에 있는 사람들의 행동을 규제하는 관념이나 관습을 의문시하는데 이르고, 그 사람들이 가지고 있는 믿음을 거부하고, 그 사람들이 따르는 것보다 더 좋은 생활방식을 보는 데에 이른다면, 침묵과 우연한 말이나 일반적인 태도로써, 자기는 다른 사람들과 다르며 그들과는 의견도 공유하고 있지 않다는 것을 겉으로 드러내지 않는 다는 것은, 자기 자신의 추론의 진실을 확신하고 있는 한, 거의 불가능한 일이다. 어떤 사람은 소크라테스와 같이 자신들의 사상을 감추기보다는 죽음에 직면하는 것을 더 좋아하는 사람도 있었고, 오늘날도 있을 것이다. 따라서 사상의 자유란, 적어도 가치 있는 의미에 있어서는, 언론의 자유를 포함하는 것이다.

존 배그넬 버리: 사상의 자유사

제 4장 동명사

Basic Reading 4

1. 매우 소수의 사람만이 그들이 만족할 때까지 여행을 즐길 수 있다. 왜냐하면 그것은 많은 시간과 돈을 요구하기 때문이다.

2. 우리는 같은 마을에 살았기 때문에 나는 때때로 그와 만나는 것을 거의 피할 수가 없었다.

3. 그는 문제의 여성이 역장에게 말을 걸고 역장이 그녀를 기차로 배웅하였던 것을 기억하였다.

4. 나는 내가 약속한 바대로 어제 출석하지 못한 것에 대하여 진지하게 사과해야 한다; 그러나 대단히 중요한 예상치 못한 일이 내가 당신의 집으로 나서는 바로 그 순간에 내 걸음을 취소시켰다.

5. 내 남편이 은퇴했을 때, 우리는 더 작은 집을 사기로 결정했다. 우리는 처음에 도시에서 벗어나 이사갈 것을 고려했으나 나는 그렇게 하는 것을 정말로 좋아하지 않았다. 나는 시골지역에 사는 것에 반대하지 않지만, 그 문제에 대하여 이야기 해본 결과 우리는 이 지역에 사는 것이 매우 익숙해 있어서 특별한 이유 없이 이웃을 떠난다는 것이 어리석다는 것을 인식하였다.

6. 많은 오래된 관습들이 해를 거듭할수록 나라에서 점차적으로 사라져 가고 있다. 그러나 그들 중에 일부는 의심할 바 없이 영원히 보존되어 후손들에게 물려줄 가치가 있다.

7. 영어에 접근하는 방법에 있어서 "어학"과 "문학" 사이의 차이는 상당히 오도(誤導)되었고 해로울 뿐만 아니라 분명히 인위적이다. 왜냐하면 두 분야 혹은 두 학문을 분리할 수 없기 때문이다.

8. 많은 미국인은 그들의 공공 교육 제도가 젊은 이들에게 기초 과목인 영문학, 작문, 수학, 그리고 과학을 가르치는 것으로 돌아갈 것을 바란다.

9. 글을 천천히 읽는 일부 독자들이 훌륭한 독자일 수 있으며, 글을 빨리 읽는 일부 독자들이 훌륭한 독자가 아닐 수 있다 – 중요한 것은 우리가 얼마나 이해하고 기억할 수 있는가 하는 것이다. 네가 생각을 흡수할 수 있는 것보다 더 빨리 읽으려고 노력하는 것은 아무 소용이 없다.

10. 도덕성의 측면에서 나의 인생 가운데 가장 위대한 업적은 내가 잘못한 사람에게 사과할 수 있다는 것이다. 나는 용서를 받기 위해서 머리를 숙여서 간청할 수 있다. 나는 모든 사람이 사과하는 법을 배워야 한다고 생각한다. 다른 사람에게 사과를 하는 것은 자신에게 굴욕감을 주기는커녕 영혼을 고양시킨다는 것을 모든 사람은 인식해야 한다.

Advanced Reading 7

자유는 평화 위에 세워지며, 다른 토대를 가질 수 없다. 전쟁과 무질서는 자유의 두 가지 큰 적이다. 우리가 향유하는 바와 같은 우리의 자유 정부는 폭력을 법으로, 육체적 충돌을 논의로 대치해 놓은 것이다. 이것은 여러 세기를 거쳐 이룩한 업적이다. 즉 이것은 자유 토론이 정의를 행하고, 정의에 관한 현명한 결론에 도달하는 가장 좋은 방식이라는 믿음에 의지하고 있다. 그러나 그것은 지켜야만 하는 그 자체의 규칙이 있다. 그것은 관용과 상호 자제를 요구한다. 그것은 소수파가 국회에서 표결에 패할 때 당분간 굴복할 것을 요구하며, 자신들의 의견을 이성과 논의로써 우세하게 할 수 있는 미래를 위하여 일하는 것에 만족할 것을 요구한다. 이런 가정 가운데 어떤 하나라도 이루어지지 않으면, 우리의 감정이 문자 그대로 말로 표현할 수 없을 정도로 너무 강하면, 소수파가 굴복하지 않으려 들어서 말을 떠나서 주먹으로 날아가면, 또는 다수파가 그들의 권력을 남용하여 소수파로 하여금 물리적인 저항을 하게끔 내몬다면, 그 때는 자유는 만사 끝장나는 것이다.

스펜서: 자유

Advanced Reading 8

매 세대는 과거를 고쳐 쓴다. 역사란 평온한 시기에는 다소 장식적인 예술이지만 위험한 시기에는 오늘의 어려운 문제에 대한 해답을 찾아내려는 긴급한 필요에 따라 기술된 기록에로 달려간다. 우리들 이전 세대에 속해 있던 다른 사람들이 서기 위해서 어떤 종류의 단단한 기반을 찾아냈는가를 우리는 알 필요가 있다. 변화하는 삶의 조건에도 불구하고 그들도 우리 자신들과 별로 다르지 않았다. 그들의 생각들은 우리 생각들의 근원이었으며, 그들도 우리들이 직면해야만 하는 상황과 동일하게 어려운 상황에 가까스로 대처하였다. 때로는 가벼운 마음으로 그 상황들에 대처하였고, 어느 정도는 그들의 희망이 승리하게도 하였다. 우리는 어떻게 그들이 그런 일을 하였는가를 알아야 할 필요가 있다.

존 도스 파소스: 주제는 자유다

제 5장 수동태

Basic Reading 5

1. 네가 남을 사랑하면 그들도 너를 사랑할 것이다. 네가 친절하게 그들에게 말하면 그들도 친절하게 네게 말할 것이다. 사랑은 사랑으로서 보답을 받고, 증오심은 증오심으로써 보답을 받는다.

2. 피로한 두뇌의 상태에서는 훌륭한 일을 수행하도록 할 수 없다. 푸른 들판을 산책함으로서 책을 연구하여 습득할 수 있는 것보다 훨씬 많은 것을 얻을 수 있는 일이 종종 있다.

3. 토마토는 원래 아메리카가 원산지이다. 감자 역시 아메리카가 원산지이다. 이 두 식품은 처음에 스페인에 전해졌고, 스페인에서 유럽의 다른 지역들로 전파되었다.

4. 사람들을 소개하는 데는 여러 가지 규칙이 있다. 일반적으로 나이가 적은 사람이 연장자에게, 손님이 주인이나 안주인에게, 한 사람이 여러 사람에게 소개된다.

5. 남자와 여자가 (서로에게) 소개될 경우, 그들은 악수를 할 수도 있고 또는 하지 않을 수도 있다.

6. 많은 나라에서는 개인적인 서비스에 대한 요금이 정해져 있다. 호텔이나 식당의 계산서에 서비스에 대한 일정한 비율의 요금이 추가 될 수 있다. 다른 곳에서는 서비스가 행해질 때마다 고객이 팁을 주도록 요구될 수 있다.

7. 그리스 사람들은 올림피아 평원에서 최초의 올림픽 경기를 개최했다. 그 당시에는 그리스가 많은 나라로 나뉘어 있었다, 이들 나라에서 온 가장 우수한 운동선수들이 그 경기에 참가하도록 초청 받았다. 경기 우승자들은 상을 받았다. 최고상은 왕관이었는데, 그것은 올리브잎으로 만든

것이었다.

8. 지금은 존재하지 않는 많은 동물들의 해골과 뼈가 바위 속에 보존된 채 발견되어 오고 있다. 이 유물들은 화석이라고 불린다. 대부분의 화석은 물의 작용의 결과로 형성된 바위에서 발견되므로, 이들 고대 동물들이 물가에서 또는 물 속에서 살았다는 것을 우리는 알 수 있다.

9. 잃어버린 재산은 근면과 절약으로, 잃어버린 지식은 공부로, 잃어버린 건강은 절제와 약으로 되찾을 수 있지만, 잃어버린 시간은 영원히 잃게 된다고 사람들은 현명하게도 말한다.

10. 건강은 매우 귀중한 보물이지만 그것의 가치는 건강을 잃을 때까지는 좀처럼 인식되지 않는다. 토마스 카알라일은 개인의 경험을 기초로 기록하고 있다: "건강한 자는 자신의 건강에 대하여 인식하지 못하고 병든자만이 인식한다." 특히 젊은이는 건강을 당연히 여기는 경향이 있으며, 미래의 성공과 행복 그리고 심지어 인생 그 자체도 자신의 성장기 동안에 습득된 생활 습관에 의하여 영향을 받으며 많은 경우에 실제로 결정된다는 것을 인식하지 못하면서, 건강을 무분별하게 낭비하는 경향이 있다.

Advanced Reading 9

아무런 대답도 없었다. 어둠이 이제 완전히 깊어서 그는 자신의 발 밑에 있는 희미한 물체를 제외하고는 아무것도 전혀 볼 수 없었는데, 희미한 물체는 낙엽위에 놓인 하얀 모슬린 옷이었다.다른 만물은 암흑 속에 있는 것과도 같았다. 더어버빌은 몸을 숙여, 부드럽고 규칙적인 숨소리를 들었다. 그는 무릎을 꿇고 더 낮게 몸을 굽혔다. 그녀의 호흡이 그 자신의 얼굴을 따뜻하게 할 때까지 굽혔다. 그러자 이내 그의 빰이 그녀의 빰과 맞닿았다. 그녀는 곤하게 잠들어 있었고, 그녀의 속눈썹에는 눈물이 맺혀 있었다.
어둠과 침묵만이 주변 모든 곳을 지배하고 있었다. 그들 위에는 체이스 숲의 원시적인 주목나무와 참나무들이 솟아 있었고, 그 나무에는 태연하게 조용히 쉬고 있는 새들이 그들의 마지막 잠을 자고 있었으며, 그들의 주변에는 깡충거리는 토끼들이 살금살금 지나갔다.

토마스 하디: 더버빌가의 테스중에서

Advanced Reading 10

용서하려는 결심은 자신을 향한 측은지심에서 나온 행위이다. 분노가 풀리지 않는다면, 그것은 지속되어 자신에게 정신적, 정서적 그리고 육체적인 피해를 초래하는데, 이 점은 앞에서 논의되었다. 자기를 용서하기란 어떤 점에서 보면 용서의 가장 어려운 측면이 될 것이다. 많은 사람들은 스스로 비현실적이고 달성할 수 없는 탁월한 미덕 표준을 정한다. 이것은 우리로 하여금 명백하게 지나친 요구를 하도록 이끌며 자기를 용서하지 못하게 한다. 이것은 특히 어떤 도덕적 실수를 저지른 자신들을 용서하기를 꺼려하는 성직자들에게 적용된다. 성직자들은 타인의 고통과 상처를 다룰 때에 가장 측은지심이 강한 사람들이다. 하지만 자신들을 향한 측은지심은 슬프게도 종종 결여되어 있다.

용서는 새로운 삶의 시작

제 6장 시제

Basic Reading 6

1. 만약 네가 어린 나이에 해외에 나가게 되면, 너는 외국 사람과 그들의 관습과 예절을 접촉하게 됨으로써 네게 나중에 매우 귀중한 인생의 폭넓은 인생관을 얻게 될 것이다.

2. 지난주에 도착한 당신의 편지에 정말 감사를 드립니다. 두 달간이나 편지를 드리지 못해서 죄송합니다. 대학생활이 너무 바빠서 단지 시간이 없었어요. 제게 화를 내지 마세요. 함께 머무는 영국인 가족들은 좋은가요? 새 영어강좌는 벌써 시작하셨나요? 모든 일이 잘되기를 바랍니다.

3. 20년 동안, 미국의 교육방식은 음악, 미술, 요리, 개인의 금전관리, 영화제작과 같은 다양한 과목들의 강좌를 제공해 왔다. 이로 인하여 글을 쓰고, 계산하고, 생각하는 기본적인 기능들에 대해서는 소홀하게 되었다고 많은 사람들은 믿는다.

4. 로버트는 수잔과 사귀고 있었고 그녀와의 결혼을 생각하고 있었다. 그는 알고 싶었다. 그녀의 자매들이 어떤 여자들이고, 그녀의 아버지가 어떤 분인지, 그리고 그녀의 어머니가 돌아가신지는 얼마나 되었는지를.

5. 종교적 믿음은 인생의 폭풍우로부터 피신하기 위하여 우리가 도망칠 수 있는 피난처가 아니다. 오히려 그것은 사람들로 하여금 그 폭풍우를 희망과 마음의 평화를 가지고 정면으로 맞이할 수 있게 해주는 내적 영혼의 힘이다. 종교적 믿음은 어려운 시기에 보통 인간들을 위대함으로 올려주는 기적적인 힘을 가지고 있다. 종교적 믿음은 하나님의 약속 안에서 발견할 수 있다.

6. 남북 전쟁 중 가장 암울한 때에, 링컨은 일리노이 주 스프링필드에 사는 옛 친구에게 편지를 써서 워싱턴으로 와줄 것을 부탁했다. 링컨은 그와 함께 의논하고 싶은 문제들이 있다고 말했다. 그 옛 이웃은 백악관으로 찾아왔고 링컨은 노예를 해방시키는 것에 관해 그에게 이야기했다. 몇 시간 동안 이야기한 후 링컨은 그의 옛 친구와 악수를 하며 잘 가라는 인사를 하고는, 그의 의견을 묻지도 않고서 그를 일리노이로 되돌려 보냈다. 링컨은 혼자서 모든 이야기를 다 했던 것이다. 그것이 그의 마음을 정리해 주는 것 같았다. "이야기를 한 뒤 그는 편안해 하는 것 같았죠." 라고 그 옛 친구는 말했다. 링컨은 조언을 원했던 것이 아니었다. 그는 단지 그가 이야기할 수 있는, 다정하고 따뜻한 마음으로 들어주는 사람을 원했던 것이다. 그것이 곤경에 처했을 때 우리 모두가 원하는 것이다.

7. <미녀와 야수>에서 한 젊은 아가씨가 무서운 괴물을 만난다. 그의 분노로부터 그녀의 가족을 구하기 위해 그녀는 그와 함께 살 것을 동의한다. 결국 그를 알게 됨으로써 그녀는 혐오감을 극복하고 심지어는 그를 사랑하게 된다. 기적이 일어나서 그는 본래 왕자의 모습으로 돌아온다. 이 이야기는 사랑의 힘으로 누군가를 더 나은 존재로 변화시킬 수 있으며 우리가 여성이라면 그렇게 하는 것이 우리의 의무라는 문화적인 가설을 강조하고 있는 것처럼 보인다.

8. 우리 자신을 다른 동물들과 비교해 본다면, 우리가 가지고 있는 모든 기관은 하나를 제외하고는 전적으로 아무 특징이 없다. 인간보다 다른 동물들이 더 힘이 세고, 더 빠르며, 감각이 더 예민하고, 더 예리하며, 더 잘 견디는 등 비교해 보면

끝이 없다. 한 가지 예외는 물론 우리 두뇌이다. 우리는 현존하는 다른 어떤 동물의 두뇌보다 우월하다고 볼 수 있는 두뇌를 가지고 있다. 적어도 인간의 두뇌만이 유일하게 기술문명을 일으켰으며, 인간의 두뇌만이 추상적인 사고를 할 수 있다고 하는 것이 널리 인정되고 있다.

9. 쉬운 영어를 쓰는 것은 어려운 일이다. 교과서를 통해서 문학을 배운 사람은 일찍이 아무도 없었다. 나는 작문수업을 받아 본 적이 없다. 나는 자연스럽게 그리고 나 스스로 글을 쓰는 법을 배웠다. 나는 우연히 성공한 것이 아니라 참을성 있게 열심히 노력하여 성공하였다.

10. 그는 신사로 대학에 간 것이 아니었고, 신사가 되어 돌아온 것도 아니었다. 그는 바보로 대학에 갔고, 유식한 체하는 자가 되어 돌아왔다. 그의 원래의 어리석음에 엄청난 자만심이 보태졌던 것이다.

Advanced Reading 11

영어와 미국의 말은 같은 언어이다. 그러나 최초의 식민정착 이래 흘러간 3세기 이상 동안에 두 언어는 서로 다른 방식으로 발달했다. 영국에서는 사라진 많은 오래된 영어 관용어가 미국에서는 보존되어 있다는 사실은 잘 알려지지 않았다. 부분적으로 삶의 상이한 조건들을 통해서, 그리고 부분적으로는 많은 나라들에서 온 거대한 이민자들을 흡수하는 과정에서 다른 언어로부터 많은 영향을 받음으로써 미국 영어는 새로운 언어방식을 발전시켰다. 영어와 미국영어의 주된 차이점은 말의 리듬과 억양이다.
그러나 미국영어가 영국 영어에 매우 크게 영향을 미쳤다는 것은 분명하다. 이것은 상업과 영화와 재정에 있어서 미국이 주도적인 위치를 차지하고 있다는 단순한 사실보다 더 광범위한 일련의 상황에 기인한 것이다. 은유적인 표현 속에 깃든 생생함과 강력함이 많은 미국영어의 특징이다. 그러므로 특히 새로운 언어적 경험을 하고자 가장 열망하는 젊은이들에 의해서 이러한 선택이 구어 영어에 받아들여진다는 것은 자연스러운 것이다.

워런: 영어

Advanced Reading 12

앨리스는 땅에 넘어지더니 부들부들 떨고 있었다. 그녀는 자신이 한 일에 너무도 놀라서, 그 남자가 가버렸을 때에도 감히 일어나지 못하고 겨우 손과 무릎으로 기어서 풀밭을 지나 집에까지 갔다. 자신의 방에 이르자 그녀는 문에 빗장을 걸고 경대를 문 쪽으로 가로질러 끌어당겼다. 그녀의 몸은 오한이나 든 듯 떨렸고 그녀의 두 손도 잠옷을 입기도 어려울 만큼 떨렸다. 침대 속으로 들어가자 그녀는 베개에 얼굴을 묻고 가슴 저리게 울었다. "나에게 무슨 문제가 있는 거지?" "나는 주의하지 않으면 끔찍한 일을 저지를 거야"라고 그녀는 생각했다. 그리고는 벽 쪽으로 얼굴을 돌려, 와인스버그에서 조차 많은 사람들이 홀로 살다가 죽어가야만 한다는 사실을 억지로 용감하게 직시하려고 애쓰기 시작했다.

셔우드 앤더슨: 와인스버그 오하이오

제 7장 조동사

Basic Reading 7

1. 젊은이가 배워야 할 첫 번째 교훈은 자신이 별로 아는 것이 없다는 것이다; 더 빠르고 더 철저히 이 교훈을 학습하게 되면 될수록, 마음의 평화를 위해서도 더 좋을 것이며, 그의 인생의 성공에도 도움이 될 것이다.

2. 내가 그날 나중에 내 이야기를 전달했을 때, 나는 그들에게 이 경험에 대하여 말했고, 남자(사람)라면, 가능하다면 혼자서, 바다에 나가서 하늘과 대양과 더불어 얼마간의 시간을 보내볼 것을 제안하였다.

3. 나는 나의 건강을 위해서 때때로 여행을 떠나고자 한다.

4. 그녀는 여배우였음으로 많은 사람들의 시선과 무대에 서있는 것에 익숙했다.

5. 아르키메데스는 어떤 일이 불가능하다고 말하는 가장 마지막 사람이었다. 그는 힘든 문제를 해결하는 데 대단한 희열을 느꼈다. 그리고 어떤 질문이 그를 당황하게 했을 때 그는 그 해답을 찾을 때까지 연구에 몰두하곤 했다.

6. 우리의 초기 인류의 조상들은 신중한 정책에 근거하여 행동했을 리가 없고 본능적인 절차, 즉 부족 내에서는 우정과 다른 사람들에게는 적대감이라는 이중적인 과정에 의해서 자극 받았음이 틀림없다.

7. 세상의 의견을 경멸하지 말라; (세상의 의견을 경멸하려거든) 차라리 당신이 촛불을 사용할 수 있기 때문에 태양 빛에 신경을 쓰지 않는다고 말하는 편이 낫다.

8. 임의적으로 이용할 수 있는 제한된 시간을 가진 사람들이 런던이 가지고 있는 많은 명소와 보화들을 적절히 살펴보는데 있어서 실망하는 것은 당연하다.

9. 당신이 지금 직면해야 할 한 가지 사실이 있다. 즉, 가장 쉬운 것이 당신에게 좀처럼 가장 좋은 것이 아니다. 수고로움이 인류에게 가장 커다란 축복 중에 하나였다.

10. 인류에게 더 많은 지성과, 더 많은 번영, 그리고 더 많은 자유를 부여하는 방향에서 세계의 성장을 저지하려고 하는 것은, 차라리 철도의 트랙을 가로질러 몸을 던짐으로 힘센 철로의 진행을 차단하려 하는 편이 더 나을 것이다.

Advanced Reading 13

청소년 시절 내내 나는 게으름뱅이로 알려졌고 대표적 게으른 소년으로 지적됐다. 그러나 나는 나의 은밀한 목적을 추구하는데 항상 바빴는데, 그것은 글쓰기를 배우는 것이었다. 어디를 가든지 나는 두 권의 책을 끼고 다녔는데, 한 권은 읽기 위한 것이었고, 다른 한 권은 쓰기 위한 공책이었다. 특히, 내 마음을 흡족하게 하는 것을 읽게 될 때 나는 즉시 앉아서 그 작가의 문체를 모방하여 써보려고 애를 썼다. 시골길을 산보할 때에는 내가 본 것에다 적절한 말을 붙여 보려고 애를 썼다. 이렇게 함으로써 유익함을 얻었든 얻지 못하였든 나는 이것이 글쓰기를 배우는 길이라고 믿는다.

로버트 스티븐슨 : 기억과 회상

Advanced Reading 14

비록 우리들이 우리의 육체를 중요하게 생각할지라도, 육체는 실제 우리의 매우 작은 부분에 불과하다. 인간의 참다운 생명은 육체에 있지 않고 인간이 육체를 가지고 하는 행위 속에 있다. 태어나기 전에는 우리는 우리의 도구들을 한데 모아 놓고, 태어나서는 우리는 그 도구들을 사용하며, 그렇게 하여 우리들의 도구나 도구상자에 있지 않고 우리들이 도구를 가지고 행하는 일에 있는 우리의 진실한 삶을 형성해 내는 것이다. 한 겨울밤에 런던의 한끝에서 다른 끝에 이르기까지 수천명의 사람들을 끌어당기는 것은 그 음악 작품을 쓴 육체가 아니라 헨델의 음악작품이다. 이것이 바로 진정한 헨델이며, 그는 우리 가운데서 육체 속에 살아 있던 기간보다도 죽고 난 후 122년 동안이나 우리 가운데서 더 많은 생명력을 가지고 있다.

사무엘 버트러: 그의 노트중에서

제 8장 접속사 / 전치사

Basic Reading 8

1. 사람은 자기의 모든 여가시간에 일을 하거나 혹은 오락에 이용하도록 노력하여야 한다. 단순히 낭비된 시간은 자신에 대해서도, 또 사회에 대해서도 절대적인 손실이기 때문이다.

2. 책은 사람과 같기 때문에 독서는 가치가 있다. 권투선수가 실제 시합을 위해서 펀칭백이나 연습상대와 연습을 하는 것과 마찬가지로 당신도 진짜 사람들과의 관계를 위해 책으로 당신 자신을 훈련할 수 있다.

3. 나는 이 편지를 보자마자 그것이 내가 찾고 있었던 편지였다고 결론을 내렸다.

4. 배가 그 항구를 떠난 후로 5일 동안 바다와 하늘을 제외하고는 아무 것도 볼 수가 없었다. 마침내 여섯째 날 우리는 멀리서 작은 섬을 찾아냈다.

5. 18세기가 되어서야 비로소 과학적 연구 작업 결과들이 가치 있는 지식들을 처음으로 과학기술자들에게 제공하기 시작했다.

6. 어떠한 어려움에 직면해도, 우리는 극복하기 위하여 서로 서로 도울 것이다.

7. 네가 어떤 일에 종사하든지, 몸과 마음을 바쳐 그 일에 전념하지 않는다면, 결코 성공하기를 희망할 수 없다.

8. 학식 있는 사람들이 어떤 책에 대해 어떤 훌륭한 평가를 내려도, 그들이 아무리 만장일치로 그 책을 훌륭하게 평가하여도, 그 책이 당신의 흥미

를 끌지 못한다면 당신과 아무런 상관이 없다.

9. 의사소통은 두 사람 혹은 그 이상 개인들의 합동 노력을 요구하는 사회적 활동이다. 단지 문장만을 만들어 내는 대화는, 그 결과가 아무리 훌륭하게 형성되고 우아하다고 해도, 그 자체로써 의사소통을 이루어 내지 못한다.

10. 우리가 이 지구상에서 어디를 가도, 우리는 같은 것을 발견할 것이다. 우리의 집이 아무리 누추해도 집과 같은 곳은 없다. 그가 무슨 말을 해도 결국은 자기 집으로 돌아 올 것이다.

11. 예술작품을 창조하는 것은 기적의 결과가 아니다. 그것은 준비를 요구한다. 아무리 토양이 비옥해도 그 토양에 영양분이 공급되어야 한다. 사려 깊은 사고의 노력을 통해 예술가는 자신의 개성을 확대하며, 깊이와 다양성을 추구해야 한다.

12. 이러한 힘든 과업에도 불구하고, 그는 글쓰기를 배웠다. 무엇보다도, 그는 혼자 힘으로 생각하는 법을 배웠다.

13. 일단 존이 어떤 생각을 갖게 되면, 그는 너무나 완고해서 누구도 그를 설득해서 그만두게 할 수가 없었다.

14. 그들은 나무 속을 뚫고 앞으로 나갔지만, 결국 여전히 커다란 숲 속에 남아 있게 되었음을 발견하였다.

15. 갑자기 멀리서 나는 사람의 모습을 발견했는데, 놀랍게도 곧 그 여행자는 여성이라는 것을 알아차렸다.

16. 나는 너의 설명을 들었기 때문에, 더욱 더 네 의견에 동의하고 싶다.

Advanced Reading 15

그는 멕시코 만류에서 조각배를 타고 혼자서 고기잡이를 하는 노인이었다. 그런데 한 마리의 고기도 잡지 못한 채 지금까지 팔십 사일을 보냈다. 처음 사십일 동안에는 한 소년이 그와 함께 있었다. 그러나 고기를 한 마리도 잡지 못한 채 사십일이 지나자 그 소년의 부모는 아들에게 그 노인은 틀림없이 끝내 '살라오' 신세가 됐다고 말해 주었다. 그것은 가장 나쁜 불행을 뜻하는 말이다. 그래서 그 소년은 부모의 명령으로 다른 배로 옮겨갔으며, 그 배는 첫 주에 꽤 큰 고기를 세 마리 잡았다. 노인이 매일 빈 조각배로 돌아오는 것을 보면 소년은 슬픈 생각이 나서, 언제나 그에게 달려 내려가서 돌돌 감긴 낚시 줄이나 갈퀴 또는 작살과 돛대에 감겨 있는 돛을 운반하는 것을 도와주기도 했다. 이 돛은 밀가루 자루로 꿰맨 것이었고, 그래서 감겨있는 모습이 영원한 패배의 깃발처럼 보였다.

헤밍웨이: 노인과 바다 중에서

Advanced Reading 16

뉴스는 중요한 사건을 즉각 취재한다. 뉴스는 또한 사실과 정보를 제공해준다. 게다가 뉴스는 광고를 팔고/혹은 신문과 잡지를 팔아서 돈을 버는 일종의 사업이다. 때로 뉴스는 사람들을 통제하는 방법으로서의 선전이거나 그릇된 정보일 때도 있다. 그러나 어떤 뉴스이건 간에 온통 우리 주변에 있다. 우리들은 그 정보의 홍수에서 벗어날 수가 없다. 매일 우리는 신문, 잡지, 텔레비전, 그리고 컴퓨터 인터넷에서 쏟아지는 정보의 폭탄을 맞는다.
'뉴스'가 의심할 바 없는 진실한 것을 항상 의미하는 것은 아니다. 뉴스가 사실에 근거하고 있는 것처럼 보일지라도, 이런 사실은 해석될 뿐만 아니라 그것들을 보도하기 위하여 미디어가 선택한 방식으로 보도된다. 가령 뉴스로 전해지는 어떤 정보는 실제 기자들에 의해서 형성된 이론들이나 단순한 생각이다. 더구나 많은 저널리스트들과 기자들은 어떤 이야기를 더욱 흥미 있게 만들기 위해서 새로운 사건을 극화하거나 선정적으로 만든다. 불행하게도, 선정주의는 종종 진실을 왜곡하고 그것이 희생시키는 사람들에게 격심한 고통을 불러오기도 한다. 그러므로 뉴스 소비자로서의 우리들은 뉴스와 미디어에 대하여 비판적으로 생각하는 법을 공부해야만 하며, 무엇이 진실인가를 생각하는 법을 공부해야만 한다.

제 9장 관계사

Basic Reading 9

1. 한 사람의 인격이 한 사람의 재산보다 그의 행복에 훨씬 더 많은 기여를 한다는 것은 상당히 분명하다.

2. 그는 다른 사람이 자기 아들에 관하여 이야기한 것을 믿지 않았으며, 설상가상으로, 그는 소위 상식을 완전히 상실했다.

3. 한편으로는 악화된 건강, 재정상 염려, 그녀의 아이들에 대한 걱정으로, 한편으로는 사업 경영에 대한 과로로 가엾은 그 여인은 쓰러졌다.

4. 독서가 마음에 대한 관계는 운동이 몸에 대한 관계와 같다. 전자에 의해서는 건강이 보존되고, 강화되며, 상쾌하게 된다; (마음의 건강인) 미덕은 후자에 의해서 살아 약동하고, 소중히 여겨지며, 확실하게 된다.

5. 어떠한 경우에서든지 교육이 할 수 있는 모든 것은 우리로 하여금 우리 자신을 잘 활용할 수 있도록 가르치는 것이다; 만약 우리가 더불어 시작해 볼 별로 신통치 않은 존재라면 상당한 양의 교육도 우리에게 어떤 효력을 줄 수 없다.

6. 누구나 자기가 잘못했다고 고백하는 것을 결코 부끄러워해서는 안 된다. 바꾸어 말하면, 그것은 자신이 어제보다 오늘 더 현명해졌다는 것을 말하는 것뿐이다.

7. 교육만이 질에서 최고이며 양에서 무한한 인생의 즐거움으로 우리를 안내할 수 있다.

8. 개인의 관점으로부터 그는 자신의 능력을 최대한 활용할 수 있는 일을 해야 한다. 실제로 사람들은 자신의 능력을 요구하는 직업들을 선택하는 것을 보게 되며, 그리고 직업 길잡이에서 이것은 주요한 고려사항 가운데 하나이다.

9. 어떤 사회를 이해하기 위해서, 우리는 먼저 그 사회의 가치 기준을 살펴보아야 한다. 여전히 미국에서 가장 중요한 의미를 갖고 있는 가치들은 자유, 독립, 경쟁, 개인주의, 평등이다.

10. 인구 전문가들은 세계 인구가 다음 세기(21세기)에 200억에 도달 할 수 있음을 전망한다. 그러나 이 수치는 이 지구가 지탱할 수 있는 최대한의 인구라고 그들은 경고한다. 우리가 이 한계에 도달했을 때, 인류에게 무슨 일이 일어날까?

11. 그가 마을에 접근했을 때 그는 많은 사람들을 만났으나, 그가 알았던 어떤 사람도 만나지 못했다. 이러한 사실은 다소 그를 놀라게 했다. 왜냐하면 그는 자신이 그 시골 지역의 모든 사람들과 안면이 있다고 생각했었다. 그들의 의상 또한 그가 익숙해 있던 의상과 다른 패션으로 되어 있었다.

12. 그와 대화를 나누어 본 사람들 가운데서, 다양한 주제에 대한 그의 준비된 많은 정보, 지적이고 방향이 바로 잡힌 질문, 그리고 다른 사람의 말을 들어줄 수 있는 그의 대단한 역량에 놀라지 않는 사람을 만나본 적이 없다.

13. 내 말들이 실현될 때가 틀림없이 올 것이다. 그러나 그 때가 실제로 도달했을 때, 나는 죽은 지가 상당히 오래 되었을 것이다.

14. 모든 습득된 나쁜 습관은 후에 훌륭한 습관에 장벽이 된다; 유년기 최초 습관 형성이 그렇게 중요한 이유는 바로 그 때문이다.

15. 이 세상에서 가장 슬픈 장면중의 하나는 힘든 생존 경쟁 때문에 그가 가진 모든 건강과 체격을 희생한 젊은이의 모습이다.

16. 무절제는 우리가 빠질 수 있는 가장 경멸할 만하고 기분 나쁜 습관들 중의 하나이다. 그것은 또한 가장 위험한 것 중의 하나이다. 그것은 극기심의 부족에서 생겨나며, 그것은 남아있을 수 있는 모든 극기심마저도 파괴시켜 버린다.

17. 사랑이 있는 곳은 어디에나 증오, 양심, 질투, 분노가 반드시 존재한다.

18. 아인슈타인 부인은 그녀의 남편이 사고하는 데 있어서는 질서를 좋아했으나, 생활하는 데 있어서는 질서를 좋아하지 않았다고 말하곤 했다. 그는 하고자 원하는 것은 무엇이든지 하고, 그가 하고자 원할 때는 언제든지 하였다. 그리고 그는 단지 두 개의 행동 규칙을 가지고 있었다. 첫째는 어떤 규칙도 갖지 않는다는 것이며, 둘째는 다른 사람의 견해로부터 독립한다는 것이다.

19. 내가 알고 있는 은행가는 그의 작업 시간을 통제하여 이제는 많은 시간을 보트에서 그의 가족과 함께 보낸다. 그의 시간을 주의 깊게 계획하는 방법을 통하여, 새로운 업무를 경영하며, 그의 매일 매일 일정을 그의 장기 계획에 맞추게 하는 것이 훨씬 더 쉽다는 것을 발견하였다.

20. 우리의 아시아 문화는 우리가 하는 모든 것에 있어서 중용(中庸)의 도를 가르쳐 준다. 그것은 우리가 자연을 정복하는 것이 아니라 자연과

더불어 조화를 이루며 사는 것이다. 우리는 높은 혈압과 심장 발작을 일으키는 쥐경주에 참여하는 것을 거절하여야 한다. 훌륭한 인생의 특성은, 내게 있어서는, 자연에 가깝게 단순히 사는 것으로 구성된 것으로 여겨진다.

21. 우리가 살고 있는 세상은 빠르게 변하고 있다. 그리고 우리의 언어는 세상과 더불어 변한다. 모든 살아있는 언어는 성장하고 변한다. 언어를 사용하는 사람들이 새로운 단어들을 창조하고, 오래된 의미 대신에 새로운 의미를 찾아냄에 따라서 언어는 변한다.

22. 내가 알고 있는 미국인들에게 그들이 자녀를 두는 이유를 최근에 물었을 때, 그들은 가족의 가치, 그들이 되기를 소망하는 종류의 사람들, 그들이 후세에 남겨주고 싶은 종류의 세상에 대하여 이야기하였다.

Advanced Reading 17

지금은 꽤 상쾌한 저녁이다. 이 때는 온몸이 하나의 감각기관이 되어 모든 땀 구멍을 통해서 기쁨을 들이마신다. 나는 자연의 일부가 되어 이상하리만큼 자유롭게 자연 속을 오간다. 내가 셔츠만 입은 채 돌이 많이 깔린 연못가를 거닐 때, 특이하게 내게 매혹적으로 다가오는 것은 없지만, 이 모든 주변 것들이 유달리 내 마음을 흡족하게 한다. 이제 어둠이 내렸지만, 바람은 여전히 불면서 숲에서 포효하며, 물결은 여전히 철썩거린다. 어떤 생물들은 자신들의 노래 가락으로 다른 생물들을 달래준다. 휴식에는 결코 끝이 없는 법이다. 가장 야성적인 동물들은 휴식을 끝내고, 이제 먹이 감을 찾아 나선다. 여우와 스컹크와 산토끼들이 이제는 두려움 없이 들과 숲을 돌아다닌다. 그들은 활기찬 생명의 나날을 연결시켜주는 고리이자 자연의 야경꾼들이다.

내 가장 가까운 이웃이라 해보았자 일 마일이나 떨어져 살고 있고, 내 집에서 반 마일 거리에 있는 언덕배기를 제외하고는 어떤 곳에서 봐도 집 한 채 볼 수 없다. 유독 나만이 숲으로 한계 지워진 지평선을 소유하고 있는 것이다. 한편 연못과 인접한 철로가 먼 광경으로 보이고, 다른 편으로는 숲 속의 길을 둘러싸고 있는 울타리의 모습이 먼 광경으로 보인다. 그러나 대체로 내가 사는 곳은 평원만큼 고독하다. 뉴잉글랜드가 아시아나 아프리카와 같은 셈이다. 말하자면, 나는 내 자신만의 해와 달과 별 그리고 작은 세상을 소유하고 있는 것이다. 밤에는 나그네가 내 집 옆을 지나가거나 문을 두드리는 적이 결코 없었다.

헨리 데이비드 소로우: 고독중에서

Advanced Reading 18

근대 유럽과 미국의 역사는 정치적, 경제적 그리고 인간을 속박해온 정신적 족쇄로부터 자유를 획득하기 위한 노력으로 집중된다. 자유를 위한 투쟁은 억압받은 사람들 즉 새로운 자유를 원하는 사람들이 방어할만한 특권을 가졌던 사람들에 대항한 싸움이었다. 어떤 계급이 지배에서 스스로 해방되고자 싸우는 동안에는 그 싸움은 그와 같은 인간의 자유를 위한 싸움으로 믿어졌고, 그래서 하나의 이상에 호소를 할 수 있었으며, 억압받은 모든 사람들 속에 뿌리 밖은 자유에 대한 열망에 호소를 할 수 있었다. 자유를 위한 길고도 실질적으로 계속된 투쟁의 과정에서 그러나, 승리가 획득되고 새로운 특권들이 수호되어야할 때에, 어느 단계에서 압제에 대항하여 싸웠던 계급들은 자유의 적들과 한편이 되었다.

많은 실패에도 불구하고 자유는 전투에서 승리

했다. 많은 사람들이 자유 없이 살기보다는 압제에 대항하여 싸우다가 죽는 것이 더 낫다는 신념 아래 그러한 전투에서 죽어갔다. 그와 같은 죽음은 자신들의 개성에 대한 최고의 주장이었다. 역사는 인간이 자신을 지배하고, 스스로 결정을 내리고 생각하며 적절하게 본 바대로 느끼는 것이 가능했다는 것을 입증하는 것처럼 보였다. 인간의 잠재력을 온전히 표현하는 것이야말로 사회적 발전이 급격하게 접근하고 있던 목표처럼 보였다. 경제적 자유주의, 정치적 민주주의, 종교적 자율성 그리고 사생활의 개인주의란 자유에 대한 열망을 표현한 말이었고, 동시에 인류로 하여금 그러한 것의 실현에 더욱 가까이 다가가게 하는 것처럼 보였다.

에리히 프롬: 자유 중에서

제10장 법

Basic Reading 10

1. 당신이 수다스런 미국인을 우연히 만나게 된다할지라도 결코 당신이 질문 받은 모든 질문을 답변하도록 강요받지 않는다.

2. 만약 낯선 사람이 초대장이나 소개서 없이 예절 바른 영국인을 방문한다면, 그는 자기의 사생활을 과감히 침입한 것으로 간주할 것이다. 주일날은 이러한 방문을 할 적절한 날이 아니고; 주말이 이러한 목적을 위하여 선정되어야 한다.

3. 만약 우리가 인생과 행복에 대하여 영속적으로 불확실하게 의식하면, 우리는 쉽게 음울하게 되며, 일과 즐거움 모두에서 우리의 열정을 잃게 될 것이다.

4. 만약 그날 아침 습관적인 기차를 탔더라면, 그는 폭발이 일어날 시점에 폭발의 중심부에 근접해 있었을 것이다.

5. 만약 내가 그것을 먹기 전에 그것이 무엇인지를 듣게 되었었다면 나는 결코 먹지 않았을 것이라고 생각한다. 그러나 사실 그것은 상당히 맛이 좋은 것으로 판명되었다.

6. 나는 훌륭히 충고 해 주신 분들을 비웃는 부류의 사람에 결코 속하지 않았다. 반대로 만약 내가 내 출생 이후로 내가 들은 모든 훌륭한 충고를 이행했더라면 나는 지금 더 훌륭한 사람이 되었을 것이라고 인식했다.

7. 인생이 모두 고통과 쓰라린 환멸인 것만은 아니다. 만약 인생이 고통과 환멸뿐이라면, 인생은

견딜 수 없을 것이고 살만한 가치가 없을 것이다. 우리는 나이 들어감에 따라 인생의 시련과 고난을 철학적으로 수용하는 법을 배운다. 우리는 우리의 과실을 통해서 지혜를 배운다. 때때로 실수를 하게 됨으로써 진정으로 올바로 사는 법을 알게 된다.

8. 철갑옷이 아니었다면 그는 전사했을 것이다. 실상은 그의 투구 일부만을 잃었다.

9. 그의 쾌활한 기질이 아니었더라면, 그렇게 민감한 체구를 가지고서 스스로 부과한 그렇게 많은 일을 끝내지 못했을 것이다.

10. 하지만 전체적으로 현대 과학기술은 과학자가 없었더라면 불가능했을 것이며, 과학기술이 더 복잡해지면 복잡해질수록 과학자의 역할은 더 중심적이 된다.

11. 그는 결혼하자마자, 그가 죽게 될 경우 아내의 나머지 일생동안 정기적인 수입을 보장해 줄 보험증권에 가입하였다.

12. 만약 우리가 운명의 모든 변화를 알 수 있다면, 인생은 너무나 희망, 두려움, 환희 혹은 실망으로 가득 차 있어서 우리에게 단 한 순간의 참된 평정도 제공할 수 없을 것이다.

13. 나는 젊은 시절에 독서를 지도해 줄 양식 있는 누군가를 알고 있었더라면 좋았을 것이라고 진심으로 소망한다. 내게 아무런 이득이 되지 못했던 책에 내가 낭비했던 그 시간들을 회생해 볼 때 한숨이 절로 난다.

14. "내가 학창시절에 그것을 배웠더라면" 혹은 "내가 더 많은 교육을 받았더라면"이라고 성인들이 말하는 것을 들었을 것이다. 왜 그들이 그렇게 느끼는지를 너는 생각해 보았는가? 아마 그것은 그들이 생각하기로는 만약 그들이 조금 더 많이 배웠거나 혹은 더 잘 교육받았더라면 인생이 더 흥미로웠을 것이고, 혹은 더 좋은 직업을 얻을 수 있었을 것이라고 생각하기 때문이다.

15. 내가 아는 가장 행복한 사람들은 그들의 일이 돈을 벌기 위한 것이 아니라 단지 즐거움을 얻기 위해 행하는 취미생활과 같은 활동들로 접근하는 사람들이다. 운 좋은 사람들은 그들의 일로부터 회피하지 않는다; 그들은 일 속으로 들어간다. 실제적으로 그들은 일을 하지 않는 것보다는 차라리 일을 할 것이다.

16. 만약 네가 가령 천 달러의 돈이 있다면 너는 무엇을 하겠는가?

17. 인간은 자신이 죽어야 한다는 것을 아는 유일한 존재이며, 인간은 경험을 통해서만 이 사실을 안다. 아이가 혼자 자라서 무인도로 보내진다면, 고양이 혹은 식물이 죽음에 대하여 알지 못하는 것처럼 죽음에 대한 생각을 하지 못할 것이다.

18. 어려움으로부터 탈출하려고 해봐야 소용이 없다. 왜냐하면 그것들은 틀림없이 당신을 따라잡을 것이기 때문이다. 그 어려움에 담대히 직면해 봐라. 그러면 그것들은 종종 사라져 버릴 것이다.

19. 사람들은 운동에 할애할 시간이 없다고 말한다. 그들에게 '운동할 시간을 찾아야 한다. 그렇지 않으면 아파서 침대에 누워있을 시간을 찾아야 할 것이다' 고 아무리 빨리 말하여도 지나치

지 않다.

Advanced Reading 19

또 다른 인기 있는 식용 동물은 돼지이다. 인간들이 어떻게 여지껏 돼지들을 길들였는지는 신비로운 일이다. 야생 상태에서 돼지는 극도로 사나운 짐승이기 때문이다. 아시아와 아프리카에서 야생 돼지에 몰래 접근했던 사냥꾼들은 돼지가 호랑이보다 더 위험하다고 말한다. 돼지는 한층 더 심하게 물어뜯을 수 있을 뿐만 아니라 지능지수에서 가장 높은 원숭이 바로 다음 순위를 차지할 만큼 영악하기도 하다. 조오지 오웰은 자신의 풍자소설 '동물농장'의 주인공 혹은 악당을 돼지로 삼으면서 적에 돼지의 지능에 찬사를 보냈다. 그 소설 이야기에서, 우리가 기억하듯이, 돼지들은 다른 어떤 동물들 보다 훨씬 더 영악하여 (자신들의 인간 주인을 최초로 더 나은 꾀로 속인 후) 농장을 접수하며 독재자들로서 농장을 통치한다.

Advanced Reading 20

나는 인간이 견뎌낼 뿐만 아니라 이길 것이라 믿고 있습니다. 인간만이 모든 생물들 가운데서 고갈되지 않은 자신의 목소리를 낼 수 있다는 이유에서가 아니라 인간은 영혼, 즉 연민과 희생과 인내를 가능하게 하는 정신을 가지고 있다는 이유에서 불멸입니다. 시인과 작가의 임무는 이런 것들을 쓰는 것입니다. 그의 특권은 마음을 격려함으로써, 인류의 과거 영광이었던 용기와 명예와 희망과 자긍심과 동정과 측은지심과 희생을 상기시킴으로써 인간으로 하여금 인내하게 돕는 것입니다. 시인의 목소리는 인간에 대한 기록에 불과할 필요는 없습니다. 그것은 재산가 중 하나가 될 수 있으며, 인간으로 하여금 인내하여 승리하게 돕는 기둥 가운데 하나가 될 수 있습니다.

윌리엄 포크너: 노벨상 수상 연설중에서

제11장 일치 / 화법

Basic Reading 11

1. 대학 졸업 후 나는 정규직 일을 구하기가 매우 어렵다는 것을 깨달았다. 그래서 나는 단지 용돈을 벌기 위해 시간제 웨이트리스 일을 하기로 하였다. 그러던 어느 날 식사시중을 들던 나는 손님 두 사람이 하는 말을 우연히 듣게 되었다. 한 사람이 자기 비서가 갑자기 그만두었다고 설명하면서 어떻게 해야 할지 모르겠다고 말했다. 나는 식사 시중들던 일을 즉시 멈추고 그 사람에게 그 일자리에 나를 고려해 줄 수 있는지 물어 보았다. 그는 몹시 놀랐지만, 다음날 면접을 하기로 하였다. 간단히 말해, 대화를 가로막은 나의 용기 덕분에 그 일자리를 구할 수 있었다.

2. 운동의 중요성을 깨닫지 못하는 사람들은 거의 없다. 그러나 많은 사람들은 일상생활에서 그것을 실천하지 않는다. 그들의 가장 흔한 핑계는 "시간이 없어."이다. 그런 사람들에 대한 나의 대답은 "그것은 궁색한 변명이다."라는 것이다. 매일 이를 닦고, 매일 먹고, 매일 자는 것처럼, 운동도 매일 할 수 있다. 규칙적인 운동을 하면, 잠을 적게 자도 기분이 더 상쾌할 것이고, 일도 훨씬 더 능률적으로 하게 될 것이다. 그 결과, 실제로 운동에 할애한 시간보다 더 많은 시간을 벌게 될 것이다.

3. 언어는 결코 가만히 서 있지 않는다. 모든 언어는 그것이 죽게 될 때까지, 다시 말하여 더 이상 사용되지 않게 될 때까지 끊임없이 변화의 상태에 있게 된다. 우리가 말하고 글로 표현하는 영어는 우리의 할아버지 대에서 말하고 쓰던 영어가 아니고, 또한 할아버지 대의 영어는 엘리자베스 여왕 시대의 영어와도 똑같지 않다. 우리가 과거로 거슬러 올라갈수록 우리는 우리 선조들이 사용한 언어가 더욱 낯선 것임을 알게 되고 마침내 우리는 마치 그것이 외국어나 되는 것처럼 우리에게 매우 낯선 영어에 접하게 된다.

4. 미국에서는 개인적인 독립심과 자부심에 대한 생각이 매우 강해서 흔히 부모나 성년이 된 자녀는 따로 사는 것을 선택한다.

5. 나의 아내와 아이들이 화목하게 살아간다면 나는 행복하다. 나의 모든 가족이 희노애락을 함께 나누며 서로 의사 소통을 원만히 할 때 나는 행복하다.

6. 어떤 과학자들은 적은 양의 적포도주가 우리 건강에 적어도 한 가지 좋은 영향을 끼칠지도 모른다는 사실을 알아냈다. 그 연구 결과는 적포도주가 혈액 속의 콜레스테롤 수치를 낮출 수 있다는 것을 암시한다. 그러나, 최근의 한 연구는 콜레스테롤의 수치를 낮추는 것이 알코올이 아님을 보여 준다. 다시 말하자면, 의사들은 콜레스테롤을 낮추는 것은 바로 포도라는 사실을 알게 되었다. 이런 결과로, 콜레스테롤 수치가 높은 사람들은 포도를 먹음으로써 같은 결과를 얻을 수 있다.

7. 인생이란 전투를 위해서 젊은이가 갖출 수 있는 최선의 장비는 양심과 상식과 건강이다. 떳떳한 양심만큼 훌륭한 친구는 없다. 떳떳치 못한 양심만큼 위험한 적은 없다. 양심은 우리를 왕이나 노예가 되게 한다.

8. 직업만족도와 관련되는 요소는 많다. 개인차가 있을 수는 있지만, 대부분의 사람들은 직업이 근로자에게 정신적인 도전을 제공해야 한다는데 동의한다. 사람들은 그들의 직업이 의미있고

재미있는 것이라고 느껴야 한다. 그리고 물론, 특히 직업으로부터 만족감을 얻지 못하는 개인들에게는 임금이 대단히 중요하다. 쾌적한 작업 환경, 높은 임금, 정신적 도전을 제공하는 직업은 대부분의 사람들이 찾고자 하는 것이다. 사람들은 각자 성취감을 느끼고 싶어한다.

9. 20세기 이전에는 수백만 명의 사람들이 병원에서 불필요하게 죽어갔다. 그때로 거슬러 올라가 보면, 의사들은 업무 도중에 손을 씻지 않았다. 그들은 세균에 대해서 그리고 그것들이 어떻게 퍼져 나가는지에 대해서 거의 몰랐다. 의사들은 한 수술을 끝내고는 즉시 또 다른 수술을 시작하곤 했다. 그때 그들은 자신들이 이 사람에게서 저 사람에게로 세균을 옮기고 있다는 사실을 결코 깨닫지 못한 채로 환자들을 검진하곤 했다. 많은 경우에 그들은 치료하고자 했던 사람들을 심각하게 감염시켰다.

10. 니콜에게
내 아들이 메리라는 여자와 결혼할 예정이다. 메리는 지난 7개월 동안 매주 일요일에 우리 집에서 저녁을 먹었다. 난 항상 좋은 음식을 차려 주었다. 메리는 잘 먹었고 음식들을 좋아했다. 하지만, 그 애는 한 번도 설거지하는 것을 도와주겠다고 하거나 심지어 자기가 먹은 그릇을 부엌에 가져다 놓겠다고 한 적도 없었다. 내 아들은 메리가 손님이기 때문에 그럴 필요가 없다고 생각하고 있다. 나는 내 아들이 옳지 않다고 말하고 있는데, 너라면 무슨 말을 하겠니?
시카고에서 조안

Advanced Reading 21

어린이에게 이차방정식을 풀도록 가르치는 요점은 무엇일까? 이 질문에 대한 전통적인 대답이 있다. 그 대답은 이렇다. 즉 마음은 도구이이니까, 먼저 그것을 연마하고, 그 다음에 그것을 사용하라. 이차방정식을 푸는 힘을 획득한 것은 마음을 연마하는 과정의 일부이다. 이제 이 대답 속에는 확실히 오랜 시대 동안 그 대답을 살아 있도록 하는 충분한 진리가 있다. 그러나 그 절반의 진리에도 불구하고, 그것은 현대세계의 천재를 질식시킬만한 근본적인 오류를 구체화시킨다. 나는 정신을 죽은 도구에 이처럼 유추시킨 것에 대하여 첫 번째로 책임질 사람이 누구인지 모른다. 내가 아는 범위 내에서는 그리스의 7인의 현자 가운데 한 명일지도 모르고, 그들 모두로 구성된 위원회일지도 모른다. 최초 시발자가 누구였든 간에, 저명한 사람들이 그 대답에 계속적으로 시인을 함으로써 그것이 획득한 권위에 대하여 의심할 수가 없다.

알프레스 화이트헤드: 교육의 목적

Advanced Reading 22

세계의 오랜 역사 속에서, 극소수의 세대들만이 자유가 최대의 위험에 빠져있을 시기에 자유를 수호하는 역할을 부여받았습니다. 나는 이 책임을 회피하지 않고, 그것을 환영합니다. 나는 우리들 중 어느 누구도 어떤 다른 사람들이나 어떤 다른 세대와 입장을 바꾸기를 원하지 않을 것이라 믿습니다. 우리가 이 노력에 기울이는 힘과 믿음 그리고 헌신은 우리 조국과 조국에 봉사하는 모든 사람들을 밝혀줄 것입니다. 그리고 그 불에서 타오르는 불빛은 세계를 참으로 밝혀줄 수 있을 것입니다.
그러므로, 나의 동료 미국인들이여, 여러분의 조국이 여러분을 위해서 무엇을 할 수 있는가를 묻지 마시고, 여러분이 여러분의 조국을 위하여 무것을 할 수 있는가를 물으십시오.
나의 동료 세계 시민여러분이여! 미국이 여러분을 위하여 무엇을 할 것인가를 묻지 마시고, 우리가 함께 인간의 자유를 위하여 무엇을 할 수 있는가를 물으십시오.
끝으로, 여러분이 미국시민이든 세계시민이든지 간에, 우리가 여러분에게 요구하는 것과 동일한 수준의 힘과 희생을 여기 있는 우리에게 요구하십시오. 우리의 유일하고 확실한 보상인 양심을 가지고, 우리 행위에 대한 최후의 심판인 역사와 더불어, 우리가, 하나님의 축복과 도움을 구하되 여기 지상에서의 하나님의 일이 진실로 우리 자신의 일임에 틀림없다는 것을 알고서, 사랑하는 이 나라를 이끌고 가기 위하여 다 함께 전진하십시다.

존 에프 케네디

제12장 형용사 / 부사

Basic Reading 12

1. 대기오염의 근원이 항상 공장에 제한된 것만은 아니라는 사실을 우리는 간과하는 경향이 있다.

2. 다른 종류의 읽을 거리는 다른 종류의 독서법을 요구한다. 우선 독자는 수중에 어떤 유형의 읽을 거리를 가지고 있는 것인지를 파악해야 한다; 그리고 그는 그 자료를 적절히 읽어야 한다. 우리 눈에 잡히는 모든 읽기 자료들이 같은 비중으로 읽을 가치가 있는 것은 아니고, 또한 같은 우리의 관심을 요구하지도 않는다.

3. 존 삼촌은 내 돌아가신 아버지를 매우 닮아서 나는 삼촌을 볼 때마다 아버지를 생각한다.

4. 혼자서 시골지역을 산보할 때마다 방대한 대륙에 대한 자신의 무지에 대하여 놀란다.

5. 많은 사람이 책들을 소유하고 있는데 매우 소수 사람들만이 책을 이용하는 법을 안다.

6. 그가 이른 나이에 죽은 것은 그의 음주 습관 때문이라고 많은 사람은 생각한다. 보통 그는 자신을 거의 통제하지 못했다.

7. 유럽의 자유에 대한 위협은 미국의 자유에 대한 위협이다. 워싱턴에서 행정이 반드시 그러한 위협에 대하여 응수해야 하는 이유가 바로 그 때문이다. — 그것은 단지 선의에 입각해서가 아니라 필요에 의한 것이다.

8. 이상하게 들릴지 모르지만, 내가 런던에 온 것은 사람들을 만나기 위해서가 아니라 나의 더 많

은 고독을 위해서 이다. 왜냐하면 나는 내가 사는 작은 마을에서 너무 잘 알려져서 내가 마을에 나가기만 하면 즉시 대화에 참여하게 되기 때문이다.

9. 어떤 사람이 현명하지 못하기 때문에 낙담해서는 안 된다. 왜냐하면 수많은 현명하지 못한 사람들이 그들의 꾸준한 노력으로 인생에서 성공했기 때문이다.

10. 당신은 책들을 선택함에 있어서 아무리 신중해도 지나치지 않는다. 한 권의 책은 당신의 이웃에게 비유할 수 있다; 만약 그 이웃이 선한 사람이면, 그 관계가 아무리 오래 지속되어도 지나침이 없고, 만약 악한 사람이라면 아무리 빨리 청산해도 지나침이 없다.

11. 굶주리고 비열한 사람들이 결코 난폭하고 조잡하지 않기를 기대하는 것은 효과 없는 일이다.

12. 내 인생의 전체적인 확신은 이제 고독은 내 자신과 몇몇 다른 고독한 사람들에게 특이한 진귀하고 호기심이 가는 현상이기보다는 인간 존재의 중심적이고 피할 수 없는 사실이라고 하는 믿음에 기반을 두고 있다.

Advanced Reading 23

필수로 해야 하는 자원봉사 때문에 97년 매릴랜드 고등학교 학급의 많은 구성원들은 화를 내고 불평했다. 미래의 상급생들은 하지만 아마도 그 프로그램이 폐지되었으니까 저항자로서 있지는 않을 것이다. 존 말로니 같은 학생들은 이미 공인된 지역사회 봉사의 필수시간을 마쳤다. 보위 고등학교 이 학년은 보위 지역에 있는 라킨-세이스 양육 및 원기 회복원에서 일 주일에 이틀 밤을 자원 봉사함으로써 제8학년에서 자신의 시간을 획득했다.
그는 셔플보드 놀이, 카드놀이, 나이 많은 시민들과 다른 게임을 했다. 그는 또한 그들을 위해서 파티 계획을 짜는 것을 도왔으며, 그들이 적적하지 않도록 그들의 방을 방문했다.
열 다섯 살인 존은 자원봉사를 마치지 않았다. 일 주일에 한번 그는 포레스트빌 지역에 있는 프린스 조오지 군 동물보호소에서 동물들을 비비오 테이프로 촬영한다. 그가 촬영한 테이프는 동물들의 보금자리를 발견하기를 기대하면서 보위 지역 대중들이 볼 수 있는 텔레비전 채널에서 방영된다.

Advanced Reading 24

네가 말한 것은 책읽기를 좋아한다는 것이군. 그래 나는 그 덕분에 기쁘구나. 셰익스피어와 거의 같은 시대에 산 사람인데, 프란시스 베이컨의 수필을 알고 있니? 그의 수필에는 책읽기에 관한 좋은 것들이 많이 있지. 그 가운데서 몇 개가 여기 있는데, "공부하는 것에 관해서"란 수필에서 뽑은 것이야.
'어떤 책은 맛보아야 하고, 다른 책은 꿀꺽 삼켜야하고, 또 어떤 책은 가끔 씹어서 소화시켜야한다.'
'논박하거나 싸우기 위해서 책을 읽지 말라, 믿지도 말고 당연하게 받아들이지도 말라, 재담과 담론을 찾지도 말라 오직 숙고하고 생각하기 위해서 책을 읽어라.'
이 보다 더 좋은 충고는 해 줄 수가 없구나. 첫 번째 인용문은 다른 종류의 책을 읽는 법을 알려주는 것이야.
대부분의 여행에 관한 책들은 '맛을 보아야' 한

다. 그런 책은 대충 읽는 것으로 충분하며, 여기저기 조금씩 읽어도 된다. 네가 범죄소설 (아가시 크리스티, 시몬 그리고 오늘날 인기 있는 작가들의) 을 좋아한다면, 네가 나와 같다면, 그런 책들은 재빨리 읽어라. 너는 그런 책들은 '꿀꺽 삼키게' 될 거야. 그리고 다음에는 네가 천천히 그리고 주의 깊게 읽어야할 책이 있다. 너의 관심을 끄는 중요한 주제에 관한 책이라면 너는 그것을 씹어서 소화하기를 원할 거야. 그리고 책의 저자가 말하는 것을 숙고하기 원할 거야 그리고 저자의 생각과 논증을 깊게 생각하기를 원할 거야.

A. S. 혼비: 독서에 대하여 중에서

제13장 비교

Basic Reading 13

1. 이러한 충동 구매의 상승은 셀프서비스 상점의 성장과 일치한다. 고객에게 시중을 드는 점원이 근무하는 잡화점에서 충동구매를 하는 것이 셀프서비스 가게에서 고객이 충동구매를 하는 것보다 약 반 배쯤 된다는 다른 연구보고서가 나와 있다.

2. 여성이 근육의 발달에 있어서 남성처럼 그렇게 튼튼하지 않지만 평균적으로 질병에 더 걸리지 않으며, 사소한 질병으로 고통을 자주 호소하지만 여성이 더 오래 산다는 것을 의학적 증거는 보여준다.

3. 인생에서 정말로 중요한 것은 재능이 아니라 성격이다.

4. 자연을 연구함에 있어서, 그것에 대한 설명은 사실들과 일관성이 있어야 할 뿐 아니라 가능한 단순하고 단도직입적이어야 한다.

5. 그 기선은 안락함과 호화로움에 있어서 미진한 점이 전혀 없었다.

6. 노예들 자신에 관하여, 그들이 주인의 명령들에 만족하여 복종하기만 하면, 그들은 대규모 농장에서 상당히 유복한 것처럼 보였다.

7. 우리가 경험할 수 있는 가장 아름답고 심오한 감정은 신비감이다. 그것은 모든 참된 예술과 과학의 원천이다. 이러한 감정이 익숙지 않고, 놀라움에 걸음을 멈출 수 없으며 경외심에 넋을 빼앗길 수 없는 사람은 죽은 사람과 마찬가지이다; 그

의 눈은 감긴 것이다.

8. 더 많이 책을 읽어감에 따라, 그 주제는 내게 더욱 더 복잡하게 보이며, 나는 나의 무지를 더욱 더 의식하게 된다.

9. 현대 삶 속에서 신경과민의 피로감으로부터 탈출하는 것은 매우 어려운 문제이다. 우선 모든 작업시간 내내 그리고 직장과 집 사이의 출퇴근 시간에 더욱 더, 도시 노동자는 소음에 노출되어 있다. 그는 의식적으로 대부분의 소음을 듣지 않으려고 애를 쓰지만, 그럼에도 불고하고, 그 소리를 듣지 않으려는 의식적인 노력 때문에 더욱 더 그를 지치게 만들어 버리는 것이 사실이다.

10. 만약 자신을 제외하고는 아무도 자신의 일기를 읽지 않는다고 확신되는 일기를 쓴다면, 그는 아마도 완벽하게 참된 일기를 기록할 것이다. 다르게 기록할 동기가 없는 것이다. 그는 목욕탕에서 자신을 보는 것을 부끄러워하지 않는 것처럼, 그의 행동이 선하건 악하건 발생한 그대로 기록하는 것을 부끄러워하지 않을 것이다.

11. 그러나 단념은 행복을 정복하는 데 있어서 담당하는 역할이 또한 있으며, 이 역할은 노력이 담당하는 역할 못지 않게 필수적인 것이다. 현명한 사람은 막아낼 수 있는 불행 아래에 그냥 앉아 있지도 않을 것이지만, 피할 수 없는 불행에 시간과 감정을 낭비하지도 않을 것이다.

12. 두 다리로 걷는 것이 원숭이들에게 부자연스럽고 힘든 일인 것처럼 생각하는 일은 인간에게 있어서 마찬가지로 부자연스럽고 힘든 일이다. 우리가 해야 할 생각 이상을 하는 경우가 드물고 생각을 하지 않으려는 우리의 성향은 우리가 가장 편안하다고 느낄 때 일반적으로 가장 크다. 사고의 노동을 싫어하는 인간의 반감이 사적인 일에서처럼 공적인 삶에서도 마찬가지로 분명하기 때문에, 인류는 편하고 번영하는 시대에는 역사에 남을 만한 생각을 별로 할 수 없었다.

13. 돈으로 행복을 얻는 것보다 더 쉬운 것은 없는데 그러나 세상의 부자들은 그 반대로 입증합니다.

14. 그는 주변의 어떤 의사보다도 더 많은 사람을 진료했지만, 그는 항상 가난한 사람들으르 돌봤기 때문에 더 적은 돈을 벌었다.

15. 우리의 국민들이 돈을 버는 것이 가장 중요하다는 환상에 집착하는 한, 우리의 대학과 종합대학교들은 계속해서 돈을 버는 법을 젊은이들에게 가르치려고 노력할 것이다.

16. 어떤 경험도 외국어를 배우는 것보다 더욱 문화적으로 시야를 넓혀주는 것은 없다. 세계에서 우리와 다르게 일을 처리하는 사람들이 있다는 것을 설득력 있게 입증하는 방법으로 외국어를 배우는 것보다 더 나은 것은 없다.

17. 예절은 약함의 표명이 아니라 상식의 표시이다. 예절은 "우리가 필요 없이 싸우지 맙시다"라고 말하는 인류의 인사방법이다 – 그리고 사업에서, 사랑과 결혼에 있어서, 매일 매일 업무에서 예절보다 더 고상한 지혜는 없다.

18. 내가 판단하는 한 그는 보통의 감각기준에서 볼 때, 지금까지 살아 있었던 어떤 사람보다 야망과는 가장 무관한 사람이었다. 만약 그가 승진에 승진을 거듭했다면, 그것은 고용주의 관심

을 끌기 위해서 자신을 드러냈기 때문이 아니라 그의 고용주가 그의 승진을 주장했기 때문이다.

19. 수줍어하는 사람은 보통 아무런 이유 없이 수줍어해 왔음을 발견하며, 그리고 실제로 누구도 자기에 대해서 조금의 주의도 기울이지 않는다.

20. 현재 가장 문명화된 나라에서 언론의 자유는 당연한 것으로 여겨지며, 완전히 단순한 것으로 보인다. 우리는 언론의 자유에 매우 익숙해 있어서 그것을 천부적인 권리로 간주한다. 그러나 이 권리는 상당히 최근에서야 획득된 것이며, 이 권리를 획득하는 과정은 피의 호수로 이루어진 것이었다. 자신의 견해를 출판하고 모든 의문 사항을 토의하는 것은 나쁜 일이 아니라 좋은 일이라는 것을 가장 개화된 사람들에게 설득하는 것은 여러 세기의 시간이 소요되었다.

21. 나의 관심을 끈 첫 번째 과목은 종교였다. 왜냐하면 내가 살고 있는 이 세계가 생각해 볼 유일한 세계인지, 아니면 이 세계를 앞으로 다가올 삶에 대해서 나를 준비 시키는 단지 시련의 장소로 여겨야 하는지를 결정하는 일이 나에게는 가장 중요한 일로 보였기 때문이었다.

Advanced Reading 25

삼 천 년 동안 시인들은 자신들의 상상력에 황홀해 하기도하고 감동을 받기도 했으며 당혹해하기도 했습니다. 어느 짧고도 요약적인 에세이에서 나는 기껏해야 그런 신비의 어떤 조그만 모퉁이를 들어올리기를 바랄 수 있을 뿐이었습니다. 하지만 그것은 중요한 모퉁이입니다. 질문컨대, 우리가 상상할 때 마음속에서는 무슨 일이 일어나는 것일까요? 여러분은 제게서 이에 대한 답변이 꽤 독특하다는 것을 들을 것입니다. 말하자면 이렇습니다. 우리는 상상력의 작용을 묘사할 수 있다는 사실입니다. 그리고 제가 하는 바와 같이 우리가 그것을 묘사를 할 때, 상상력이란 특별한 인간의 재능임이 명백해 집니다. 상상하기란 시인의 마음이나 화가의 마음 혹은 과학자의 마음을 특징짓는 것이 아니라 인간의 마음을 특징짓는 행위입니다.

자코브 브론스키: 상상력의 범위 중에서

Advanced Reading 26

모든 개인은 자신들의 믿음을 공식화하고 표현하고 자기 자신의 결정을 하는데 가능한 최대한 자유로워야하는가 아니면 어떤 종류의 통치 집단으로부터 지시 받고 통제 받는 사회의 유기적 조직체에 합병되어야 하는가? 정부는 개인의 권리와 복지를 보호하기 위해서 존재하는가 아니면 개인이 전적으로 국가에 종속되어야 하는가? 개방된 사회와 폐쇄된 사회간의 이런 갈등은, 그것이 지금 새롭고 더욱 강한 형식을 가장하고 있다고 해도, 결코 20세기의 특유한 것은 아니다.
폐쇄된 사회의 신봉자들은 미래란 자신들 것이라고 주장한다. 그러나 실제로 이것은 새로운 상황이 아니라 매우 오래된 상황이다. 원시인들은 폐쇄된 사회에 살았다. 꽉 짜여진 부족집단에 속해서, 그들은 개인의 권리이나 독립에 대한 아무런 의식도 갖지 못했다. 원시적인 조건하에서는 그와 같은 태도가 생존에 필요했다. 부족이 자연의 장애물에 대처하고, 그들의 적들과 맞서 자신들의 생명을 유지할 수 있었던 것은 모든 부족 구성원들의 의심 없는 복종과 지속적인 일치단결을 통하는 길뿐이었다.
그러나 인류가 발전의 수준에 이르기 시작하자

부족적인 일치단결은 점차로 생존에 불필요하게 되었고 대신에 더 많은 발전에 장애물이 되었다. 진보란 이제 새로운 아이디어와 새로운 생활 방식을 탐험하도록 개인을 자유롭게 함으로써 가장 잘 촉진될 수 있게 되었다.

헨리 밤포드 파커: 열린 사회에서의 개인의 권리 중에서

제14장 명사 / 관사 / 대명사

Basic Reading 14

1. 만약 네가 배울 준비가 되어 있다면, 세상 모든 것이 너의 스승이다. 심지어 나무 한 토막, 하늘에 있는 구름 한 조각, 나무에 앉아 있는 새 또는 어린아이로부터 너는 무엇인가를 배울 수 있다. 어린 소년으로부터의 충고 한 마디, 또는 책 속에 있는 한 구절이 네가 현명한 사람이 되도록 도와줄 것이다.

2. 다른 언어를 아는 것은 여러 가지 이점을 준다. 그것은 다른 문화로 통하는 창이기 때문이다. 왜냐하면 어떤 사회가 세상을 어떻게 생각하고 어떻게 보는가 하는 것이 언어를 통해 표현되기 때문이다. 다른 언어를 아는 것은 우리가 모두에게 흔히 있는 문제들을 처리하는 다른 방법들을 제공한다. 게다가 요즘에는 외국인 파트너가 있는 것이 흔하기 때문에, 다른 언어를 알고 있는가 아니면 모르고 있는가 하는 것은 사업 세계에서 중요하다. 마지막으로 다른 언어를 이해하는 것은 자신의 문화를 새로운 시각으로 볼 수 있게 해준다.

3. 여러분 신체의 특정 부위에 있는 어떤 박테리아는 여러분에게 해가 될 수 있다. 하지만 많은 박테리아는 여러분의 생명에 중요하다. 몸 안의 음식물 분해를 돕는 박테리아가 없다면 여러분은 커다란 곤경에 빠질 것이다. 사실, 어떤 식으로든 몸 안에 있는 박테리아를 모두 제거해 버린다면, 여러분은 음식물을 소화시킬 수 없기 때문에 굶어 죽게 될 것이다.

4. 아마 미국을 이해할 수 있는 가장 싼 방법은 버스를 타고 여행하는 것이다. 그레이하운드 버

스는 미국의 시골과 모든 대도시를 횡단 운행한다. 그 버스들은 운전사들이 여러 정류장에서 차를 바꾸어 운행하면서 밤낮으로 운행된다. 이런 방법의 여행은 여러분들에게 미국의 실체를 알 수 있는 기회와 흥미로운 사람들을 만날 수 있는 기회를 제공해 줄 것이다.

5. 사실 읽을 가치가 있는 책은 모두 과학 서적을 읽는 것과 똑같은 방식으로 읽혀져야 한다. 즉 즐거움만을 위해서 읽혀서는 안되고; 그리고 모든 읽을 가치가 있는 책은 과학 서적이 가지고 있는 것과 같은 양의 가치를 지녀야 한다, 물론 그 가치가 전혀 다른 종류이기는 하지만.

6. 두 개의 동전은 매우 비슷하게 보여서 동전 하나를 다른 하나와 구별하는 것은 어려웠다.

7. 아는 것과 행동하는 것은 별개이다. 많은 사람들이 일찍 자고 일찍 일어나는 것이 건강에 유익하다는 것을 알지만, 매우 소수의 사람들만이 그것을 실행한다.

8. 만일 박식한 사람들이 중요하고 읽을 만하다고 여기는 책에 당신이 지루함을 느끼면, 자신에게 정직해져서 아마도 어려움이 책에 있는 것이 아니라 당신에게 있다고 솔직히 인정하라. 지금은 재미없거나 어려워 보이는 책이 당신이 지적으로 보다 성숙해졌을 때에는 이해하기가 쉽고 읽기에 흥미진진한 것으로 종종 판명될 것이다.

9. 어느 책도 글을 어떻게 쓰는지를 가르쳐 주지 않는다. 아무리 책을 많이 읽어도 글을 어떻게 쓰는지를 가르쳐 주지 않는다. 독서는 필수적이고, 실질적인 책이 도움을 줄 수 있다. 그러나 작가가 될 수 있는 싹을 가지고 있지 않는 한, 다시 말하여 글을 쓰고자 하는 막을 수 없는 의지가 없는 한, 성공할 수 없는 법이다. 더군다나 글로써 성공을 거두고자 한다면 열심히 노력을 해야 한다.

10. 워싱턴은 말을 하는 데 매우 신중하였으며, 상대방을 이용하거나 논쟁에서 일시적인 승리를 노린다거나 하는 일은 결코 하지 않았다.

11. 사회과학의 방법론은 자연과학의 방법론과 필연적으로 차이가 난다. 그것은 하나의 기본적인 이유에서 차이가 나고, 또 차이가 나는 점은 사회과학의 연구자가 자신이 다루는 자료의 외부가 아닌 내부에 존재한다는 점이다. 인간은 외적 자연을 연구하는 것과 똑같은 방법으로 인간을 연구할 수 없다.

Advanced Reading 27

대학이란 하나의 공동체입니다. 공동체는 개인적인 끈으로 함께 묶여진 사람들로 구성됩니다. 교수와 학생간의 관계는 개인적인 관계입니다. 거기에는 상호 관심이 있어야 하며, 상호 도움이 있어야 합니다. 어떤 기계적인 장치도 이런 개인적인 유대관계를 대신할 수는 없습니다. 어떤 텔레비전 스크린도 우리들의 반응에 대해 반응을 할 수 없으며, 우리들의 즐거움과 슬픔을 나눌 수 없으며, 또 대학 휴게실에 차 한 잔이나 콜라 한 잔을 마시면서 사소한 이야기를 나눌 수가 없습니다. 교육을 기계화하고, 교육을 비개인화 하는 것은 교육에서 가장 귀중한 구성인자를 박탈해 버리는 것입니다. 어떤 대가를 치르더라도 이런 개인적인 요소를 소중히 합시다. 번더빌트 대학은 운 좋게도 우리가 서로를 알고, 서로 관심을 갖기에 지나치게 크지 않습니다. 번더빌트 대학은 우리가 친구가 되는데 지나치게 크지도 않습니다.

랜달 스트워트: 우리가 대학에 다니는 이유

Advanced Reading 28

언어가 우리들의 일상생활 가운데 많은 부분을 차지하고 있기 때문에 일부 사람들은 호흡이나 눈 깜박거림과 같이 다소 자동적이며 자연발생적인 행위로서 언어를 간주하게 된다. 물론 우리가 그 문제를 조금이라도 생각한다면, 우리는 언어에 관해서 자동적인 것은 아무것도 없다는 것을 깨닫게 된다. 어린이들은 그들의 모국어를 배워야하며 오랜 시간이 걸리는 필요한 훈련을 받아야 한다. 언어란 유전적으로 전해지는 것이 아니다. 그것은 집중적인 교육을 통해서만이 한 세대에서 다음세대로 전해질 수 있는 기술이다. 언어가 우리들의 사회적 행위상 하는 엄청나게 큰 역할을 깨닫기는 쉽지 않다. 언어가 없다면 사회는 어떻게 될까? 물론 말로써 의사소통하는 수단이나 글쓰기가 불가능할 것이다. 그 이유는 이런 모든 것이 궁극적으로 구어에 의존하기 때문이다. 우리는 동물처럼 다른 사람들의 행위를 하거나 관찰함으로써 배워야만 할 것이다. 언어가 없다면 과거의 경험을 재창조하여 그것을 다른 사람들에게 전달할 수 있는 길이 없을 것이기 때문이다.

해리 호이저: 언어와 문화

제15장 특수구문

Basic Reading 15

1. 공공의 문제는 광범위하고 매우 복잡해서 그 문제를 적절히 이해하기를 희망할 수 있는 사람들은 단지 소수의 사람들뿐이다.

2. 그는 보통 말을 삼가는 편이다. 그러나 만약 그가 말을 하게 되면, 항상 정곡을 찌르는 말을 한다.

3. 영어로 글을 쓰거나 말하는 것은 학문이 아니라 기술이다. 기준이 될 만한 규칙은 없다: 단지 구체적인 어휘가 추상적인 어휘보다 더 좋으며, 어떤 사실을 짧게 기술하는 것이 최선이라는 일반적인 원리가 있을 뿐이다. 단지 어법에 올바르다는 것만으로는 결코 훌륭한 글쓰기를 보장해 주지 못한다.

4. 나는 부유한 사람으로 간주되며, 실제로 그렇다. 나는 네게 지혜롭고 선하게 성장할 모든 기회를 줄 수 있다. 그러나 나는 너를 빈둥거리게 방치할 정도로 부유하지도 않으며, 그렇게 할 의사도 결코 없다.

5. 초기에 진심어린 악수는 우정을 보여주는 것이 아니고 불신을 보여주는 것이었다. 오른손을 습관적으로 사용하는 것은 우연히 시작되지 않았다. 그것은 다른 사람의 무기를 다루는 손을 고정시키는 예방 조치였다.

6. 갈릴레오는 망원경의 건조를 진행시켰고, 그 동안 줄곧 제품의 질을 향상시켰으며 망원경의 성능을 확대하여 마침내 삼십 배를 확대하는 망원경을 건설하였다. 대물렌즈의 직경이 얼마나

되었는지를 우리는 모르지만 아마 2 인치 혹은 그 보다 조금 더 길었을 것이다. 그 크기가 얼마였든지 망원경은 그 시대 사람들에게 틀림없이 마법사의 도구처럼 보였을 것이다.

7. 충고는 겨울철의 눈과 같다: 충고를 부드럽게 하면 할수록, 더 오래 남아있게 되며, 그 충고는 더욱 더 마음 속 깊게 파고든다.

8. 건전한 교육은 어떤 학생의 머리를 여러 가지 사실과 이론들로 채워서 학교를 내보내도록 하는 것을 의미하지 않는다. 교육은 두뇌만이 아닌 몸 전체의 발달을 진정으로 도모하는 것이다.

9. 어떤 사람에게 인생은 즐거움이고, 다른 사람에게는 고통이다. 그러나 의무에 복종하는 것이야말로, 어떤 대가를 지불하고 위험을 감수한다 해도, 고도로 문명화된 삶의 본질이다.

10. 의심할 바 없이, 자동화는 적절히 적용된다면 인류에게 현저한 이득을 줄 수 있지만, 고용과 사회적인 삶에 관한 문제를 또한 일으킬 것이다.

11. 이상적인 사회는 모든 남자와 여자로 하여금 그들의 타고난 능력들을 최대한 활용하게 할 수 있을 것이다.

12. 그러나 음악에 무관심한 것은 위대한 인물들과 선한 사람들의 상당히 보편적인 특징이라는 것을 경험적으로 우리에게 말해 준다.

Advanced Reading 29

동양이 정신적이고 서양은 물질적이라고 말하는 것이 오랫동안 유행이 되어 왔다. 그러나 부주의하게 말해진 많은 일들처럼 그것은 사실이 아니다. 동양은 서양보다 더 정신적이지도 덜 정신적이지도 않다. 그리고 서양은 동양보다 더 물질적이지도 덜 물질적이지도 않다. 이 말은 동양 사람이나 서양 사람이나 똑같다는 말이다. 사람들은 굶주리기보다는 식사하기를 더 좋아하고, 집이 없는 것보다는 집을 소유하는 것을 더 좋아하고, 병들기 보다는 건강하기를 더 좋아하고, 단명하기보다는 장수하기를 더 좋아하고, 슬프기 보다는 행복하기기를 더 좋아한다. 그렇다면 정신적인 동양과 물질적인 서양이라는 신화는 어디에서 왔을까? 그것은 일종의 사실에 근거를 두고 있다. 이 사실은 이렇게 단순하게 말해질 수 있다: 동양 사람들은 삶을 즐기기를 좋아한다. 그들은 생활과 식사와 잠과 가족과 놀기와 그들의 아내와 가족과 이야기하는 소박한 즐거움 누릴 시간적 여유가 없을 정도까지 힘들게 일하지 않으려한다. 그들은 하나의 직업으로도 생활비를 낼 수 있다면 두 개의 직업을 떠맡지 않으려 할 것이다. 두 개의 직업이란 자신들의 시간을 소모하고 마음을 산란스럽게 하니까. 그들은 일에 대하여 끊임없이 생각하기를 원하지 않는다. 그들은 일에 대하여 끝없이 생각하기를 원하지 않는다. 그렇다고 그들이 게으른 것은 전혀 아니다.

펄 벅: 동양과 서양

Advanced Reading 30

먼저 과학이 할 수 있는 것과 할 수 없는 것, 즉 과학의 고유한 영역과 기능을 고려해보자. 과학은 정확한 물리적 현상과 사회적 현상에 도달하기 위해서 그것들을 연구한다. 과학은 사물이 어떻게 움직이는가를 기술하려한다. 과학은 천체의 움직임, 원자의 내부 작용, 생리학적 과정, 사회적 움직임 또는 인간의 행위를 다룬다. 프란시스 베이컨은 과학은 우리에게 힘을 제공한다고 말함으로써 그 질문에 답한다. 과학은 우리로 하여금 우리가 살고 있는 세계의 물리적 현상과 사회적 현상에 대하여 어느 정도 지배력과 통제력을 행사할 수 있도록 해준다. 그 질문에 답하는 다른 방법은 과학은 우리로 하여금 물건을 생산할 수 있도록 해준다고 말하는 것이다.

엔지니어나 의사에 의해서 응용이 되면 과학은 다리를 건설하게 하거나 건강을 회복시키도록 도와준다. 그러나 동일한 지식이 또한 우리가 아는 바와 같이 사물을 파괴하고 인간을 불구로 만들거나 죽이기 위해서 사용될 수도 있다. 바꿔 말하면 과학은 좋은 목적뿐만 아니라 나쁜 목적을 추구하는 것을 촉진할 수 있는 수단을 우리에게 제공한다. 과학 그 자체는 도덕적으로 중립적인데 즉 그 수단이 사용되는 목적의 가치에는 무관심할 뿐만 아니라 전적으로 어떠한 도덕적 방향을 가리켜 줄 수도 없다.

모티머 애드러: 과학 시대의 철학